THE NAVARRE BIBLE: STANDARD EDITION

SAINT MATTHEW'S GOSPEL

VOLUMES IN THIS SERIES

Standard Edition

NEW TESTAMENT
St Matthew's Gospel
St Mark's Gospel
St Luke's Gospel
St John's Gospel
Acts of the Apostles
Romans and Galatians
Corinthians
Captivity Letters
Thessalonians and Pastoral Letters
Hebrews
Catholic Letters
Revelation

OLD TESTAMENT
The Pentateuch
Joshua–Kings [Historical Books 1]
Chronicles–Maccabees [Historical Books 2]
The Psalms and the Song of Solomon
Wisdom Books
Major Prophets
Minor Prophets

Reader's (Omnibus) Edition
The Gospels and Acts
The Letters of St Paul
Revelation, Hebrews and Catholic Letters

Single-volume, large-format New Testament

THE NAVARRE BIBLE

Saint Matthew's Gospel

in the Revised Standard Version and New Vulgate
with a commentary by members of the
Faculty of Theology of the University of Navarre

FOUR COURTS PRESS • DUBLIN
SCEPTER PUBLISHERS • NEW YORK

Typeset by Carrigboy Typesetting Services for
FOUR COURTS PRESS LTD
7 Malpas Street, Dublin 8, Ireland
www.fourcourtspress.ie
Distributed in North America by
SCEPTER PUBLISHERS, INC.
P.O. Box 211, New York, NY 10018–0004
www.scepterpublishers.org

Nihil obstat: Stephen J. Greene, censor deputatus
Imprimi potest: J. O'Carroll, Diocesan Administrator, 15 October 1987

The translation of introductions and commentary was made by Michael Adams.

A catalogue record for this title is available from the British Library.
First edition 1988; Second edition 1991, reprinted many times;
Third edition (reset and repaged) 2005
Reprinted 2007; 2012; 2016; 2018; 2022.

ISBN 978–1–85182–900–2

Library of Congress Cataloging-in-Publication Data [for first volume in this series]

Bible. O.T. English. Revised Standard. 1999.
    The Navarre Bible. – North American ed.
        p.   cm
    "The Books of Genesis, Exodus, Leviticus, Numbers, Deuteronomy in the Revised
        Standard Version and New Vulgate with a commentary by members of the
        Faculty of Theology of the University of Navarre."
    Includes bibliographical references.
    Contents: [1] The Pentateuch.
    ISBN 1–889334–21–9 (hardback: alk. paper)
I. Title.
    BS891.A1   1999.P75   99–23033
    221.7'7—dc21   CIP

The title "Navarre Bible" is © Four Courts Press 2003.

ACKNOWLEDGMENTS
Quotations from Vatican II documents are based on the translation in Vatican Council II:
The Conciliar and Post Conciliar Documents, ed. A. Flannery, OP (Dublin 1981).

The New Vulgate text of the Bible can be accessed via
http://www.vatican.va.archive/bible/index.htm

Printed and bound in England by CPI Group (UK) Ltd, Croydon.

Contents

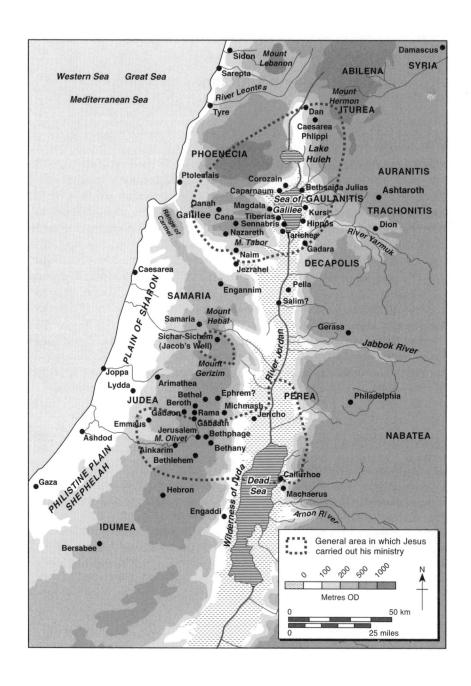

Palestine in the time of Jesus

Preface and Preliminary Notes

The Commentary
The distinguishing feature of the *Navarre Bible* is its commentary on the biblical text. Compiled by members of the Theology faculty of the University of Navarre, Pamplona, Spain, this commentary draws on writings of the Fathers, texts of the Magisterium of the Church, and works of spiritual writers, including St Josemaría Escrivá, the founder of Opus Dei; it was he who in the late 1960s entrusted the faculty at Navarre with the project of making a translation of the Bible and adding to it a commentary of the type found here.

The commentary, which is not particularly technical, is designed to explain the biblical text and to identify its main points, the message God wants to get across through the sacred writers. It also deals with doctrinal and practical matters connected with the text.

The first volume of the *Navarre Bible* (the English edition) came out in 1985—first, twelve volumes covering the New Testament; then seven volumes covering the Old Testament. Many reprints and revised editions have appeared over the past twenty years. All the various volumes are currently in print.

The Revised Standard Version
The English translation of the Bible used in the *Navarre Bible* is the Revised Standard Version (RSV) which is, as its preface states, "an authorized revision of the American Standard Version, published in 1901, which was a revision of the King James Version [the "Authorized Version"], published in 1611".

The RSV of the entire Bible was published in 1952; its Catholic edition (RSVCE) appeared in 1966. The differences between the RSV and the RSVCE New Testament texts are listed in the "Explanatory Notes" in the end-matter of this volume. Whereas the Spanish editors of what is called in English the "Navarre Bible" made a new translation of the Bible, for the English edition the RSV has proved to be a very appropriate choice of translation. The publishers of the *Navarre Bible* wish to thank the Division of Christian Education of the National Council of the Churches of Christ in the USA for permission to use that text.

The Latin Text
This volume also carries the official Latin version of the New Testament in the *editio typica altera* of the New Vulgate (Vatican City, 1986).

Preface

The headings within the biblical text have been provided by the editors (they are not taken from the RSV). A full list of these headings, giving an overview of the New Testament, can be found at the back of the volume.

An asterisk *inside the biblical text* signals an RSVCE "Explanatory Note" at the end of the volume.

References in the biblical text indicate parallel texts in other biblical books. All these marginal references come from the *Navarre Bible* editors, not the RSV.

Abbreviations

1. BOOKS OF HOLY SCRIPTURE

Acts	Acts of the Apostles	1 Kings	1 Kings
Amos	Amos	2 Kings	2 Kings
Bar	Baruch	Lam	Lamentations
1 Chron	1 Chronicles	Lev	Leviticus
2 Chron	2 Chronicles	Lk	Luke
Col	Colossians	1 Mac	1 Maccabees
1 Cor	1 Corinthians	2 Mac	2 Maccabees
2 Cor	2 Corinthians	Mal	Malachi
Dan	Daniel	Mic	Micah
Deut	Deuteronomy	Mk	Mark
Eccles	Ecclesiastes (Qoheleth)	Mt	Matthew
Esther	Esther	Nah	Nahum
Eph	Ephesians	Neh	Nehemiah
Ex	Exodus	Num	Numbers
Ezek	Ezekiel	Obad	Obadiah
Ezra	Ezra	1 Pet	1 Peter
Gal	Galatians	2 Pet	2 Peter
Gen	Genesis	Phil	Philippians
Hab	Habakkuk	Philem	Philemon
Hag	Haggai	Ps	Psalms
Heb	Hebrews	Prov	Proverbs
Hos	Hosea	Rev	Revelation (Apocalypse)
Is	Isaiah	Rom	Romans
Jas	James	Ruth	Ruth
Jer	Jeremiah	1 Sam	1 Samuel
Jn	John	2 Sam	2 Samuel
1 Jn	1 John	Sir	Sirach (Ecclesiasticus)
2 Jn	2 John	Song	Song of Solomon
3 Jn	3 John	1 Thess	1 Thessalonians
Job	Job	2 Thess	2 Thessalonians
Joel	Joel	1 Tim	1 Timothy
Jon	Jonah	2 Tim	2 Timothy
Josh	Joshua	Tit	Titus
Jud	Judith	Wis	Wisdom
Jude	Jude	Zech	Zechariah
Judg	Judges	Zeph	Zephaniah

Abbreviations

2. OTHER ABBREVIATIONS

ad loc.	*ad locum*, commentary on this passage	f	and following (*pl.* ff)
AAS	*Acta Apostolicae Sedis*	ibid.	*ibidem*, in the same place
Apost.	Apostolic	in loc.	*in locum,* commentary on this passage
can.	canon		
chap.	chapter	loc.	*locum*, place or passage
cf.	*confer*, compare	par.	parallel passages
Const.	Constitution	Past.	Pastoral
Decl.	Declaration	RSV	Revised Standard Version
Dz-Sch	Denzinger-Schönmetzer, *Enchiridion Biblicum* (4th edition, Naples & Rome, 1961)	RSVCE	Revised Standard Version, Catholic Edition
		SCDF	Sacred Congregation for the Doctrine of the Faith
Enc.	Encyclical	sess.	session
Exhort.	Exhortation	v.	verse (*pl.* vv.)

"Sources quoted in the Commentary", which appears at the end of this book, explains other abbreviations used.

Introduction to
the Gospel according to Matthew

With the help of God we are going to enter a golden city, more precious than all the gold the world contains. Let us notice what its foundations are made of, and find its gates to be composed of sapphires and precious stones. In Matthew we have the best of guides. Matthew is the door by which we enter, and we must enter eagerly, for if the guide notices that someone is distracted, he will exclude him from the city. What a magnificent and truly stately city it is; not like our cities, which are a mixture of streets and palaces. Here all are palaces. Let us, then, open the gates of our soul, let us open our ears, and as we prepare reverently to cross its threshold, let us adore the King who holds sway therein. What immense splendour shall we not find when we enter![1]

THE AUTHOR

As is the case with many other sacred books, the name of the author does not appear in the text of this Gospel. This fact is significant in itself: it indicates that the author was not writing a book of his own; he was bearing witness, briefly and in written form, to Jesus' life on earth, his teachings, his redemptive passion and death, and his glorious resurrection. He was seeking to show that Jesus of Nazareth, a descendant of David, a descendant of Abraham according to the flesh, who was virginally conceived in the pure womb of Mary by the working of the Holy Spirit, was the Messiah promised in the Old Testament prophecies; that he was the Incarnate Son of God, the Saviour of mankind, who had come to set men free from the slavery of sin, from the devil and from eternal death. In the presence of the divine and human majesty of Jesus Christ, St Matthew makes no appearance. Jesus is what matters, and what he said, and what he did.

However, the constant Tradition of the Church from earliest times identifies the human author of this Gospel as the apostle St Matthew, one of the first

---

1. St John Chrysostom, *Hom. on St Matthew*, 1, 8.

Twelve, whom Jesus himself called when he was working at his job as a "pub-lican", that is, as a tax collector.

We have referred to St Matthew as being the "human author" of the first Gospel, the reason being that the principal author of the sacred books is God himself, who "inspired" the human authors, or hagiographers, in their literary work and "by supernatural power so moved and impelled them to write—he so assisted them when writing—that the things which he ordered, and those only, they, first, rightly understood, then willed faithfully to write down, and finally expressed in apt words and with infallible truth".[2]

However, when he communicates his grace to men, God, in his providence, does not destroy nature—in this case, the human qualities of the writers; rather, he raises nature on to a new level, perfects it and uses it to suit his pur-pose, in the same kind of way as a musician brings out all the qualities of a good violin. In two important respects, however, the comparison does not fit: firstly, because God, as well as using the writer as his instrument, also created him and endowed him with those qualities which he wanted him to have, to equip him to perform the task he planned for him; and secondly, because the sacred writer is not an inert instrument in God's hands: he is a living instru-ment, gifted with all his faculties. By virtue of this divine inspiration, a sacred book—in its entirety—is the end-product of close collaboration between God and the particular writer: each and every part of the book is really and in the proper sense of the word a work composed by God and a work composed by his instrument, the hagiographer; but, first and foremost, it is God's book, because God is its principal author.

St Matthew's Gospel, therefore—like any other biblical text—has charac-teristics of its own, which we will later examine. These help to identify the human author and they combine perfectly with the divine hallmark that is to be found in all the books of Holy Scripture.

Much less is known about St Matthew than about certain other New Testament authors, such as St Peter, St Paul and St John. We do know that very soon after being called to be an apostle, the immense joy he felt over his voca-tion led him to give a large dinner-party for his old friends and colleagues, a party attended by Jesus and by Matthew's new companions in the apostolate (cf. Mt 9:10–13; Mk 2:15–17; Lk 5:29–32). St Luke describes it as a "great feast" for "a large company": this shows that Matthew was well-to-do, had many friends and was held in high regard in Capernaum, despite the low opin-ion the Jews generally had of tax collectors.

St Matthew himself tells about how Jesus first called him (cf. Mt 9:9–12). When Jesus addressed him personally, in affectionate and at the same time imperative terms, Matthew immediately left his position as a tax collector and

---

2. Leo XIII, Enc. *Providentissimus Deus*.

"followed him" (cf. Mt 9:9; Mk 2:14; Lk 5:27). From St Luke (5:27) we learn that Matthew was also known as Levi, and St Mark (2:14) further specifies him as "Levi the son of Alphaeus".

Later on, St Matthew received a further call from our Lord: after spending a night in prayer Jesus chose him to be one of the twelve apostles (cf. Mt 10:1–14; Mk 3:13–19; Lk 6:12–16; 9:1–2; Acts 1:13). We find him involved in those episodes of our Lord's life where the Twelve are present—or the Eleven after Judas' betrayal. He was, therefore, an eye-witness of the life of Christ.

After the events reported in the Gospels and in the Acts of the Apostles, the New Testament tells us nothing further about Matthew's life. According to an ancient tradition reflected in Christian writers of the second to fourth centuries (St Irenaeus, Clement of Alexandria, Eusebius etc.), Matthew stayed in Palestine for some years, working with the other apostles, preaching the Gospel and ministering to the early Church. He would have written his Gospel towards the end of that period.

In later years he evangelized other countries, but no hard historical evidence is available in this connexion. Some documents speak of his ministering mainly in Abyssinia and Persia. The place, circumstances and date of his martyrdom are unclear.

DATE OF COMPOSITION

Written testimonies going back as early as the beginning of the second century assure us that St Matthew was the first to write down the Gospel of Jesus Christ "in the language of the Hebrews". This would have been the language spoken at that time by the Jews of Palestine; it is difficult to say exactly whether the evangelist used Hebrew or Aramaic, because no copy of the original text is extant nor any description of it—merely references to its existence. All we can say is that most scholars think that it must have been written in Aramaic. However, the Greek text of this Gospel was very soon accepted as canonical; Christian documents going back to the end of the first century show that it was widely known and used; these are: the *Didache*, written between AD 80 and 100; the *First Letter* of Pope St Clement of Rome, written between 92 and 101; the so-called *Letter of Barnabas*, written between 96 and 98; the *Letters* of St Ignatius of Antioch, martyred around the year 107; the writings of St Polycarp, who died in 156; etc.

We know that St Matthew wrote his (Aramaic) Gospel before the other evangelists wrote theirs; the estimated date is around the year 50. We do not know the date of composition of the Greek text, which is the one we have. Nor do we know whether the Greek editor was St Matthew himself or some other early Christian. The most likely date for this text is around the year 70. In any event, the original text (Aramaic or Hebrew) of St Matthew is to be dated prior to the destruction of Jerusalem (the year 70) and indeed prior to St Paul's journey to Rome (the year 60). In view of the general agreement among the Fathers and ancient ecclesiastical writers and the unanimous tradition of the Church from the beginning, our Greek Matthew, the only Matthew text used as canonical, is substantially identical with the original Matthew written in the language of the Jews.

AUTHENTICITY AND CANONICITY

The authenticity of the original Jewish-language text of St Matthew has never been questioned by the Church: in other words, it was always held that the apostle St Matthew is the author of the Gospel which bears his name. Similarly the Church has always regarded the Greek text as canonical.

THE PURPOSE OF THIS GOSPEL

The primary purpose of St Matthew's Gospel is identical with that of the other three. St John sums up this purpose very well in these words: "Now Jesus did many other signs in the presence of his disciples, which are not written in this book; but these are written that you may believe that Jesus is the Christ, the Son of God, and that believing you may have life in his name" (Jn 20:30–31). His purpose is also to show, in the first place, that Jesus of Nazareth is the Christ or Messiah promised and announced in the Old Testament, that is, that the ancient prophecies find their fulfilment in Christ; and that this messiahship consists in Jesus being the Son of God, that is, that Jesus Christ is God. This truth is illustrated and explained by providing a rich account of our Lord's teaching and reporting certain aspects or episodes of his life among men. Finally, "the Kingdom of God" or "the Kingdom of heaven", predicted in the Old Testament, has now come to pass and been made visible in the life of Jesus and in that of the messianic people he founded and convoked—the Church. That Church is the perfecting of the ancient people of God—Israel—and is the visible beginning of the definitive and perfect Kingdom of heaven, to which all are called; but only those will be finally chosen who have responded generously to God's call.

To put it another way, the first Gospel sets out to proclaim in writing the "Good News", which the apostles preached orally—news to the effect that the salvation of Israel and of mankind, promised by God in the Old Testament, has now been brought into the world by Jesus Christ, the Messiah and the Son of God; men are enabled to know this by the marvellous account given in the Gospel, in which Jesus' words and works explain each other and reach their climax in his redemptive sacrifice, his passion and death, followed by his glorious resurrection.

CONTENT

In broad outline the content of the first Gospel can be summed up as follows: the birth and infancy of Jesus; the announcement by John the Baptist, the Precursor, that Christ is about to begin his mission; Jesus' public ministry in Galilee and the calling of the twelve apostles: here he begins to reveal his messiahship and divinity, through his teaching and miracles; journeys Jesus makes with his disciples, doing good, curing the sick, teaching—in other words fulfilling what the Old Testament prophecies said about him; the last stage of his public ministry in Judea and Jerusalem; the account of his passion and death; his glorious resurrection; and post-resurrection appearances.

An outstanding feature of this Gospel is its account of five long discourses of Jesus; these, and the narrative parts of the Gospel, shed light on each other and lead the reader into the drama of Christ's death and the joy of his resurrection.

It is really not possible to fit St Matthew's Gospel into any kind of rigid structure. However, the following outline may be of some help:

1. *Birth and infancy of Jesus* (chaps. 1–2). A selection of the basic historical facts which illustrate and explain the following truths of faith: Jesus is the Messiah descended from David, the Saviour promised in the Old Testament; the Son of God, conceived by the action of the Holy Spirit and born of the Virgin Mary; the *Emmanuel* or *God-with-us* prophesied by Isaiah, protected during his infancy by a special providence of God (the fatherly care given him by St Joseph and the maternal affection of the Blessed Virgin Mary); the King of Israel, adored even by Gentiles (the wise men). The sober accounts—simple yet profound—comprising these two chapters already bring in quite a number of the basic truths about the divine and human mystery of Jesus Christ.

2. *Prelude to the public ministry of Jesus* (3:1—4:11). This takes place in regions which for centuries lived in hope of salvation—the Judean desert and the river Jordan. Here we find the Baptist's prophetic announcement of the imminence of the Kingdom of God; his exhortation to conversion and

penance; the baptism of Jesus, accompanied by the revelation that he is the Son of God made man; and the temptations of Jesus in the wilderness.

PART ONE: JESUS' MINISTRY IN GALILEE
The beginnings of the message of salvation, the calling of the disciples and the convocation of the new people of God (4:12–25).

3. *The sermon on the mount.* Jesus, the supreme Teacher, Lawgiver and Prophet: the "discourse on the mount" (chaps. 5–7), the first of the five great discourses and a summary of the new Law of the Kingdom of God; Jesus, God made man, teaches a most sublime doctrine never heard before, in words simple yet totally demanding; this is the way of salvation which man must follow. This discourse is a kind of distillate of the teachings of Jesus the Messiah on evangelical holiness.

4. *The miracles of the Messiah* (chaps. 8–9). Following on these words or teachings, St Matthew's Gospel presents an array of miracles, whereby our Lord backs up his teaching with divine authority. These miracles also mean that the salvation promised in the Old Testament has come about in the person of Jesus. Also, the curing of the sick shows that men are being set free from sin, because sin is the ultimate cause of illness and mortality in man. These two chapters are, then, a kind of summary of "the words of the Messiah".

5. *From the old to the new people of God.* The first sending forth of the disciples, the "apostolic discourse", the hardening of the hearts of the religious leaders of Israel against Jesus' messiahship (chaps. 10–12); Jesus trains his twelve apostles for their immediate mission and for the future (chap. 10). In reaction to the proclamation of Jesus as Messiah—through his words and works and his convocation of the new messianic people (chaps. 3–10)—the Jewish leaders grow more and more opposed to him (chaps. 11–12). The scene is being set for their rejection of him, their plotting of his death, and the foundation of the Church as the new people of God.

6. *The parables of the Kingdom* (chap. 13). Despite this, Jesus continues to reveal to the people the mystery of the Kingdom of God, or Kingdom of heaven. This he does by means of parables—a teaching method suited to the capacity of his listeners. These parables contain a substantial proportion of his teaching concerning the Church which he will found; from a small beginning it will grow until the end of time. This "parabolic discourse" ends with a visit to Nazareth, where Jesus encounters the incredulity of his fellow-townsmen. This brings to an end what we might call the first part of St Matthew's Gospel.

7. *Jesus withdraws to the border country* (13:53—16:20). In view of the growing antagonism of the Jewish religious authorities and the martyrdom of John the Baptist, Jesus makes a series of evangelical journeys in the regions adjoining Israel. His disciples accompany him. These journeys are an advance indication of the universality of the Gospel; but they also act as a form of retreat, enabling Jesus to continue his ministry undisturbed, and to avoid precipitating his passion. Jesus teaches his disciples, with an eye to founding his Church. Outside Israel proper, in Caesarea Philippi, Peter makes a confession of faith in Jesus as Messiah, and Jesus promises to make Peter the head of his Church (Mt 16:13–20).

PART TWO: JESUS' MINISTRY ON THE WAY TO JERUSALEM
8. *Towards Judea and Jerusalem* (16:21—17:27). The transfiguration of Jesus and new teachings (chap. 17): Jesus' divinity is revealed to his disciples.

9. *The discourse on the Church* (chap. 18): so called because it contains specific teaching about the life of the future Church, and the authority of the apostles and their successors.

Various teachings of Jesus—on marriage and virginity, poverty, humility, etc. (chap. 19); the parable of the labourers in the vineyard; the third announcement of the Passion, etc. (chap. 20).

PART THREE: JESUS' MINISTRY IN JERUSALEM
10. *Cleansing of the temple. Controversies* (21:1—23:39). This begins with his messianic entry into the Holy City and the temple (21:1–17), followed by teaching concerning Christ's authority (21:18–27) and three great allegorical parables (21:28—22:14) on salvation history and the mystery of the Church. Then comes an account of controversies with the Pharisees (22:15–46) in which they bring up various questions in the hope that Jesus will provide them with grounds for indicting him. These events lead to Jesus' invective against the scribes and Pharisees ("Woe to him ...": 23:13–36) and his lament over the destruction of Jerusalem (23:37–39).

11. *The eschatological discourse.* This section ends with Jesus' prophecies about the destruction of Jerusalem and the end of the world—the "eschatological discourse" (chaps. 24–25): the prophecies (24:1–36) are followed by teaching about the vigilance required of a Christian (24:37—25:30). Our Lord illustrates his teaching by three parables—that of the unjust servant (24:45–51), that of the ten virgins (25:1–13), and the parable of the talents (25:14–30). The eschatological discourse ends with teaching on the Last Judgment, where Jesus himself will be the judge (25:31–46).

12. *The passion, death and resurrection of Jesus* (chaps. 26–28). Like the other three Gospels, St Matthew's devotes considerable space to its account of the passion and death of the Son of God, which embraces the truths every Christian should know regarding the sacrifice of the Messiah. Two chapters cover the period from the anointing at Bethany (26:6–13), to the death of Jesus on the cross (27:45–56), his burial (27:57–61) and the placing of the guard over the tomb (27:62–66). At various points the Passion account throws light on Old Testament prophecies which predicted the Passion in one way or another.

Also like the other Gospels, St Matthew's ends with Jesus' victory over death through his glorious resurrection—a message of immense joy, hope and faith. It tells how the tomb was found to be empty (28:1–8, 11–15) and of the appearances of the risen Jesus to the holy women (28:9–10) and to the apostles (28:16–17). The Gospel ends with the proclamation of the absolute lordship of Jesus Christ, now glorified (28:18), and his charge to his disciples to preach the Gospel throughout the world, baptizing in the name of the three divine persons (28:19–20).

SPECIAL FEATURES

The Gospel of St Matthew is a divine and human work. God is the principal author of the book, and his purpose goes beyond that of the human author, his instrument. St Matthew—man, apostle and evangelist—does speak to us through these pages: but, above all, God himself is speaking. This means that no matter how much honest effort is put into studying and explaining this Gospel—or any other part of Holy Scripture—we can never grasp its full meaning. God's purpose in inspiring a particular man to write this book is to reveal to us something about himself and to entrust this text to his Church, which will make it comprehensible to us and helpful to our sanctification and eternal salvation. St Matthew's Gospel is one of the most precious of all the many gifts God has given us in Scripture; we should thank God for it, in the first instance; but we should also be grateful to the man who, with the help of divine inspiration, took pains to write it.

THE GOSPEL OF THE DISCOURSES OF THE LORD

St Matthew's Gospel has been called "the Gospel of the Discourses of the Lord" because of the five long discourses it contains. Through these we can hear Jesus' words and be present when he preaches. However, we should not forget that, since the Gospel was written under the inspiration of the Holy Spirit and has God as its principal author, the entire text—not just these discourses—is truly the word of God, and "all that the hagiographer (or sacred writer) affirms should be regarded as affirmed by the Holy Spirit".[3]

These five discourses are: the discourse on the mount (chaps. 5–7); the apostolic discourse (chap. 10); the parabolic discourse (chap. 13); the discourse on the Church (chap. 18); and the eschatological discourse (chaps. 24–25). There are also shorter discourses—such as Christ's indictment of the Pharisees and scribes (23:13–36) and some of his controversies with the Pharisees (12:25–45). Usually these discourses are preceded by other passages describing the development of events; the discourse part and narrative part of the account combine to help us understand the deep meaning of the works and words of Jesus.

THE GOSPEL OF FULFILMENT

Although each of the four Gospels was written for all men in all ages, God also wrote them for a particular immediate readership. In the case of Matthew, the text was obviously written in a manner suited to Christians of Jewish background—its immediate readers—as well as for later generations. Matthew, for example, is at pains to show that all the Old Testament finds its fulfilment in the person and work of Christ: at particularly important points in Jesus' life, the evangelist expressly points out that "this took place to fulfil what the Lord had spoken by the prophet" or words to that effect (cf., e.g., Mt 1:23; 2:6, 15, 17–18; 3:3–4; 4:4, 14–16; 5:17; 21:4–5, 16; 26:31; 27:9–10). This feature of his Gospel has led to its being called "the Gospel of fulfilment". Insight into the Old Testament in the light of the New is not unique to St Matthew's Gospel, for it was something Jesus was always teaching to his disciples and something that the Holy Spirit also revealed to them—it is the science of "understanding the Scriptures" (cf., e.g., Lk 24:32, 45; Acts 8:35)—but it was clearly an important factor in the evangelization of Jews and in their subsequent catechesis.

JESUS, THE REJECTED MESSIAH

In countless ways all the books of the New Testament show that Jesus is the promised Messiah, the Christ, the Lord (*Kyrios*) and the Son of God; and they also reveal the mystery of God, one essence and three persons.

But within this general teaching common to them all, it is clear from the particular accents it carries that Matthew's Gospel was addressed in the first instance to Christians of Jewish background. In keeping with what has been said about the "Gospel of fulfilment", it points out that the beginning of

---

3. Vatican II, *Dei Verbum*, 11.

Christ's public preaching is the dawn of messianic light (cf. Mt 4:13–17) fore-told by the prophet Isaiah (cf. Is 8:23—9:1); similarly the first cures Jesus per-forms (cf. Mt 8:16–17) are presented as fulfilling the words of the prophets, particularly Isaiah (cf. Is 53:4–5).

And, above all, the first Gospel contains teaching and events which dra-matically emphasize the mystery of the rejection of Jesus, the promised Messiah, by the rulers of the Jews, and by many of the people, whom those rulers succeeded in misleading. Guided by the light of divine inspiration, the evangelist confronts this mystery in various ways: sometimes, when report-ing how the scribes, Pharisees and chief priests react against Jesus, or when narrating the way he suffers during his passion, he stresses that all this, far from frustrating God's plan, was foreseen and predicted by the Old Testament prophets and fulfils what they predicted would happen (cf. Mt 12:17; 13:35; 26:54, 56; 27:9; etc.). At other times he explains that this rejec-tion of the Messiah by Israel is in line with and a culmination of a whole his-tory of infidelity to God's generosity and love (cf., e.g., Mt 21:28–44; 23:9–33). In any event the Gospel shows the pain Christ feels over Israel's failure to respond to his love and the punishment that lies in store for it if it fails to mend its ways (cf. Mt 23:37–39).

THE GOSPEL OF THE KINGDOM

St Matthew refers 51 times to "the Kingdom", St Mark 14 times and St Luke 39. But whereas the two last-mentioned speak of "the Kingdom of God", Matthew on all but five occasions uses the phrase "the Kingdom of heaven". This must certainly have been the phrase Jesus normally used, given the Jewish custom of the time not to utter the name of God—out of respect—but instead to use other equivalent terms such as "of heaven". The Kingdom of God comes into being with the arrival of Christ (cf. note on Mt 3:2) and, espe-cially in the parables, Jesus explains what its features are (cf. note on Mt 13:3). The first Gospel is called the "Gospel of the Kingdom" because it throws so much light on these features.

THE DIVINITY OF JESUS

Christ's divinity is affirmed in various ways in this Gospel. From the conception of Jesus by the action of the Holy Spirit (Mt 1:20) to the trinitarian formula for Baptism at the end (Mt 28:19), the first Gospel asserts and stresses that Jesus, the Christ, is the Son of God. In numerous passages it mentions the relationship between the Father and the Son: Jesus is the Son of the Father, the Father is God, and the Son is equal to the Father. Some passages also place the Father, the Son and the Holy Spirit on the same level (the most famous being that just mentioned: Mt 28:19). What this means is that the revelation of the Blessed Trinity, a revelation expressly made by Jesus Christ, is affirmed in St Matthew's Gospel by the revelation that Jesus is the Son of the Father, and God like him.

In the light of this essential truth, that Jesus is the Son of God, all the other messianic titles which the Old Testament used in prophecies about the Saviour fall into place—Son of David, Son of man, Messiah, Lord.

THE GOSPEL OF THE CHURCH

This Gospel has also been called the "ecclesiastical Gospel" or the "Gospel of the Church". One reason for this is that the actual word "church" appears three times (cf. Mt 16:18; 18:17 twice). Another is that the Church, even without being expressly named, can be seen to be in the background of the narrative: it is hinted at in different ways in quite a few parables; its foundation is announced and explicitly expressed when Peter is promised the primacy (cf. Mt 16:17–19); its beginning can in some way be seen in the discourse in chapter 18; it is figuratively depicted in some episodes such as that of the calming of the storm (cf. Mt 8:23–27); it is cast in the role of the new, true Israel in the parable of the wicked tenants of the vineyard (cf. Mt 21:33–45); and its role as universal vessel of salvation is based on the apostolic charge which our Lord gives at the end of the Gospel. In effect, the Church forms a background to the entire text of this Gospel and is ever-present in the mind and heart of the evangelist—as it is in the mind and heart of Jesus Christ.

LITERARY STYLE

From what has been said about its content and structure it can be seen that the Gospel also has strong literary unity: every paragraph is written in line with the writer's purpose; this affects both the content of the writing and the context in which it is placed. As the reader grows more familiar with the text he notices more hints, more symbolism and additional teaching developing themes already covered quite elaborately.

The precision with which Matthew articulates Jesus' teaching comes across very clearly. He writes in a concise, sober and thoughtful style, and a person making his way through the book will find that it enters into his soul and brings him face to face with the powerful yet tender mystery of Jesus Christ.

Many commentators have pointed out that St Matthew's particular style has the effect of making many of his phrases easy to recognize: we often find ourselves quoting Matthew's version in preference to other Gospel accounts. For this reason his Gospel has been called the first Gospel of Christian catechesis.

ST MATTHEW'S GOSPEL IN THE LIFE OF THE CHURCH

From the end of the first century—in references by Pope St Clement—there is overwhelming evidence of predominant use of the St Matthew text in the teachings of the Church's Magisterium. The early Fathers are forever quoting it and many later Fathers commented on it (for example, there are ninety long homilies by St John Chrysostom) as did the great teachers of the Middle Ages (for example, St Thomas Aquinas) and later ecclesiastical writers.

THE GOSPEL ACCORDING TO MATTHEW

The Revised Standard Version, with notes

1. BIRTH AND INFANCY OF JESUS

The ancestry of Jesus Christ

1 ¹The book of the genealogy of Jesus Christ, the son of David, the son of Abraham.*

²Abraham was the father of Isaac, and Isaac the father of Jacob, and Jacob the father of Judah and his brothers, ³and Judah the father of Perez and Zerah by Tamar, and Perez the father of Hezron, and Hezron the father of Ram,ᵃ ⁴and Ramᵃ the father of Amminadab, and Amminadab the father of Nahson, and Nahson the father of Salmon, ⁵and Salmon the father of Boaz by Rahab, and Boaz the father of Obed by Ruth, and Obed the father of Jesse, ⁶and Jesse the father of David the king.

And David was the father of Solomon by the wife of Uriah, ⁷and Solomon the father of Rehoboam, and Rehoboam the father of Abijah, and Abijah the father of Asa,ᵇ ⁸and Asaᵇ the father of

Lk 3:23–38
1 Chron 17:11
Gen 5:1; 22:1

Gen 21:3, 12; 25:26; 29:35; 49:10

1 Chron 1:34

1 Chron 2:5, 9
Gen 38:29f
Ruth 4:18–22
1 Chron 2:10f
Ruth 4:13–17

2 Sam 12:24

1 Chron 3:10–16

1:1. This verse is a kind of title to St Matthew's entire Gospel. The promises God made to Abraham for the salvation of mankind (Gen 12:3) are fulfilled in Jesus Christ, as is Nathan's prophecy to King David of an everlasting kingdom (2 Sam 7:12–16).

The genealogy presented here by St Matthew shows Jesus' human ancestry and also indicates that salvation history has reached its climax with the birth of the Son of God through the working of the Holy Spirit. Jesus Christ, true God and true man, is the expected Messiah.

The genealogy is presented in a framework of three series, each consisting of fourteen links which show the progressive development of salvation history.

For the Jews (and for other Eastern peoples of nomadic origin) genealogical trees were of great importance because a person's identity was especially linked to family and tribe, with place of birth taking secondary importance. In the case of the Jewish people there was the added

religious significance of belonging by blood to the chosen people.

In Christ's time each family still kept a careful record of its genealogical tree, since because of it people acquired rights and duties.

1:6. Four women are named in these genealogies—Tamar (cf. Gen 38; 1 Chron 2:4), Rahab (cf. Josh 2:6, 17). Bathsheba (cf. 2 Sam 11:2, 24) and Ruth (cf. Book of Ruth). These four foreign women, who in one way or another are brought into the history of Israel, are one sign among many others of God's design to save all men.

By mentioning sinful people, God's ways are shown to be different from man's. God will sometimes carry out his plan of salvation by means of people whose conduct has not been just. God saves us, sanctifies us and chooses us to do good despite our sins and infidelities—and he chose to leave evidence of this at various stages in the history of our salvation.

a. Greek *Aram* **b.** Greek *Asaph*

Jehoshaphat, and Jehoshaphat the father of Joram, and Joram the father of Uzziah, [9]and Uzziah the father of Jotham, and Jotham the father of Ahaz, and Ahaz the father of Hezekiah, [10]and Hezekiah the father of Manasseh, and Manasseh the father of Amos,[c]

Ezra 1:32

and Amos[c] the father of Josiah, [11]and Josiah the father of Jechoniah and his brothers, at the time of the deportation to Babylon.

1 Chron 3:17
Ezra 3:2

[12]And after the deportation to Babylon: Jechoniah was the father of Shealtiel,[d] and Shealtiel[d] the father of Zerubbabel, [13]and Zerubbabel the father of Abiud, and Abiud the father of Eliakim, and Eliakim the father of Azor, [14]and Azor the father of Zadok, and Zadok the father of Achim, and Achim the father of Eliud,[15] and Eliud the father of Eleazar, and Eleazar the father of Matthan, and Matthan the father of Jacob, [16]and Jacob the father of Joseph the husband of Mary, of whom Jesus was born, who is called Christ.*

1:11. The deportation to Babylon, described in 2 Kings 24–25, fulfilled the prophets' warning to the people of Israel and their kings that they would be punished for their infidelity to the commandments of the Law of God, especially the first commandment.

1:16. Jewish genealogies followed the male line. Joseph, being Mary's husband, was the legal father of Jesus. The legal father is on a par with the real father as regards rights and duties. This fact provides a sound basis for recognizing St Joseph as Patron of the whole Church, since he was chosen to play a very special role in God's plan for our salvation; with St Joseph as his legal father, Jesus the Messiah has David as his ancestor.

Since it was quite usual for people to marry within their clan, it can be concluded that Mary belonged to the house of David. Several early Fathers of the church testify to this—for example, St Ignatius of Antioch, St Irenaeus, St Justin and Tertullian, who base their testimony on an unbroken oral tradition.

It should also be pointed out that when St Matthew comes to speak of the birth of Jesus, he uses an expression which is completely different from that used for the other people in the genealogy. With these words the text positively teaches that Mary conceived Jesus while still a virgin, without the intervention of man.

1:18. St Matthew relates here how Christ was conceived (cf. Lk 1:25–38): "We truly honour and venerate (Mary) as Mother of God, because she gave birth to a person who is at the same time both God and man" (St Pius V, *Catechism*, 1, 4, 7).

According to the provisions of the Law of Moses, engagement took place about one year before marriage and enjoyed almost the same legal validity. The marriage proper consisted, among other ceremonies, in the bride being brought solemnly and joyously to her husband's house (cf. Deut 20:7)

From the moment of engagement onwards, a certificate of divorce was needed in the event of a break in the relationship between the couple. The entire account of Jesus' birth teaches, through

---

c. Other authorities read *Amon* **d.** Greek *Salathiel*

[17]So all the generations from Abraham to David were fourteen generations, and from David to the deportation to Babylon fourteen generations, and from the deportation to Babylon to the Christ fourteen generations.

The virginal conception of Jesus, and his birth
[18]Now the birth of Jesus Christ[f] took place in this way. When his mother Mary had been betrothed to Joseph, before they came together she was found to be with child of the Holy Spirit; [19]and her husband Joseph, being a just man and unwilling to put her to shame, resolved to send her away quietly. [20]But as he considered this, behold, an angel of the Lord appeared to him in a dream, saying, "Joseph, son of David, do not fear to take Mary your wife,

Lk 1:35

the fulfilment of the prophecy of Isaiah 7:14 (which is expressly quoted in vv. 22–23) that: 1) Jesus has David as his ancestor since Joseph is his legal father; 2) Mary is the Virgin who gives birth according to the prophecy; 3) the Child's conception without the intervention of man was miraculous.

1:19. "St Joseph was an ordinary sort of man on whom God relied to do great things. He did exactly what the Lord wanted him to do, in each and every event that went to make up his life. That is why Scripture praises Joseph as a 'just man' (Mt 1:19). In Hebrew a just man means a good and faithful servant of God, someone who fulfils the divine will (cf. Gen 7:1; 18:23–32; Ezek 18:5ff; Prov 12:10), or who is honourable and charitable towards his neighbour (cf. Tob 7:6; 9:6). So a just man is someone who loves God and proves his love by keeping God's commandments and directing his whole life towards the service of his brothers, his fellow men" (St Josemaría Escrivá, *Christ Is Passing By*, 40).

Joseph considered his spouse to be holy despite the signs that she was going to have a child. He was therefore faced with a situation he could not explain. Precisely because he was trying to do God's will, he felt obliged to put her away; but to shield her from public shame he decided to send her away quietly.

Mary's silence is admirable. Her perfect surrender to God even leads her to the extreme of not defending her honour or innocence. She prefers to suffer suspicion and shame rather than reveal the work of grace in her. Faced with a fact which was inexplicable in human terms she abandons herself confidently to the love and providence of God. God certainly subjected the holy souls of Joseph and Mary to a severe trial. We ought not be surprised if we also undergo difficult trials in the course of our lives. We ought to trust in God during them, and remain faithful to him, following the example Mary and Joseph gave us.

1:20. God gives his light to those who act in an upright way and who trust in his power and wisdom when faced with situations which exceed human understanding. By calling him the son of David, the angel reminds Joseph that he is the prov-

f. Other ancient authorities read *of the Christ*

Lk 1:31; 2:21
Acts 4:12

Is 7:14
Lk 2:7

for that which is conceived in her is of the Holy Spirit; [21]she will bear a son, and you shall call his name Jesus, for he will save his people from their sins." [22]All this took place to fulfil what the Lord had spoken by the prophet:
[23]"Behold, a virgin shall conceive and bear a son,
and his name shall be called Emmanuel"

---

idential link which joins Jesus with the family of David, according to Nathan's messianic prophecy (cf. 2 Sam 7:12). As St John Chrysostom says: "At the very start he straightaway reminds him of David, of whom the Christ was to spring, and he does not wish him to be worried from the moment he reminds him, through naming his most illustrious ancestor, of the promise made to all his lineage" (*Hom. on St Matthew*, 4).

"The same Jesus Christ, our only Lord, the Son of God, when he assumed human flesh for us in the womb of the Virgin, was not conceived like other men, from the seed of man, but in a manner transcending the order of nature, that is, by the power of the Holy Spirit, so that the same person, remaining God as he was from eternity, became man, which he was not before" (St Pius V, *Catechism*, 1, 4, 1).

1:21. According to the Hebrew root, the name of Jesus means "saviour". After our Lady, St Joseph is the first person to be told by God that salvation has begun. "Jesus is the proper name of the God-man and signifies 'Saviour', a name given him not accidentally, or by the judgment or will of man, but by the counsel and command of God" [...]. All other names which prophecy gave to the Son of God—Wonderful Counsellor, Mighty God, Everlasting Father, Prince of Peace (cf. Is 9:6)—are comprised in this one name Jesus; for while they partially signified the salvation which he was to bestow

on us, this name included the force and meaning of all human salvation" (St Pius V, *Catechism*, 1, 3, 5 and 6).

1:23. "Emmanuel": the prophecy of Isaiah 7:14, quoted in this verse, foretold about seven hundred years in advance that God's salvation would be marked by the extraordinary event of a virgin giving birth to a child. The Gospel here, therefore, reveals two truths.

The first is that Jesus is in fact the God-with-us foretold by the prophet. This is how Christian tradition has always understood it. Indeed the Church has officially condemned an interpretation denying the messianic sense of the Isaiah text (cf. Pius VI, Brief *Divina*, 1779). Christ is truly God-with-us, therefore, not only because of his God-given mission but because he is God made man (cf. Jn 1:14). This does not mean that Jesus should normally be called Emmanuel, for this name refers more directly to the mystery of his being the Incarnate Word. At the Annunciation the angel said that he should be called Jesus, that is, Saviour. And that was the name St Joseph gave him.

The second truth revealed to us by the sacred text is that Mary, in whom the prophecy of Isaiah 7:14 is fulfilled, was a virgin before and during the birth itself. The miraculous sign given by God that salvation had arrived was precisely that a woman would be a virgin and a mother at the same time. "Jesus Christ came forth from his mother's womb without injury

(which means God with us). [24]When Joseph woke from sleep, he did as the angel of the Lord commanded him; he took his wife, [25]but knew her not until she had borne a son;* and he called his name Jesus.

---

to her maternal virginity. This immaculate and perpetual virginity forms, therefore, the just theme of our eulogy. Such was the work of the Holy Spirit, who at the conception and birth of the Son so favoured the Virgin Mother as to impart fruitfulness to her while preserving inviolate her perpetual virginity" (St Pius V, *Catechism*, 1, 4, 8).

1:25. St John Chrysostom, addressing himself to St Joseph, comments: "Christ's conception was the work of the Holy Spirit, but do not think this divine economy has nothing to do with you. For although it is true that you had no part in the generation of Christ, and that the Virgin remained inviolate, nevertheless, what pertains to a father (not injuring the honour of virginity) that do I give you— the naming of the child. For 'you shall call his name'. Although you have not generated him, you will act as a father to him. Hence it is that, beginning with giving him his name, I associate you intimately with the one who is to be born" (*Hom. on St Matthew*, 4).

Following the Greek text strictly, the New Vulgate version says: "et non cognoscebat eam, *donec* peperit filium". The literal English translation is: "and he knew her not *until* she had borne a son". The word "*donec*" (until) of itself does not direct our attention to what happened afterwards; it simply points out what has happened up to that moment, that is, the virginal conception of Jesus Christ by a unique intervention of God. We find the same word in John 9:18, where it says that the Pharisees did not believe in the miraculous cure of the man blind from

birth "until" (*donec*) they called his parents. However, neither did they believe afterwards. Consequently, the word "until" does not refer to what happens later.

The Vulgate adds after "*filium*" the words "*suum primogenitum*", which in the Bible simply means "the first son", without implying that there are any other children (cf. Ex 13:2). This Latin variant gives no ground whatsoever for thinking that our Lady had other children later. See the note on Lk 2:7.

The Church has always taught that the perpetual virginity of our Lady is a truth to be held by Catholics. For example, the following are the words of the Lateran Council of AD 649: "If anyone does not profess according to the holy Fathers, that in the proper and true sense, the holy, ever-virgin, immaculate Mary is the Mother of God, since in this last age not with human seed but of the Holy Spirit she properly and truly conceived the Divine Word, who was born of God the Father before all ages, and gave him birth without any detriment to her virginity, which remained inviolate even after his birth: let such a one be condemned" (can. 3).

St Jerome gives the following reasons why it was fitting that the Mother of God, as well as being a virgin, should also be married: first, so that Mary's child would be clearly a descendant of King David (through the genealogy of St Joseph); second, to ensure that on having a son her honour would not be questioned nor any legal penalty be imposed on her; third, so that during the flight into Egypt she would have the help and pro-

The adoration of the Magi

Lk 2:1–7

Num 24:17

2 [1]Now when Jesus was born in Bethlehem of Judea in the days of Herod the king, behold, wise men from the East came to Jerusalem, saying, [2]"Where is he who has been born king of the Jews? For we have seen his star in the East, and have come to

---

tection of St Joseph. He even points to a fourth possible reason, expressly taken from St Ignatius Martyr, and to which he seems to give less importance—that the birth of Jesus would go unnoticed by the devil, who would have no knowledge of the virginal conception of our Lord (cf. *Comm. on Matthew*, 1, 1).

2:1. "King Herod": four different Herods are mentioned in the New Testament. The first is Herod the Great, referred to in this passage and in the next; the second, his son, Herod Antipas, who had St John the Baptist beheaded (Mt 14:1–12) and who abused our Lord during his passion (Lk 23:7–11); the third, Herod Agrippa I, a grandson of Herod the Great, who executed the apostle St James the Greater (Acts 12: 1–3), imprisoned St Peter (Acts 12:4–7), and died suddenly and mysteriously (Acts 12:20–23). The fourth, Herod Agrippa II, was Herod Agrippa I's son. It was before him that St Paul answered Jewish accusations when he was a prisoner in Caesarea (Acts 25:23).

Herod the Great, who appears here, was the son of non-Jewish parents. He came to power with the aid and as a vassal of the Romans. He was a consummate politician and among other things he rebuilt the temple in Jerusalem on a lavish scale. Herod the Great had a persecution complex; everywhere he saw rivals to his throne. He was notorious for his cruelty: he killed over half of his ten wives, some of his children and many people of standing. This information derives largely from the Jewish historian

Flavius Josephus, who wrote towards the end of the first century, and it confirms the cruel picture drawn in the Gospels.

"Wise men": these were learned men, probably from Persia, who devoted themselves to the study of the stars. Since they were not Jews, they can be considered to be the very first Gentiles to receive the call to salvation in Christ. The adoration of the wise men forms part of the very earliest documented tradition: the scene is already depicted at the beginning of the second century in the paintings in the catacombs of St Priscilla in Rome.

2:2. The Jews had made known throughout the East their hope of a Messiah. The wise men knew about this expected Messiah, king of the Jews. According to ideas widely accepted at the time, this sort of person, because of his significance in world history, would have a star connected with his birth. God made use of these ideas to draw to Christ these representatives of the Gentiles who would later be converted

"The star had been hidden from them so that, on finding themselves without their guide, they would have no alternative but to consult the Jews. In this way the birth of Jesus would be made known to all" (St John Chrysostom, *Hom. on St Matthew*, 7). Chrysostom also points out that "God calls them by means of the things they are most familiar with: and he shows them a large and extraordinary star so that they would be impressed by its size and beauty" (ibid., 6). God called the wise men in the midst of their ordinary occupations, and he still calls people in

worship him." ³When Herod the king heard this, he was troubled, and all Jerusalem with him; ⁴and assembling all the chief priests and scribes of the people, he inquired of them where the Christ was to be born. ⁵They told him, "In Bethlehem of Judea; for so it is written by the prophet:

Mic 5:2
Jn 7:42

---

that way. He called Moses when he was shepherding his flock (Ex 3:1–3), Elisha the prophet ploughing his land with oxen (1 Kings 19:19–20), Amos looking after his herd (Amos 7:15). ... "What amazes you seems natural to me: that God has sought you out in the practice of your profession! That is how he sought at first, Peter and Andrew, James and John, beside their nets, and Matthew, sitting in the custom-house. And—wonder of wonders!—Paul, in his eagerness to destroy the seeds of Christianity" (St Josemaría Escrivá, *The Way*, 799).

"Like the Magi we have discovered a star—a light and a guide in the sky of our soul. 'We have seen his star in the East and have come to worship him (Mt 2:2).' We have had the same experience. We too noticed a new light shining in our soul and growing increasingly brighter. It was a desire to live a fully Christian life, a keenness to take God seriously" (St J. Escrivá, *Christ Is Passing By*, 32).

2:4. In all Jewish circles at the time of Jesus, the hope was widespread that the Messiah would come soon. The general idea was that he would be a king, like a new and even greater David. Herod's worry is therefore all the more understandable: he governed the Jews with the aid of the Romans and cruelly and jealously guarded his crown. Due to his political ambition and his lack of religious sense, Herod saw a potential Messiah-King as a dangerous rival to his own worldly power.

In the time of our Lord, both Herod's monarchy and the occupying Romans (through their procurators) recognized the Sanhedrin as the representative body of the Jewish people. The Sanhedrin was, therefore, the nation's supreme council which ruled on day-to-day affairs, both religious and civil. The handling of the more important questions needed the approval of either the king (under Herod's monarchy) or the Roman procurator (at the time of the direct Roman occupation of Palestine). Following Exodus 24:1–9 and Numbers 11:16, the Sanhedrin was composed of seventy-one members presided over by the high priest. The members were elected from three groupings: 1) the chief priests, that is, the leaders of the principal priestly families; it was these families who appointed the high priest (the chief priests also included anybody who had formerly held the high priesthood); 2) the elders, or the leaders of the most important families; 3) the scribes, who were teachers of the Law or experts on legal and religious matters; the majority of these scribes belonged to the party or school of the Pharisees. In this passage of St Matthew only the first and third of the above groups are mentioned. This is understandable since the elders would have no authority in the matter of the birth of the Messiah—a purely religious question.

2:5–6. The prophecy referred to in this passage is Micah 5:1. It is worth noting that Jewish tradition interpreted this prophecy as predicting the Messiah's exact place of birth and as referring to a particular person. The second text thus teaches us once more that the prophecies of the Old Testament are fulfilled in Jesus Christ.

⁶'And you, O Bethlehem, in the land of Judah,
are by no means least among the rulers of Judah;
for from you shall come a ruler
who will govern my people Israel.'"
⁷Then Herod summoned the wise men secretly and ascertained
from them what time the star appeared; ⁸and he sent them to
Bethlehem, saying, "Go and search diligently for the child, and
when you have found him bring me word, that I too may come
and worship him." ⁹When they had heard the king they went their
way; and lo, the star which they had seen in the East went before
them, till it came to rest over the place where the child was.
¹⁰When they saw the star, they rejoiced exceedingly with great

2:8. Herod tried to find out exactly where the Child was—not, of course, to adore him, as he said, but to dispose of him. Such was Herod's exclusively political view of things. Yet neither his shrewdness nor his wickedness could prevent God's plans from being fulfilled. Despite Herod's ambition and his scheming, God's wisdom and power were going to bring salvation about.

2:9. "It might happen at certain moments of our interior life—and we are nearly always to blame—that the star disappears, just as it did to the wise kings on their journey. [...] What should we do if this happens? Follow the example of those wise men and ask. Herod used knowledge to act unjustly. The Magi use it to do good. But we Christians have no need to go to Herod nor to the wise men of this world. Christ has given his Church sureness of doctrine and a flow of grace in the sacraments. He has arranged things so that there will always be people to guide and lead us, to remind us constantly of our way" (St Josemaría Escrivá, *Christ Is Passing By*, 34).

2:10. "Why were they so happy? Because those who had never doubted received proof from the Lord that the star had not disappeared. They had ceased to contem-

plate it visibly, but they kept it always in their souls. Such is the Christian's vocation. If we do not lose faith, if we keep our hope in Christ who will be with us 'until the consummation of the world' (Mt 28:20), then the star reappears. And with this fresh proof that our vocation is real, we are conscious of a greater joy which increases our faith, hope and love" (*Christ Is Passing By*, 35).

2:11. The gifts they offered—gold, frankincense and myrrh—were those most valued in the East. People feel the need to give gifts to God to show their respect and faith. Since they cannot give themselves as a gift, which is what they would wish, they give instead what is most valuable and dear to them.

The prophets and the psalmists foretold that the kings of the earth would pay homage to God at the time of the Messiah (Is 49:23). They would offer him their treasures (Is 60:5) and adore him (Ps 72:10–15). Through this action of the wise men and the offering of their gifts to Jesus, these prophecies begin to be fulfilled.

The Council of Trent expressly quotes this passage when it underlines the veneration that ought to be given to Christ in the Eucharist: "The faithful of Christ venerate this most holy sacrament with

joy; [11]and going into the house they saw the child with Mary his
mother, and they fell down and worshipped him. Then, opening
their treasures, they offered him gifts, gold and frankincense and
myrrh. [12]And being warned in a dream not to return to Herod, they
departed to their own country by another way.

Ps 72:10–15
Is 60:6

The flight into Egypt. The massacre of the Innocents

[13]Now when they had departed, behold, an angel of the Lord
appeared to Joseph in a dream and said, "Rise, take the child and
his mother, and flee to Egypt, and remain there till I tell you; for
Herod is about to search for the child, to destroy him." [14]And he
rose and took the child and his mother by night, and departed to

Ex 2:15

---

the worship of latria which is due to the
true God. [...] For in this sacrament we
believe that the same God is present
whom the eternal Father brought into the
world, saying of him, 'Let all God's
angels worship him' (Heb 1:6; cf. Ps
97:7). It is the same God whom the Magi
fell down and worshipped (cf. Mt 2:11)
and, finally, the same God whom the
apostles adored and worshipped (cf. Mt
28:17)" (*De SS. Eucharistia*, chap. 5).

St Gregory Nazianzen has also commented on this verse, as follows: "Let us
remain in adoration; and to him, who, in
order to save us, humbled himself to such
a degree of poverty as to take our flesh,
let us offer him not only incense, gold
and myrrh (the first as God, the second as
king, and the third as one who sought
death for our sake), but also spiritual
gifts, more sublime than those which can
be seen with the eyes" (*Oratio*, 19).

2:12. The involvement of the wise men
in the events at Bethlehem ends with yet
another act of respectful obedience and
cooperation with God's plans. Christians
also should be receptive to the specific
grace and mission God has given them.
They should persevere in this even if it
means having to change any personal
plans they may have made.

2:14. St John Chrysostom, commenting
on this passage, draws particular attention to Joseph's faithfulness and obedience: "On hearing this, Joseph was not
scandalized, nor did he say, 'This is hard
to understand. You yourself told me not
long ago that he would save his people,
and now he is not able to save even himself. Indeed, we have to flee and under-
take a journey and be away for a long
time...'. But he does not say any of
these things, because Joseph is a faithful
man. Neither does he ask when they will
be coming back, even though the angel
had left it open when he said 'and
remain there till I tell you'. This does not
hold him back: on the contrary, he
obeys, believes and endures all the trials
with joy" (*Hom. on St Matthew*, 8).

It is worth noting also how God's
way of dealing with his chosen ones contains light and shade: they have to put up
with intense sufferings side by side with
great joy: "It can be clearly seen that
God, who is full of love for man, mixes
pleasant things with unpleasant ones, as
he did with all the saints. He gives us neither dangers nor consolations in a continual way, but rather he makes the lives of
the just a mixture of both. This is what he
did with Joseph" (ibid.).

Hos 11:1 Egypt, [15]and remained there until the death of Herod. This was to fulfil what the Lord had spoken by the prophet, "Out of Egypt have I called my son."

[16]Then Herod, when he saw that he had been tricked by the wise men, was in a furious rage, and he sent and killed all the male children in Bethlehem and in all that region who were two years old or under, according to the time which he had ascertained

Jer 31:15 from the wise men. [17]Then was fulfilled what was spoken by the prophet Jeremiah:

Gen 35:19 [18]"A voice was heard in Ramah,
wailing and loud lamentation,
Rachel weeping for her children;
she refused to be consoled,
because they were no more."

Return to Nazareth

[19]But when Herod died, behold, an angel of the Lord appeared in

Ex 4:19 a dream to Joseph in Egypt, saying, [20]"Rise, take the child and his

---

2:15. The text of Hosea 11:1 speaks of a child who comes out of Egypt and is a son of God. This refers in the first place to the people of Israel whom God brought out of Egypt under Moses' leadership. But this event was a symbol or prefiguration of Jesus, the head of the Church, the new people of God. It is in him that this prophecy is principally fulfilled. The sacred text gives a quotation from the Old Testament in the light of its fulfilment in Jesus Christ. The Old Testament achieves its full meaning in Christ, and, in the words of St Paul, to read it without keeping in mind Jesus is to have one's face covered by a veil (cf. 2 Cor 3:12–18).

2:16–17. Concerning Herod, see the note on Matthew 2:1. God permitted Herod to be wicked and cruel in trying to kill the Child. His cruel behaviour also fulfils the prophecy of Jeremiah 31:15. The Church regards these children as the first martyrs to give their lives for Christ. Martyrdom brought them justification (that is, salvation) and gave them the same grace as

Baptism gives; their martyrdom is, in fact, Baptism by blood. St Thomas Aquinas comments on this passage in the following way: "How can it be said that they died for Christ, since they could not use their freedom? [...] God would not have allowed that massacre if it had not been of benefit to those children. St Augustine says that to doubt that the massacre was good for those children is the same as doubting that Baptism is of use to children. For the Holy Innocents suffered as martyrs and confessed Christ *non loquendo, sed moriendo*, not by speaking, but by dying" (*Comm. on St Matthew*, 2, 16).

2:18. Ramah was the city in which Nebuchadnezzar, king of Babylon, concentrated the Israelites he had taken prisoner. Since Ramah was in the land of Benjamin, Jeremiah puts this lament for the children of Israel in the mouth of Rachel, the mother of Benjamin and Joseph. So great was the misfortune of those exiled to Babylon that Jeremiah says poetically that Rachel's sorrow is too great to allow

mother, and go to the land of Israel, for those who sought the child's life are dead." [21]And he rose and took the child and his mother, and went to the land of Israel. [22]But when he heard that Archelaus reigned over Judea in place of his father Herod, he was afraid to go there, and being warned in a dream he withdrew to the district of Galilee. [23]And he went and dwelt in a city called Nazareth, that what was spoken by the prophets might be fulfilled, "He shall be called a Nazarene."

Lk 1:26; 2:39
Is 11:1; 53:2
Jn 1:46

2. PRELUDE TO THE PUBLIC MINISTRY OF JESUS

John the Baptist preaching in the wilderness

3 [1]In those days came John the Baptist, preaching in the wilderness of Judea, [2]"Repent,* for the kingdom of heaven

Mk 1:2–8
Lk 3:3–18;
1:13; 4:17

of consolation. "Rachel was buried in the racecourse near Bethlehem. Since her grave was nearby and the property belonged to her son, Benjamin (Ramah was of the tribe of Benjamin), the children beheaded in Bethlehem could reasonably be called Rachel's children" (St John Chrysostom, *Hom. on St Matthew*, 9).

2:22. History tells us that Archelaus was ambitious and cruel like his father. By the time Joseph returned from Egypt, the new king was quite notorious. "In the different circumstances of his life, St Joseph never refuses to think, never neglects his responsibilities. On the contrary, he puts his human experience at the service of faith. When he returns from Egypt, learning 'that Archelaus reigned over Judea in place of his father Herod, he was afraid to go there'. In other words, he had learned to work within the divine plan. And to confirm that he was doing the right thing, Joseph received an instruction to return to Galilee" (St J. Escrivá, *Christ Is Passing By*, 42).

2:23. Nazareth, where the Annunciation had taken place (Lk 1:26), was a tiny and

insignificant Palestinian village. It was located in Galilee, the most northerly part of the country. The term "Nazarene" refers to Jesus' geographic origin, but his critics used it as a term of abuse when he began his mission (Jn 1:46). Even in the time of St Paul the Jews tried to humiliate the Christians by calling them Nazarenes (Acts 24:5). Many prophets predicted that the Messiah would suffer poverty and contempt (Is 52:2ff.; Jer 11:19; Ps 22) but the words "he shall be called a Nazarene" are not to be found as such in any prophetic text. They are, rather, as St Jerome points out, a summary of the prophets' teaching in a short and expressive phrase. However, St Jerome himself (cf. *Comm. in Isaiah*, 11:1) says that the name "Nazarene" fulfils the prophecy of Isaiah 11:1: Christ is the "shoot" (*nezer*, in Hebrew) of the entire race of Abraham and David.

3:1. The expression "in those days" does not specify the exact time of the event in question. It is sometimes used merely as an opening phrase to mark the beginning

35

Is 40:3
Jn 1:23
is at hand." [3]For this is he who was spoken of by the prophet
Isaiah when he said,

"The voice of one crying in the wilderness:
Prepare the way of the Lord,
make his paths straight."

---

of a new episode. In this case, in fact, it can be calculated that some twenty-five years have elapsed since the Holy Family's return from Egypt. This is only an estimate, because the exact date of their return has not been established.

On the date of the start of John the Baptist's preaching, see Luke 3:1–3.

The word "wilderness" has a wider meaning here than we give it today. It does not refer to a sandy or rocky desert, but rather to arid regions, low in vegetation.

3:2. "Repent": Christ's redeeming work ushers in a new era in the Kingdom of God. This brings such advance in salvation history, that what is required from now on is a radical change in man's behaviour towards God. The coming of the Kingdom means that God has intervened in a special way to save mankind, but it also implies that we must be open to God's grace and reform our ways. Christ's life on earth compels people to take a stand—either for God or against him ("He who is not with me is against me, and he who does not gather with me scatters": Lk 11:23). Given man's sinful state after original sin, the newly-arrived Kingdom requires that all men repent of their past life. To put it another way, they have to stop going away from God and instead try to get closer to him. Since sin hinders this conversion, it is impossible to turn back to God without performing acts of penance. Conversion is not simply a question of making a good resolution to mend our ways; we have to fulfil that resolution, even if we find it difficult. Penance grows only where there is

humility—and everyone should admit sincerely that he is a sinner (cf. 1 Jn 1:8–10). Obedience also goes hand in hand with penance; everyone ought to obey God and keep his commandments (cf. 1 Jn 2:3–6).

The literal translation of the Greek is "Repent". But precisely because the very essence of conversion consists in doing penance, as we have said, the New Vulgate has *paenitentaim agite* ("do penance"). This translation conveys the deeper meaning of the text.

Man's whole life, in fact, consists in constantly correcting his behaviour, and therefore implies a continual doing of penance. This turning back to God was preached continually by the prophets in the Old Testament. Now, however, with the coming of Christ, this penance and turning to God are absolutely essential. That Christ took on our sins and suffered for us does not excuse us from making a true conversion; on the contrary, it demands it of us (cf. Col 1:24).

"Kingdom of heaven": this expression is identical to "Kingdom of God". The former is the one most used by St Matthew, and is more in line with the Jewish turn of phrase. Out of reverence, the Jews avoided pronouncing the name of God and substituted other words for it, as in this case. "Kingdom of God" or "Kingdom of heaven" was a concept used already in the Old Testament and in religious circles at the time of Christ. But it occurs particularly frequently in Jesus' preaching.

The phrase "Kingdom of God" can refer in a general way to God's dominion

⁴Now John wore a garment of camel's hair, and a leather girdle around his waist; and his food was locusts and wild honey. ⁵Then went out to him Jerusalem and all Judea and all the region about the Jordan, ⁶and they were baptized by him in the river Jordan, confessing their sins.*

2 Kings 1:18

---

over creatures; but normally, as in this text, it refers to God's sovereign and merciful involvement in the life of his people. Man's rebellion and sin broke the order originally established in creation. To re-establish it, God's intervention was needed again; this consisted in the redeeming work of Christ, Messiah and Son of God. It was preceded by a series of preliminary stages in salvation history throughout the Old Testament. Consequently, the Kingdom of God, announced as imminent by John the Baptist, is brought into being by Jesus. However, this is an entirely spiritual one and does not have the nationalistic dimension expected by Jesus' contemporaries. He comes to save his people and all mankind from the slavery of sin, from death and from the devil, thereby opening up the way of salvation.

In the period between the first and second comings of Christ, this Kingdom of God (or Kingdom of heaven) is, in fact, the Church. The Church makes Christ (and therefore also God) present among all peoples and calls them to eternal salvation. The Kingdom of God will be brought to completion only at the end of this world, that is, when our Lord comes to judge the living and the dead at the end of time. Then God will reign over the blessed in a perfect way.

In the passage we are considering, John the Baptist, the last of the Old Testament prophets, preaches the imminence of the Kingdom of God, ushered in by the coming of the Messiah.

3:3. By quoting Isaiah 40:3, St Matthew makes it clear that St John the Baptist has a mission as a prophet. This mission has two purposes—first, to prepare the people to receive the Kingdom of God; second, to testify before the people that Jesus is the Messiah who is bringing that Kingdom.

3:4. The Gospel gives a brief outline of the extremely austere life of St John the Baptist. His style of life is in line with that of certain Old Testament prophets and is particularly reminiscent of Elijah (cf. 2 Kings 1:8; 2:8–13ff). The kinds of food and dress described are of the most rudimentary for the region in question. The locust was a kind of grasshopper; the wild honey probably refers to substances excreted by certain local shrubs rather than to bees' honey. In view of the imminent coming of the Messiah, John underlines, with his example, the attitude of penance preceding great religious festivals (similarly, in its Advent liturgy the Church puts John before us as a model and invites us to practise mortification and penance). In this way, the point made in the previous verse (concerning John's view of his mission as precursor of Christ) is fulfilled. A Christian's entire life is a preparation for his meeting with Christ. Consequently, mortification and penance play a significant part in his life.

3:6. John's baptism did not have the power to cleanse the soul from sin as Christian baptism does. The latter is a sacrament, a sign, which produces the grace it signifies. Concerning the value of John's baptism, see the note on Mt 3:11.

37

Gen 3:15

Rom 2:28f;
4:12
Jn 8:33, 39

Lk 13:7–9
Jn 15:6

Jn 1:15, 26f, 33

Acts 1:5

[7]But when he saw many of the Pharisees and Sadducees coming for baptism, he said to them, "You brood of vipers! Who warned you to flee from the wrath to come? [8]Bear fruit that befits repentance, [9]and do not presume to say to yourselves, 'We have Abraham as our father'; for I tell you, God is able from these stones to raise up children to Abraham. [10]Even now the axe is laid to the root of the trees; every tree therefore that does not bear good fruit is cut down and thrown into the fire.

[11]"I baptize you with water for repentance, but he who is coming after me is mightier than I, whose sandals I am not worthy

---

3:7. St John reproaches the Pharisees and Sadducees for their attitude towards him. His preaching and baptism are not simply one more purification rite. Rather, they demand a true interior conversion of the soul, as a necessary predisposition to reach the grace of faith in Jesus. In the light of this explanation, we can understand why the prophetic words of St John the Baptist were so hard-hitting; as it turned out, most of these people did not accept Jesus as the Messiah.

"Pharisees": these constituted the most important religious group in Jesus' time. They kept the Law of Moses rigorously and also the oral traditions which had built up around it. They gave as much importance to these latter, indeed, as to the Law itself. They strongly opposed the influence of Greek paganism and totally rejected the homage paid to the Roman emperor. Among them there were men of great spiritual eminence and sincere piety; but there were many others who exaggerated pharisaical religiosity to the extreme of fanaticism, pride and hypocrisy. It was this perversion of the true Israelite religion that John the Baptist (and later our Lord) castigated.

"Sadducees": the Sadducees constituted a smaller religious group than the Pharisees, but they included many influential people, most of them from the main priestly families. They accepted the written Law, but, unlike the Pharisees, they rejected oral tradition. They also rejected certain important truths, such as the resurrection of the dead.

On the political front, they went along easily with the terms dictated by the Romans, and they acquiesced in the introduction of pagan customs into the country. Their opposition to Christ was even more pronounced than that of the Pharisees.

3:9–10. St John the Baptist's listeners believe their salvation is assured because they are descendants of Abraham according to the flesh. But St John warns them that to pass God's judgment it is not enough to belong to the chosen people; they must also yield the good fruit of a holy life. If they fail to do this, they will be thrown into the fire, that is, into hell, the eternal punishment, because they did not do penance for their sins. See the note on Mt 25:46.

3:11. St John the Baptist did not limit himself to preaching penance and repentance; he encouraged people to receive his baptism. This baptism was a way of interiorly preparing them and helping them to realize that the coming of Christ was imminent. By his words of encouragement and by their humble recognition of their sins, they were prepared to

to carry; he will baptize you with the Holy Spirit and with fire. ¹²His winnowing fork is in his hand, and he will clear his threshing floor and gather his wheat into the granary, but the chaff he will burn with unquenchable fire."

Jesus is baptized

¹³Then Jesus came from Galilee to the Jordan to John, to be baptized by him. ¹⁴John would have prevented him, saying, "I need to

Mk 1:9–11
Lk 3:21f
Jn 1:31–34

---

receive Christ's grace through Baptism with fire and the Holy Spirit. To put it another way, John's baptism did not produce justification, whereas Christian Baptism is the sacrament of initiation, which forgives sin and bestows sanctifying grace. The effectiveness of the sacrament of Christian Baptism is expressed in Catholic teaching when it says that the sacrament gives grace *ex opere operato*. This means that grace is given by virtue of Christ who acts through the sacrament, and not by virtue of the merits of either the minister or the recipient of the sacrament. "When Peter baptizes, it is Christ who baptizes [...]. When Judas baptizes, it is Christ who baptizes" (St Augustine, *In Ioann. Evang.*, 6).

The word "fire" points in a metaphorical way to the effectiveness of the Holy Spirit's action in totally wiping out sins. It also shows the life-giving power of grace in the person baptized. Foremost among the personal qualities of St John the Baptist is his remarkable humility; he resolutely rejects the temptation of accepting the dignity of Messiah which the crowds apparently wanted to bestow on him. Carrying the sandals of one's master was a job for the lowest of servants.

3:12. Verses 10 and 12 refer to judgment by the Messiah. This judgment has two parts: the first occurs throughout each man's life and ends in the Particular Judgment immediately after death; the second occurs at the time of the Last Judgment. Christ is the judge in both instances. Let us remember the words of St Peter in Acts 10:42: "And he commanded us to preach to the people, and to testify that he [Jesus] is the one ordained by God to be judge of the living and the dead." The judgment will give to each person the reward or punishment merited by his good or bad actions.

It is worth noting that the word "chaff" does not refer only to bad deeds; it refers also to useless ones, for example, lives lacking in service to God and men. God will judge us, therefore, for our omissions and our lost opportunities.

"Don't let your life be barren. Be useful. Make yourself felt. Shine forth with the torch of your faith and your love. With your apostolic life, wipe out the trail of filth and slime left by the unclean sowers of hatred. And set aflame all the ways of the earth with the fire of Christ that you bear in your heart" (St Josemaría Escrivá, *The Way*, 1).

3:13. Jesus spent about thirty years (Lk 3:23) in what is normally called his "hidden life". We should marvel at the silence of the Incarnate Word of God during this period. There may be many reasons why he waited so long before beginning his public ministry, but one factor may have been the Jewish custom whereby rabbis did not carry out their function as teachers until they were thirty

be baptized by you, and do you come to me?" [15]But Jesus answered him, "Let it be so now; for thus it is fitting for us to fulfil all righteousness." Then he consented.* [16]And when Jesus was baptized, he went up immediately from the water, and behold, the heavens were opened[g] and he saw the Spirit of God descending like a dove, and alighting on him; [17]and lo, a voice from

1 Pet 4:14
Ezek 1:1

Mt 17:5
Ps 2:7

years old. Whatever the reason, by his long years of work beside St Joseph, our Lord teaches all Christians the sanctifying value of ordinary life and work.

The Baptist prepares the people to receive the Messiah, according to God's plan; and it is only then that Jesus commences his public life.

3:14. St. John's reluctance to baptize Jesus is not surprising since he had given such forthright witness to Him. Jesus did not need to be baptized by John since he had no sin, but he chose to receive this baptism (see the note on v. 15) before beginning to preach, so to teach us to obey all God's commands (he had already subjected himself to circumcision, presentation to the temple and being redeemed as the first-born). God wished to humble himself even to the extent of submitting to the authority of others.

3:15. "Righteousness" (or "justice") has a very deep meaning in the Bible; it refers to the plan which God, in his infinite goodness and wisdom, has marked out for man's salvation. Consequently, "to fulfil all righteousness" should be understood as fulfilling God's will and designs. Thus we could translate "fulfil all righteousness" as; "fulfil everything laid down by God". Jesus comes to receive John's baptism and hence recognizes it as a stage in salvation history—a stage foreseen by God as a final and immediate preparation for the messianic

era. The fulfilment of any one of these stages can be called an act of righteousness. Jesus, who has come to fulfil his Father's will (Jn 4:34), is careful to fulfil that saving plan in all its aspects. See the note on Mt 5:6.

3:16. Jesus possessed the fullness of the Holy Spirit from the moment of his conception. This is due to the union of human nature and divine nature in the person of the Word (the dogma of the hypostatic union). Catholic teaching says that in Christ there is only one person (who is divine) but two natures (divine and human). The descent of the Spirit of God spoken of in the text indicates that just as Jesus was solemnly commencing his messianic task, so the Holy Spirit was beginning his action through him. There are many texts in the Old Testament which speak of the showing forth of the Holy Spirit in the future Messiah. This sign of the Spirit gave St John the Baptist unmistakable proof of the genuineness of his testimony concerning Christ (cf. Jn 1:29–34). The mystery of the Holy Trinity is revealed in the baptism of Jesus: the Son is baptized; the Holy Spirit descends on him in the form of a dove; and the voice of the Father gives testimony about his Son. Christians must be baptized in the name of the three divine persons. "If you have sincere piety, the Holy Spirit will descend on you also and you will hear the voice of the Father saying to you from above: 'This was not

g. Other ancient authorities add *to him* h. Or *my Son, my* (or *the*) *Beloved*

heaven, saying, "This is my beloved son,[h] with whom I am well pleased."

Is 42:1

Jesus fasts and is tempted

Mk 1:12f
Lk 4:1–13

4 [1]Then Jesus was led up by the Spirit into the wilderness to be tempted by the devil. [2]And he fasted forty days and forty

Heb 4:15
Ex 34:28
1 Kings 19:8

---

my son, but now after Baptism he has been made my son'" (St Cyril of Jerusalem, *De Baptismo*, 14).

3:17. Literally, as the RSV points out, "This is my Son, my (*or* the) Beloved". When the expression "the beloved" goes with "the son", normally it refers to an only son (cf. Gen 16; Jer 6:26; Amos 8:10; Zech 12:10). Repetition of the article and the solemnity of the passage show that, in the language of the Bible, Jesus is not just one more among the adopted sons of God, nor even the greatest of them. Rather, it declares strongly and correctly that Jesus is "the Son of God", the Only-begotten, who is totally different from other men because of his divine nature (cf. Mt 7:21; 11:27; 17:5; Jn 3:35; 5:20; 20:17; etc.).

Here we can see the fulfilment of the messianic prophecies, especially Isaiah 42:1, which is applied now to Jesus through the voice of the Father speaking from heaven.

4:1. Jesus, our Saviour, allowed himself to be tempted because he so chose; and he did so out of love for us and to instruct us. However, since he was perfect, he could only be tempted externally. Catholic teaching tells us that there are three levels of temptation: 1) suggestion, that is, external temptation, which we can undergo without committing any sin; 2) temptation, in which we take a certain delight, whether prolonged or not, even though we do not give clear consent; this level of temptation has now become

internal and there is some sinfulness in it; 3) temptation to which we consent; this is always sinful, and, since it affects the deepest part of the soul, is definitely internal. By allowing himself to be tempted, Jesus wanted to teach us how to fight and conquer our temptations. We will do this by having trust in God and prayer, with the help of God's grace and by having fortitude.

Jesus' temptations in the desert have a deep significance in salvation history. All the most important people throughout sacred history were tempted—Adam and Eve, Abraham, Moses, and the chosen people themselves. Similarly with Jesus. By rejecting the temptations of the devil, our Lord atones for the falls of those who went before him and those who come after him. He is an example for us in all the temptations we were subsequently to have, and also for the battles between the Church and the power of the devil. Later Jesus teaches us in the Our Father to ask God to help us with his grace not to fall at the time of temptation.

4:2. Before beginning his work as Messiah, that is, before promulgating the New Law or New Testament, Jesus prepares himself by prayer and fasting in the desert. Moses acted in the same way before proclaiming, in God's name, the Old Law on Mount Sinai (Ex 34:28), Elijah, too, journeyed for forty days in the desert to fulfil the Law (1 Kings 19:5–8).

The Church follows Jesus' footsteps by prescribing the yearly Lenten fast. We

Gen 3:1–7 nights, and afterward he was hungry. ³And the tempter came and
said to him, "If you are the Son of God, command these stones to
Deut 8:3 become loaves of bread." ⁴But he answered, "It is written,
Wis 16:26
  'Man shall not live by bread alone,
  but by every word that proceeds from the mouth of God.'"
⁵Then the devil took him to the holy city, and set him on the pin-
Ps 91:11f nacle of the temple, ⁶and said to him, "If you are the Son of God,
throw yourself down; for it is written,

---

should practise Lent each year with this spirit of piety. "It can be said that Christ introduced the tradition of forty days fast into the Church's liturgical year, because he himself 'fasted forty days and forty night' before beginning to teach. By this Lenten fast the Church is in a certain sense called every year to follow her Master and Lord if she wishes to preach his Gospel effectively" (John Paul II, General Audience, 28 February 1979). In the same way, Jesus' withdrawal into the desert invites us to prepare ourselves by prayer and penance before any important decision or action.

4:3. Jesus has fasted for forty days and forty nights. Naturally he is very hungry and the devil makes use of this opportunity to tempt him. Our Lord rejects the temptation and in doing so he uses a phrase from Deuteronomy (8:3). Although he could do this miracle, he prefers to continue to trust his Father since performing the miracle is not part of his plan of salvation. In return for this trust, angels come and minister to him (Mt 4:11).

Miracles in the Bible are extraordinary and wonderful deeds done by God to make his words or actions understood. They do not occur as isolated outpourings of God's power but rather as part of the work of Redemption. What the devil proposes in this temptation would be for Jesus' benefit only and therefore could not form part of the plan for Redemption. This suggests that the devil, in tempting

him in this way, wanted to check if Jesus is the "Son of God". For, although he seems to know about the voice from heaven at Jesus' baptism, he cannot see how the Son of God could be hungry. By the way he deals with the temptation, Jesus teaches us that when we ask God for things we should not ask in the first place for what we can obtain by our own efforts. Neither should we ask for what is exclusively for our own convenience, but rather for what will help towards our holiness or that of others.

4:4. Jesus' reply is an act of trust in God's fatherly providence. God led him into the desert to prepare him for his messianic work, and now he will see to it that Jesus does not die. This point is underlined by the fact that Jesus' reply evokes Deuteronomy 8:3, where the sons of Israel are reminded how Yahweh fed them miraculously with manna in the desert. Therefore, in contrast to the Israelites who were impatient when faced with hunger in the desert, Jesus trustingly leaves his well-being to the Father's providence. The words of Deuteronomy 8:3, repeated here by Jesus, associate "bread" and "word" as having both come from the mouth of God: God speaks and gives his Law; God speaks and makes manna appear as food.

Also, manna is commonly used in the New Testament (see, for example, Jn 6:32–58) and throughout Tradition as a symbol of the Eucharist.

'He will give his angels charge of you,'

and

'On their hands they will bear you up,
lest you strike your foot against a stone.'"

[7]Jesus said to him, "Again it is written, 'You shall not tempt the
Lord your God.'" [8]Again, the devil took him to a very high mountain, and showed him all the kingdoms of the world and the glory

Deut 6:16

Deut 34:1
Rev 21:10

The Second Vatican Council points
out another interesting aspect of Jesus'
word when it proposes guidelines for
international cooperation in economic
matters: "In many instances there exists a
pressing need to reassess economic and
social structures, but caution must be
exercised with regard to proposed solutions which may be untimely, especially
those which offer material advantage
while militating against man's spiritual
nature and advancement. For 'man shall
not live by bread alone, but by every
word that proceeds from the mouth of
God'" (*Gaudium et spes*, 86).

4:5. Tradition suggests that this temptation occurred at the extreme southeast
corner of the temple wall. At this point,
the wall was at its highest, since the
ground beneath sloped away steeply to
the Cedron river. Looking down from
this point one could easily get a feeling
of vertigo. St Gregory the Great (*In
Evangelia homiliae*, 16) says that if we
consider how our Lord allowed himself
to be treated during his passion, it is not
surprising that he allowed the devil also
to treat him as he did.

4:6. "Holy Scripture is good, but heresies arise through its not being understood
properly" (St Augustine, *In Ioann. Evang.*,
18, 1). Catholics should be on their guard
against arguments which, though they
claim to be founded on Scripture, are
nevertheless untrue. As we can see in this
passage of the Gospel, the devil can also

set himself up at times as an interpreter
of Scripture, quoting it to suit himself.
Therefore, any interpretation which is not
in line with the teaching contained in the
Tradition of the Church should be rejected. The error proposed by a heresy
normally consists in stressing certain passages to the exclusion of others, interpreting them at will, losing sight of the
unity that exists in Scripture and the fact
that the faith is all of a piece.

4:7. Jesus rejects the second temptation
as he did the first; to do otherwise would
have been to tempt God. In rejecting it,
he uses a phrase from Deuteronomy
(6:16): "You shall not put the Lord your
God to the test". In this way he alludes
also to the passage in Exodus where the
Israelites demand a miracle of Moses.
The latter replies, "Why do you put the
Lord to the proof?" (Ex 17:2).

To tempt God is the complete opposite of having trust in him. It means pre-
sumptuously putting ourselves in the way
of an unnecessary danger, expecting God
to help us by an exceptional use of his
power. We would also tempt him if, by
our unbelief and arrogance, we were to
ask him for signs of proof. The very first
lesson from this passage of the Gospel is
that if ever a person were to ask or
demand extraordinary proofs or signs
from God, he would clearly be tempting
him.

4:8–10. The third temptation is the most
pseudo-messianic of the three: Jesus is

Deut 6:13

of them; [9]and he said to him, "All these I will give you, if you will fall down and worship me." [10]Then Jesus said to him, "Begone, Satan! for it is written,

'You shall worship the Lord your God
and him only shall you serve.'"

Jn 1:51
Heb 1:6, 14

[11]Then the devil left him, and behold, the angels came and ministered to him.

PART ONE

Jesus' ministry in Galilee

Mk 1:14f
Lk 4:14f
Jn 2:12; 4:43

Jesus begins to preach

[12]Now when he heard that John had been arrested, he withdrew into Galilee; [13]and leaving Nazareth he went and dwelt in

---

urged to appropriate to himself the role of an earthly messianic king of the type so widely expected at the time. Our Lord's vigorous reply, "Begone, Satan!" is an uncompromising rejection of an earthly messianism—an attempt to reduce his transcendent, God-given mission to a purely human and political use. By his attitude, Jesus, as it were, rectifies and makes amends for the worldly views of the people of Israel. And, for the same reason, it is a warning to the Church, God's true Israel, to remain faithful to its God-given mission of salvation in the world. The Church's pastors should be on the alert and not allow themselves to be deceived by this temptation of the devil.

"We should learn from Jesus' attitude in these trials. During his life on earth he did not even want the glory that belonged to him. Though he had the right to be treated as God, he took the form of a servant, a slave (cf. Phil 2:6–7). And so the Christian knows that all glory is due to

God and that he must not make use of the sublimity and greatness of the Gospel to further his own interests or human ambitions.

"We should learn from Jesus. His attitude in rejecting all human glory is in perfect balance with the greatness of his unique mission as the beloved Son of God who takes flesh to save men [...]. And the Christian, who, following Christ, has this attitude of complete adoration of the Father, also experiences our Lord's loving care: 'because he cleaves to me in love. I will deliver him; I will protect him, because he knows my name' (Ps 90:14)" (St Josemaría Escrivá, *Christ Is Passing By*, 62).

4:11. If we struggle constantly, we will attain victory. And nobody is crowned without having first conquered: "Be faithful unto death, and I will give you the crown of life" (Rev 2:10). By coming to minister to Jesus after he rejects the

Capernaum by the sea, in the territory of Zebulun and Naphtali,
¹⁴that what was spoken by the prophet Isaiah might be fulfilled:
   ¹⁵"The land of Zebulun and the land of Naphtali,   Is 8:23; 9:1
      toward the sea, across the Jordan, Galilee of the Gentiles Jn 7:52
      —¹⁶the people who sat in darkness have seen a great light Lk 1:78f
      and for those who sat in the region and shadow of death Jn 1:9
      light has dawned."
¹⁷From that time Jesus began to preach, saying, "Repent, for the
kingdom of heaven is at hand."

---

temptations, the angels teach us the interior joy given by God to the person who fights energetically against the temptation of the devil. God has given us also powerful defenders against such temptations—our guardian angels, on whose aid we should call.

4:15–16. Here St Matthew quotes the prophecy of Isaiah 8:23—9:1. The territory referred to (Zebulun, Naphtali, the way of the sea, the land beyond the Jordan), was invaded by the Assyrians in the period 734–721 BC, especially during the reign of Tilgathpilneser III. A portion of the Jewish population was deported and sizeable numbers of foreigners were planted in the region to colonize it. For this reason it is referred to in the Bible henceforward as the "Galilee of the Gentiles".

The evangelist, inspired by God, sees Jesus' coming to Galilee as the fulfilment of Isaiah's prophecy. This land, devastated and abused in Isaiah's time, will be the first to receive the light of Christ's life and preaching. The messianic meaning of the prophecy is, therefore, clear.

4:17. See the note on Mt 3:2. This verse indicates the outstanding importance of the first step in Jesus' public ministry, begun by proclaiming the imminence of the Kingdom of God. Jesus' words echo John the Baptist's proclamation: the

second part of this verse is the same, word for word, as Matthew 3:2. This underlines the role played by St John the Baptist as prophet and precursor of Jesus. Both St John and our Lord demand repentance, penance, as a prerequisite to receiving the Kingdom of God, now beginning. God's rule over mankind is a main theme in Christ's Revelation, just as it was central to the whole Old Testament. However, in the latter, the Kingdom of God had an element of theocracy about it: God reigned over Israel in both spiritual and temporal affairs and it was through him that Israel subjected other nations to her rule. Little by little, Jesus will unfold the new-style Kingdom of God, now arrived at its fullness. He will show it to be a Kingdom of love and holiness, thereby purifying it of the nationalistic misconceptions of the people of this time.

The King invites everyone without exception to this Kingdom (cf. Mt 22:1–14). The banquet of the Kingdom is held on this earth and has certain entry requirements which must be preached by the proponents of the Kingdom: "Therefore the eucharist celebration is the centre of the assembly of the faithful over which the priest presides. Hence priests teach the faithful to offer the divine Victim to God the Father in the sacrifice of the Mass, and with the Victim to make an offering of their whole lives. In the

The first disciples are called

Mk 1:16–20
Lk 5:1–11
Jn 1:40f

Ezek 47:10

Mt 19:27

[18]As he walked by the Sea of Galilee, he saw two brothers, Simon who is called Peter and Andrew his brother, casting a net into the sea; for they were fishermen. [19]And he said to them, "Follow me, and I will make you fishers of men." [20]Immediately they left their nets and followed him. [21]And going on from there he saw two other brothers, James the son of Zebedee and John his brother, in the boat with Zebedee their father, mending their nets, and he called to them. [22]Immediately they left the boat and their father, and followed him.

Mk 1:39
Lk 4:15, 44
Acts 10:38

[23]And he went about all Galilee, teaching in their synagogues and preaching the gospel of the kingdom and healing every disease and every infirmity among the people. [24]So his fame spread

---

spirit of Christ the pastor, they instruct them to submit their sins to the Church with a contrite heart in the sacrament of Penance, so that they may be daily more and more converted to the Lord, remembering his words: 'Repent, for the Kingdom of heaven is at hand'" (Vatican II, *Presbyterorum ordinis*, 5).

4:18–22. These four disciples had already met our Lord (Jn 1:35–42), and their brief meeting with him seems to have had a powerful effect on their souls. In this way Christ prepared their vocation, a fully effective vocation which moved them to leave everything behind so as to follow him and be their disciples. Standing out above their human defects (which the Gospels never conceal), we can see the exemplary generosity and promptness of the apostles in answering God's call.

The thoughtful reader cannot fail to be struck by the delightful simplicity with which the evangelists describe the calling of these men in the midst of their daily work. "God draws us from the shadows of our ignorance, our groping through history, and, no matter what our occupation in the world, he calls us in a loud voice, as he once called Peter and

Andrew" (St Josemaría Escrivá, *Christ Is Passing By*, 45).

"This divine and human dialogue completely changed the lives of John and Andrew, and Peter and James and so many others. It prepared their hearts to listen to the authoritative teaching which Jesus gave them beside the Sea of Galilee" (ibid., 108).

We should notice the words Sacred Scripture uses to describe the alacrity with which these apostles follow our Lord. Peter and Andrew "immediately" left their nets and followed him. Similarly, James and John "immediately" left their boats and their father and followed him. God passes by and calls us. If we do not answer him "immediately", he may continue on his way and we could lose sight of him. When God passes us by, he may do so rapidly; it would be sad if we were to fall behind because we wanted to follow him while still carrying many things that are only a dead weight and a nuisance.

Concerning Christ's call to men in the midst of their ordinary work, see the note on Mt 2:2.

4:23. "Synagogue": this word comes from the Greek and designates the build-

throughout all Syria and they brought him all the sick, those
afflicted with various diseases and pains, demoniacs, epileptics,
and paralytics, and he healed them. ²⁵And great crowds followed
him from Galilee and the Decapolis and Jerusalem and Judea and
from beyond the Jordan.

Mk 6:55

Mk 3:7f
Lk 6:17–19

3. THE SERMON ON THE MOUNT

The Beatitudes

5 ¹Seeing the crowds, he went up on the mountain, and when he
sat down his disciples came to him. ²And he opened his
mouth and taught them, saying:

Lk 6:20–49

ing where the Jews assembled for religious ceremonies on the sabbath and other feast days. Such ceremonies were non-sacrificial in character (sacrifices could be performed only in the temple of Jerusalem). The synagogue was also the place where the Jews received their religious training. The word was also used to designate local Jewish communities within and without Palestine.

4:24. "Epileptic" (or, in some translations, "lunatic"): this word was applied in a very general way to those who had illnesses related to epilepsy. The disease was popularly regarded as being dependent on the phases of the moon (Latin: *luna*).

4:23–25. In these few lines, the evangelist gives us a very fine summary of the various aspects of Jesus' work. The preaching of the gospel or "good news" of the Kingdom, the healing of diseases, and the casting out of devils are all specific signs of the Messiah's presence, according to Old Testament prophecies (Is 35:5–6; 61:1; 40:9; 52:7).

5:1. The discourse, or sermon, on the mount takes up three full chapters of St Matthew's Gospel—chapters 5–7. It is

the first of the five great discourses of Jesus which appear in this Gospel and contains a considerable amount of our Lord's teaching.

It is difficult to reduce this discourse to one single theme, but the various teachings it contains could be said to deal with these five points: 1) the attitude a person must have for entering the Kingdom of heaven (the Beatitudes, the salt of the earth, the light of the world, Jesus and his teaching, the fullness of the Law); 2) uprightness of intention in religious practices (here the Our Father would be included); 3) trust in God's fatherly providence; 4) how God's children should behave towards one another (not judging one's neighbour, respect for holy things, the effectiveness of prayer and the golden rule of charity); 5) the conditions for entering the Kingdom (the narrow gate, false prophets and building on rock).

5:2. "He taught them": this refers both to the disciples and to the multitude, as can be seen at the end of the Sermon.

5:3–12. The Beatitudes form, as it were, the gateway to the Sermon on the Mount. In order to understand the Beatitudes properly, we should bear in mind that

Is 57:15; 61:1
Mt 11:5
Lk 4:18
³"Blessed are the poor in spirit, for theirs is the kingdom of heaven.

Ps 126:6
Is 61:2

Ps 37:11
⁴"Blessed are those who mourn, for they shall be comforted.
⁵"Blessed are the meek, for they shall inherit the earth.

they do not promise salvation only to the particular kinds of people listed here: they cover everyone whose religious dispositions and moral conduct meet the demands which Jesus lays down. In other words, the poor in spirit, the meek, those who mourn, those who hunger and thirst after righteousness, the merciful, the pure in heart, the peacemakers and those who suffer persecution in their search for holiness—these are not different people or kinds of people but different demands made on everyone who wants to be a disciple of Christ.

Similarly, salvation is not being promised to different groups in society but to everyone, no matter what his or her position in life, who strives to follow the spirit and to meet the demands contained in the Beatitudes.

All the Beatitudes have an eschatological meaning, that is, they promise us definitive salvation, not in this world, but in the next. But the spirit of the Beatitudes does give us, in this life, peace in the midst of tribulation. The Beatitudes imply a completely new approach, quite at odds with the usual way man evaluates things: they rule out any kind of pharisaical religiosity, which regards earthly happiness as a blessing from God and a reward for good behaviour, and unhappiness and misfortune as a form of punishment. In all ages the Beatitudes put spiritual good on a much higher plane than material possessions. The healthy and the sick, the powerful and the weak, the rich and the poor—all are called, independently of their circumstances, to the deep happiness that is experienced by those who live up to the Beatitudes which Jesus teaches.

The Beatitudes do not, of course, contain the entire teaching of the Gospel, but they do contain, in embryo, the whole programme of Christian perfection.

5:3. This text outlines the connexion between poverty and the soul. This religious concept of poverty was deeply rooted in the Old Testament (cf., e.g., Zeph 2:3ff). It was more to do with a religious attitude of neediness and of humility towards God than with material poverty: that person is poor who has recourse to God without relying on his own merits and who trusts in God's mercy to be saved. This religious attitude of poverty is closely related to what is called "spiritual childhood". A Christian sees himself as a little child in the presence of God, a child who owns nothing: everything he has comes from God and belongs to God. Certainly, spiritual poverty, that is, Christian poverty, means one must be detached from material things and practise austerity in using them. God asks certain people—religious—to be legally detached from ownership and thereby bear witness to others of the transitoriness of earthly things.

5:4. "Those who mourn": here our Lord is saying that those are blessed who suffer from any kind of affliction—particularly those who are genuinely sorry for their sins, or are pained by the offences which others offer God, and who bear their suffering with love and with a spirit of atonement.

"You are crying? Don't be ashamed of it. Yes, cry: men also cry like you, when they are alone and before God.

48

⁶"Blessed are those who hunger and thirst for righteousness, for they shall be satisfied.
⁷"Blessed are the merciful, for they shall obtain mercy.
⁸"Blessed are the pure in heart, for they shall see God.

Rev 7:16f

Jas 2:13

Ps 24:4; 51:10; 73:1
Jn 3:2f

Each night, says King David, I soak my bed with tears. With those tears, those burning manly tears, you can purify your past and supernaturalize your present life" (St J. Escrivá, *The Way*, 216).

The Spirit of God will console with peace and joy, even in this life, those who weep for their sins, and later he will give them a share in the fullness of happiness and glory in heaven: these are the blessed.

5:5. "The meek": those who patiently suffer unjust persecution; those who remain serene, humble and steadfast in adversity, and do not give way to resentment or discouragement. The virtue of meekness is very necessary in the Christian life. Usually irritableness, which is very common, stems from a lack of humility and interior peace.

"The earth": this is usually understood as meaning our heavenly fatherland.

5:6. The notion of righteousness (or justice) in Holy Scripture is an essentially religious one (cf. notes on Mt 1:19 and 3:15; Rom 1:17; 1:18–32; 3:21–22 and 24). A righteous person is one who sincerely strives to do the will of God, which is discovered in the commandments, in one's duties of state in life and through one's life of prayer. Thus, righteousness, in the language of the Bible, is the same as what nowadays is usually called "holiness" (1 Jn 2:29; 3:7–10; Rev 22:11; Gen 15:6; Deut 9:4).

As St Jerome comments (*Comm. on Matthew*, 5, 6), in the fourth Beatitude our Lord is asking us not simply to have a vague desire for righteousness: we should hunger and thirst for it, that is, we should love and strive earnestly to seek what makes a man righteous in God's eyes. A person who genuinely wants to attain Christian holiness should love the means that the Church, the universal vehicle of salvation, offers all men and teaches them to use—frequent use of the sacraments, an intimate relationship with God in prayer, a valiant effort to meet one's social, professional and family responsibilities.

5:7. Mercy is not just a matter of giving alms to the poor but also of being understanding towards other people's defects, overlooking them, helping them cope with them and loving them despite whatever defects they may have. Being merciful also means rejoicing and suffering with other people.

5:8. Christ teaches us that the source of the quality of human acts lies in the heart, that is, in a man's soul, in the depth of his spirit. "When we speak of a person's heart, we refer not just to his sentiments, but to the whole person in his loving dealings with others. In order to help us understand divine things, Scripture uses the expression 'heart' in its full meaning, as the summary and source, expression and ultimate basis, of one's thoughts, words and actions. A man is worth what his heart is worth" (St J. Escrivá, *Christ Is Passing By*, 164).

Cleanness of heart is a gift of God, which expresses itself in a capacity to love, in having an upright and pure attitude to everything noble. As St Paul says, "whatever is true, whatever is honourable, whatever is just, whatever is pure, whatever is lovely, whatever is gracious,

49

Rev 22:4
Heb 12:14
Sir 4:11
1 Pet 3:14

9"Blessed are the peacemakers, for they shall be called sons of God.

10"Blessed are those who are persecuted for righteousness' sake, for theirs is the kingdom of heaven.

1 Pet 4:14

11"Blessed are you when men revile you and persecute you and utter all kinds of evil against you falsely on my account.

Jas 5:10
Heb 11:33–38

12"Rejoice and be glad, for your reward is great in heaven, for so men persecuted the prophets who were before you.

Salt of the earth and light of the world

Mk 9:50
Lk 14:34f

13"You are the salt of the earth; but if salt has lost its taste, how shall its saltness be restored? It is no longer good for anything except to be thrown out and trodden under foot by men.

---

if there is any excellence, if there is anything worthy of praise, think about these things" (Phil 4:8). Helped by God's grace, a Christian should strive to cleanse his heart and acquire this purity, the reward for which is the vision of God.

5:9. The translation "peacemakers" well conveys the active meaning of the original text—those who foster peace, in themselves and in others and, as a basis for that, try to be reconciled and to reconcile others with God. Being at peace with God is the cause and the effect of every kind of peace. Any peace on earth not based on this divine peace would be vain and misleading.

"They shall be called sons of God": this is an Hebraicism often found in Sacred Scripture; it is the same as saying "they will be sons of God". St John's first letter (3:1) provides a correct exegesis of this Beatitude: "See what love the Father has given us, that we should be called children of God; and so we are".

5:10. What this Beatitude means, then, is: blessed are those who are persecuted because they are holy, or because they are striving to be holy, for theirs is the Kingdom of heaven.

Thus, blessed is he who suffers persecution for being true to Jesus Christ and

who does so not only patiently but joyfully. Circumstances arise in a Christian's life that call for heroism—where no compromise is admissible: either one stays true to Jesus Christ whatever the cost in terms of reputation, life or possessions, or one denies him. St Bernard (*Sermon on the Feast of All Saints*) says that the eighth Beatitude is as it were the prerogative of Christian martyrs. Every Christian who is faithful to Jesus' teaching is in fact a "martyr" (a witness) who reflects or acts in accordance with this Beatitude, even if he does not undergo physical death.

5:11–12. The Beatitudes are the conditions Jesus lays down for entering the Kingdom of heaven. This verse, in a way summing up the preceding ones, is an invitation to everyone to put this teaching into practice. The Christian life, then, is no easy matter, but it is worthwhile, given the reward that Jesus promises.

5:13–16. These verses are calling to that apostolate which is part and parcel of being a Christian. Every Christian has to strive for personal sanctification, but he also has to seek the sanctification of others. Jesus teaches us this, using the very expressive simile of salt and light. Salt preserves food from corruption; it

Jn 8:12
Rev 21:10f
Mk 4:21
Lk 8:16; 11:33
Eph 5:8f
1 Pet 2:12

[14]"You are the light of the world. A city set on a hill cannot be hid. [15]Nor do men light a lamp and put it under a bushel, but on a stand, and it gives light to all the house. [16]Let your light so shine before men, that they may see your good works and give glory to your Father who is in heaven.

Jesus and his teaching, the fullness of the Law

Lk 4:21
Rom 3:31; 10:4

[17]"Think not that I have come to abolish the law and the prophets; I have come not to abolish them but to fulfil them.* [18]For truly I

---

also brings out its flavour and makes it more pleasant; and it disappears into the food; the Christian should do the same among the people around him.

"You are salt, apostolic soul. '*Bonum est sal*: salt is a useful thing', we read in the holy Gospel; '*si autem sal evanuerit*: but if the salt loses its taste', it is good for nothing, neither for the land nor for the manure heap; it is thrown out as useless. You are salt, apostolic soul. But if you lose your taste ..." (St Josemaría Escrivá, *The Way*, 921).

Good works are the fruit of charity, which consists in loving others as God loves us (cf. Jn 15:12). "I see now," St Thérèse of Lisieux writes, "that true charity consists in bearing with the faults of those about us, never being surprised at their weaknesses, but edified at the least sign of virtue. I see above all that charity must not remain hidden in the bottom of our hearts: 'nor do men light a lamp and put it under a bushel, but on a stand, and it gives light to all in the house.' It seems to me that this lamp is the symbol of charity; it must shine out not only to cheer up those we love best but all in the house" (*The Autobiography of a Saint*, chap. 9).

Apostolate is one of the clearest expressions of charity. The Second Vatican Council emphasized the Christian's duty to be apostolic. Baptism and Confirmation confer this duty, which is also a right (cf. *Lumen gentium*, 33), so much so that,

because the Christian is part of the Mystical Body, "a member who does not work at the growth of the body to the extent of his possibilities must be considered useless both to the Church and to himself " (*Apostolicam actuositatem*, 2). "Laymen have countless opportunities for exercising the apostolate of evangelization and sanctification. The very witness of a Christian life, and good works done in a supernatural spirit, are effective in drawing men to the faith and to God; and that is what the Lord has said: 'Let your light shine before men, that they may see your good works and give glory to your Father who is in heaven' " (ibid., 6).

"The Church must be present to these groups [those who do not even believe in God] through those of its members who live among them or have been sent to them. All Christians by the example of their lives and the witness of their word, wherever they live, have an obligation to manifest the new man, which they put on in Baptism, and to reveal the power of the Holy Spirit by whom they were strengthened at Confirmation, so that others, seeing their good works, might glorify the Father and more perfectly perceive the true meaning of human life and the universal solidarity of mankind" (*Ad gentes*, 11; cf. 36).

5:17–19. In this passage Jesus stresses the perennial value of the Old Testament, it is the word of God; because it has a

Lk 16:17; 21:33 say to you, till heaven and earth pass away, not an iota, not a dot, will pass from the law until all is accomplished. [19]Whoever then Jas 2:10 relaxes one of the least of these commandments and teaches men 1 Cor 15:9 so, shall be called least in the kingdom of heaven; but he who does them and teaches them shall be called great in the kingdom of heaven. [20]For I tell you, unless your righteousness exceeds that of the scribes and Pharisees, you will never enter the kingdom of heaven.

Ex 20:13; 21:12
Lev 24:17
Deut 17:8 [21]"You have heard that it was said to the men of old, 'You shall not kill; and whoever kills shall be liable to judgment.' [22]But I say 1 Jn 3:15 to you that every one who is angry with his brother[i] shall be liable

---

divine authority it deserves total respect. The Old Law enjoined precepts of a moral, legal and liturgical type. Its moral precepts still hold good in the New Testament because they are for the most part specific, divine-positive, promulgations of the natural law. However, our Lord gives them greater weight and meaning. But the legal and liturgical precepts of the Old Law were laid down by God for a specific stage in salvation history, that is, up to the coming of Christ; Christians are not obliged to observe them (cf. St Thomas Aquinas, *Summa theologiae*, 1–2, 108, 3 ad 3).

The law promulgated through Moses and explained by the prophets was God's gift to his people, a kind of anticipation of the definitive Law which the Christ or Messiah would lay down. Thus, as the Council of Trent defined, Jesus not only "was given to men as a redeemer in whom they are to trust, but also as lawgiver whom they are to obey" (*De iustificatione*, can. 21).

5:20. "Righteousness": see the note on Mt 5:6. This verse clarifies the meaning of the preceding verses. The scribes and Pharisees had distorted the spirit of the Law, putting the whole emphasis on its

external, ritual observance. For them exact and hyper-detailed but external fulfilment of the precepts of the Law was a guarantee of a person's salvation: "if I fulfil this I am righteous, I am holy and God is duty bound to save me". For someone with this approach to sanctification it is really not God who saves: man saves himself through external works of the Law. That this approach is quite mistaken is obvious from what Christ says here; in effect what he is saying is: to enter the Kingdom of God the notion of righteousness or salvation developed by the scribes and Pharisees must be rejected. In other words, justification or sanctification is a grace from God; man's role is one of cooperating with that grace by being faithful to it. Elsewhere Jesus gives the same teaching in an even clearer way (cf. Lk 18:9–14, the parable of the Pharisee and the tax collector).

It was also the origin of one of St Paul's great battles with the "Judaizers" (see Gal 3 and Rom 2–5).

5:21–26. Verses 21–26 give us a concrete example of the way that Jesus Christ brought the Law of Moses to its fulfilment, by explaining the deeper meaning of the commandments of that law.

---

i. Other ancient authorities insert *without cause*

to judgment; whoever insults[j] his brother shall be liable to the council, and whoever says, 'You fool!' shall be liable to the hell[k] of fire. [23]So if you are offering your gift at the altar, and there remember that your brother has something against you, [24]leave your gift there before the altar and go; first be reconciled to your brother, and then come and offer your gift. [25]Make friends quickly with your accuser, while you are going with him to court, lest your accuser hand you over to the judge, and the judge to the guard, and you be put in prison; [26]truly, I say to you, you will never get out till you have paid the last penny.

Mk 11:25

Mt 18:35
Lk 12:58f
1 Pet 5:8

5:22. By speaking in the first person ("but I say to you") Jesus shows that his authority is above that of Moses and the prophets; that is to say, he has divine authority. No mere man could claim such authority.

"Insults": practically all translations of this passage transcribe the original Aramaic words, *raca* (cf. RSV note below). It is not an easy word to translate. It means "foolish, stupid, crazy". The Jews used it to indicate utter contempt; often, instead of verbal abuse they would show their feelings by spitting on the ground.

"Fool" translates an even stronger term of abuse than *raca*—implying that a person has lost all moral and religious sense, to the point of apostasy.

In this passage our Lord points to three faults which we commit against charity, moving from internal irritation to showing total contempt. St Augustine comments that three degrees of faults and punishments are to be noted. The first is the fault of feeling angry; to this corresponds the punishment of "judgment". The second is that of passing an insulting remark, which merits the punishment of "the council". The third arises when anger quite blinds us: this is punished by "the hell of fire" (cf. *De Serm. Dom. in monte*, 2, 9).

"The hell of fire": literally, "*Gehenna* of fire", meaning, in the Jewish language of the time, eternal punishment. This shows the gravity of external sins against charity—gossip, backbiting, calumny etc. However, we should remember that these sins stem from the heart; our Lord focusses our attention, first, on internal sins—resentment, hatred etc.—to make us realize that that is where the root lies and that it is important to nip anger in the bud.

5:23–24. Here our Lord deals with certain Jewish practices of his time, and in doing so gives us perennial moral teaching of the highest order. Christians, of course, do not follow these Jewish ritual practices; to keep our Lord's commandment we have ways and means given us by Christ himself. Specifically, in the New and definitive Covenant founded by Christ, being reconciled involves going to the sacrament of Penance. In this sacrament the faithful "obtain pardon from God's mercy for the offence committed against him, and are, at the same time, reconciled with the Church which they have wounded by their sins" (Vatican II, *Lumen gentium*, 11).

In the New Testament, the greatest of all offerings is the Eucharist. Although

---

j. Greek *says Raca to* (an obscure term of abuse) **k.** Greek *Gehenna*

Ex 20:14
Job 31:1
2 Pet 2:14
Mt 18:8f
Mk 9:43, 47
Col 3:5

²⁷"You have heard that it was said, 'You shall not commit adultery.' ²⁸But I say to you that every one who looks at a woman lustfully has already committed adultery with her in his heart. ²⁹If your right eye causes you to sin, pluck it out and throw it away; it is better that you lose one of your members than that your whole

---

one has a duty to go to Mass on Sundays and holy days of obligation, an essential condition before receiving Holy Communion is that one be in the state of grace.

It is not our Lord's intention here to give love of neighbour priority over love of God. There is an order in charity: "You shall love the Lord your God with all your heart, with all your soul and with all your strength. This is the great and first commandment" (Mt 22:37–38). Love of one's neighbour, which is the second commandment in order of importance (cf. Mt 22:39), derives its meaning from the first. Brotherhood without parenthood is inconceivable. An offence against charity is, above all, an offence against God.

5:27–30. This refers to a sinful glance at any woman, be she married or not. Our Lord fills out the precepts of the Old Law, where only adultery and the coveting of one's neighbour's wife were considered sinful.

"Lustfully": feeling is one thing, consenting another. Consent presupposes that one realizes the evil of these actions (looking, imagining, having impure thoughts) and freely engages in them.

Prohibition of vices always implies a positive aspect—the contrary virtue. Holy purity, like every other virtue, is something eminently positive; it derives from the first commandment and is also directed to it: "You shall love the Lord your God *with all* your heart, *with all* your soul, and *with all* your mind" (Mt 22:37). "Purity is a consequence of the love that prompts us to commit to Christ

our soul and body, our faculties and senses. It is not something negative; it is a joyful affirmation" (St Josemaría Escrivá, *Christ Is Passing By*, 5). This virtue demands that we use all the resources available to us, to the point of heroism if necessary.

"Right eye", "right hand", refers to whatever we value most. Our Lord lays it on the line and is not exaggerating. He obviously does not mean that we should physically mutilate ourselves, but that we should fight hard without making any concessions, being ready to sacrifice anything which clearly could put us in the way of offending God. Jesus' graphic words particularly warn us about one of the most common occasions of sin, reminding us of how careful we need to be guarding our sight. King David, by indulging his curiosity, went on to commit adultery and crime. He later wept over his sins and led a holy life in the presence of God (cf. 2 Sam 11 and 12).

"The eyes! Through them many iniquities enter the soul. So many experiences like David's! If you guard your sight you will have assured the guard of your heart" (St Josemaría Escrivá, *The Way*, 183).

Among the ascetical methods of protecting the virtue of holy purity are: frequent Confession and Communion; devotion to our Lady; a spirit of prayer and mortification; guarding of the senses; flight from occasions of sin; and striving to avoid idleness by always being engaged in doing useful things. There are two further means which are particularly relevant today: "Decorum and modesty are younger brothers of purity" (ibid.,

body be thrown into hell.k* [30]And if your right hand causes you to sin, cut it off and throw it away; it is better that you lose one of your members than that your whole body go into hell.k

[31]"It was also said, 'Whoever divorces his wife, let him give her a certificate of divorce.' [32]But I say to you that every one who

Mk 10:4–12
Deut 24:1

---

128). Decorum and modesty are a sign of good taste, of respect for others and of human and Christian dignity. To act in accord with this teaching of our Lord, the Christian has to row against the current in a paganized environment and bring his influence for good to bear on it.

"There is need for a crusade of manliness and purity to counteract and undo the savage work of those who think that man is a beast. And that crusade is your work" (ibid., 121).

5:31–32. The Law of Moses (Deut 24:1), which was laid down in ancient times, had tolerated divorce due to the hardness of heart of the early Hebrews. But it had not specified clearly the ground on which divorce might be obtained. The rabbis worked out different sorts of interpretations, depending on which schools they belonged to—solutions ranging from very lax to quite rigid. In all cases, only husbands could repudiate wife, not vice versa. A woman's inferior position was eased somewhat by the device of a written document whereby the husband freed the repudiated woman to marry again if she wished. Against these rabbinical interpretations, Jesus re-establishes the original indissolubility of marriage as God instituted it (Gen 1:27; 2:24; cf. Mt 19:4–6; Eph 1:31; 1 Cor 7:10).

[The RSVCE carries a note which reads: "unchastity": The Greek word used here appears to refer to marriages which were not legally marriages, because they were either within the for-

bidden degrees of consanguinity (Lev 18:6–16) or contracted with a Gentile. The phrase "except on the ground of unchastity" does not occur in the parallel passage in Lk 16:18. See also Mt 19:9 (Mk 10:11–12), and especially 1 Cor 7:10–11, which shows that the prohibition is unconditional.] The phrase "except on the ground of unchastity" should not be taken as indicating an exception to the principle of the absolute indissolubility of marriage that Jesus has just re-established. It is almost certain that the phrase refers to unions accepted as marriage among some pagan peoples, but prohibited as incestuous in the Mosaic Law (cf. Lev 18) and in rabbinical tradition. The reference, then, is to unions radically invalid because of some impediment. When persons in this position were converted to the true faith, it was not that their union could be dissolved; it was declared that they had never in fact been joined in true marriage. Therefore, this phrase does not go against the indissolubility of marriage, but rather reaffirms it.

On the basis of Jesus' teaching and guided by the Holy Spirit, the Church has ruled that in the specially grave case of adultery it is permissible for a married couple to separate, but without the marriage bond being dissolved; therefore, neither party may contract a new marriage.

The indissolubility of marriage was unhesitatingly taught by the Church from the very beginning; she demanded practi-

---

k. Greek *Gehenna*

55

Lk 16:18
1 Cor 7:10f

divorces his wife, except on the ground of unchastity,* makes her an adulteress; and whoever marries a divorced woman commits adultery.

Ex 20:7
Lev 19:12
Num 30:2
Mt 23:16–22

³³"Again you have heard that it was said to the men of old, 'You shall not swear falsely, but shall perform to the Lord what you have sworn.' ³⁴But I say to you, Do not swear at all, either by

cal and legal recognition of this doctrine, expounded with full authority by Jesus (Mt 19:3–9; Mk 10:1–12; Lk 16:18) and by the apostles (1 Cor 6:16; 7:10–11, 39; Rom 7:2–8; Eph 5:31f). Here, for example, are just a few texts from the Magisterium on this subject: "Three blessings are ascribed to matrimony [...]. The third is the indissolubility of matrimony—indissoluble because it signifies the indivisible union of Christ with the Church. Although a separation from bed maybe permitted by reason of marital infidelity, nevertheless it is not permitted to contract another matrimony since the bond of a marriage lawfully contracted is perpetual" (Council of Florence, *Pro Armeniis*).

"If anyone says that the marriage bond can be dissolved by reason of heresy, domestic incompatibility, or willful desertion by one of the parties, let him be anathema" (Council of Trent, *De Sacram. matr.*, can. 5).

"If anyone says that the Church is in error when she has taught and does teach according to the doctrine of the Gospels and apostles that the marriage bond cannot be dissolved because of adultery on the part of either the husband or the wife; and that neither party, not even the innocent one who gave no cause for the adultery, can contract another marriage while the other is still living; and that adultery is committed both by the husband who dismisses the adulterous wife and marries again and by the wife who dismisses her adulterous husband and marries again: let him be anathema" (ibid., can. 7).

"Taking our starting point from that Encyclical, which is concerned almost entirely with vindicating the divine institution of matrimony, its dignity as a Sacrament, and its perpetual stability, let us first recall this immutable, inviolable and fundamental truth: matrimony was not instituted or re-established by men but by God; not men, but God, the Author of nature, and Christ our Lord, the restorer of nature, provided marriage with its laws, confirmed it and elevated it; and consequently those laws can in no ways be subject to human wills or to any contrary pact made even by the contracting parties themselves. This is the teaching of Sacred Scripture; it is the constant and universal Tradition of the Church; it is the solemnly defined doctrine of the Council of Trent, which uses the words of Holy Scripture to proclaim and establish that the perpetual indissolubility of the marriage bond, its unity and stability, derive from God himself" (Pius XI, *Casti connubii*).

"It is true that before the coming of Christ the perfection and strictness of the original law were modified to the extent that Moses, because of the hardness of their hearts, allowed even the members of God's people to give a bill of divorce for certain reasons. But Christ, by virtue of his power as supreme Lawgiver, revoked this concession and restored the law to its original perfection by those words which must never be forgotten: 'What God hath jointed together let no man put asunder'" (ibid.).

heaven, for it is the throne of God, [35]or by the earth, for it is his footstool, or by Jerusalem, for it is the city of the great King. [36]And do not swear by your head, for you cannot make one hair white or black. [37]Let what you say be simply 'Yes' or 'No'; anything more than this comes from evil.[1]

[38]"You have heard that it was said, 'An eye for an eye and a tooth for a tooth.' [39]But I say to you, Do not resist one who is evil.

Is 66:1
Acts 7:49
Ps 48:2

2 Cor 1:17
Jas 5:12

Lev 24:19f

Jn 18:22f

"For the good of the parties, of the children, and of society this sacred bond no longer depends on human decision alone. For God himself is the author of marriage [...]. The intimate union of marriage (as a mutual giving of two persons) and the good of the children demand total fidelity from the spouses and require an unbreakable unity between them" (Vatican II, *Gaudium et spes*, 48).

5:33–37. The Law of Moses absolutely prohibited perjury or violation of oaths (Ex 20:7; Num 30:3; Deut 23:22). In Christ's time, the making of sworn statements was so frequent and the casuistry surrounding them so intricate that the practice was being grossly abused. Some rabbinical documents of the time show that oaths were taken for quite unimportant reasons. Parallel to this abuse of oath-taking there arose no less ridiculous abuses to justify non-fulfilment of oaths. All this meant great disrespect for the name of God. However, we do know from Holy Scripture that oath-taking is lawful and good in certain circumstances: "If you swear, 'As the Lord lives', in truth, in justice, and in uprightness, then nations shall bless themselves in him, and in him shall they glory" (Jer 4:2).

Jesus here lays down the criterion that his disciples must apply in this connexion. It is based on re-establishing mutual trust, nobility and sincerity. The

devil is "the father of lies" (Jn 8:44). Therefore, Christ's Church cannot permit human relationships to be based on deceit and insincerity. God is truth, and the children of the Kingdom must, therefore, base mutual relationships on truth. Jesus concludes by praising sincerity. Throughout his teaching he identifies hypocrisy as one of the main vices to be combatted (cf., e.g., Mt 23:13–32), and sincerity as one of the finest of virtues (cf. Jn 1:47).

5:38–42. Among the Semites, from whom the Israelites stemmed, the law of vengeance ruled. It led to interminable strife and countless crimes. In the early centuries of the chosen people, the law of retaliation was recognized as an ethical advance, socially and legally: no punishment could exceed the crime, and any punitive retaliation was outlawed. In this way, the honour of the clans and families was satisfied, and endless feuds avoided.

As far as New Testament morality is concerned, Jesus establishes a definitive advance: a sense of forgiveness and absence of pride play an essential role. Every legal framework for combating evil in the world, every reasonable defence of personal rights, should be based on morality. The last three verses refer to mutual charity among the children of the Kingdom, a charity which presupposes and enhances justice.

---

1. Or *the evil one*

Lev 19:18
1 Cor 6:7

But if any one strikes you on the right cheek, turn to him the other also; [40]and if any one would sue you and take your coat, let him have your cloak as well; [41]and if any one forces you to go one mile, go with him two miles. [42]Give to him who begs from you, and do not refuse him who would borrow from you.

Lev 19:18
Ex 23:4f
Rom 12:14, 20
Lk 23:34
Acts 7:59
Eph 5:1

[43]"You have heard that it was said, 'You shall love your neighbour and hate your enemy.' [44]But I say to you, Love your enemies and pray for those who persecute you, [45]so that you may be sons of your Father who is in heaven; for he makes his sun rise on the evil and on the good, and sends rain on the just and on the unjust. [46]For if you love those who love you, what reward have you? Do not even the tax collectors do the same? [47]And if you salute only your brethren, what more are you doing than others? Do not even

Lev 19:2

the Gentiles do the same? [48]You, therefore, must be perfect, as your heavenly Father is perfect.

5:43. The first part of this verse—"You shall love your neighbour"—is to be found in Leviticus 19:18. The second part—"hate your enemy"—is not in the Law of Moses. However, Jesus' words refer to a widespread rabbinical interpretation which understood "neighbours" as meaning "Israelites". Our Lord corrects this misinterpretation of the Law: for him everyone is our neighbour (cf. the parable of the Good Samaritan in Lk 10:25–37).

5:43–47. This passage sums up the teaching which precedes it. Our Lord goes so far as to say that a Christian has no personal enemies. His only enemy is evil as such—sin—but not the sinner. Jesus himself puts this into practice with those who crucified him, and he continues to act in the same way towards sinners who rebel against him and despise him. Consequently, the saints have always followed his example—like St Stephen, the first martyr, who prayed for those who were putting him to death. This is the apex of Christian perfection—to love, and pray for, even those who persecute and calumniate us. It is the distinguishing mark of the children of God.

5:46. "Tax collectors": the Roman Empire had no officials of its own for the collection of taxes; in each country it used local people for this purpose. These were free to engage agents (hence we find references to "chief tax collectors": cf. Lk 19:2). The global amount of tax for each region was specified by the Roman authorities; the tax collectors levied more than this amount, keeping the surplus for themselves: this led them to act rather arbitrarily, which was why the people hated them. In the case of the Jews, insult was added to injury by the fact that the chosen people were being exploited by Gentiles.

5:48. Verse 48 is, in a sense, a summary of the teaching in this entire chapter, including the Beatitudes. Strictly speaking, it is quite impossible for a created being to be as perfect as God. What our Lord means here is that God's own perfection should be the model that every faithful Christian tries to follow, even though he realizes that there is an infinite distance between himself and his Creator. However, this does not reduce the force of this commandment; it sheds more light

An upright intention in almsgiving, prayer and fasting

6 [1]"Beware of practising your piety before men in order to be seen by them; for then you will have no reward from your Father who is in heaven.

[2]"Thus, when you give alms, sound no trumpet before you, as the hypocrites do in the synagogues and in the streets, that they may be praised by men. Truly, I say to you, they have their reward. [3]But when you give alms, do not let your left hand know what your right hand is doing, [4]so that your alms may be in secret; and your Father who sees in secret will reward you.

Rom 12:8

[5]"And when you pray, you must not be like the hypocrites; for they love to stand and pray in the synagogues and at the street corners, that they may be seen by men. Truly, I say to you, they have their reward. [6]But when you pray, go into your room and shut the

2 Sam 4:33
Is 26:20

---

on it. It is a difficult commandment to live up to, but also with this we must take account of the enormous help grace gives us to go so far as to tend towards divine perfection. Certainly, the perfection that we should imitate does not refer to the power and wisdom of God, which are totally beyond our scope; here the context seems to refer primarily to love and mercy. Along the same lines, St Luke quotes these words of our Lord: "Be merciful, even as your Father is merciful" (Lk 6:36; cf. the note on Lk 6:20–49).

Clearly, the "universal call to holiness" is not a recommendation but a commandment of Jesus Christ. "Your duty is to sanctify yourself. Yes, even you. Who thinks that this task is only for priests and religious? To everyone, without exception, our Lord said: 'Be ye perfect, as my heavenly Father is perfect'" (St J. Escrivá, *The Way*, 291). This teaching is sanctioned by chapter 5 of Vatican II's Constitution *Lumen gentium*, where it says (at no. 40): "The Lord Jesus, divine teacher and model of all perfection, preached holiness of life (of which he is the author and maker) to each and every one of his disciples without distinction: 'You, therefore, must be perfect,

as your heavenly Father is perfect' [...]. It is therefore quite clear that all Christians in any state or walk of life are called to the fullness of Christian life and to the perfection of love, and by this holiness a more human manner of life is fostered also in earthly society."

6:1–18. "Piety", here, means good works (cf. the note on Mt 5:6). Our Lord is indicating the kind of spirit in which we should do acts of personal piety. Almsgiving, fasting and prayer were the basic forms taken by personal piety among the chosen people—which is why Jesus refers to these three subjects. With complete authority he teaches that true piety must be practised with an upright intention, in the presence of God and without any ostentation. Piety practised in this way implies exercising our faith in God who sees us—and also in the safe knowledge that he will reward those who are sincerely devout.

6:5–6. Following the teaching of Jesus, the Church has always taught us to pray even when we were infants. By saying "you" (singular) our Lord is stating quite unequivocally the need for personal pray-

door and pray to your Father who is in secret; and your Father who sees in secret will reward you.*

⁷"And in praying do not heap up empty phrases as the Gentiles do; for they think that they will be heard for their many words. ⁸Do not be like them, for your Father knows what you need before you ask him. ⁹Pray then like this:

---

er—relating as child to Father, alone with God.

Public prayer, for which Christ's faithful assemble together, is something necessary and holy; but it should never displace obedience to this clear commandment of our Lord: "When you pray, go into your room and shut the door and pray to your Father."

The Second Vatican Council reminds us of the teaching and practice of the Church in its liturgy, which is "the summit towards which the activity of the Church is directed; it is also the fount from which all her power flows [...]. The spiritual life, however, is not limited solely to participation in the liturgy. The Christian is indeed called to pray with others, but he must also enter into his bedroom to pray to his Father in secret; furthermore, according to the teaching of the apostle, he must pray without ceasing (1 Thess 5:17)" (*Sacrosanctum Concilium*, 10 and 12).

A soul who really puts his Christian faith into practice realizes that he needs frequently to get away and pray alone to his Father, God. Jesus, who gives us this teaching about prayer, practised it during his own life on earth: the holy Gospel reports that he often went apart to pray on his own: "At times he spent the whole night in an intimate conversation with his Father. The apostles were filled with love when they saw Christ pray" (St J. Escrivá, *Christ Is Passing By*, 119; cf. Mt 14:23; Mk 1:35; Lk 5:16; etc.). The apostles followed the Master's example, and

so we see Peter going up to the rooftop of the house to pray in private, and receiving a revelation (cf. Acts 10:9–16). "Our life of prayer should also be based on some moments that are dedicated exclusively to our conversation with God, moments of silent dialogue" (*Christ Is Passing By*, 119).

6:7–8. Jesus condemns the superstitious notion that long prayers are needed to attract God's attention. True piety is not so much a matter of the amount of words as of the frequency and the love with which the Christian turns towards God in all the events, great or small, of his day. Vocal prayer is good, and necessary; but the words count only if they express our inner feelings.

6:9–13. The Our Father is, without any doubt, the most commented-on passage in all Holy Scripture. Numerous great Church writers have left us commentaries full of poetry and wisdom. The early Christians, taught by the precepts of salvation, and following the divine commandment, centred their prayer on this sublime and simple form of words given them by Jesus. And the last Christians, too, will raise their hearts to say the Our Father for the last time when they are on the point of being taken to heaven. In the meantime, from childhood to death, the Our Father is a prayer which fills us with hope and consolation. Jesus fully realized how helpful this prayer would be to us. We are grateful to him for giving it to us,

Our Father who art in heaven,
Hallowed be thy name.
¹⁰Thy kingdom come,
Thy will be done,
On earth as it is in heaven.

Lk 11:2–4
Jn 17:6
Mt 7:11

Lk 22:42

---

to the apostles for passing it on to us and, in the case of most Christians, to our mothers for teaching it to us in our infancy. So important is the Lord's Prayer that from apostolic times it has been used, along with the Creed, the Ten Commandments and the Sacraments, as the basis of Christian catechesis. Catechumens were introduced to the life of prayer by the Our Father, and our catechisms today use it for that purpose. St Augustine says that the Lord's Prayer is so perfect that it sums up in a few words everything man needs to ask God for (cf. *Sermons*, 56). It is usually seen as being made up of an invocation and seven petitions—three to do with praise of God and four with the needs of men.

6:9. It is a source of great consolation to be able to call God "our Father"; Jesus, the Son of God, teaches men to invoke God as Father because we are indeed his children, and should feel towards him in that way.

"The Lord [...] is not a tyrannical master or a rigid and implacable judge; he is our Father. He speaks to us about our lack of generosity, our sins, our mistakes; but he does so in order to free us from them, to promise us his friendship and his love [...]. A child of God treats the Lord as his Father. He is not obsequious and servile, he is not merely formal and well-mannered: he is completely sincere and trusting" (St J. Escrivá, *Christ Is Passing By*, 64).

"Hallowed be thy name": in the Bible a person's "name" means the same as the person himself. Here the name of God

means God himself. Why pray that his name be hallowed, sanctified? We do not mean sanctification in the human sense—leaving evil behind and drawing closer to God—for God is holiness itself. God, rather, is sanctified when his holiness is acknowledged and honoured by his creatures—which is what this first petition of the Our Father means (cf. *St Pius V Catechism*, 4, 10).

6:10. "Thy kingdom come": this brings up again the central idea of the Gospel of Jesus Christ—the coming of the Kingdom. The Kingdom of God is so identical with the life and work of Jesus Christ that the Gospel is referred to now as the Gospel of Jesus Christ, now as the Gospel of the Kingdom (Mt 9:35). On the notion of Kingdom of God see the commentary on Matthew 3:2 and 4:17. The coming of the Kingdom of God is the realization of God's plan of salvation in the world. The Kingdom establishes itself in the first place in the core of man's being, raising him up to share in God's own inner life. This elevation has, as it were, two stages—the first, in this life, where it is brought about by grace; the second, definitive stage in eternal life, where man's elevation to the supernatural level is fully completed. We for our part need to respond to God spontaneously, lovingly and trustingly.

"Thy will be done": this third petition expresses two desires. The first is that man identify humbly and unconditionally with God's will—abandonment in the arms of his Father God. The second is that the will of God be fulfilled, that man

Jn 17:11, 15

[11]Give us this day our daily bread;[m]
[12]And forgive us our debts,
As we also have forgiven our debtors;
[13]And lead us not into temptation,
But deliver us from evil.[n]

---

cooperate with it in full freedom. For example, God's will is to be found in the moral aspect of the divine law—but this law is not forced on man. One of the signs of the coming of the Kingdom is man's loving fulfilment of God's will. The second part of the petition, "on earth as it is in heaven", means that, just as the angels and saints in heaven are fully at one with God's will, so—we desire—should the same thing obtain on earth.

Our effort to do God's will proves that we are sincere when we say the words, "Thy will be done." For our Lord says, "Not every one who says to me, 'Lord, Lord' shall enter the kingdom of heaven, but he who does the will of my Father who is in heaven" (Mt 7:21). "Anyone, then, who sincerely repeats this petition, 'Fiat voluntas tua', must, at least in intention, have done this already" (St Teresa of Avila, *Way of Perfection*, chap. 36).

6:11. In making this fourth petition, we are thinking primarily of our needs in this present life. The importance of this petition is that it declares that the material things we need in our lives are good and lawful. It gives a deep religious dimension to the support of life: what Christ's disciple obtains through his own work is also something for which he should implore God—and he should receive it gratefully as a gift from God. God is our support in life: by asking God to support him and by realizing that it is God who is providing this support, the Christian

avoids being worried about material needs. Jesus does not want us to pray for wealth or to be attached to material things, but to seek and make sober use of what meets our needs. Hence, in Matthew as well as in Luke (Lk 11:2), there is reference to having enough food for every day. This fourth petition, then, has to do with moderate use of food and material things—far from the extremes of opulence and misery, as God already taught in the Old Testament: "Give me neither poverty nor riches; feed me with the food which is needful for me, lest I be full, and deny thee, and say, 'Who is the Lord?' or lest I be poor, and steal, and profane the name of my God" (Prov 30:8).

The Fathers of the Church interpreted the bread asked for here not only as material food but also as referring to the Blessed Eucharist, without which our spirit cannot stay alive.

According to the *St Pius V Catechism* (cf. 4, 13, 21) the Eucharist is called our daily bread because it is offered daily to God in the Mass and because we should worthily receive it, every day if possible, as St Ambrose advises: "If the bread is daily, why do you take it only once a year [...]? Receive daily what is of benefit to you daily! So live that you may deserve to receive it daily!" (*De Sacramentis*, 5, 4).

6:12. "Debts": clearly, here, in the sense of sin. In the Aramaic of Jesus' time the same word was used for offence and debt. In this fifth petition, then, we admit

---

m. Or *our bread for the morrow*

62

[14]For if you forgive men their trespasses, your heavenly Father also will forgive you; [15]but if you do not forgive men their trespasses, neither will your Father forgive your trespasses.

Mk 11:25f

that we are debtors because we have offended God. The Old Testament is full of references to man's sinful condition. Even the "righteous" are sinners. Recognizing our sins is the first step in every conversion to God. It is not a question of recognizing that we have sinned in the past but of confessing our present sinful condition. Awareness of our sinfulness makes us realize our religious need to have recourse to the only One who can cure it. Hence the advantage of praying insistently, using the Lord's Prayer to obtain God's forgiveness time and again.

The second part of this petition is a serious call to forgive our fellow-men, for we cannot dare to ask God to forgive us if we are not ready to forgive others. The Christian needs to realize what this prayer implies: unwillingness to forgive others means that one is condemning oneself (see the notes on Mt 5:23–24 and 18:21–35).

6:13. "And lead us not into temptation": "We do not ask to be totally exempt from temptation, for human life is one continuous temptation (cf. Job 7:1). What, then, do we pray for in this petition? We pray that the divine assistance may not forsake us, lest having been deceived, or worsted, we should yield to temptation; and that the grace of God may be at hand to succour us when our strength fails, to refresh and invigorate us in our trials" (St Pius V, *Catechism*, 4, 15, 14).

In this petition of the Our Father we recognize that our human efforts alone do not take us very far in trying to cope with temptation, and that we need to have

humble recourse to God, to get the strength we need. For, "God is strong enough to free you from everything and can do you more good than all the devils can do you harm. All that God decrees is that you confide in him, that you draw near him, that you trust him and distrust yourself, and so be helped; and with this help you will defeat whatever hell brings against you. Never lose hold of this firm hope [...] even if the demons are legion and all kinds of severe temptations harass you. Lean upon Him, because if the Lord is not your support and your strength, then you will fall and you will be afraid of everything" (St John of Avila, *Sermons*, 9, First Sunday of Lent).

"But deliver us from evil": in this petition, which, in a way, sums up the previous petitions, we ask the Lord to free us from everything our enemy does to bring us down; we cannot be free of him unless God himself frees us, in response to our prayers.

This sentence can also be translated as "Deliver us from the evil one", that is to say, the devil, who is in the last analysis the author of all evils to which we are prone.

In making this request we can be sure that our prayer will be heard because Jesus Christ, when he was on the point of leaving this world, prayed to the Father for the salvation of all men: "I do not pray that thou shouldst take them out of the world, but that thou shouldst keep them from the evil one" (Jn 17:15).

6:14–15. In vv. 14 and 15 St Matthew gives us a sort of commentary of our Lord on the fifth petition of the Our Father.

n. Or *the evil one*. Other authorities, some ancient, add, in some form, *For thine is the kingdom and the power and the glory, for ever. Amen*

Is 58:5–9

[16]"And when you fast, do not look dismal, like the hypocrites, for they disfigure their faces that their fasting may be seen by men. Truly, I say to you, they have their reward. [17]But when you fast, anoint your head and wash your face, [18]that your fasting may not be seen by men but by your Father who is in secret; and your Father who sees in secret will reward you.

Trust in God's fatherly providence

Lk 12:33f
Col 3:1f

[19]"Do not lay up for yourselves treasures on earth, where moth and rust[o] consume and where thieves break in and steal, [20]but lay up for yourselves treasures in heaven, where neither moth nor rust[o] consumes and where thieves do not break in and steal. [21]For where your treasure is, there will your heart be also.

Lk 11:34–36

[22]"The eye is the lamp of the body. So, if your eye is sound, your whole body will be full of light; [23]but if your eye is not

---

A God who forgives is a wonderful God. But if God, who is thrice-holy, has mercy on the sinner, how much more ought we forgive others—we sinners, who know from our own experience the wretchedness of sin. No one on earth is perfect. Just as God loves us, even though we have defects, and forgives us, we should love others, even though they have defects, and forgive them. If we wait to love people who have no defects, we shall never love anyone. If we wait until others mend their ways or apologize, we will scarcely ever forgive them. But then we ourselves will never be forgiven. "All right: that person has behaved badly towards you. But, haven't you behaved worse towards God?" (St Josemaría Escrivá, *The Way*, 686).

Thus, forgiving those who have offended us makes us like our Father, God: "In loving our enemies there shines forth in us some likeness to God our Father, who, by the death of his Son, ransomed from everlasting perdition and reconciled to himself the human race, which before was most unfriendly and hostile

to him" (St Pius V, *Catechism*, 4, 14, 19).

6:16–18. Starting from the traditional practice of fasting, our Lord tells us the spirit in which we should practise mortification of our senses: we should do so without ostentation, avoiding praise, discreetly; that way Jesus' words will not apply to us: "they have their reward"; it would have been a very bad deal. "The world admires only spectacular sacrifice, because it does not realize the value of sacrifice that is hidden and silent" (St Josemaría Escrivá, *The Way*, 185).

6:19–21. The idea here is very clear: man's heart yearns for a treasure that will give him security and happiness. However, every treasure in the form of earthly goods—wealth, property—becomes a constant source of worry, because there is always the risk we will lose it or because the effort to protect it is such a strain.

Against this, Jesus teaches us here that our true treasure lies in good works and an upright life, which will be eter-

o. Or *worm*

sound, your whole body will be full of darkness. If then the light in you is darkness, how great is the darkness!

[24]"No one can serve two masters; for either he will hate the one and love the other, or he will be devoted to the one and despise the other. You cannot serve God and mammon.*

[25]"Therefore I tell you, do not be anxious about your life, what you shall eat or what you shall drink, nor about your body, what you shall put on. Is not life more than food, and the body more than clothing? [26]Look at the birds of the air; they neither sow nor reap nor gather into barns, and yet your heavenly Father feeds them. Are you not of more value than they? [27]And which of you by being anxious can add one cubit to his span of life?[p] [28]And why are you anxious about clothing? Consider the lilies of the field, how they grow; they neither toil nor spin; [29]yet I tell you, even Solomon in all his glory was not arrayed like one of these. [30]But if God so

Side references:
Lk 16:9, 13
Lk 12:22–31
Phil 4:6
1 Pet 5:7
1 Tim 6:6
Heb 13:5
1 Kings 10

---

nally rewarded by God in heaven. That indeed is a treasure which one never loses, a treasure on which Christ's disciple should put his heart.

Jesus closes the teaching contained in the preceding verses with a kind of refrain (v. 21). He is not saying that people should be unconcerned about earthly things; what he does say is that no created thing can be "the treasure", the ultimate aim, of man. What man should do is make his way to God, sanctify himself and give all glory to God, by making right use of the noble things of the earth: "Whether you eat or drink, or whatever you do, do all to the glory of God" (1 Cor 10:31; cf. Col 3:17).

6:22–23. Here is another jewel of Jesus' wisdom teaching. It begins with a sentence that is then immediately explained. The Master uses the simile of the eye as a lamp which provides the body with light. Christian exegesis has seen this "eye", this "lamp", as meaning the motivation behind our behaviour. St Thomas explains it in this way: "The eye refers to

motive. When a person wants to do something, he first forms an intention: thus, if your intention is sound—simple and clear—that is to say, if it is directed towards God, your whole body, that is, all your actions, will be sound, sincerely directed towards good" (St Thomas Aquinas, *Comm. on St Matthew*, 6, 22–23).

6:24. Man's ultimate goal is God; to attain this goal he should commit himself entirely. But in fact some people do not have God as their ultimate goal, and instead choose wealth of some kind—in which case wealth becomes their god. Man cannot have two absolute and contrary goals.

6:25–32. In this beautiful passage Jesus shows us the value of the ordinary things of life, and teaches us to put our trust in God's fatherly providence. Using simple examples and comparisons taken from everyday life, he teaches us to abandon ourselves into the arms of God.

6:27. The word "span" could be translated as "stature", but "span" is closer to

p. Or *to his stature*

clothes the grass of the field, which today is alive and tomorrow is thrown into the oven, will he not much more clothe you, O men of little faith? [31]Therefore do not be anxious, saying, 'What shall we eat?' or 'What shall we drink?' or 'What shall we wear?' [32]For the Gentiles seek all these things; and your heavenly Father knows that

Rom 14:17
1 Kings 3:13f
Ps 37:4, 25

you need them all. [33]But seek first his kingdom and his righteous-ness, and all these things shall be yours as well.

Ex 16:19

[34]"Therefore do not be anxious about tomorrow, for tomorrow will be anxious for itself. Let the day's own trouble be sufficient for the day.

Various precepts. Do not judge

Rom 2:1
1 Cor 4:5
Mk 4:24

7 [1]"Judge not, that you be not judged. [2]For with the judgment you pronounce you will be judged, and the measure you give

the original (cf. Lk 12:25). A "cubit" is a measure of length which can metaphori-cally refer to time.

6:33. Here again the righteousness of the Kingdom means the life of grace in man—which involves a whole series of spiritual and moral values and can be summed up in the notion of "holiness". The search for holiness should be our pri-mary purpose in life. Jesus is again insist-ing on the primacy of spiritual demands. Commenting on this passage, Pope Paul VI says: "Why poverty? It is to give God, the Kingdom of God, the first place in the scale of values which are the object of human aspirations. Jesus says: 'Seek first his kingdom and his righteousness.' And he says this with regard to all the other temporal goods, even necessary and legitimate ones, with which human desires are usually concerned. Christ's poverty makes possible that detachment from earthly things which allows us to place the relationship with God at the peak of human aspirations" (General Audience, 5 January 1977).

6:34. Our Lord exhorts us to go about our daily tasks serenely and not to worry

uselessly about what happened yesterday or what may happen tomorrow. This is wisdom based on God's fatherly provi-dence and on our own everyday experi-ence: "He who observes the wind will not sow; and he who regards the clouds will not reap" (Eccles 11:4).

What is important, what is within our reach, is to live in God's presence and make good use of the present moment: "Do your duty 'now', without looking back on 'yesterday', which has already passed, or worrying over 'tomorrow', which may never come for you" (St Josemaría Escrivá, *The Way*, 253).

7:1. Jesus is condemning any rash judg-ments we make maliciously or carelessly about our brothers' behaviour or feelings or motives. "Think badly and you will not be far wrong" is completely at odds with Jesus' teaching.

In speaking of Christian charity St Paul lists its main features: "Love is patient and kind [...]. Love bears all things, believes all things, hopes all things, endures all things" (1 Cor 13:4, 5, 7). Therefore, "Never think badly of anyone, not even if the words or conduct of the person in question give you good

will be the measure you get. ³Why do you see the speck that is in your brother's eye, but do not notice the log that is in your own eye? ⁴Or how can you say to your brother, 'Let me take the speck out of your eye,' when there is the log in your own eye? ⁵You hypocrite, first take the log out of your own eye, and then you will see clearly to take the speck out of your brother's eye.

Respect for holy things
⁶"Do not give dogs what is holy; and do not throw your pearls before swine, lest they trample them under foot and turn to attack you.

Effectiveness of prayer
⁷"Ask, and it will be given you; seek, and you will find; knock, and it will be opened to you. ⁸For every one who asks receives,

Mk 11:24
Lk 11:9–13
Jer 29:13f
Jn 14:13; 16:23

---

grounds for doing so" (St Josemaría Escrivá, *The Way*, 442).

"Let us be slow to judge. Each one sees things from his own point of view, as his mind, with all its limitations, tells him, and through eyes that are often dimmed and clouded by passion" (ibid., 451).

7:1–2. As elsewhere, the verbs in the passive voice ("you will be judged", "the measure you will be given") have God as their subject, even though he is not explicitly mentioned: "Do not judge *others*, that you be not judged *by God*." Clearly the judgment referred to here is always a condemnatory judgment; therefore, if we do not want to be condemned by God, we should never condemn our neighbour. "God measures out according as we measure out and forgives as we forgive, and comes to our rescue with the same tenderness as he sees us having towards others" (Fray Luis de León, *Exposición del Libro de Job*, chap. 29).

7:3–5. A person whose sight is distorted sees things as deformed, even though in fact they are not deformed. St Augustine gives this advice: "Try to acquire those virtues which you think your brothers

lack, and you will no longer see their defects, because you will not have them yourselves" (*Enarrationes in Psalmos*, 30, 2, 7). In this connexion, the saying "A thief thinks that everyone else is a thief" is in line with this teaching of Jesus.

Besides: "To criticize, to destroy, is not difficult; any unskilled labourer knows how to drive his pick into the noble and finely-hewn stone of a cathedral. To construct: that is what requires the skill of a master" (St Josemaría Escrivá, *The Way*, 456).

7:6. Jesus uses a popular saying to teach discernment in the preaching of the word of God and distribution of the means of sanctification. The Church has always heeded this warning, particularly in the sense of respect with which she administers the sacraments—especially the Holy Eucharist. Filial confidence does not exempt us from the sincere and profound respect that should imbue our relations with God and with holy things.

7:7–11. Here the Master teaches us in a number of ways about the effectiveness of prayer. Prayer is a raising of mind and heart to God to adore him, to praise him,

and he who seeks finds, and to him who knocks it will be opened. [9]Or what man of you, if his son asks him for bread, will give him a stone? [10]Or if he asks for a fish, will give him a serpent? [11]If you then, who are evil, know how to give good gifts to your children, how much more will your Father who is in heaven give good things to those who ask him!

Jas 1:17

The golden rule

Lk 6:31
Rom 13:8–10

[12]So whatever you wish that men would do to you, do so to them; for this is the law and the prophets.

The narrow gate

Lk 13:24
Jn 10:7, 9

[13]"Enter by the narrow gate; for the gate is wide and the way is easy,[q] that leads to destruction, and those who enter by it are

---

to thank him and to ask him for what we need (cf. St Pius X, *Catechism*, 255). Jesus emphasizes the need for petitionary prayer, which is the first spontaneous movement of a soul who recognizes God as his Creator and Father. As God's creature and child, each of us needs to ask him humbly for everything.

In speaking of the effectiveness of prayer, Jesus does not put any restriction: "Every one who asks receives", because God is our Father. St Jerome comments: "It is written, to everyone who asks it will be given; so, if it is not given to you, it is not given to you because you do not ask; so, ask and you will receive" (*Comm. on Matthew*, 7). However, even though prayer in itself is infallible, sometimes we do not obtain what we ask for. St Augustine says that our prayer is not heard because we ask "aut mali, aut male, aut mala." "*Mali*" (= evil people): because we are evil, because our personal dispositions are not good; "*male*" (= badly): because we pray badly, without faith, not persevering, not humbly; "*mala*" (= bad things): because we ask for bad things, that is, things which are

not good for us, things which can harm us (cf. *De civitate Dei*, 20, 22 and 27; *De Serm. Dom. in monte*, 2, 27, 73). In the last analysis, prayer is ineffective when it is not true prayer. Therefore, "Pray. In what human venture could you have greater guarantes of success?" (St Josemaría Escrivá, *The Way*, 96).

7:12. This "golden rule" gives us a guideline to realize our obligations towards and the love we should have for others. However, if we interpreted it superficially it would become a selfish rule; it obviously does not mean "*do ut des*" ("I give you something so that you will give me something") but that we should do good to others unconditionally: we are clever enough not to put limits on how much we love ourselves. This rule of conduct will be completed by Jesus' "new commandment" (Jn 13:34), where he teaches us to love others as he himself has loved us.

7:13–14. "Enter": in St Matthew's Gospel this verb often has as its object the "Kingdom of heaven" or equivalent

---

q. Other ancient authorities read *for the way is wide and easy*

many. [14]For the gate is narrow and the way is hard, that leads to life, and those who find it are few.

Acts 14:22

False prophets

[15]"Beware of false prophets, who come to you in sheep's clothing but inwardly are ravenous wolves. [16]You will know them by their fruits. Are grapes gathered from thorns, or figs from thistles? [17]So, every sound tree bears good fruit, but the bad tree bears evil fruit. [18]A sound tree cannot bear evil fruit, nor can a bad tree bear good fruit. [19]Every tree that does not bear good fruit is cut down and thrown into the fire. [20]Thus you will know them by their fruits.

Acts 20:29

Gal 5:19–22
Jas 3:12

Jn 15:2, 6

---

expressions (life, the marriage feast, the joy of the Lord, etc.). We can interpret "enter" as an imperious invitation.

The way of sin is momentarily pleasant and calls for no effort, but it leads to eternal perdition. Following the way of a generous and sincere Christian life is very demanding—here Jesus speaks of a narrow gate and a hard way—but it leads to Life, to eternal salvation.

The Christian way involves carrying the cross. "For if a man resolve to submit himself to carrying this cross—that is to say, if he resolve to desire in truth to meet trials and to bear them in all things for God's sake, he will find in them all great relief and sweetness wherewith he may travel upon this road, detached from all things and desiring nothing. Yet, if he desire to possess anything—whether it comes from God or from any other source—with any feeling of attachment, he has not stripped and denied himself in all things; and thus he will be unable to walk along this narrow path or to climb upward by it" (St John of the Cross, *Ascent of Mount Carmel*, book 2, chap. 7, 7).

7:15–20. There are many references in the Old Testament to false prophets, perhaps the best-known being Jeremiah 23:9–40 which condemns the impiety of those prophets who "prophesied by Baal and led my people Israel astray"; "who prophesy to you, filling you with vain hopes; they speak visions of their own minds, not from the mouth of the Lord […]. I did not send the prophets, yet they ran. I did not speak to them, yet they prophesied"; they "lead my people astray by their lies and their recklessness, when I did not send them or charge them; so that they do not profit this people at all".

In the life of the Church the Fathers see these false prophets, as of whom Jesus speaks, in heretics, who apparently are pious and reformist but who in fact do not have Christ's sentiments (cf. St Jerome, *Comm. on Matthew*, 7). St John Chrysostom applies this teaching to anyone who appears to be virtuous but in fact is not, and thereby misleads others.

How are false prophets and genuine prophets to be distinguished? By the fruit they produce. Human nobility and divine inspiration combine to give the things of God a savour of their own. A person who truly speaks the things of God sows faith, hope, charity, peace and understanding; whereas a false prophet in the Church of God, in his preaching and behaviour, sows division, hatred, resentment, pride and sensuality (cf. Gal 5:16–25). However, the main characteristic of a false prophet is that he separates the people of

Rom 2:13
Jas 1:22, 25; 2:14
1 Cor 12:3

Lk 13:25–27
1 Cor 13:1f
Jer 14:14; 27:15

2 Tim 2:19
Ps 6:8

Doing the will of God

[21]"Not every one who says to me, 'Lord, Lord,' shall enter the kingdom of heaven, but he who does the will of my Father who is in heaven. [22]On that day many will say to me, 'Lord, Lord, did we not prophesy in your name, and cast out demons in your name, and do many mighty works in your name?' [23]And then will I declare to them, 'I never knew you; depart from me, you evildoers.'

Building on rock

[24]"Every one then who hears these words of mine and does them will be like a wise man who built his house upon the rock; [25]and the rain fell, and the floods came, and the winds blew and beat

God from the Magisterium of the Church, through which Christ's teaching is declared to the world. Our Lord also indicates that these deceivers are destined to eternal perdition.

7:21–23. To be genuine, prayer must be accompanied by a persevering effort to do God's will. Similarly, in order to do his will it is not enough to speak about the things of God: there must be consistency between what one preaches—what one says—and what one does: "The kingdom of God does not consist in talk but in power" (1 Cor 4:20); "Be doers of the word, and not hearers only, deceiving yourselves" (Jas 1:22).

Christians, "holding loyally to the Gospel, enriched by its resources, and joining forces with all who love and practise justice, have shouldered a weighty task on earth and they must render an account of it to him who will judge all men on the last day. Not every one who says 'Lord, Lord' will enter the Kingdom of heaven, but those who do the will of the Father, and who manfully put their hands to the work" (Vatican II, *Gaudium et spes*, 93).

To enter the Kingdom of heaven, to be holy, it is not enough, then, to speak eloquently about holiness. One has to practise what one preaches, to produce fruit that accords with one's words. Fray Luis de León puts it very graphically: "Notice that to be a good Christian it is not enough just to pray and fast and hear Mass; God must find you faithful, like another Job or Abraham, in times of tribulation" (*Guide for Sinners*, book 1, part 2, chap. 21).

Even if a person exercises an ecclesiastical ministry that does not assure his holiness; he needs to practise the virtues he preaches. Besides, we know from experience that any Christian (clerical, religious or lay) who does not strive to act in accordance with the demands of the faith he professes, begins to weaken in his faith and eventually parts company also with the teaching of the Church. Anyone who does not live in accordance with what he says, ends up saying things that are contrary to faith.

The authority with which Jesus speaks in these verses reveals him as sovereign Judge of the living and the dead. No Old Testament prophet ever spoke with this authority.

7:22. "That day": a technical formula in biblical language meaning the day of the Judgment of the Lord or the Last Judgment.

upon that house, but it did not fall, because it had been founded on the rock. ²⁶And every one who hears these words of mine and does not do them will be like a foolish man who built his house upon the sand; ²⁷and the rain fell, and the floods came, and the winds blew and beat against that house, and it fell; and great was the fall of it."

Ezek 33:10f

Jesus teaches with authority

²⁸And when Jesus finished these sayings, the crowds were astonished at his teaching, ²⁹for he taught them as one who had authority, and not as their scribes.

Mk 1:22
Lk 4:32
Jn 7:46

7:23. This passage refers to the Judgment where Jesus will be the Judge. The sacred text uses a verb which means the public proclamation of a truth. Since in this case Jesus Christ is the Judge who makes the declaration, it takes the form of a judicial sentence.

7:24–27. These verses constitute the positive side of the previous passage. A person who tries to put Christ's teaching into practice, even if he experiences personal difficulties or lives during times of upheaval in the life of the Church or is surrounded by error, will stay firm in the faith, like the wise man who builds his house on rock.

Also, if we are to stay strong in times of difficulty, we need, when things are calm and peaceful, to accept little contradictions with a good grace, to be very refined in our relationship with God and with others, and to perform the duties of our state in life in a spirit of loyalty and abnegation. By acting in this way we are laying down a good foundation, maintaining the edifice of our spiritual life and repairing any cracks that make their appearance.

7:28–29. Jesus' listeners could clearly see the radical difference between the style of teaching of the scribes and Pharisees, and the conviction and confidence with which Jesus spoke. There is nothing tentative about his words; they leave no room for doubt; he is clearly not giving a mere opinion. Jesus spoke with absolute command of the truth and perfect knowledge of the true meaning of the Law and the Prophets; indeed he often spoke on his own authority (cf. Mt 5:22, 28, 32, 38, 44), and with the very authority of God (cf. Mk 2:10; Mt 28:18). All this conferred a singular force and authority on his words, such as had never been known in Israel (cf. Lk 19:48; Jn 7:46).

Chapters 8 and 9 of St Matthew deal with a series of miracles worked by our Lord. The first Christians had vivid experience of the fact that the glorified Jesus was still present in his Church, confirming its teaching by signs, by miracles (Mk 16:20; Acts 14:3).

And so, St Matthew, after giving the nucleus of Jesus' public teaching in the Sermon on the Mount (chapters 5–7), goes on now to gather a number of miracles to support our Lord's words. Some commentators call this section— chaps. 8 and 9—"the works of the Messiah", parallelling what they called "the words of the Messiah" (the discourse on the mount). In chapters 5–7 we see Jesus as the supreme lawgiver and master who

4. MIRACLES OF THE MESSIAH

Curing of a leper

Mk 1:40–44
Lk 5:12–14

Mk 7:36
Lk 17:14
Lev 13:49;
14:2–32

8 ¹When he came down from the mountain, great crowds followed him; ²and behold, a leper came to him and knelt before him, saying, "Lord, if you will, you can make me clean." ³And he stretched out his hand and touched him, saying, "I will; be clean." And immediately his leprosy was cleansed.* ⁴And Jesus said to him, "See that you say nothing to any one; but go, show yourself to the priest, and offer the gift that Moses commanded, for a proof to the people."ʳ

The centurion's faith

Lk 7:1–10
Jn 4:47

⁵As he entered Capernaum, a centurion came forward to him, beseeching him ⁶and saying, "Lord, my servant is lying paralyzed at home, in terrible distress." ⁷And he said to him, "I will come and heal him." ⁸But the centurion answered him, "Lord, I am not

---

teaches with divine authority, a unique authority superior to that held by Moses and the prophets. Now, in chapters 8 and 9, he is shown as endowed with divine authority over disease, death, the elements and evil spirits. These miracles worked by Jesus Christ accredit the divine authority of his teaching.

8:1. The Gospel draws attention, for the third time, to the huge crowds that flocked to Jesus: literally, "many multitudes followed him". This shows the popularity he had achieved: he was so popular that the Sanhedrin (the great council of the Jewish nation) dared not arrest him for fear of what the people would do (cf. Mt 21:46; 26:5; Mk 14:2). Later on, they would accuse him before Pilate of stirring up the whole country from Judea to Galilee. And we will see Herod Antipas' eagerness to meet Jesus, of whom he has heard so much (cf. Mt 14:1). In contrast to this huge popularity, we find the elders opposing him and

deceiving the people into calling for Jesus' execution (cf. Mt 27:20–22).

8:2. The Fathers have taken the following meaning from this cure: leprosy is a vivid image of sin; it is ugly, disgusting, very contagious and difficult to cure. We are all sinners and we are all in need of God's forgiveness and grace (cf. Rom 3:23–24). The leper in the Gospel knelt down before Jesus, in all humility and trust, begging to be made clean. If we have recourse to our Saviour with that kind of faith, we can be sure that he will cure the wretchedness of our souls. We should often address Christ with this short prayer, borrowed from the leper: "Lord, if you will, you can make me clean."

8:4. According to the Law of Moses (Lev 14), if a leper is cured of his disease, he should present himself to a priest, who will register the cure and give him a certificate which he needs to be reintegrated into the civil and religious life of Israel.

r. Greek *to them*

worthy to have you come under my roof; but only say the word, and my servant will be healed. [9]For I am a man under authority, with soldiers under me; and I say to one, 'Go,' and he goes, and to another, 'Come,' and he comes, and to my slave, 'Do this,' and he does it." [10]When Jesus heard him, he marvelled, and said to those who followed him, "Truly, I say to you, not even[s] in Israel have I found such faith. [11]I tell you, many will come from east and west and sit at table with Abraham, Isaac, and Jacob in the kingdom of heaven, [12]while the sons of the kingdom will be thrown into the outer darkness; there men will weep and gnash their teeth." [13]And to the centurion Jesus said, "Go; be it done for you as you have believed." And the servant was healed at that very moment.

Lk 13:28f
Is 49:12; 59:19
Mal 1:11
Ps 107:3

Curing of Peter's mother-in-law

[14]And when Jesus entered Peter's house, he saw his mother-in-law lying sick with a fever; [15]he touched her hand, and the fever left her, and she rose and served him.

Mk 1:29–34
Lk 4:38–41
1 Cor 9:5

Other cures

[16]That evening they brought to him many who were possessed with demons; and he cast out the spirits with a word, and healed

---

Leviticus also prescribes the purifications and sacrifice he should offer. Jesus' instruction to the leper is, then, in keeping with the normal way of fulfilling what the laws laid down.

8:5–13. "Centurion": an officer of the Roman army in control of one hundred men. This man's faith is still an example to us. At the solemn moment when a Christian is about to receive Jesus in the Blessed Eucharist, the Church's liturgy places on his lips and in his heart these words of the centurion, to enliven his faith: "Lord, I am not worthy ...".

The Jews of this time regarded any Jew who entered a Gentile's house as contracting legal impurity (cf. Jn 19:28; Acts 11:2–3). This centurion has the deference not to place Jesus in an embarrassing position in the eyes of his fellow Israelites. He shows that he is convinced

that Jesus has power over disease and illness; he suggests that if Jesus just says the word, he will do what is needed without having actually to visit the house; he is reasoning, in a simple, logical way, on the basis of his own professional experience. Jesus avails of this meeting with a Gentile believer to make a solemn prophecy to the effect that his Gospel is addressed to the world at large; all men, of every nation and race, of every age and condition, are called to follow Christ.

8:14–15. After his body—or soul—is healed, everyone is called to "rise up" from his previous position, to serve Jesus Christ. No laments, no delays; instead one should make oneself immediately available to the Lord.

8:16–17. The expulsion of evil spirits is one of the main signs of the establish-

s. Other ancient authorities read *with no one*

Is 53:4
Jn 1:29, 36
all who were sick. [17]This was to fulfil what was spoken by the prophet Isaiah, "He took our infirmities and bore our diseases."

Following Christ is not easy

Mk 4:35
Lk 8:22
Lk 9:57–60
2 Cor 8:9

1 Kings 19:20
[18]Now when Jesus saw great crowds around him, he gave orders to go over to the other side. [19]And a scribe came up and said to him, "Teacher, I will follow you wherever you go." [20]And Jesus said to him, "Foxes have holes, and birds of the air have nests; but the Son of man has nowhere to lay his head." [21]Another of the disciples said to him, "Lord let me first go and bury my father." [22]But

---

ment of the Kingdom of God (cf. Mt 12:8). Similarly, the healing of diseases, which ultimately are the result of sin, is one of the signs of the "works of the Messiah" proclaimed by the prophets (cf. Is 29:18; 35:5–6).

8:18–22. From the very outset of his messianic preaching, Jesus rarely stays in the same place; he is always on the move. He "has nowhere to lay his head" (Mt 8:20). Anyone who desires to be with him has to "follow him". This phrase "following Jesus" has a very precise meaning: it means being his disciple (cf. Mt 19:28). Sometimes the crowds "follow him"; but Jesus' true disciples are those who "follow him" in a permanent way, that is, who keep on following him: being a "disciple of Jesus" and "following him" amount to the same thing. After our Lord's ascension, "following him" means being a Christian (cf. Acts 8:26). By the simple and sublime fact of Baptism, every Christian is called, by a divine vocation, to be a full disciple of our Lord, with all that that involves.

The evangelist here gives two specific cases of following Jesus. In the case of the scribe our Lord explains what faith requires of a person who realizes that he has been called; in the second case—that of the man who has already said "yes" to Jesus—he reminds him of what his com-

mitment entails. The soldier who does not leave his position on the battlefront to bury his father, but instead leaves that to those in the rearguard, is doing his duty. If service to one's country makes demands like that on a person, all the more reason for it to happen in the service of Jesus Christ and his Church.

Following Christ, then, means we should make ourselves totally available to him; whatever sacrifice he asks of us we should make: the call to follow Christ means staying up with him, not falling behind; we either follow him or lose him. In the sermon on the mount (Mt 5–7) Jesus explained what following him involves—a teaching that we find summarized in even the most basic catechism of Christian doctrine: a Christian is a man who believes in Jesus Christ—a faith he receives at Baptism—and is duty bound to serve him. Through prayer and friendship with the Lord every Christian should try to discover the demands which this service involves as far as he personally is concerned.

8:20. "The Son of man": this is one of the expressions used in the Old Testament to refer to the Messiah. It appeared first in Daniel 7:14 and was used in Jewish writings in the time of Jesus. Until our Lord began to preach, it had not been understood in all its depth. The title "the Son

Jesus said to him, "Follow me, and leave the dead to bury their own dead."

Jn 1:43; 5:25
Rom 16:13

The calming of the storm

²³And when he got into the boat, his disciples followed him. ²⁴And behold, there arose a great storm on the sea, so that the boat was being swamped by the waves; but he was asleep. ²⁵And they went and woke him, saying, "Save us, Lord; we are perishing." ²⁶And he said to them, "Why are you afraid, O men of little faith?" Then he rose and rebuked the winds and the sea; and there was a great calm. ²⁷And the men marvelled, saying, "What sort of man is this, that even winds and sea obey him?"

Mk 4:36–41
Lk 8:23–35
Ps 4:8

Ps 107:25ff

of man" did not fit in very well with Jewish hopes of an earthly Messiah; this was why it was Jesus' favourite way of indicating that he was the Messiah— thereby avoiding any tendency to encourage Jewish nationalism. In the prophecy of Daniel just mentioned this messianic title has a transcendental meaning; by using it Jesus was able discreetly to proclaim that he was the Messiah and yet avoid people interpreting his role in a political sense. After the Resurrection the apostles at last realized that "Son of man" meant nothing less than "Son of God".

8:22. "Leave the dead to bury their own dead": although this sounds very harsh, it is a style of speaking which Jesus did sometimes use. Here the "dead" clearly refers to those whose interest is limited to perishable things and who have no aspirations towards the things that last forever.

"If Jesus forbade him," St John Chrysostom comments, "it was not to have us neglect the honour due to our parents, but to make us realize that nothing is more important than the things of heaven and that we ought to cleave to these and not to put them off even for a little while, though our engagements be ever so indis-

pensable and pressing" (*Hom. on St Matthew*, 27).

8:23–27. This remarkable miracle left a deep impression on Jesus' disciples, as can be seen from the fact that the first three evangelists all report it. Christian Tradition has applied this miracle in various ways to the life of the Church and the experience of the individual soul. From earliest times Christian art and literature have seen the boat as representing the Church, which also has to make its way around hazards which threaten to capsize it. Indeed, very early on, Christians were persecuted in various ways by Jews of their time, and were misunderstood by the public opinion of a pagan society—which also began to persecute them. Jesus' sleeping through the storm has been applied to the fact that sometimes God seems not to come to the Church's rescue during persecution. Following the example of the apostles in the boat, Christians should seek Jesus' help, borrowing their words, "Save us, Lord; we are perishing". Then, when it seems we can bear it no longer, Jesus shows his power: "He rose and rebuked the winds and the sea; and there was a great calm"—but first rebuking us for being men of little faith. Quite often Gospel

The demoniacs of Gadara

Mk 5:1–17
Lk 8:26–37

Lk 4:41
2 Pet 2:4

²⁸And when he came to the other side, to the country of the Gadarenes,ᵗ two demoniacs met him, coming out of the tombs, so fierce that no one could pass that way. ²⁹And behold, they cried out, "What have you to do with us, O Son of God? Have you come here to torment us before the time?"* ³⁰Now a herd of many swine was feeding at some distance from them. ³¹And the demons begged him, "If you cast us out, send us away into the herd of swine." ³²And he said to them, "Go." So they came out and went into the swine; and behold, the whole herd rushed down the steep bank into the sea, and perished in the waters. ³³The herdsmen fled, and going into the city they told everything, and what had happened to the demoniacs. ³⁴And behold, all the city came out to

accounts are meant to serve as examples to us: they epitomize the future history of the Church and of the individual Christian soul.

8:28. Most Gospel codexes and the New Vulgate say "Gadarenes"; but the Vulgate and parallel texts in Mark and Luke have "Gerasenes". Both names are possible; the two main towns in the area were Gerasa and Gadara. The event reported here could have happened close to both towns (limits were not very well defined), though the swine running down into the lake or sea of Galilee makes Gadara somewhat more likely. "Gergesenes" was a suggestion put forward by Origen.

8:28–34. In this episode Jesus once more shows his power over the devil. That it occurred in Gentile territory (Gerasa and Gadara were in the Decapolis, east of Jordan) is borne out by the fact that Jews were forbidden to raise swine, which the Law of Moses declared to be unclean. This and other instances of expulsion of demons narrated in the Gospel are referred to in the Acts of the Apostles,

when St Peter addresses Cornelius and his household: "he went about doing good and healing all that were oppressed by the devil" (Acts 10:38). It was a sign that the Kingdom of God had begun (cf. Mt 12:28).

The attitude of local people towards this miracle reminds us that meeting God and living a Christian life require us to subordinate personal plans to God's designs. If we have a selfish or materialistic outlook we fail to appreciate the value of divine things and push God out of our lives, begging him to go away, as these people did.

9:1. "His own city": Capernaum (cf. Mt 4:13 and Mk 2:1).

9:2–6. The sick man and those who bring him to Jesus ask him to cure the man's physical illness; they believe in his supernatural powers. As in other instances of miracles, our Lord concerns himself more with the underlying cause of illness, that is, sin. With divine largesse he gives more than he is asked for, even though people do not appreciate this. St Thomas Aquinas says that Jesus Christ

t. Other ancient authorities read *Gergesenes*; some, *Gerasenes*

meet Jesus; and when they saw him, they begged him to leave their neighbourhood.

Curing of a paralyzed man

9 [1] And getting into a boat he crossed over and came to his own city. [2] And behold, they brought to him a paralytic, lying on his bed; and when Jesus saw their faith he said to the paralytic, "Take heart, my son; your sins are forgiven." [3] And behold, some of the scribes said to themselves, "This man is blaspheming." [4] But Jesus, knowing[u] their thoughts, said, "Why do you think evil in your hearts? [5] For which is easier, to say, 'Your sins are forgiven,' or to say, 'Rise and walk'? [6] But that you may know that the Son of man has authority on earth to forgive sins"—he then said to

Mk 2:1–12
Lk 5:16–26

Mk 2:7

Jn 2:25

---

acts like a good doctor: he cures the cause of the illness (cf. *Comm. on St Matthew*, 9, 1–6).

9:2. The parallel passage of St Mark adds a detail that helps us understand this scene better and explains why the text refers to "their faith": in Mark 2:2–5 we are told that there was such a crowd around Jesus that the people carrying the bed could not get near him. So they had the idea of going up onto the roof and making a hole and lowering the bed down in front of Jesus. This explains his "seeing their faith".

Our Lord was pleased by their boldness, a boldness which resulted from their lively faith which brooked no obstacles. This nice example of daring indicates how we should go about putting charity into practice—also how Jesus feels towards people who show real concern for others: he cures the paralytic who was so ingeniously helped by his friends and relatives; even the sick man himself showed daring by not being afraid of the risk involved.

St Thomas comments on this verse as follows: "This paralytic symbolizes the sinner lying in sin"; just as the paralytic cannot move, so the sinner cannot help himself. The people who bring the paralytic along represent those who, by giving him good advice, lead the sinner to God" (*Comm. on St Matthew*, 9, 2). In order to get close to Jesus the same kind of holy daring is needed, as the saints show us. Anyone who does not act like this will never make important decisions in his life as a Christian.

9:3–7. Here "to say" obviously means "to say and mean it", "to say producing the result which your words imply". Our Lord is arguing as follows: which is easier—to cure the paralytic's body or to forgive the sins of his soul? Undoubtedly, to cure his body; for the soul is superior to the body and therefore diseases of the soul are the more difficult to cure. However, a physical cure can be seen, whereas a cure of the soul cannot. Jesus proves the hidden cure by performing a visible one.

The Jews thought that any illness was due to personal sin (cf. Jn 9:1–3); so when they heard Jesus saying, "Your sins are forgiven", they reasoned in their

---

u. Other ancient authorities read *seeing*

the paralytic—"Rise, take up your bed and go home." [7]And he rose and went home. [8]When the crowds saw it, they were afraid, and they glorified God, who had given such authority to men.

The call of Matthew

Mk 2:13–17
Lk 5:27–32
[9]As Jesus passed on from there, he saw a man called Matthew sitting at the tax office; and he said to him, "Follow me." And he rose and followed him.

[10]And as he sat at table[v] in the house, behold, many tax collectors and sinners came and sat down with Jesus and his disciples.

---

minds as follows: only God can forgive sins (cf. Lk 5:21); this man says that he has power to forgive sins; therefore, he is claiming a power that belongs to God alone—which is blasphemy. Our Lord, however, forestalls them, using their own arguments: by curing the paralytic by just saying the word, he shows them that since he has the power to cure the effects of sin (which is what they believe disease to be), then he also has power to cure the cause of illness (sin); therefore, he has divine power.

Jesus Christ passed on to the apostles and their successors in the priestly ministry the power to forgive sins: "Receive the Holy Spirit. If you forgive sins of any, they are forgiven; if you retain the sins of any, they are retained" (Jn 20:22–23). "Truly, I say to you, whatever you bind on earth shall be bound in heaven, and whatever you loose on earth shall be loosed in heaven" (Mt 18:18). Priests exercise this power in the sacrament of Penance: in doing so they act not in their own name but in Christ's—*in persona Christi*, as instruments of the Lord.

Hence the respect, veneration and gratitude with which we should approach Confession: in the priest we should see Christ himself, God himself, and we should receive the words of absolution firmly believing that it is Christ who is uttering them through the priest. This is why the minister does not say: "Christ absolves you ...", but rather "I absolve you from your sins ...": he speaks in the first person, so fully is he identified with Jesus Christ himself (cf. St Pius V, *Catechism*, 2, 5, 10).

9:9. "Tax office": a public place for the payment of taxes. On "following Jesus", see the note on Mt 8:18–22.

The Matthew whom Jesus calls here is the apostle of the same name and the human author of the first Gospel. In Mark 2:14 and Luke 5:27 he is called Levi the son of Alphaeus or simply Levi.

In addition to Baptism, through which God calls all Christians (cf. the note on Mt 8:18–22), the Lord can also extend, to whomever he chooses, a further calling to engage in some specific mission in the Church. This second calling is a special grace (cf. Mt 4:19–21; Mk 1:17-20; Jn 1:39; etc.) additional to the earlier calling through Baptism. In other words, it is not man who takes the initiative; it is Jesus who calls, and man who responds to this call by his free personal decision: "You did not choose me, but I chose you" (Jn 15:16).

---

v. Greek *reclined*

[11]And when the Pharisees saw this, they said to his disciples, "Why does your teacher eat with tax collectors and sinners?" [12]But when he heard it, he said, "Those who are well have no need of a physician, but those who are sick. [13]Go and learn what this means, 'I desire mercy, and not sacrifice.' For I came not to call the righteous, but sinners."

Lk 15:2

Hos 6:6
1 Sam 15:22
Mt 18:11

A discussion on fasting

[14]Then the disciples of John came to him, saying, "Why do we and the Pharisees fast,[w] but your disciples do not fast?" [15]And

Mk 2:18–22
Lk 5:33–38;
18:12

Matthew's promptitude in "following" Jesus' call is to be noted. When God speaks, a soul may be tempted to reply, "Tomorrow; I'm not ready yet." In the last analysis this excuse, and other excuses, are nothing but a sign of selfishness and fear (different from that fear which can be an additional symptom of vocation: cf. Jon 1). "Tomorrow" runs the risk of being too late.

As in the case of the other apostles, St Matthew is called in the midst of the ordinary circumstances of his life: "What amazes you seems natural to me: that God has sought you out in the practice of your profession! That is how he sought the first, Peter and Andrew, James and John, beside their nets, and Matthew, sitting in the custom-house. And—wonder of wonders!—Paul, in his eagerness to destroy the seeds of Christianity" (St Josemaría Escrivá, *The Way*, 799).

9:10–11. The attitude of these Pharisees, who are so prone to judge others and classify them as just men or sinners, is at odds with the attitude and teaching of Jesus. Earlier on, he said, "Judge not, that you be not judged" (Mt 7:1), and elsewhere he added, "Let him who is without sin among you be the first to throw a stone at her" (Jn 8:7). The fact is that all of us are sinners; and our Lord has come

to redeem all of us. There is no basis, therefore, for Christians to be scandalized by the sins of others, since any one of us is capable of committing the vilest of sins unless God's grace were to come to our aid.

9:12. There is no reason why anyone should be depressed when he realizes he is full of failings: recognition that we are sinners is the only correct attitude for us to have in the presence of God. He has come to seek all men, but if a person considers himself to be righteous, by so doing he is closing the door to God; all of us in fact are sinners.

9:13. Here Jesus quotes Hosea 6:6, keeping the hyperbole of the Semitic style. A more faithful translation would be "I desire mercy *more than* sacrifice". It is not that our Lord does not want the sacrifices we offer him: he is stressing that every sacrifice should come from the heart, for charity should imbue everything a Christian does—especially his worship of God (see 1 Cor 13:1–13; Mt 5:23–24).

9:14–17. This passage is interesting, not so much because it tells us about the sort of fasting practised by the Jews of the time—particularly the Pharisees and

w. Other ancient authorities add *much* or *often*

Jn 3:29

Jesus said to them, "Can the wedding guests mourn as long as the bridegroom is with them? The days will come, when the bridegroom is taken away from them, and then they will fast. [16]And no one puts a piece of unshrunk cloth on an old garment, for the patch tears away from the garment, and a worse tear is made. [17]Neither is new wine put into old wineskins; if it is, the skins burst, and the wine is spilled, and the skins are destroyed; but new wine is put into fresh wineskins, and so both are preserved."

Jn 1:17

The raising of Jairus' daughter and the curing of the woman with a haemorrhage

Mk 5:22–43
Lk 8:41–56

[18]While he was thus speaking to them, behold, a ruler came in and knelt before him, saying, "My daughter has just died; but come and lay your hand on her, and she will live." [19]And Jesus rose and followed him, with his disciples.

[20]And behold, a woman who had suffered from a hemorrhage for twelve years came up behind him and touched the fringe of his

---

John the Baptist's disciples—but because of the reason Jesus gives for not requiring his disciples to fast in that way. His reply is both instructive and prophetic. Christianity is not a mere mending or adjusting of the old suit of Judaism. The redemption wrought by Jesus involves a total regeneration. Its spirit is too new and too vital to be suited to old forms of penance, which will no longer apply.

We know that in our Lord's time Jewish theology schools were in the grip of a highly complicated casuistry to do with fasting, purifications etc, which smothered the simplicity of genuine piety. Jesus' words point to that simplicity of heart with which his disciples might practise prayer, fasting and almsgiving (cf. Mt 6:1–18 and notes to same). From apostolic times onwards it is for the Church, using the authority given it by our Lord, to set out the different forms fasting should take in different periods and situations.

9:15. "The wedding guests": literally, "the sons of the house where the wedding is

being celebrated"—an expression meaning the bridegroom's closest friends. This is an example of how St Matthew uses typical Semitic turns of phrase, presenting Jesus' manner of speech.

This "house" to which Jesus refers has a deeper meaning; set beside the parable of the guests at the wedding (Mt 22:1ff), it symbolizes the Church as the house of God and the body of Christ: "Moses was faithful in all God's house as a servant, to testify to the things that were to be spoken later, but Christ was faithful over God's house as a son. And we are his house if we hold fast our confidence and pride in our hope" (Heb 3:5–6). The second part of the verse refers to the violent death Jesus would meet.

9:18–26. Here are two miracles which occur almost simultaneously. From parallel passages in Mark (5:21–43) and Luke (8:40–56) we know that the "ruler" (of the synagogue) referred to here was called Jairus. The Gospels report Jesus raising three people to life— this girl, the son of the widow of Nain, and Lazarus.

garment; [21]for she said to herself, "If I only touch his garment, I shall be made well." [22]Jesus turned, and seeing her he said, "Take heart, daughter; your faith has made you well." And instantly the woman was made well. [23]And when Jesus came to the ruler's house, and saw the flute players, and the crowd making a tumult, [24]he said, "Depart; for the girl is not dead but sleeping." And they laughed at him. [25]But when the crowd had been put outside, he went in and took her by the hand, and the girl arose. [26]And the report of this went through all that district.

Jn 11:11, 14, 25

Curing of two blind men. The dumb devil

[27]And as Jesus passed on from there, two blind men followed him, crying aloud, "Have mercy on us, Son of David." [28]When he entered the house, the blind men came to him; and Jesus said to them, "Do you believe that I am able to do this?" They said to him, "Yes, Lord." [29]Then he touched their eyes, saying, "According to your faith be it done to you." [30]And their eyes were opened.

In each case the identity of the person is clearly given.

This account shows us, once again, the role faith plays in Jesus' saving actions. In the case of the woman with the hemorrhage we should note that Jesus is won over by her sincerity and faith: she does not let obstacles get in her way. Similarly, Jairus does not care what people will say; a prominent person in his city, he humbles himself before Jesus for all to see.

9:18. "Knelt before him": the eastern way of showing respect to God or to important people. In the liturgy, especially in the presence of the Blessed Eucharist, reverences are a legitimate and appropriate external sign of internal faith and adoration.

9:23. "The flute players": engaged to provide music at wakes and funerals.

9:24. "Depart, for the girl is not dead, but sleeping": Jesus says the same thing about Lazarus: "Our friend Lazarus has fallen asleep, but I go to awaken him" (Jn 11:11).

Although Jesus speaks of sleep, there is no question of the girl—or Lazarus, later—not being dead. For our Lord there is only one true death—that of eternal punishment (cf. Mt 10:28).

9:27–34. The evangelist shows people's different reactions to miracles. Everyone admits that God is at work in these events—everyone, that is, except the Pharisees who attribute them to the power of the devil. A pharisaical attitude so hardens a person's heart that he becomes closed to any possibility of salvation. The fact that the blind men recognize Jesus as the Messiah (they call him "Son of David": v. 27) may have exasperated the Pharisees. Despite Jesus' sublime teaching, despite his miracles, they remain entrenched in their opposition.

In the light of this episode it is easy enough to see that the paradox is true: there are blind people who in fact see God and seers who see no trace of him.

9:30. Why did our Lord not want them to publicize the miracle? Because his

And Jesus sternly charged them, "See that no one knows it." [31]But they went away and spread his fame through all that district.

[32]As they were going away, behold, a dumb demoniac was brought to him. [33]And when the demon had been cast out, the dumb man spoke; and the crowds marvelled, saying, "Never was anything like this seen in Israel." [34]But the Pharisees said, "He casts out demons by the prince of demons."

The need for good pastors

[35]And Jesus went about all the cities and villages, teaching in their synagogues and preaching the gospel of the kingdom, and healing every disease and every infirmity. [36]When he saw the crowds, he had compassion for them, because they were harassed and help-

Mk 6:34

---

plan was to gradually manifest himself as the Messiah, the Son of God. He did not want to anticipate events which would occur in their own good time; nor did he want the crowd to start hailing him as Messiah King, because their notion of messiah was a nationalistic, not a spiritual one. However, the crowd did in fact proclaim him when he worked the miracles of the loaves and the fish (Jn 6:14–15): "When the people saw the sign which he had done, they said, 'This is indeed the prophet who is to come into the world!' Perceiving then that they were about to come and take him by force to make him king, Jesus withdrew again to the hills by himself."

9:31. St Jerome (cf. *Comm. on Matthew*, 9, 31) says that the blind men spread the news of their cure, not out of disobedience to Jesus, but because it was the only way they could find to express their gratitude.

9:35. The Second Vatican Council uses this passage when teaching about the message of Christian charity which the Church should always be spreading: "Christian charity is extended to all without distinction of race, social condition or

religion, and seeks neither gain nor gratitude. Just as God loves us with a gratuitous love, so too the faithful, in their charity, should be concerned for mankind, loving it with that same love with which God sought man. As Christ went about all the towns and villages healing every sickness and infirmity, as a sign that the Kingdom of God had come, so the Church, through its children, joins itself with men of every condition, but especially with the poor and afflicted, and willingly spends herself for them" (*Ad gentes*, 12).

9:36. "He had compassion for them": the Greek verb is very expressive; it means "he was deeply moved". Jesus was moved when he saw the people, because their pastors, instead of guiding them and tending them, led them astray, behaving more like wolves than genuine shepherds of their flock. Jesus sees the prophecy of Ezekiel 34 as now being fulfilled; in that passage God, through the prophet, upbraids the false shepherds of Israel and promises to send them the Messiah to be their new leader.

"If we were consistent with our faith when we looked around us and contemplated the world and its history, we

less, like sheep without a shepherd. [37]Then he said to his disciples, "The harvest is plentiful, but the labourers are few; [38]pray therefore the Lord of the harvest to send out labourers into his harvest."

Num 27:17
Ezek 34:5
Lk 10:2

5. FROM THE OLD TO THE NEW PEOPLE OF GOD

The calling of the twelve apostles

10 [1]And he called to him his twelve disciples and gave them authority over unclean spirits, to cast them out, and to heal every disease and every infirmity. [2]The names of the twelve apostles are these: first, Simon, who is called Peter, and Andrew his

Mk 6:7–13
Lk 9:1–5

Mk 3:14–19
Lk 6:13–16
Jn 1:40–49

---

would be unable to avoid feeling in our own hearts the same sentiments that filled the heart of our Lord" (St J. Escrivá, *Christ Is Passing By*, 133). Reflection on the spiritual needs of the world should lead us to be tirelessly apostolic.

9:37–38. After contemplating the crowds neglected by their shepherds, Jesus uses the image of the harvest to show us that that same crowd is ready to receive the effects of Redemption: "I tell you, lift up your eyes, and see now the fields are already white for harvest" (Jn 4:35). The field of the Jewish people cultivated by the prophets—most recently by John the Baptist—is full of ripe wheat. In farmwork, the harvest is lost if the farmer does not reap at the right time; down the centuries the Church feels a similar need to be out harvesting because there is a big harvest ready to be won.

However, as in the time of Jesus, there is a shortage of labourers. Our Lord tells us how to deal with this: we should pray God, the Lord of the harvest, to send the necessary labourers. If a Christian prays hard, it is difficult to imagine his not feeling urged to play his part in this apostolate. In obeying this commandment to pray for labourers, we should pray especially for there to be no lack of good shepherds, who will be able to equip others with the necessary means of sanctification needed to back up the apostolate.

In this connexion Paul VI reminds us: "the responsibility for spreading the Gospel that saves belongs to everyone— to all those who have received it! The missionary duty concerns the whole body of the Church; in different ways and to different degrees, it is true, but we must all of us be united in carrying out this duty. Now let the conscience of every believer ask himself: Have I carried out my missionary duty? Prayer for the Missions is the first way of fulfilling this duty" (Angelus Address, 23 October 1977).

10:1–4. Jesus calls his twelve apostles after recommending to them to pray to the Lord to send labourers into his harvest (cf. Mt 9:38). Christians' apostolic action should always, then, be preceded and accompanied by a life of constant prayer: apostolate is a divine affair, not a merely human one. Our Lord starts his Church by calling twelve men to be, as it were, twelve patriarchs of the new people of God, the Church. This new people is

brother; James the son of Zebedee, and John his brother; ³Philip
and Bartholomew; Thomas and Matthew the tax collector; James
the son of Alphaeus, and Thaddaeus;ˣ ⁴Simon the Cananaean, and
Judas Iscariot, who betrayed him.

The apostles' first mission

Acts 13:46
Jer 50:6
Lk 10:9

⁵These twelve Jesus sent out, charging them, "Go nowhere among
the Gentiles, and enter no town of the Samaritans,* ⁶but go rather

established not by physical but by spiritual generation. The names of those apostles are specifically mentioned here. They
were not scholarly, powerful or important
people: they were average, ordinary
people who responded faithfully to the
grace of their calling—all of them, that
is, except Judas Iscariot. Even before his
death and resurrection Jesus confers on
them the power to cast out unclean spirits
and cure illnesses—as an earnest sign of
and as training for the saving mission
which he will entrust to them.

The Church reveres these first Christians in a very special way and is proud to
carry on their supernatural mission, and
to be faithful to the witness they bore to
the teaching of Christ. The true Church is
absent unless there is uninterrupted apostolic succession and identification with
the spirit which the apostles made their
own.

"Apostle": this word means "sent";
Jesus sent them out to preach his
Kingdom and pass on his teaching. The
Second Vatican Council, in line with
Vatican I, "confesses" and "declares" that
the Church has a hierarchical structure:
"The Lord Jesus, having prayed at length
to the Father, called to himself those
whom he willed and appointed twelve to
be with him, whom he might send to
preach the Kingdom of God (cf. Mk
3:13–19; Mt 10:1–10). These apostles
(cf. Lk 6:13) he constituted in the form of

a college or permanent assembly, at the
head of which he placed Peter, chosen
from among them (cf. Jn 21:15–17). He
sent them first of all to the children of
Israel and then to all peoples (cf. Rom
1:16), so that, sharing in his power, they
might make all peoples his disciples
and sanctify and govern them (cf. Mt
28:16–20; Mk 16:15; Lk 24:45–48; Jn
20:21–23) and thus spread the Church
and, administering it under the guidance
of the Lord, shepherd it all days until the
end of the world (cf. Mt 28:28)" (*Lumen
gentium*, 19).

10:1. In this chapter St Matthew describes
how Jesus, with a view to the spreading
of the Kingdom of God which he inaugu-
rates, decides to establish a Church,
which he does by giving special powers
and training to these twelve men who are
its seed.

10:5–15. After revealing his intention to
found the Church by choosing the
Twelve (vv. 1–4), in the present passage
he shows that he intends to start training
these first apostles. In other words, from
early on in his public ministry he began
to lay the foundations of his Church.
Everyone needs doctrinal and apostolic
training to follow his Christian calling.
The Church has a duty to teach, and the
faithful have a parallel duty to make that
teaching their own. Therefore, every

x. Other ancient authorities read *Lebbaeus* or *Lebbaeus called Thaddaeus*

to the lost sheep of the house of Israel. [7]And preach as you go, saying, 'The kingdom of heaven is at hand.' [8]Heal the sick, raise the dead, cleanse lepers, cast out demons. You received without pay, give without pay. [9]Take no gold, nor silver, nor copper in your belts, [10]no bag for your journey, nor two tunics, nor sandals,

Acts 20:33

Lk 10:4
1 Tim 5:18

Christian should avail himself or herself of the facilities for training which the Church offers—which will vary according to a person's circumstances.

10:5–6. In his plan of salvation God gave certain promises (to Abraham and the patriarchs), a Covenant and a Law (the Law of Moses), and sent the prophets. The Messiah would be born into this chosen people, which explains why the Messiah and the Kingdom of God were to be preached to the house of Israel before being preached to Gentiles. Therefore, in their early apprenticeship, Jesus restricts the apostles' area of activity to the Jews, without this taking from the worldwide scope of the Church's mission. As we will see, much later on he charges them to "go and make disciples of all nations" (Mt 28:19); "Go into all the world and preach the Gospel to the whole creation" (Mk 16:16). The apostles also, in the early days of the spread of the Church, usually sought out the Jewish community in any new city they entered, and preached first to them (cf. Acts 13:46).

10:7–8. Previously, the prophets, when speaking of the messianic times, had used imagery suited to the people's spiritual immaturity. Now, Jesus, in sending his apostles to proclaim that the promised Kingdom of God is imminent, lays stress on its spiritual dimension. The powers mentioned in verse 8 are the very sign of the Kingdom of God or the reign of the Messiah proclaimed by the prophets. At first (chaps. 8 and 9) it is Jesus who exer-

cises these messianic powers; now he gives them to his disciples as proof that his mission is divine (Is 35:5–6; 40:9; 52:7; 61:1).

10:9. "Belts": twin belts, stitched together leaving space where coins and other small, heavy objects could be secreted and carried.

10:9–10. Jesus urges his disciples to set out on their mission without delay. They should not be worried about material or human equipment: God will make up any shortfall. This holy audacity in setting about God's work is to be found throughout the history of the Church: if Christians had bided their time, waiting until they had the necessary material resources, many, many souls would never have received the light of Christ. Once a Christian is clear in his mind about what God wants him to do, he should not stay at home checking to see if he has the wherewithal to do it. "In your apostolic undertakings you are right—it's your duty—to consider what means the world can offer you (2 + 2 = 4), but don't forget—ever!—that, fortunately, your calculations must include another term: God + 2 + 2 ..." (St Josemaría Escrivá, *The Way*, 471).

However, that being said, we should not try to force God's hand, to have him do something exceptional, when in fact we can meet needs by our own efforts and work. This means that Christians should generously support those who, because they are totally dedicated to the spiritual welfare of their brethren, have

Num 18:31

Lk 10:5f

Lk 10:10–12
Acts 13:51;
18:6

Lk 20:47

nor a staff; for the labourer deserves his food. [11]And whatever town or village you enter, find out who is worthy in it, and stay with him until you depart. [12]As you enter the house, salute it. [13]And if the house is worthy, let your peace come upon it; but if it is not worthy, let your peace return to you. [14]And if any one will not receive you or listen to your words, shake off the dust from your feet as you leave that house or town. [15]Truly, I say to you, it shall be more tolerable on the day of judgment for the land of Sodom and Gomorrah than for that town.

Lk 10:3
Jn 10:12
Acts 20:29
Rom 16:19
Eph 5:15

Mk 13:9–13
Lk 21:12–17
Mt 24:9; 24:14
Acts 25:23; 27:24

Jesus' instructions to the apostles

[16]"Behold, I send you out as sheep in the midst of wolves; so be wise as serpents and innocent as doves. [17]Beware of men; for they will deliver you up to councils, and flog you in their synagogues, [18]and you will be dragged before governors and kings for my

---

no time left over to provide for themselves: in this connexion see Jesus' promise in Mt 10:40–42.

10:11–15. "Peace" was, and still is, the normal Jewish form of greeting. On the apostles' lips it is meant to have a deeper meaning—to be a sign of God's blessing which Jesus' disciples, who are his envoys, pour out on those who receive them. The commandment our Lord gives here affects not only this specific mission; it is a kind of prophecy which applies to all times. His messenger does not become discouraged if his word is not well received. He knows that God's blessing is never ineffective (cf. Is 55:11), and that every generous effort a Christian makes will always produce fruit. The word spoken in apostolate always brings with it the grace of conversion: "Many of those who heard the word believed; and the number of the men came to about five thousand" (Acts 4:4; cf. 10:44; Rom 10:17).

Man should listen to this word of the Gospel and believe in it (Acts 13:48; 15:7). If he accepts it and stays faithful to it his soul is consoled, he obtains peace

(Acts 8:39) and salvation (Acts 11:4–18). But if he rejects it, he is not free from blame and God will judge him for shutting out the grace he was offered.

10:16–23. The instructions and warnings Jesus gives here apply right through the history of the Church. It is difficult for the world to understand the way of God. Sometimes there will be persecutions, sometimes indifference to the Gospel or failure to understand it. Genuine commitment to Jesus always involves effort— which is not surprising, because Jesus himself was a sign of contradiction; indeed, if that were not the experience of a Christian, he would have to ask himself whether he was not in fact a worldly person. There are certain worldly things a Christian cannot compromise about, no matter how much they are in fashion. Therefore, Christian life inevitably involves nonconformity with anything that goes against faith and morals (cf. Rom 12:2). It is not surprising that a Christian's life often involves choosing between heroism and treachery. Difficulties of this sort should not make us afraid: we are not alone, we can count on

sake, to bear testimony before them and the Gentiles. [19]When they deliver you up, do not be anxious how you are to speak or what you are to say; for what you are to say will be given to you in that hour; [20]for it is not you who speak, but the Spirit of your Father speaking through you. [21]Brother will deliver up brother to death, and the father his child, and children will rise against parents and have them put to death; [22]and you will be hated by all for my name's sake. But he who endures to the end will be saved. [23]When they persecute you in one town, flee to the next; for truly, I say to you, you will not have gone through all the towns of Israel, before the Son of man comes.

[24]"A disciple is not above his teacher, nor a servant[y] above his master; [25]it is enough for the disciple to be like his teacher, and the servant[y] like his master. If they have called the master of the house Beelzebul, how much more will they malign those of his household.

Lk 12:11f

Jn 14:26
1 Cor 2:4

Mic 7:6

Jn 15:21

Lk 6:40
Jn 13:16;
15:20
Mt 12:24

---

the powerful help of our Father God to give us strength and daring.

10:20. Here Jesus teaches the completely supernatural character of the witness he asks his disciples to bear. The documented accounts of a host of Christian martyrs prove that he has kept this promise: they bear eloquent witness to the serenity and wisdom of often uneducated people, some of them scarcely more than children. The teaching contained in this verse provides the basis for the fortitude and confidence a Christian should have whenever he has to profess his faith in difficult situations. He will not be alone, for the Holy Spirit will give him words of divine wisdom.

10:23. In interpreting this text, the first thing is to reject the view of rationalists who argue that Jesus was convinced that soon he would come in glory and the world would come to an end. That interpretation is clearly at odds with many passages of the Gospel and the New Testament. Clearly, Jesus refers to himself when he speaks of the "Son of man", whose glory will be manifested in this way. The most cogent interpretation is that Jesus is referring here, primarily, to the historical event of the first Jewish war against Rome, which ended with the destruction of Jerusalem and of the temple in the year 70, and which led to the scattering of the Jewish people. But this event, which would occur a few years after Jesus' death, is an image or a prophetic symbol of the end of the world (cf. the note on Mt 24:1). The coming of Christ in glory will happen at a time which God has not revealed. Uncertainty about the end of the world helps Christians and the Church to be ever-vigilant.

10:24–25. Jesus uses these two proverbs to hint at the future that awaits his disciples: their greatest glory will consist in imitating the Master, being identified with him, even if this means being despised and persecuted as he was before them: his example is what guides a Christian; as he himself said, "I am the way, and the truth, and the life" (Jn 14:6).

y. Or *slave*

Lk 12:2–9
Mk 4:22
Lk 8:17

Jas 4:12

[26]"So have no fear of them; for nothing is covered that will not be revealed, or hidden that will not be known. [27]What I tell you in the dark, utter in the light; and what you hear whispered, proclaim upon the housetops. [28] And do not fear those who kill the body but cannot kill the soul; rather fear him who can destroy both soul and body in hell.[z] [29]Are not two sparrows sold for a penny? And not one of them will fall to the ground without your Father's will. [30]But even the hairs of your head are all numbered. [31]Fear not, therefore; you are of more value than many sparrows. [32]So every one who acknowledges me before men, I also will acknowledge

---

Beelzebul (cf. Lk 11:15) was the name of the idol of the ancient Philistine city of Ekron. The Jews later used the word to describe the devil or the prince of devils (cf. Mt 12:24), and their hatred of Jesus led them to the extreme of applying it to him.

To equip them for the persecution and misunderstanding which Christians will suffer (Jn 15:18), Jesus encourages them by promising to stay close to them. Towards the end of his life he will call them his friends (Jn 15:15) and little children (Jn 13:33).

10:26–27. Jesus tells his disciples not to be afraid of calumny and detraction. A day will come when everyone will come to know the whole truth about everyone else, their real intentions, the true dispositions of their souls. In the meantime, those who belong to God may be misrepresented by those who resort to lies, out of malice or passion. These are the hidden things which will be made known.

Christ also tells the apostles to speak out clearly. Jesus' divine teaching method led him to speak to the crowds in parables so that they came to discover his true personality by easy stages. After the coming of the Holy Spirit (cf. Acts 1:8), the apostles would have to preach from the rooftops about what Jesus had taught them.

We too have to make Christ's doctrine known in its entirety, without any ambiguity, without being influenced by false prudence or fear of the consequences.

10:28. Using this and other Gospel texts (Mt 5:22, 29; 18:9; Mk 9:43, 45, 47; Lk 12:5), the Church teaches that hell exists; there those who die in mortal sin suffer eternal punishment (cf. St Pius V, *Catechism*, 1, 6, 3), in a manner not known to us in this life (cf. St Teresa of Avila, *Life*, chap. 32). See the notes on Lk 16:19–31.

Therefore, our Lord warns his disciples against false fear. We should not fear those who can only kill the body. Only God can cast body and soul into hell. Therefore God is the only one we should fear and respect; he is our Prince and Supreme Judge—not men. The martyrs have obeyed this precept of the Lord in the fullest way, well aware that eternal life is worth much more than earthly life.

10:29–31. An *as* (translated here as "penny") was a small coin of very little value. Christ uses it to illustrate how much God loves his creatures. As St Jerome says (*Comm. on Matthew*, 10:29–31): "If little birds, which are of such

z. Greek *Gehenna*

before my Father who is in heaven; ³³but whoever denies me before men, I also will deny before my Father who is in heaven.

³⁴"Do not think that I have come to bring peace on earth; I have not come to bring peace, but a sword. ³⁵For I have come to set a man against his father, and a daughter against her mother, and a daughter-in-law against her mother-in-law; ³⁶and a man's foes will be those of his own household. ³⁷He who loves father or mother more than me is not worthy of me; and he who loves son or daughter

Lk 9:26
Lk 12:51–53
Mic 7:6
Deut 33:9
Lk 14:26f

---

little value, still come under the providence and care of God, how is it that you, who, given the nature of your soul, are immortal, can fear that you are not looked after carefully by him whom you respect as your Father?" Jesus again teaches us about the fatherly providence of God, which he spoke about at length in the Sermon on the Mount (cf. Mt 6:19–34).

10:32–33. Here Jesus tells us that public confession of our faith in him—whatever the consequences—is an indispensable condition for eternal salvation. After the Judgment, Christ will welcome those who have given testimony of their faith and condemn those whom fear caused to be ashamed of him (cf. Mt 7:23; 25:41; Rev 21:8). The Church honours as "confessors" those saints who have not undergone physical martyrdom but whose lives bore witness to the Catholic faith. Although every Christian should be ready to die for his faith, most Christians are called to be confessors of the faith.

10:34–37. Our Lord has not come to bring a false and earthly peace—the sort of tranquillity the self-seeking person yearns for; he wants us to struggle against our own passions and against sin and its effects. The sword he equips us with for this struggle is, in the words of Scripture, "the sword of the Spirit which is the word of God" (Eph 6:17), "lively and active, sharper than any two-edged

sword, piercing to the division of soul and spirit, of joints and marrow, and discerning the thoughts and intentions of the heart" (Heb 4:12).

The word of God in fact leads to these divisions mentioned here. It can lead, even within families, to those who embrace the faith being regarded as enemies by relatives who resist the word of truth. This is why our Lord goes on (v. 37) to say that nothing should come between him and his disciple—not even father, mother, son or daughter: any and every obstacle (cf. Mt 5:29–30) must be avoided.

Obviously these words of Jesus do not set up any opposition between the first and fourth commandments (love for God above all things and love for one's parents): he is simply indicating the order of priorities. We should love God with all our strength (cf. Mt 22:37), and make a serious effort to be saints; and we should also love and respect—in theory and in practice—the parents God has given us; they have generously cooperated with the creative power of God in bringing us into the world and there is so much that we owe them. But love for our parents should not come before love of God; usually there is no reason why these two loves should clash, but if that should ever happen, we should be quite clear in mind and in heart about what Jesus says here. He has in fact given us an example to follow on this point: "How is it that you sought me? Did you not know that I must

Lk 17:33
Jn 12:25

Lk 10:16
Jn 12:44;
13:20

Mk 9:41

more than me is not worthy of me; [38]and he who does not take his cross and follow me is not worthy of me. [39]He who finds his life will lose it, and he who loses his life for my sake will find it.

[40]"He who receives you receives me, and he who receives me receives him who sent me. [41]He who receives a prophet because he is a prophet shall receive a prophet's reward, and he who receives a righteous man because he is a righteous man shall receive a righteous man's reward. [42]And whoever gives to one of these little ones even a cup of cold water because he is a disciple, truly, I say to you, he shall not lose his reward."

Messengers from John the Baptist

11 [1]And when Jesus had finished instructing his twelve disciples, he went on from there to teach and preach in their cities.

---

be in my Father's house?" (Lk 2:49)—his reply when, as a youth, Mary and Joseph found him in the temple of Jerusalem after a long search. This event in our Lord's life is a guideline for every Christian—parent or child. Children should learn from it that their affection for their parents should never come before their love for God, particularly when our Creator asks us to follow him in a way that implies special self-giving on our part; parents should take the lesson that their children belong to God in the first place, and therefore he has a right to do with them what he wishes, even if this involves sacrifice, even heroic sacrifice. This teaching of our Lord asks us to be generous and to let God have his way. In fact, however, God never lets himself be outdone in generosity. Jesus has promised a hundredfold gain, even in this life, and later on eternal life (cf. Mt 19:29), to those who readily respond to his holy will.

10:38–39. The teaching contained in the preceding verses is summed up in these two succinct sentences. Following Christ, doing what he asks, means risking this present life to gain eternal life.

"People who are constantly concerned with themselves, who act above all for their own satisfaction, endanger their eternal salvation and cannot avoid being unhappy even in this life. Only if a person forgets himself and gives himself to God and to others, in marriage as well as in any other aspect of life, can he be happy on this earth, with a happiness that is a preparation for, and a foretaste of, the joy of heaven" (St Josemaría Escrivá; *Christ Is Passing By*, 24). Clearly, Christian life is based on self-denial: there is no Christianity without the cross.

10:40. To encourage the apostles and to persuade others to receive them, our Lord affirms that there is an intimate solidarity, or even a kind of identity, between himself and his disciples. God in Christ, Christ in the apostles: this is the bridge between heaven and earth (cf. 1 Cor 3:21–23).

10:41–42. A prophet's mission is not essentially one of announcing future events; his main role is that of communicating the word of God (cf. Jer 11:2; Is 1:2). The righteous man, the just man, is

90

²Now when John heard in prison about the deeds of the Christ, he sent word by his disciples ³and said to him, "Are you he who is to come, or shall we look for another?"* ⁴And Jesus answered them, "Go and tell John what you hear and see: ⁵the blind receive their sight and the lame walk, lepers are cleansed and the deaf hear, and the dead are raised up, and the poor have good news preached to them. ⁶And blessed is he who takes no offence at me."

⁷As they went away, Jesus began to speak to the crowds concerning John: "What did you go out into the wilderness to behold? A reed shaken by the wind? ⁸Why then did you go out? To see a manª clothed in soft raiment? Behold, those who wear soft raiment are in kings' houses. ⁹Why then did you go out? To see a prophet?ᵇ Yes, I tell you, and more than a prophet. ¹⁰This is he of whom it is written,

'Behold, I send my messenger before thy face,
who shall prepare thy way before thee.'

Lk 7:18–35
Mt 14:3

Mal 3:1
Dan 9:26

Is 35:5f; 61:1
Lk 4:18

Lk 1:76

Mal 3:1
Mk 1:2
Jn 3:28

---

he who obeys the Law of God and follows his paths (cf. Gen 6:9; Is 3:10). Here Jesus tells us that everyone who humbly listens to and welcomes prophets and righteous men, recognizing God in them, will receive the reward of a prophet and a righteous man. The very fact of generously receiving God's friends will gain one the reward that they obtain. Similarly, if we should see God in the least of his disciples (v. 42), even if they do not seem very important, they are important, because they are envoys of God and of his Son. That is why he who gives them a glass of cold water—an alms, or any small service—will receive a reward, for he has shown generosity to our Lord himself (cf. Mt 25:40).

11:1. In chapters 11 and 12 the Gospel records the obduracy of the Jewish leaders towards Jesus, despite hearing his teaching (chaps. 5–7) and seeing the miracles which bear witness to the divine nature of his person and his doctrine (chaps. 8–9).

11:2. John knew that Jesus was the Messiah (cf. Mt 3:13–17). He sent his disciples to him so that they could shed their mistaken notions about the kind of Messiah to expect, and come to recognize Jesus.

11:3–6. Jesus replies to the Baptist's disciples by pointing to the fact that they are witnessing the signs that the ancient prophecies said would mark the advent of the Messiah and his Kingdom (cf. Is 35:5, 61:1; etc.). He says, in effect, that he is the prophet who "was to come". The miracles reported in the Gospel (chaps. 8–9) and the teaching given to the people (chaps. 5–7) prove that Jesus of Nazareth is the expected Messiah.

11:6. Jesus here corrects the mistaken idea which many Jews had of the Messiah, casting him in the role of a powerful earthly ruler—a far cry from the humble attitude of Jesus. It is not surprising that he was a stumbling block to Jews (cf. Is 8:14–15; 1 Cor 1:23).

---

a. Or *What then did you go out to see? A man ...*   **b.** Other ancient authorities read *What then did you go out to see? A prophet?*

Lk 16:16;
13:24
Jn 6:15

Mal 3:23
Mt 17:10–13

[11]Truly, I say to you, among those born of women there has risen no one greater than John the Baptist; yet he who is least in the kingdom of heaven is greater than he. [12]From the days of John the Baptist until now the kingdom of heaven has suffered violence,[c] and men of violence take it by force. [13]For all the prophets and the law prophesied until John; [14]and if you are willing to accept it, he is Elijah who is to come. [15]He who has ears to hear,[d] let him hear.

Jesus reproaches his contemporaries

Prov 29:9

[16]"But to what shall I compare this generation? It is like children sitting in the market places and calling to their playmates,
[17] 'We piped to you, and you did not dance;
we wailed, and you did not mourn.'

11:11. With John the Old Testament is brought to a close and we are on the threshold of the New. The Precursor had the honour of ushering Christ in, making him known to men. God had assigned him the exalted mission of preparing his contemporaries to hear the Gospel. The Baptist's faithfulness is recognized and proclaimed by Jesus. The praise he receives is a reward for his humility: John, realizing what his role was, had said, "He must increase, but I must decrease" (Jn 3:30).

St John the Baptist was the greatest in the sense that he had received a mission unique and incomparable in the context of the Old Testament. However, in the Kingdom of heaven (the New Testament) inaugurated by Christ, the divine gift of grace makes the least of those who faithfully receive it greater than the greatest in the earlier dispensation. Once the work of our redemption is accomplished, God's grace will also be extended to the just of the Old Alliance. Thus, the greatness of John the Baptist, the Precursor and the last of the prophets, will be enhanced by the dignity of being made a son of God.

11:12. "The Kingdom of heaven has suffered violence": once John the Baptist announces that the Christ is already come, the powers of hell redouble their desperate assault, which continues right through the lifetime of the Church (cf. Eph 6:12). The situation described here seems to be this: the leaders of the Jewish people, and their blind followers, were waiting for the Kingdom of God the way people wait for a rightful legacy to come their way; but while they rest on the laurels of the rights and rewards they think their race entitles them to, others, the men of violence (literally, attackers) are taking it, as it were, by force, by fighting the enemies of the soul—the world, the flesh and the devil.

"This violence is not directed against others. It is a violence used to fight your own weaknesses and miseries, a fortitude, which prevents you from camouflaging your own infidelities, a boldness to own up to the faith even when the environment is hostile" (St Josemaría Escrivá, *Christ Is Passing By*, 82).

This is the attitude of those who fight their passions and do themselves violence, thereby attaining the Kingdom of

c. Or *has been coming violently* d. Other ancient authorities omit *to hear*

¹⁸For John came neither eating nor drinking, and they say, 'He has a demon'; ¹⁹the Son of man came eating and drinking, and they say, 'Behold, a glutton and a drunkard, a friend of tax collectors and sinners!' Yet wisdom is justified by her deeds."ᵉ

Jesus reproaches cities for their unbelief

²⁰Then he began to upbraid the cities where most of his mighty works had been done, because they did not repent. ²¹"Woe to you, Chorazin! woe to you, Bethsaida! for if the mighty works done in you had been done in Tyre and Sidon, they would have repented long ago in sackcloth and ashes. ²²But I tell you, it shall be more tolerable on the day of judgment for Tyre and Sidon than for you. ²³And you, Capernaum, will you be exalted to heaven? You shall

Lk 10:12–15

Jn 3:6

Is 14:13, 15

heaven and becoming one with Christ. As Clement of Alexandria puts it: "The Kingdom of heaven does not belong to those who sleep and who indulge all their desires, but to those who fight against themselves" (*Quis dives salvetur?*, 21).

11:14. John the Baptist is Elijah, not in person, but by virtue of his mission (cf. Mt 17:10–13; Mk 9:10–12).

11:16–19. Making reference to a popular song or a child's game of his time, Jesus reproaches those who offer groundless excuses for not recognizing him. From the beginning of human history the Lord has striven to attract all men to himself: "What more was there to do for my vineyard, that I have not done in it?" (Is 5:4), and often he has been rejected: "When I looked for it to yield grapes, why did it yield wild grapes?" (Is 5:4).

Our Lord also condemns calumny: some people do try to justify their own behaviour by seeing sin where there is only virtue. "When they find something which is quite obviously good," St Gregory the Great says, "they pry into it to see if there is not also some badness

hidden in it" (*Moralia*, 6, 22). The Baptist's fasting they interpret as the work of the devil; whereas they accuse Jesus of being a glutton. The evangelist has to report these calumnies and accusations spoken against our Lord; otherwise, we would have no notion of the extent of the malice of those who show such furious opposition to Him who went about doing good (Acts 10:38). On other occasions Jesus warned his disciples that they would be treated the same way as he was (cf. Jn 15:20).

The works of Jesus and John the Baptist, each in their own way, lead to the accomplishment of God's plan for man's salvation: the fact that some people do not recognize him does not prevent God's plan being carried into effect.

11:21–24. Chorazin and Bethsaida were thriving cities on the northern shore of the lake of Gennesaret, not very far from Capernaum. During his public ministry Jesus often preached in these cities and worked many miracles there; in Capernaum he revealed his teaching about the Blessed Eucharist (cf. Jn 6:51ff).

e. Other ancient authorities read *children* (Luke 7:35)

be brought down to Hades. For if the mighty works done in you had been done in Sodom, it would have remained until this day. [24]But I tell you that it shall be more tolerable on the day of judgment for the land of Sodom than for you."

Jesus thanks his Father

Lk 10:21f
1 Cor 1:26–29
Sir 51:1
Acts 17:24
Jn 3:35; 17:2
Phil 2:9
Mt 16:7
Gal 1:15f
Mt 12:20
Jer 31:24

[25]At that time Jesus declared, "I thank thee, Father, Lord of heaven and earth, that thou hast hidden these things from the wise and understanding and revealed them to babes; [26]yea, Father, for such was thy gracious will.[f] [27]All things have been delivered to me by my Father; and no one knows the Son except the Father, and no one knows the Father except the Son and any one to whom the Son chooses to reveal him.* [28]Come to me, all who labour and are

---

Tyre, Sidon, Sodom and Gomorrah, the main cities of Phoenicia—all notorious for loose living—were classical examples of divine punishment (cf. Ezek 26–28; Is 23).

Here Jesus is pointing out the ingratitude of people who could know him but who refuse to change. On the day of Judgment (vv. 22 and 24) they will have more explaining to do: "Every one to whom much is given, of him will much be required" (Lk 12:48).

11:25–26. The wise and understanding of this world, that is, those who rely on their own judgment, cannot accept the revelation which Christ has brought us. Supernatural outlook is always connected with humility. A humble person, who gives himself little importance, sees; a person who is full of self-esteem fails to perceive supernatural things.

11:27. Here Jesus formally reveals his divinity. Our knowledge of a person shows our intimacy with him, according to the principle given by St Paul: "For what person knows a man's thoughts except the spirit of the man which is in

him?" (1 Cor 2:11). The Son knows the Father by the same knowledge as that by which the Father knows the Son. This identity of knowledge implies oneness of nature; that is to say, Jesus is God just as the Father is God.

11:28–30. Our Lord calls everyone to come to him. We all find things difficult in one way or another. The history of souls bears out the truth of these words of Jesus. Only the Gospel can fully satisfy the thirst for truth and justice that sincere people feel. Only our Lord, our Master—and those to whom he passes on his power—can sooth the sinner by telling him, "Your sins are forgiven" (Mt 9:2). In this connexion Pope Paul VI teaches: "Jesus says now and always, 'come to me, all who labour and are heavy laden, and I will give you rest.' His attitude towards us is one of invitation, knowledge and compassion; indeed, it is one of offering, promise, friendship, goodness, remedy of our ailments; he is our comforter; indeed, our nourishment, our bread, giving us energy and life" (Homily on Corpus Christi, 13 June 1974).

---

f. Or *so it was well-pleasing before thee*

heavy laden, and I will give you rest. [29]Take my yoke upon you, and learn from me; for I am gentle and lowly in heart, and you will find rest for your souls. [30]For my yoke is easy, and my burden is light."

Sir 51:33f
Jer 6:16
1 Kings 12:4
Ps 2:3
1 Jn 5:3

The law of the sabbath

12 [1]At that time Jesus went through the grainfields on the sabbath; his disciples were hungry, and they began to pluck ears of grain and to eat. [2]But when the Pharisees saw it, they said to him, "Look, your disciples are doing what is not lawful to do on the sabbath." [3]He said to them, "Have you not read what David did, when he was hungry, and those who were with him: [4]how he entered the house of God and ate the bread of the Presence, which

Mk 2:23–28
Lk 6:1–5
Deut 5:14;
23:26

Ex 20:10

1 Sam 21:7

Lev 24:9

"Come to me": the Master is addressing the crowds who are following him, "harassed and helpless, like sheep without a shepherd" (Mt 9:36). The Pharisees weighed them down with an endless series of petty regulations (cf. Acts 15:10), yet they brought no peace to their souls. Jesus tells these people, and us, about the kind of burden he imposes: "Any other burden oppresses and crushes you, but Christ's actually takes weight off you. Any other burden weighs down, but Christ's gives you wings. If you take a bird's wings away, you might seem to be taking weight off it, but the more weight you take off, the more you tie it down to the earth. There it is on the ground, and you wanted to relieve it of a weight; give it back the weight of its wings and you will see how it flies" (St Augustine, *Sermons*, 126). "All you who go about tormented, afflicted and burdened with the burden of your cares and desires, go forth from them, come to me, and I will refresh you and you shall find for your souls the rest which your desires take from you" (St John of the Cross, *Ascent of Mount Carmel*, book 1, chap. 7, 4).

12:2. "The sabbath": this was the day the Jews set aside for worshipping God.

God himself, the originator of the sabbath (Gen 2:3), ordered the Jewish people to avoid certain kinds of work on this day (Ex 20:8–11; 21:13; Deut 5:14) to leave them free to give more time to God. As time went by, the rabbis complicated this divine precept: by Jesus' time they had extended to thirty-nine the list of kinds of forbidden work.

The Pharisees accuse Jesus' disciples of breaking the sabbath. In the casuistry of the scribes and the Pharisees, plucking ears of corn was the same as harvesting, and crushing them was the same as milling—types of agricultural work forbidden on the sabbath.

12:3–8. Jesus rebuts the Pharisees' accusation by four arguments—the example of David, that of the priests, a correct understanding of the mercy of God and Jesus' own authority over the sabbath.

The first example, which was quite familiar to the people, who were used to listening to the Bible being read, comes from 1 Samuel 21:2–7: David, in flight from the jealousy of King Saul, asks the priest of the shrine at Nob for food for his men; the priest gave them the only bread he had, the holy bread of the Presence; this was the twelve loaves that were

Num 28:9

it was not lawful for him to eat nor for those who were with him, but only for the priests? ⁵Or have you not read in the law how on the sabbath the priests in the temple profane the sabbath, and are guiltless? ⁶I tell you, something greater than the temple is here.

Hos 6:6

⁷And if you had known what this means, 'I desire mercy, and not sacrifice,' you would not have condemned the guiltless. ⁸For the Son of man is lord of the sabbath."

Curing of the man with a withered hand

Mk 3:1–6
Lk 6:6–11;
14:3

⁹And he went on from there, and entered their synagogue. ¹⁰And behold, there was a man with a withered hand. And they asked him, "Is it lawful to heal on the sabbath?" so that they might accuse him. ¹¹He said to them, "What man of you, if he has one sheep and it falls into a pit on the sabbath, will not lay hold of it

Lk 14:5

and lift it out? ¹²Of how much more value is a man than a sheep! So it is lawful to do good on the sabbath." ¹³Then he said to the man, "Stretch out your hand." And the man stretched it out, and it

Jn 5:16

was restored, whole like the other. ¹⁴But the Pharisees went out and took counsel against him, how to destroy him.*

Jesus, the servant of God

Mk 3:7–12

¹⁵Jesus, aware of this, withdrew from there. And many followed him, and he healed them all, ¹⁶and ordered them not to make him

---

placed each week on the golden altar of the sanctuary as a perpetual offering from the twelve tribes of Israel (Lev 24:5–9). The second example refers to the priestly ministry to perform the liturgy, priests had to do a number of things on the sabbath but did not thereby break the law of sabbath rest (cf. Num 28:9). On the two other arguments, see the notes on Mt 9:13 and Mk 2:26–27, 28.

12:9–13. Jesus corroborates his teaching by performing this miracle: it is lawful to do good on the sabbath; no law should get in the way of doing good. He therefore rejects the interpretation given by the Pharisees; they are polarized on the letter of the law, to the detriment of God's honour and men's welfare. The very same people who are scandalized by

our Lord's miracle are quite ready to plot his death, even on the sabbath (v. 14).

12:17–21. Once again the sacred text points out the contrast between the contemporary mistaken Jewish notion of a spectacular messianic kingdom and the discernment which Jesus asks of those who witness and accept his teaching and miracles. By providing this long quotation from Isaiah (42:1–4), the evangelist is giving us the key to the teaching contained in chapters 11 and 12: in Jesus the prophecy of the Servant of Yahweh is fulfilled: the lovable and gentle teacher has come to bring the light of truth.

When narrating the passion of our Lord, the Gospels will once again remind us of the figure of the Servant of Yahweh, to show that in Jesus the suffering and

known. [17]This was to fulfil what was spoken by the prophet Is 42:1–4; 41:9
Isaiah:
> [18]"Behold my servant whom I have chosen,
>   my beloved with whom my soul is well pleased.
> I will put my Spirit upon him,
>   and he shall proclaim justice to the Gentiles.
> [19]He will not wrangle or cry aloud,
>   nor will any one hear his voice in the streets;
> [20]he will not break a bruised reed
>   or quench a smouldering wick,
> till he brings justice to victory;
> [21]and in his name will the Gentiles hope."

Allegations by the Pharisees. The sin against the Holy Spirit

Mk 3:22–30
Lk 11:14–26,
20, 32

[22]Then a blind and dumb demoniac was brought to him, and he healed him, so that the dumb man spoke and saw. [23]And all the people were amazed, and said, "Can this be the Son of David?" [24]But when the Pharisees heard it they said, "It is only by Beelzebul,* the prince of demons, that this man casts out demons." [25]Knowing their thoughts, he said to them, "Every kingdom divided against itself is laid waste, and no city or house divided against itself will stand; [26]and if Satan casts out Satan, he is divided against himself; how then will his kingdom stand? [27]And

expiatory aspect of the death of the Servant finds fulfilment (cf. Mt 27:30, with reference to Is 50:6; Mt 8:17 and Is 53:4; Jn 1:38 and Is 53:9–12; etc.).

12:17. Isaiah 42:1–4 speaks of a humble servant, beloved of God, chosen by God. And in fact Jesus, without ceasing to be the Son of God, one in substance with the Father, took the form of a servant (cf. Phil 2:6). This humility led him to cure and care for the poor and afflicted of Israel, without seeking acclaim.

12:18. See the note on Mt 3:16.

12:19. The justice proclaimed by the Servant, who is filled with the Holy Spirit, is not a noisy virtue. We can see the loving, gentle way Jesus worked his miracles, performing righteousness in all

humility. This is how he brings about the triumph of his Father's justice, his plan of revelation and salvation—very quietly and very effectively.

12:20. According to many Fathers, including St Augustine and St Jerome, the bruised reed and the smouldering wick refer to the Jewish people. They also stand for every sinner, for our Lord does not seek the sinner's death but his conversion, and his life (cf. Ezek 33:11). The Gospels often bear witness to this reassuring truth (cf. Lk 15:11–32, the parable of the prodigal son; Mt 18:12–24, the parable of the lost sheep; etc.).

12:22–24. Here is a case of possession by the devil. This consists in an evil spirit taking over a human body. Possession is normally accompanied by certain forms

1 Jn 3:8
1 Thess 2:16

Is 49:24
1 Jn 4:4

Mk 9:40
Jn 11:52

Heb 6:4, 6;
10:26
1 Jn 5:16

Lk 12:10
1 Tim 1:13

if I cast out demons by Beelzebul, by whom do your sons cast them out? Therefore they shall be your judges. [28]But if it is by the Spirit of God that I cast out demons, then the kingdom of God has come upon you. [29]Or how can one enter a strong man's house and plunder his goods, unless he first binds the strong man? Then indeed he may plunder his house. [30]He who is not with me is against me, and he who does not gather with me scatters. [31]Therefore I tell you, every sin and blasphemy will be forgiven men, but the blasphemy against the Spirit will not be forgiven.* [32]And whoever says a word against the Son of man will be forgiven; but whoever speaks against the Holy Spirit will not be forgiven, either in this age or in the age to come.

[33]"Either make the tree good, and its fruit good; or make the tree bad, and its fruit bad; for the tree is known by its fruit. [34]You

---

of illness or disease—epilepsy, dumbness, blindness ... . Possessed people have lost their self-control; when they are in the trance of possession they are tools of the devil. The evil spirit who has mastery over them sometimes gives them supernatural powers; at other times he torments the person, and may even drive him to suicide (cf. Mt 8:16; 8:28–34; 17:14–21; Mk 1:26; Lk 7:21).

The expulsion of devils by invoking Jesus' name has special significance in the history of salvation. It proves that the coming of Jesus marks the beginning of the Kingdom of God and that the devil has been dispossessed of his territory (Jn 12:31). "The seventy returned with joy, saying 'Lord, even the demons are subject to us in your name!' And he said to them, 'I saw Satan fall like lightning from heaven'" (Lk 10:17–18). Ever since Christ's coming, the devil is on the retreat—which is not to say that there are not still instances of diabolic possession.

12:30. Here Jesus sums up his whole argument against the Pharisees: they are either for him or for the devil. He said the same thing in the Sermon on the Mount: "No one can serve two masters" (Mt 6:24). Those who are not united to Jesus through faith, hope and charity, are against him—and therefore they are on the side of the devil, Jesus' enemy.

Our Lord does not mince words when it comes to asking people to adopt an attitude to his person and his Kingdom. A Christian cannot temporize; if he wants to be a true Christian he must not entertain ideas or approaches which are not in keeping with the content of Revelation and with the teaching of the Church.

Therefore, we must not compromise on matters of faith, trying to adapt Jesus' teaching to suit our convenience or because we are afraid of how other people will react to it. Our Lord wants us to adopt a clear attitude to his person *and* to his teaching.

12:31–32. God wants all men to be saved (1 Tim 2:4) and he calls everyone to repentance (2 Pet 3:9). The Redemption won by Christ is superabundant: it atones for all sins and extends to every man and woman (Rom 5:12–21). Christ gave his Church the power to forgive sins by means of the sacraments of Baptism and Penance. This power is unlimited, that is to say, the Church can pardon all sins of

brood of vipers! how can you speak good, when you are evil? For out of the abundance of the heart the mouth speaks. ³⁵The good man out of his good treasure brings forth good, and the evil man out of his evil treasure brings forth evil. ³⁶I tell you, on the day of judgment men will render account for every careless word they utter; ³⁷for by your words you will be justified, and by your words you will be condemned."

Jn 8:43
Rom 8:7
Lk 6:45

The sign of Jonah

³⁸Then some of the scribes and Pharisees said to him, "Teacher, we wish to see a sign from you." ³⁹But he answered them, "An evil and adulterous generation seeks for a sign; but no sign shall be given to it except the sign of the prophet Jonah. ⁴⁰For as Jonah was three days and three nights in the belly of the whale, so will the Son of

1 Cor 1:22

Jn 2:1f

---

all the baptized as often as they confess their sins with the right disposition. This teaching is a dogma of faith (cf. Council of Trent, *De Paenitentia*, can. 1).

The sin Jesus speaks about here is termed "sin against the Holy Spirit", because external expressions of God's goodness are specially attributed to the third person of the Blessed Trinity. Sin against the Holy Spirit is said to be unforgivable not so much because of its gravity or malice but because of the subjective disposition of the sinner in this case: his attitude shuts the door on repentance. Sin against the Holy Spirit consists in maliciously attributing to the devil the miracles and signs wrought by Christ. Thus, the very nature of this sin blocks the person's route to Christ, who is the only one who can take away the sin of the world (Jn 1:29), and the sinner puts himself outside the range of God's forgiveness. In this sense the sins against the Holy Spirit cannot be forgiven.

12:33–37. Our Lord continues his case against the Pharisees: because he is evil, the devil cannot do good things. And if the works that I do are good, as you can see they are, then they cannot have been

done by the devil; "a sound tree cannot bear evil fruit, nor can a bad tree bear good fruit" (Mt 7:18).

As on other occasions Jesus reminds people that there is a Judgment. The Magisterium of the Church explains that there is a "particular" judgment immediately after one dies, and a "general" judgment at the end of the world (cf. Benedict XII, *Benedictus Deus*).

12:39–40. This sign the Jews were asking for would have been a miracle or some other prodigy; they wanted Jesus, incongruously, to confirm his preaching—given with such simplicity—by dramatic signs. Our Lord replies by announcing the mystery of his death and resurrection, using the parallel of the case of Jonah: "No sign shall be given to it except the sign of the prophet Jonah." Jesus' glorious resurrection is the "sign" *par excellence*, the decisive proof of the divine character of his person, of his mission and of his teaching.

When St Paul (1 Cor 15:3–4) confesses that Jesus Christ "was raised on the third day in accordance with the scriptures" (words that later found their way into the Nicene-Constantinopolitan Creed, the Creed used in the Mass), he

Jn 3:5

1 Kings
10:1–10

2 Pet 2:20

man be three days and three nights in the heart of the earth. ⁴¹The men of Nineveh will arise at the judgment with this generation and condemn it; for they repented at the preaching of Jonah, and behold, something greater than Jonah is here. ⁴²The queen of the South will arise at the judgment with this generation and condemn it; for she came from the ends of the earth to hear the wisdom of Solomon, and behold, something greater than Solomon is here.

⁴³"When the unclean spirit has gone out of a man, he passes through waterless places seeking rest, but he finds none. ⁴⁴Then he says, 'I will return to my house from which I came.' And when he comes he finds it empty, swept, and put in order. ⁴⁵Then he goes and brings with him seven other spirits more evil than himself, and they enter and dwell there; and the last state of that man becomes worse than the first. So shall it be also with this evil generation."

---

must have had this passage particularly in mind. We can see another allusion to Jonah in the words our Lord spoke shortly before his ascension: "Thus it is written, that the Christ should suffer and on the third day rise from the dead" (Lk 24:45–46).

12:41–42. Nineveh was a city in Mesopotamia (modern Iraq) to which the prophet Jonah was sent. The Ninevites did penance (Jn 3:6–9) because they recognized the prophet and accepted his message; whereas Jerusalem does not wish to recognize Jesus, of whom Jonah was merely a figure. The queen of the South was the queen of Sheba in southwestern Arabia, who visited Solomon (1 Kings 10:1–10) and was in awe of the wisdom with which God had endowed the King of Israel. Jesus is also prefigured in Solomon, whom Jewish tradition saw as the epitome of the wise man. Jesus' reproach is accentuated by the example of pagan converts, and gives us a glimpse of the universal scope of Christianity, which will take root among the Gentiles.

There is a certain irony in what Jesus says about "something greater" than Jonah or Solomon having come: really,

he is infinitely greater, but Jesus prefers to tone down the difference between himself and any figure, no matter how important, in the Old Testament.

12:43. Jesus says that when demons are driven out of men they retreat into the wilderness; but that if they repossess a man they torment him in a worse way. St Peter also says that the devil prowls around like a lion seeking someone to devour (1 Pet 5:8) and that people who have been converted and revert to the depravities of their past life become worse than they were before (2 Pet 2:20). Jesus is solemnly warning the Jews of his time that if they continue to reject the light they will end up worse than they were before. The same sad truth applies to the Christian who, after being converted and reconciled to God, allows the devil to enter his soul again.

12:46–47. "Brethren": ancient Hebrew, Aramaic and other languages had no special words for different degrees of relationship, such as are found in more modern languages. In general, all those belonging to the same family, clan and even tribe were "brethren".

The true kinsmen of Jesus

⁴⁶While he was still speaking to the people, behold, his mother and his brethren* stood outside, asking to speak to him.ᵍ ⁴⁸But he replied to the man who told him, "Who is my mother, and who are my brethren?"* ⁴⁹And stretching out his hand toward his disciples, he said, "Here are my mother and my brethren! ⁵⁰For whoever does the will of my Father in heaven is my brother, and sister, and mother."

Mk 3:31–35
Lk 8:19–21
Mt 13:55

Lk 2:49

Rom 8:29
Jn 15:14

6. THE PARABLES OF THE KINGDOM

Parable of the sower. The meaning of parables

13 ¹That same day Jesus went out of the house and sat beside the sea. ²And great crowds gathered about him, so that he got into a boat and sat there; and the whole crowd stood on the beach. ³And he told them many things in parables, saying: "A

Mk 4:1–20
Lk 8:4–15

In the particular case we have here, we should bear in mind that Jesus had different kinds of relatives, in two groups—some on his mother's side, others on St Joseph's. Matthew 13:55–56 mentions, as living in Nazareth, James, Joseph, Simon and Judas ("his brethren") and elsewhere there is reference to Jesus' "sisters" (cf. Mk 6:3). But in Matthew 27:56 we are told that the James and Joseph were sons of a Mary distinct from the Blessed Virgin, and that Simon and Judas were not brothers of James and Joseph, but seemingly children of a brother of St Joseph.

Jesus, on the other hand, was known to everyone as "the son of Mary" (Mk 6:3) or "the carpenter's son" (Mt 13:55).

The Church has always maintained as absolutely certain that Jesus had no brothers or sisters in the full meaning of the term: it is a dogma that Mary was ever-Virgin (cf. the note on Mt 1:25).

12:48–50. Jesus obviously loved his Mother and St Joseph. He uses this episode to teach us that in his Kingdom human ties do not take precedence. In Luke 8:19 the same teaching is to be found. Jesus regards the person who does the will of his heavenly Father as a member of his own family. Therefore, even though it means going against natural family feelings, a person should do just that when needs be in order to perform the mission the Father has entrusted to him (cf. Lk 2:49).

We can say that Jesus loved Mary more because of the bonds between them created by grace than because he was her son by natural generation: Mary's divine motherhood is the source of all our Lady's other prerogatives; but this very motherhood is, in its turn, the first and greatest of the graces with which Mary was endowed.

13:3. Chapter 13 of St Matthew includes as many as seven of Jesus' parables,

g. Other ancient authorities insert verse 47, *Some one told him "Your mother and your brothers are standing outside, asking to speak to you"*

sower went out to sow. [4]And as he sowed, some seeds fell along the path, and the birds came and devoured them. [5]Other seeds fell on rocky ground, where they had not much soil, and immediately they sprang up, since they had no depth of soil, [6]but when the sun rose they were scorched; and since they had no root they withered away. [7]Other seeds fell upon thorns, and the thorns grew up and choked them. [8]Other seeds fell on good soil and brought forth

---

which is the reason why it is usually called "the parable discourse" or the "parabolic discourse". Because of their similarity of content and setting these parables are often called the "Kingdom parables", and also the "parables of the Lake", because Jesus taught them on the shore of Lake Gennesaret. Jesus uses these elaborate comparisons (parables) to explain certain features of the Kingdom of God, which he has come to establish (cf. Mt 3:2)—its tiny, humble origins; its steady growth; its worldwide scope; its salvific force. God calls everyone to salvation but only those attain it who receive God's call with good dispositions and who do not change their attitude; the value of the spiritual benefits the Kingdom brings— so valuable that one should give up everything to obtain them; the fact that good and bad are all mixed together until the harvest-time, or the time of God's judgment; the intimate connexion between earthly and heavenly aspects of the Kingdom, until it reaches its point of full development at the end of time.

On Jesus' lips, parables are exceptionally effective. By using parables he keeps his listeners' attention, whether they are uneducated or not, and by means of the most ordinary things of daily life he sheds light on the deepest supernatural mysteries. He used the parable device in a masterly way; his parables are quite unique; they carry the seal of his personality; through them he has graphically shown us the riches of grace, the life of the Church, the demands of the faith and

even the mystery of God's own inner life.

Jesus' teaching continues to provide every generation with light and guidance on moral conduct. By reading and reflecting on his parables one can savour the adorable humanity of the Saviour, who showed such kindness to the people who crowded around to hear him—and who shows the same readiness to listen to our prayers, despite our dullness, and to reply to our healthy curiosity when we try to make out his meaning.

13:3–8. Anyone who has visited the fertile plain to the west of the lake of Gennesaret will appreciate Jesus' touching description in the parable of the sower. The plain is crisscrossed by paths; it is streaked with rocky ground, often with the rocks lying just beneath the surface, and with the courses of rivulets, dry for most of the year but still retaining some moisture. Here and there are clumps of large thorn bushes. When the agricultural worker sows seed in this mixed kind of land, he knows that some seed will fare better than others.

13:9. Jesus did not explain this parable there and then. It was quite usual for parables to be presented in the first instance as a kind of puzzle to gain the listener's attention, excite his curiosity and fix the parable in his memory. It may well be that Jesus wanted to allow his more interested listeners to identify themselves by coming back to hear him again—as happened with his disciples.

grain, some a hundredfold, some sixty, some thirty. [9]He who has ears,[h] let him hear."

[10]Then the disciples came and said to him, "Why do you speak to them in parables?" [11]And he answered them, "To you it has been given to know the secrets of the kingdom of heaven, but to them it has not been given. [12]For to him who has will more be given, and he will have abundance; but from him who has not,

Mk 4:25
Lk 8:18

The rest—who listened out of idle curiosity or for too human reasons (to see him work miracles)—would not benefit from hearing a more detailed and deeper explanation of the parable.

13:10–13. The kind of kingdom Jesus was going to establish did not suit the Judaism of his time, largely because of the Jews' nationalistic, earthbound idea of the Messiah to come. In his preaching Jesus takes account of the different outlooks of his listeners, as can be seen in the attitudes described in the parable of the sower. If people were well disposed to him, the enigmatic nature of the parable would stimulate their interest; and Jesus later did give his many disciples a fuller explanation of its meaning; but there was no point in doing this if people were not ready to listen.

Besides, parables—as indeed any type of comparison or analogy—are used to reveal or explain something that is not easy to understand, as was the case with the supernatural things Jesus was explaining. One has to shade one's eyes to see things if the sun is too bright; otherwise, one is blinded and sees nothing. Similarly, parables help to shade supernatural brightness to allow the listener to grasp meaning without being blinded by it.

These verses also raise a very interesting question: how can divine revelation and grace produce such widely differing responses in people? What is at

work here is the mystery of divine grace —which is an unmerited gift—and of man's response to this grace. What Jesus says here underlines man's responsibility to be ready to accept God's grace and to respond to it. Jesus' reference to Isaiah (Mt 13:14–15) is a prophecy of that hardness of heart which is a punishment meted out to those who resist grace.

These verses need to be interpreted in the light of three points: 1) Jesus Christ loved everyone, including the people of his own hometown: he gave his life in order to save all men; 2) the parable is a literary form designed to get ideas across clearly: its ultimate aim is to teach, not to mislead or obscure; 3) lack of appreciation for divine grace is something blameworthy, which does merit punishment; however, Jesus did not come directly to punish anyone, but rather to save everyone.

13:12. Jesus is telling his disciples that, precisely because they have faith in him and want to have a good grasp of his teaching, they will be given a deeper understanding of divine truths. But those who do not "follow him" (cf. the note on Mt 4:18–22) will later lose interest in the things of God and will grow ever blinder: it is as if the little they have is being taken away from them.

This verse also helps us understand the meaning of the parable of the sower, a parable which gives a wonderful expla-

---

h. Other ancient authorities add here and in verse 43 *to hear*

Deut 29:4   even what he has will be taken away.* ¹³This is why I speak to

Is 6:9f   them in parables, because seeing they do not see, and hearing they
Jn 12:40   do not hear, nor do they understand. ¹⁴With them indeed is ful-
Acts 28:26f   filled the prophecy of Isaiah which says:

> 'You shall indeed hear but never understand,
> and you shall indeed see but never perceive.
> ¹⁵For this people's heart has grown dull,
> and their ears are heavy of hearing,
> and their eyes they have closed,
> lest they should perceive with their eyes,
> and hear with their ears,
> and understand with their heart,
> and turn for me to heal them.'

Lk 10:23f   ¹⁶But blessed are your eyes, for they see, and your ears, for they
hear. ¹⁷Truly, I say to you, many prophets and righteous men
longed to see what you see, and did not see it, and to hear what
you hear, and did not hear it.

---

nation of the supernatural economy of divine grace: God gives grace, and man freely responds to that grace. The result is that those who respond to grace generously receive additional grace and so grow steadily in grace and holiness; whereas those who reject God's gifts become closed up within themselves; through their selfishness and attachment to sin they eventually lose God's grace entirely. In this verse, then, our Lord gives a clear warning: with the full weight of his divine authority he exhorts us—without taking away our freedom—to act responsibly: the gifts God keeps sending us should yield fruit; we should make good use of the opportunities for Christian sanctification which are offered us in the course of our lives.

13:14–15. Only well-disposed people grasp the meaning of God's words. It is not enough just to hear them physically. In the course of Jesus' preaching the prophetic words of Isaiah come true once again.

However, we should not think that not wanting to hear or to understand was something exclusive to certain contemporaries of Jesus; each one of us is at times hard of hearing, hard-hearted and dull-minded in the presence of God's grace and saving word. Moreover, it is not enough to be familiar with the teaching of the Church: it is absolutely necessary to put the faith into practice, with all that that implies, morally and ascetically. Jesus was fixed to the wood of the cross not only by nails and by the sins of certain Jews but also by our sins—sins committed centuries later but which afflicted the most sacred humanity of Jesus Christ, who bore the burden of our sins. See the note on Mk 4:11–12.

13:16–17. In contrast with the closed attitude of many Jews who witnessed Jesus' life but did not believe in him, the disciples are praised by our Lord for their docility to grace, their openness to recognizing him as the Messiah and to accepting his teaching.

He calls his disciples blessed, happy. As he says, the prophets and just men

[18]"Hear then the parable of the sower. [19]When any one hears the word of the kingdom and does not understand it, the evil one comes and snatches away what is sown in his heart; this is what was sown along the path. [20]As for what was sown on rocky ground, this is he who hears the word and immediately receives it with joy; [21]yet he has no root in himself, but endures for a while, and when tribulation or persecution arises on account of the word, immediately he falls away.[i] [22]As for what was sown among thorns, this is he who hears the word, but the cares of the world and the delight in riches choke the word, and it proves unfruitful. [23]As for what was sown on good soil, this is he who hears the word and understands it; he indeed bears fruit, and yields, in one case a hundredfold, in another sixty, and in another thirty."

1 Tim 6:9

The parable of the weeds
[24]Another parable he put before them, saying, "The kingdom of heaven may be compared to a man who sowed good seed in his

---

and women of the Old Testament had for centuries lived in hope of enjoying one day the peace the future Messiah would bring, but they had died without experiencing this good fortune. Simeon, towards the end of his long life, was filled with joy on seeing the infant Jesus when he was presented in the temple: "he took him up in his arms and blessed God and said, 'Lord, now lettest thou thy servant depart in peace, according to thy word; for mine eyes have seen thy salvation'" (Lk 2:28–30). During our Lord's public life, his disciples were fortunate enough to see and be on close terms with him; later they would recall that incomparable gift, and one of them would begin his first letter in these words: "That which was from the beginning, which we have heard, which we have seen with our eyes, which we have looked upon and touched with our hands, concerning the word of life; [...] that which we have seen and heard we proclaim also to you, so that you may have fellowship with us;

and our fellowship is with the Father and with his Son Jesus Christ. And we are writing this that our [or: your] joy may be complete" (1 Jn 1:1–4).

This exceptional good fortune was, obviously, not theirs because of special merit: God planned it; it was he who decided that the time had come for the Old Testament prophecies to be fulfilled. In any event, God gives every soul opportunities to meet him: each of us has to be sensitive enough to grasp them and not let them pass. There were many men and women in Palestine who saw and heard the Incarnate Son of God but did not have the spiritual sensitivity to see in him what the apostles and disciples saw.

13:19. He does not understand because he does not love—not because he is not clever enough: lack of love opens the door of the soul to the devil.

13:24–25. "The situation is clear: the field is fertile and the seed is good; the

---

i. Or *stumbles*

field; ²⁵but while men were sleeping, his enemy came and sowed weeds among the wheat, and went away. ²⁶So when the plants came up and bore grain, then the weeds appeared also. ²⁷And the servants ʲ of the householder came and said to him, 'Sir, did you not sow good seed in your field? How then has it weeds?' ²⁸He said to them, 'An enemy has done this.' The servants ʲ said to him, 'Then do you want us to go and gather them?' ²⁹But he said, 'No; lest in gathering the weeds you root up the wheat along with them. ³⁰Let both grow together until the harvest; and at harvest time I will tell the reapers, Gather the weeds first and bind them in bundles to be burned, but gather the wheat into my barn.' "

Mk 4:30–32
Lk 13:18–19;
17:6

The mustard seed; the leaven

Ezek 17:23;
31:6

³¹Another parable he put before them saying, "The kingdom of heaven is like a grain of mustard seed which a man took and sowed in his field; ³²it is the smallest of all seeds, but when it has

Lord of the field has scattered the seed at the right moment and with great skill. He even has watchmen to make sure that the field is protected. If, afterwards, there are weeds among the wheat, it is because men have failed to respond, because they—and Christians in particular—have fallen asleep and allowed the enemy to approach" (St Josemaría Escrivá, *Christ Is Passing By*, 123).

13:25. This weed—cockle—looks very like wheat and can easily be mistaken for it until the ears appear. If it gets ground up with wheat it contaminates the flour and any bread made from that flour causes severe nausea when eaten. In the East personal vengeance sometimes took the form of sowing cockle among an enemy's wheat. Roman law prescribed penalties for this crime.

13:28. "When the careless servants ask the Lord why weeds have grown in his field, the explanation is obvious: '*inimicus homo hoc fecit*: an enemy has done this.'

We Christians should have been on guard to make sure that the good things placed in this world by the Creator were developed in the service of truth and good. But we have fallen asleep—a sad thing, that sluggishness of our heart! while the enemy and all those who serve him worked incessantly. You can see how the weeds have grown abundantly everywhere" (ibid., 123).

13:29–30. The end of this parable gives a symbolic explanation of why God allows evil to have its way for a time—and for its ultimate extirpation. Evil is to run its course on earth until the end of time; therefore, we should not be scandalized by the presence of evil in the world. It will be obliterated not in this life, but after death; at the Judgment (the harvest) the good will go to heaven and the bad to hell.

13:31–32. Here, the man is Jesus Christ and the field, the world. The grain of mustard seed is the preaching of the

j. Or *slaves*

grown it is the greatest of shrubs and becomes a tree, so that the birds of the air come and make nests in its branches."

Ps 104:12

[33]He told them another parable. "The kingdom of heaven is like leaven which a woman took and hid in three measures of meal, till it was all leavened."

Lk 13:20f

[34]All this Jesus said to the crowds in parables; indeed he said nothing to them without a parable. [35]This was to fulfil what was spoken by the prophet:[k]

Mk 4:33f
Ps 78:2

> "I will open my mouth in parables,
> I will utter what has been hidden
> since the foundation of the world."

The parable of the weeds explained

[36]Then he left the crowds and went into the house. And his disciples came to him, saying, "Explain to us the parable of the weeds of the field." [37]He answered, "He who sows the good seed is the

Gospel and the Church, which from very small beginnings will spread throughout the world. The parable clearly refers to the universal scope and spread of the Kingdom of God: the Church, which embraces all mankind of every kind and condition, in every latitude and in all ages, is forever developing in spite of obstacles, thanks to God's promise and aid.

13:33. This comparison is taken from everyday experience: just as leaven gradually ferments all the dough, so the Church spreads to convert all nations. The leaven is also a symbol of the individual Christian. Living in the middle of the world and retaining his Christian quality, he wins souls for Christ by his word and example: "Our calling to be children of God, in the midst of the world, requires us not only to seek our own personal holiness, but also to go out onto all the ways of the earth, to convert them into roadways that will carry souls over all obstacles and lead them to the Lord. As we take part in all temporal activities as ordinary citizens, we are to become leaven acting on the mass" (ibid., 120).

13:34–35. Revelation, God's plans, are hidden (cf. Mt 11:25) from those who are not disposed to accept them. The evangelist wishes to emphasize the need for simplicity and for docility to the Gospel. By recalling Psalm 78:2, he tells us once more, under divine inspiration, that the Old Testament prophecies find their fulfilment in our Lord's preaching.

13:36–43. While making its way on earth, the Church is composed of good and bad people, just men and sinners: they are mixed in with one another until the harvest time, the end of the world, when the Son of man, in his capacity as Judge of the living and the dead, will divide the good from the bad at the Last Judgment—the former going to eternal glory, the inheritance of the saints; the latter, to the eternal fire of hell. Although the just and the sinners are now side by side, the

k. Other ancient authorities read *the prophet Isaiah*

1 Cor 3:9

Son of man; [38]the field is the world, and the good seed means the sons of the kingdom; the weeds are the sons of the evil one, [39]and the enemy who sowed them is the devil; the harvest is the close of the age, and the reapers are angels. [40]Just as the weeds are gathered and burned with fire, so will it be at the close of the age. [41]The Son of man will send his angels, and they will gather out of his kingdom all causes of sin and all evildoers, [42]and throw them into the furnace of fire; there men will weep and gnash their teeth. [43]Then the righteous will shine like the sun in the kingdom of their Father. He who has ears, let him hear.

Jn 15:6

Zeph 1:3
Mt 25:31–46;
7:23

Dan 12:3

The hidden treasure; the pearl; the net

Lk 14:33
Phil 3:7
Prov 2:4

[44]"The kingdom of heaven is like treasure hidden in a field, which a man found and covered up; then in his joy he goes and sells all that he has and buys that field.

Prov 8:10f

[45]"Again, the kingdom of heaven is like a merchant in search of fine pearls, [46]who, on finding one pearl of great value, went and sold all that he had and bought it.

Church has the right and the duty to exclude those who cause scandal, especially those who attack its doctrine and unity; this it can do through ecclesiastical excommunication and other canonical penalties. However, excommunication has a medicinal and pastoral function— to correct those who are obstinate in error, and to protect others from them.

13:44–46. In these two parables Jesus shows the supreme value of the Kingdom of heaven, and the attitude people need if they are to attain it. The parables are very alike, but it is interesting to note the differences: the treasure means abundance of gifts; the pearl indicates the beauty of the Kingdom. The treasure is something stumbled upon; the pearl, the result of a lengthy search; but in both instances the finder is filled with joy. Faith, vocation, true wisdom, desire for heaven, are things that sometimes are discovered suddenly and unexpectedly, and sometimes after much searching (cf. St Gregory the Great, *In Evangelia homiliae*, 11). However, the

man's attitude is the same in both parables and is described in the same terms: "he goes and sells all that he has and buys it": detachment, generosity, is indispensable for obtaining the treasure.

"Anyone who understands the Kingdom which Christ proposes realizes that it is worth staking everything to obtain it […]. The Kingdom of heaven is difficult to win. No one can be sure of achieving it, but the humble cry of a repentant man can open wide its doors" (St Josemaría Escrivá, *Christ Is Passing By*, 180).

13:47. "Fish of every kind": almost all the Greek manuscripts and early translations say "All kinds of things". A dragnet is very long and about two metres wide; when it is extended between two boats it forms double or triple mesh with the result that when it is pulled in it collects all sorts of things in addition to fish— algae, weeds, rubbish etc.

This parable is rather like the parable of the cockle, but in a fishing context: the net is the Church, the sea the world.

47"Again, the kingdom of heaven is like a net which was thrown into the sea and gathered fish of every kind; 48when it was full, men drew it ashore and sat down and sorted the good into vessels but threw away the bad. 49So it will be at the close of the age. The angels will come out and separate the evil from the righteous, 50and throw them into the furnace of fire; there men will weep and gnash their teeth.

51"Have you understood all this?" They said to him, "Yes." 52And he said to them, "Therefore every scribe who has been trained for the kingdom of heaven is like a householder who brings out of his treasure what is new and what is old."*

7. JESUS WITHDRAWS TO THE BORDER COUNTRY

No one is a prophet in his own country
53And when Jesus had finished these parables he went away from there, 54and coming to his own country he taught them in their

Mk 6:1–6
Lk 4:15–30

We can easily find in this parable the dogmatic truth of the Judgment: at the end of time God will judge men and separate the good from the bad. It is interesting to note our Lord's repeated references to the last things, especially Judgment and hell: he emphasizes these truths because of man's great tendency to forget them: "All these things are said to make sure that no one can make the excuse that he does not know about them: this excuse would be valid only if eternal punishment were spoken about in ambiguous terms" (St Gregory the Great, *In Evangelia homiliae*, 11).

13:52. "Scribe": among the Jews a scribe was a religious teacher, a specialist in Holy Scripture and its application to life. Our Lord here uses this old word to refer to the apostles, who will have the role of teachers in his Church. Thus, the apostles and their successors, the bishops, are the *Ecclesia docens*, the teaching Church; they have the authority and the mission to teach. The Pope and the Bishops exercise

this authority directly and are also helped in this by priests. The other members of the Church form the *Ecclesia discens*, the learning Church. However, every disciple of Christ, every Christian who has received Christ's teaching, has a duty to pass this teaching on to others, in language they can understand; therefore, he should make sure he has a good grasp of Christian doctrine. The treasure of Revelation is so rich that it can provide teaching that applies to all times and situations. It is for the word of God to enlighten all ages and situations—not the other way around. Therefore, the Church and its pastors preach, not new things, but a single unchanging truth contained in the treasure of Revelation: for the past two thousand years the Gospel has always been "good news".

13:53–58. The Nazarenes' surprise is partly due to people's difficulty in recognizing anything exceptional and supernatural in those with whom they have been on familiar terms. Hence the

synagogue, so that they were astonished, and said, "Where did this man get this wisdom and these mighty works? [55]Is not this the carpenter's son? Is not his mother called Mary? And are not his brethren James and Joseph and Simon and Judas?* [56]And are not all his sisters with us? Where then did this man get all this?" [57]And they took offence at him. But Jesus said to them, "A prophet is not without honour except in his own country and in his own house." [58]And he did not do many mighty works there, because of their unbelief.

Jn 7:15, 52

Jn 4:44

The martyrdom of John the Baptist

Mk 6:14, 17–30
Lk 9:7–9; 3:19f

Lev 18:16; 20:21

14 [1]At that time Herod the tetrarch heard about the fame of Jesus; [2]and he said to his servants, "This is John the Baptist, he has been raised from the dead; that is why these powers are at work in him." [3]For Herod had seized John and bound him and put him in prison, for the sake of Herodias, his brother Philip's wife;[l] [4]because John said to him, "It is not lawful for you to have her." [5]And though he wanted to put him to death, he feared the people, because they held him to be a prophet. [6]But when Herod's birthday came, the daughter of Herodias danced before the company, and pleased Herod, [7]so that he promised with an oath to give her whatever she might ask. [8]Prompted by her mother, she said, "Give me the head of John the Baptist here on a

---

saying, "No one is a prophet in his own country." These old neighbours were also jealous of Jesus. Where did he acquire this wisdom? Why him rather than us? They were unaware of the mystery of Jesus' conception; surprise and jealousy cause them to be shocked, to look down on Jesus and not to believe in him: "He came to his own home, and his own people received him not" (Jn 1:11).

"The carpenter's son": this is the only reference in the Gospel to St Joseph's occupation (in Mk 6:3 Jesus himself is described as a "carpenter"). Probably in a town like Nazareth the carpenter was a general tradesman who could turn his hand to jobs ranging from metalwork to making furniture or agricultural implements.

For an explanation of Jesus' "brethren", see the note on Mt 12:46–47.

14:1. Herod the tetrarch, Herod Antipas (see the note on Mt 2:1), is the same Herod as appears later in the account of the Passion (cf. Lk 23:7ff). A son of Herod the Great, Antipas governed Galilee and Perea in the name of the Roman emperor; according to Flavius Josephus, the Jewish historian (*Jewish Antiquities*, 18, 5, 4), he was married to a daughter of an Arabian king, but in spite of this he lived in concubinage with Herodias, his brother's wife. St John the Baptist, and Jesus himself, often criticized the tetrarch's immoral life, which was in conflict with the sexual morality laid down in the Law (Lev 18:16; 20:21) and was a cause of scandal.

---

l. Other ancient authorities read *his brother's wife*

platter." [9]And the king was sorry; but because of his oaths and his guests he commanded it to be given; [10]he sent and had John beheaded in the prison, [11]and his head was brought on a platter and given to the girl, and she brought it to her mother. [12]And his disciples came and took the body and buried it; and they went and told Jesus.

First miracle of the loaves and fish

[13]Now when Jesus heard this, he withdrew from there in a boat to a lonely place apart. But when the crowds heard it, they followed him on foot from the towns. [14]As he went ashore he saw a great throng; and he had compassion on them, and healed their sick. [15]When it was evening, the disciples came to him and said, "This is a lonely place, and the day is now over; send the crowds away to go into the villages and buy food for themselves." [16]Jesus said, "They need not go away; you give them something to eat." [17]They said to him, "We have only five loaves here and two fish." [18]And he said, "Bring them here to me." [19]Then he ordered the crowds to sit down on the grass; and taking the five loaves and the two fish he looked up to heaven, and blessed, and broke and gave the loaves to the disciples, and the disciples gave them to the crowds. [20]And they all ate and were satisfied. And they took up twelve baskets full of the broken pieces left over. [21]And those who ate were about five thousand men, besides women and children.

Mk 6:31–44
Lk 9:10–17
Jn 6:1–13

2 Kings 4:44
Mk 6:45–56
Jn 6:15–21

14:3–12. Towards the end of the first century Flavius Josephus wrote of these same events. He gives additional information—specifying that it was in the fortress of Makeronte that John was imprisoned (this fortress was on the eastern bank of the Dead Sea, and was the scene of the banquet in question) and that Herodias' daughter was called Salome.

14:9. St Augustine comments: "Amid the excesses and sensuality of the guests, oaths are rashly made, which then are unjustly kept" (*Sermons*, 10). It is a sin against the second commandment of God's Law to make an oath to do something unjust; any such oath has no binding force. In fact, if one keeps it—as

Herod did—one commits an additional sin. The Catechism also teaches that one offends against this precept if one swears something untrue, or swears needlessly (cf. St Pius V, *Catechism*, 3, 3, 24). Cf. the note on Mt 5:33–37.

14:14–21. This episode must have occurred in the middle of springtime, because the grass was green (Mk 6:40; Jn 6:10). In the Near East loaves were usually made very thin, which meant it was easy to break them by hand and distribute them to those at table; this was usually done by the head of the household or the senior person at the meal. Our Lord follows this custom, and the miracle occurs when Jesus breaks the bread. The disciples then distribute it among the crowd.

Jesus walks on the water

Lk 6:12; 9:18

Lk 24:37

[22]Then he made the disciples get into the boat and go before him to the other side, while he dismissed the crowds. [23]And after he had dismissed the crowds he went up into the hills by himself to pray. When evening came, he was there alone, [24]but the boat by this time was many furlongs distant from the land,[m] beaten by the waves; for the wind was against them. [25]And in the fourth watch of the night he came to them, walking on the sea. [26]But when the disciples saw him walking on the sea, they were terrified, saying, "It is a ghost!" And they cried out for fear. [27]But immediately he spoke to them, saying, "Take heart, it is I; have no fear."

[28]And Peter answered him, "Lord, if it is you, bid me come to you on the water." [29]He said, "Come." So Peter got out of the boat and walked on the water and came to Jesus; [30]but when he saw the wind,[n] he was afraid, and beginning to sink he cried out, "Lord, save me." [31]Jesus immediately reached out his hand and caught him, saying to him, "O man of little faith, why did you doubt?"

Here again we can see Jesus' desire to have people cooperate with him.

14:22–23. It has been a very full day, like so many others. First Jesus works many cures (14:14) and then performs the remarkable miracle of the multiplication of the loaves and the fish, a symbol of the future Eucharist. The crowds who have been following him were avid for food, teaching and consolation. Jesus "had compassion on them" (14:14), curing their sick and giving them the comfort of his teaching and the nourishment of food. He continues to do the same, down the centuries, tending to our needs and comforting us with his word and with the nourishment of his own body. Jesus must have been very moved, realizing the vivifying effect the Blessed Sacrament would have on the lives of Christians—a sacrament which is a mystery of life and faith and love. It is understandable that he should feel the need to spend some hours in private to

speak to his Father. Jesus' private prayer, in an interlude between one demanding activity and another, teaches us that every Christian needs to take time out for recollection, to speak to his Father, God. On Jesus' frequent personal prayer see, for example, Mk 1:35; 6:47; Lk 5:16; 6:12. See the notes on Mt 6:5–6 and Mt 7:7–11.

14:24–33. This remarkable episode of Jesus walking on the sea must have made a deep impression on the apostles. It was one of their outstanding memories of the life they shared with the Master. It is reported not only by St Matthew, but also by St Mark (6:45–52), who would have heard about it from St Peter, and by St John (6:14–21).

Storms are very frequent on Lake Gennesaret; they cause huge waves and are very dangerous to fishing boats. During his prayer on the hill, Jesus is still mindful of his disciples; he sees them trying to cope with the wind and the

---

m. Other ancient authorities read *was out on the sea*   **n.** Other ancient authorities read *strong wind*

³²And when they got into the boat, the wind ceased. ³³And those in the boat worshipped him, saying, "Truly you are the Son of God."*

Cures in Gennesaret

³⁴And when they had crossed over, they came to land at Gennesaret. ³⁵And when the men of that place recognized him, they sent round to all that region and brought to him all that were sick, ³⁶and besought him that they might only touch the fringe of his garment; and as many as touched it were made well.

Lk 6:19

The tradition of the elders. True cleanness

15 ¹Then Pharisees and scribes came to Jesus from Jerusalem and said, ²"Why do your disciples transgress the tradition of the elders? For they do not wash their hands when they eat." ³He answered them, "And why do you transgress the commandment of God for the sake of your tradition? ⁴For God commanded,

Mk 7:1–23
Deut 4:2
Lk 11:38

---

waves and comes to their rescue once he has finished praying. This episode has applications to Christian life. The Church, like the apostles' boat, also gets into difficulties, and Jesus who watches over his Church comes to its rescue also, after allowing it wrestle with obstacles and be strengthened in the process. He gives us encouragement: "Take heart, it is I; have no fear" (14:27); and we show our faith and fidelity by striving to keep an even keel, and by calling on his aid when we feel ourselves weakening: "Lord, save me" (14:30), words of St Peter which every soul uses when he has recourse to Jesus, his Saviour. Then our Lord does save us, and we urgently confess our faith: "Truly you are the Son of God" (14:33).

14:29–31. St John Chrysostom (*Hom. on St Matthew*, 50) comments that in this episode Jesus taught Peter to realize, from his own experience, that all his strength came from our Lord and that he could not rely on his own resources, on his own weakness and wretchedness.

Chrysostom goes as far as to say that "if we fail to play our part, God ceases to help us." Hence the reproach, "O man of little faith" (14:31). When Peter began to be afraid and to doubt, he started to sink, until again, full of faith, he called out, "Lord, save me." If at any time we, like Peter, should begin to weaken, we too should try to bring our faith into play and call on Jesus to save us.

14:34–36. Learning from the faith of these people on the shore of Lake Gennesaret, every Christian should approach the adorable humanity of the Saviour. Christ—God and Man—is accessible to us in the sacrament of the Eucharist. "When you approach the tabernacle remember that *he* has been awaiting you for twenty centuries" (St Josemaría Escrivá, *The Way*, 537).

15:3–4. "For God commanded": it is interesting to note the respect and formality with which Jesus refers to the commandments of the Law of God given through Moses—in this case, the fourth

Ex 20:12;
21:17
Deut 5:16

Is 29:13

1 Tim 4:4

Jn 15:2

Lk 6:39
Jn 9:40
Rom 2:19

'Honour your father and your mother,' and, 'He who speaks evil of father or mother, let him surely die.' [5]But you say, 'If any one tells his father or his mother, What you would have gained from me is given to God,[o] he need not honour his father.'* [6]So, for the sake of your tradition, you have made void the word[p] of God. [7]You hypocrites! Well did Isaiah prophesy of you, when he said:

[8] 'This people honours me with their lips,
    but their heart is far from me;
[9]in vain do they worship me,
    teaching as doctrines the precepts of men.' "

[10]And he called the people to him and said to them, "Hear and understand: [11]not what goes into the mouth defiles a man, but what comes out of the mouth, this defiles a man." [12]Then the disciples came and said to him, "Do you know that the Pharisees were offended when they heard this saying?" [13]He answered, "Every plant which my heavenly Father has not planted will be rooted up. [14]Let them alone; they are blind guides. And if a blind

---

commandment (cf. Ex 20:12; 21:17). Following its divine Master, the Church sees the ten commandments summing up all human and Christian morality, as the divine-positive formulation of basic natural law. Each and every one of the ten commandments of the Law of God should be lovingly kept, even if this calls for heroism.

15:5–6. Over the years teachers of the Law (scribes) and priests of the temple had distorted the true meaning of the fourth commandment. In Jesus' time, they were saying that people who contributed to the temple in cash or in kind were absolved from supporting their parents: it would be sacrilegious for parents to lay claim to this *corban* (offerings for the altar). People educated in this kind of thinking felt that they were keeping the fourth commandment—in fact, fulfilling it in the best way possible—and they were praised for their piety by the religious leaders of the

nation. But what in fact it meant was that, under the cloak of piety, they were leaving elderly parents to fend for themselves. Jesus, who is Messiah and God, is the one who can correctly interpret the Law. Here he explains the proper scope of the fourth commandment, exposing the error of Jewish practice at the time.

For Christians, therefore, the fourth commandment includes affectionate help of parents if they are old or needy, even if one has other family, social or religious obligations to attend to. Children should check regularly on whether they are looking after their parents properly.

15:6–9. Jewish man-made tradition was forever adding extra little precepts or interpretations onto the Law of God; by Jesus' time these constituted almost another law. This tradition was so incredibly detailed (and sometimes quite ridiculous) that it tended to suffocate the spirit of the Law of God instead of helping a

o. Or *an offering*   **p.** Other ancient authorities read *law*

man leads a blind man, both will fall into a pit." [15]But Peter said to him, "Explain the parable to us." [16]And he said, "Are you also still without understanding? [17]Do you not see that whatever goes into the mouth passes into the stomach, and so passes on?[q] [18]But what comes out of the mouth proceeds from the heart, and this defiles a man. [19]For out of the heart come evil thoughts, murder, adultery, fornication, theft, false witness, slander. [20]These are what defile a man; but to eat with unwashed hands does not defile a man."

Gen 8:21

The Canaanite woman
[21]And Jesus went away from there and withdrew to the district of Tyre and Sidon. [22]And behold, a Canaanite woman from that region came out and cried, "Have mercy on me, O Lord, Son of David; my daughter is severely possessed by a demon." [23]But he did not answer her a word. And his disciples came and begged

Mk 7:24–30

person fulfil that Law. This is what our Lord is referring to here so bluntly. God himself, through Moses, sought to protect his Law by ordering that nothing be added to or taken from what he had commanded (cf. Deut 4:2).

15:10–20. Our Lord proclaims the true meaning of moral precepts and makes it clear that man has to answer to God for his actions. The scribes' mistake consisted in concentrating on externals and not giving pride of place to interior purity of heart. For example, they saw prayer in terms of exact recital of fixed forms of words rather than as a raising of the soul to God (cf. Mt 6:5–6). The same thing happened in the case of dietary regulations.

Jesus avails himself of the particular cases dealt with in this passage to teach us where to find the true centre of moral action: it lies in man's personal decision, good or evil, a decision that is shaped in his heart and then expressed in the form of action. For example, the

sins which our Lord lists are sins committed in the human heart prior to being acted out. In the Sermon on the Mount he already said this: "Every one who looks at a woman lustfully has already committed adultery with her in his heart" (Mt 5:28).

15:21–22. Tyre and Sidon were Phoenician cities on the Mediterranean coast, in present-day Lebanon. They were never part of Galilee but they were near its northwestern border. In Jesus' time they were outside the territory of Herod Antipas (see the note on Mt 2:1). Jesus withdrew to this area to escape persecution from Herod and from the Jewish authorities and to concentrate on training his apostles.

Most of the inhabitants of the district of Tyre and Sidon were pagans. St Matthew calls this woman a "Canaanite"; according to Genesis (10:15), this district was one of the first to be settled by the Canaanites; St Mark describes the woman as a "Syrophoenician" (Mk 7:26).

q. Or *is evacuated*

him, saying, "Send her away, for she is crying after us." [24]He answered, "I was sent only to the lost sheep of the house of Israel."* [25]But she came and knelt before him, saying, "Lord, help me." [26]And he answered, "It is not fair to take the children's bread and throw it to the dogs." [27]She said, "Yes, Lord, yet even the dogs eat the crumbs that fall from their master's table." [28]Then Jesus answered her, "O woman, great is your faith! Be it done for you as you desire." And her daughter was healed instantly.

Curing of many sick people

Mk 7:31
Mk 3:10

[29]And Jesus went on from there and passed along the Sea of Galilee. And he went up into the hills, and sat down there. [30]And great crowds came to him, bringing with them the lame, the maimed, the blind, the dumb, and many others, and they put

Mk 7:37

them at his feet, and he healed them, [31]so that the throng wondered, when they saw the dumb speaking, the maimed whole, the lame walking, and the blind seeing; and they glorified the God of Israel.

Both Gospels point out that she is a pagan, which means that her faith in our Lord is more remarkable; the same applies in the case of the centurion (Mt 8:5–13).

The Canaanite woman's prayer is quite perfect: she recognizes Jesus as the Messiah (the Son of David)—which contrasts with the unbelief of the Jews; she expresses her need in clear, simple words; she persists, undismayed by obstacles; and she expresses her request in all humility: "Have mercy on me." Our prayer should have the same qualities of faith, trust, perseverance and humility.

15:24. What Jesus says here does not take from the universal reference of his teaching (cf. Mt 28:19–20; Mk 16:15–16). Our Lord came to bring his Gospel to the whole world, but he himself addressed only the Jews; later on he will charge his apostles to preach the Gospel to pagans. St Paul, in his missionary journeys, also adopted the policy of

preaching in the first instance to the Jews (Acts 13:46).

15:25–28. This dialogue between Jesus and the woman is especially beautiful. By appearing to be harsh he so strengthens the woman's faith that she deserves exceptional praise: "Great is your faith!" Our own conversation with Christ should be like that: "Persevere in prayer. Persevere, even when your efforts seem barren. Prayer is always fruitful" (St Josemaría Escrivá, *The Way*, 101).

15:29–31. Here St Matthew summarizes Jesus' activity in this border area where Jews and pagans were living side by side. As usual he teaches and heals the sick; the Gospel account clearly echoes the prophecy of Isaiah which Christ himself used to prove that he was the Messiah (Lk 7:22): "the eyes of the blind shall be opened, and the ears of the deaf unstopped ..." (Is 35:5). "They glorified the God of Israel": this clearly refers to the Gentiles, who thought that

Second miracle of the loaves and fish

[32]Then Jesus called his disciples to him and said, "I have compas-   Mk 8:1–10
sion on the crowd, because they have been with me now three
days, and have nothing to eat; and I am unwilling to send them
away hungry, lest they faint on the way." [33]And the disciples said
to him, "Where are we to get bread enough in the desert to feed so
great a crowd?" [34]And Jesus said to them, "How many loaves
have you?" They said, "Seven, and a few small fish." [35]And com-
manding the crowd to sit down on the ground, [36]he took the seven
loaves and the fish, and having given thanks he broke them and
gave them to the disciples, and the disciples gave them to the
crowds. [37]And they all ate and were satisfied; and they took up
seven baskets full of the broken pieces left over. [38]Those who ate
were four thousand men, besides women and children. [39]And
sending away the crowds, he got into the boat and went to the
region of Magadan.

God could give the power to work miracles to Jews only. Once again the
Gentiles are seen to have more faith than
the Jews.

15:32. The Gospels speak of our
Lord's mercy and compassion towards
people's needs: here he is concerned
about the crowds who are following
him and who have no food. He always
has a word of consolation, encouragement and forgiveness: he is never indif-
ferent. However, what hurts him most
are sinners who go through life without
experiencing light and truth: he waits
for them in the sacraments of Baptism
and Penance.

15:33–38. As in the case of the first multiplication (14:13–20), the apostles provide our Lord with the loaves and the
fish. It was all they had. He also avails of
the apostles to distribute the food—the
result of the miracle—to the people. In
distributing the graces of salvation God
chooses to rely on the faithfulness and
generosity of men. "Many great things
depend—don't forget it—on whether you

and I live our lives as God wants" (St
Josemaría Escrivá, *The Way*, 755).

It is interesting to note that in both
miracles of multiplication of loaves and
fish Jesus provides food in abundance but
does not allow anything to go to waste.
All Jesus' miracles, in addition to being
concrete historical events, are also symbols of supernatural realities. Here abundance of material food also signifies
abundance of divine gifts on the level of
grace and glory: it refers to spiritual
resources and eternal rewards; God gives
people more graces than are strictly necessary. This is borne out by Christian
experience throughout history. St Paul
tells us that "where sin increased, grace
abounded all the more" (Rom 5:20); he
speaks of "the riches of his grace which
he lavished upon us" (Eph 1:8) and tells
his disciple Timothy that "the grace of our
Lord overflowed for me with the faith and
love that are in Christ Jesus" (1 Tim 1:14).

15:39. St Mark calls Magadan Dalmanu-
tha (8:10). These are the only references
to this place; we do not know its exact
location.

The Pharisees and Sadducees try to test Jesus

Mk 8:11–21
Mt 12:38
Lk 12:54–56

16 [1]And the Pharisees and Sadducees came, and to test him they asked him to show them a sign from heaven. [2]He answered them,[r] "When it is evening, you say, 'It will be fair weather; for the sky is red.' [3]And in the morning, 'It will be stormy today, for the sky is red and threatening.' You know how to interpret the appearance of the sky, but you cannot interpret the signs of the times. [4]An evil and adulterous generation seeks for a sign, but no sign shall be given to it except the sign of Jonah." So he left them and departed.

Jn 2:1
Mt 12:39f

[5]When the disciples reached the other side, they had forgotten to bring any bread. [6]Jesus said to them, "Take heed and beware of the leaven of the Pharisees and Sadducees." [7]And they discussed it among themselves, saying, "We brought no bread." [8]But Jesus, aware of this, said, "O men of little faith, why do you discuss among yourselves the fact that you have no bread? [9]Do you not yet perceive? Do you not remember the five loaves of the five thousand, and how many baskets you gathered? [10]Or the seven loaves of the four thousand, and how many baskets you gathered? [11]How is it that you fail to perceive that I did not speak about

Lk 12:1

16:1–4. On Jesus' reply to the Pharisees and the meaning of the sign of Jonah, see the note on Mt 12:39–40.

16:3. "The signs of the times": Jesus uses man's ability to forecast the weather to speak about the signs of the advent of the Messiah.

He reproaches the Pharisees for not recognizing that the messianic times have in fact arrived: "For the Lord Jesus inaugurated his Church by preaching the Good News, that is, the coming of the Kingdom of God, promised over the ages in the Scriptures: 'The time is fulfilled, and the kingdom of God is at hand' (Mk 1:15; cf. Mt 4:17). This Kingdom shone out before men in the world, in the works and in the presence of Christ. The word of the Lord is compared to a seed that is sown in a field (Mk 4:14); those who hear it with faith and are numbered

among the little flock of Christ (Lk 12:32) have truly received the Kingdom. Then, by its own power the seed sprouts and grows until the harvest (cf. Mk 4:26–29). The miracles of Jesus also demonstrate that the Kingdom has already come on earth: 'If it be by the finger of God that I cast out demons, then the kingdom of God has come upon you' (Lk 11:20; cf. Mt 12:28). But principally the Kingdom is revealed in the person of Christ himself, Son of God and Son of man, who came 'to serve, and to give his life as a ransom for many' (Mk 10:45)" (Vatican II, *Lumen gentium*, 5).

16:13–20. In this passage St Peter is promised primacy over the whole Church, a primacy which Jesus will confer on him after his resurrection, as we learn in the Gospel of St John (cf. Jn 21:15–18). This supreme authority is given to Peter for

---

r. Other ancient authorities omit the following words to the end of verse 3

bread? Beware of the leaven of the Pharisees and Sadducees." [12]Then they understood that he did not tell them to beware of the leaven of bread, but of the teaching of the Pharisees and Sadducees.

Jn 6:27

Peter's profession of faith and his primacy

[13]Now when Jesus came into the district of Caesarea Philippi, he asked his disciples, "Who do men say that the Son of man is?" [14]And they said, "Some say John the Baptist, others say Elijah, and others Jeremiah or one of the prophets."* [15]He said to them, "But who do you say that I am?" [16]Simon Peter replied, "You are the Christ, the Son of the living God."* [17]And Jesus answered him, "Blessed are you, Simon Bar-Jona! For flesh and blood has not revealed this to you, but my Father who is in heaven. [18]And I tell you, you are Peter,[s] and on this rock[t] I will build my church, and the powers of death[u] shall not prevail against it.* [19]I will give you the keys of the kingdom of heaven,* and whatever you bind on earth shall be bound in heaven, and whatever you loose on earth shall be loosed in heaven." [20]Then he strictly charged the disciples to tell no one that he was the Christ.

Mk 8:27–30
Lk 9:18–21

Jn 6:69
Gal 1:15f
Mt 17:4–5
Jn 1:42
Eph 2:20
Job 38:17
Is 38:10
Ps 9:13;
107:18
Wis 16:30
Mt 18:18
Rev 1:18

---

the benefit of the Church. Because the Church has to last until the end of time, this authority will be passed on to Peter's successors down through history. The Bishop of Rome, the Pope, is the successor of Peter.

The solemn Magisterium of the Church, in the First Vatican Council, defined the doctrine of the primacy of Peter and his successors in these terms:

"We teach and declare, therefore, according to the testimony of the Gospel that the primacy of jurisdiction over the whole Church was immediately and directly promised to and conferred upon the blessed apostle Peter by Christ the Lord. For to Simon, Christ had said, 'You shall be called Cephas' (Jn 1:42). Then, after Simon had acknowledged Christ with the confession, 'You are the Christ, the Son of the living God' (Mt 16:16), it was to Simon alone that the solemn

words were spoken by the Lord: 'Blessed are you, Simon Bar-Jona. For flesh and blood has not revealed this to you, but my Father who is in heaven. And I tell you, you are Peter, and on this rock I will build my church, and the powers of hell shall not prevail against it. I will give you the keys of the kingdom of heaven, and whatever you bind on earth shall be bound in heaven, and what you loose on earth shall be loosed in heaven' (Mt 16:17–19). And after his resurrection, Jesus conferred upon Simon Peter alone the jurisdiction of supreme shepherd and ruler over all his fold with the words, 'Feed my lambs…. Feed my sheep' (Jn 21:15–17) […].

"(Canon) Therefore, if anyone says that the blessed apostle Peter was not constituted by Christ the Lord as the Prince of all the apostles and the visible head of the whole Church militant, or that he received

s. Greek *Petros* t. Greek *petra* u. Greek *the gates of Hades*

119

PART TWO

Jesus' ministry on the way to Jerusalem

8. TOWARDS JUDEA AND JERUSALEM

Jesus foretells his passion and resurrection. The law of Christian renunciation

Mk 8:31–9:1
Lk 9:22–27
Mt 12:40
Jn 2:19

[21]From that time Jesus began to show his disciples that he must go to Jerusalem and suffer many things from the elders and chief

immediately and directly from Jesus Christ our Lord only a primacy of honour and not a true and proper primacy of jurisdiction: let him be condemned.

"Now, what Christ the Lord, supreme shepherd and watchful guardian of the flock, established in the person of the blessed apostle Peter for the perpetual safety and everlasting good of the Church must, by the will of the same, endure without interruption in the Church which was founded on the rock and which will remain firm until the end of the world. Indeed, 'no one doubts, in fact it is obvious to all ages, that the holy and most blessed Peter, Prince and head of the apostles, the pillar of faith, and the foundation of the Catholic Church, received the keys of the kingdom from our Lord Jesus Christ, the Saviour and the Redeemer of the human race; and even to this time and forever he lives', and governs, 'and exercises judgment in his successors' (cf. Council of Ephesus), the bishops of the holy Roman See, which he established and consecrated with his blood. Therefore, whoever succeeds Peter in this Chair holds Peter's primacy over the whole Church according to the plan of Christ himself [...]. For this reason, 'because of its greater sovereignty', it was always 'necessary for every church, that is, the faithful who are

everywhere, to be in agreement' with the same Roman Church [...].

"(Canon) Therefore, if anyone says that it is not according to the institution of Christ our Lord himself, that is, by divine law, that St Peter has perpetual successors in the primacy over the whole Church; or if anyone says that the Roman Pontiff is not the successor of St Peter in the same primacy: let him be condemned [...].

"We think it extremely necessary to assert solemnly the prerogative which the only-begotten Son of God deigned to join to the highest pastoral office. And so, faithfully keeping to the tradition received from the beginning of the Christian faith, for the glory of God our Saviour, for the exaltation of the Catholic religion, and for the salvation of Christian peoples, We, with the approval of the sacred council, teach and define that it is a divinely revealed dogma: that the Roman Pontiff, when he speaks *ex cathedra*, that is, when, acting in the office of shepherd and teacher of all Christians, he defines, by virtue of his supreme apostolic authority, doctrine concerning faith or morals to be held by the universal Church, possesses through the divine assistance promised to him in the person of St Peter, the infallibility with which the divine Redeemer willed his Church to be endowed in defining doctrine concerning faith or morals;

priests and scribes, and be killed, and on the third day be raised. ²²And Peter took him and began to rebuke him, saying, "God forbid, Lord! This shall never happen to you." ²³But he turned and said to Peter, "Get behind me, Satan! You are a hindrance^v to me; for you are not on the side of God, but of men."

²⁴Then Jesus told his disciples, "If any man would come after me, let him deny himself and take up his cross and follow me. ²⁵For whoever would save his life will lose it, and whoever loses his life* for my sake will find it. ²⁶For what will it profit a man, if

Is 8:14

Jn 5:29
Rom 2:6

---

and that such definitions of the Roman Pontiff are therefore irreformable because of their nature, but not because of the agreement of the Church.

"(Canon) But if anyone presumes to contradict this our definition (God forbid that he do so): let him be condemned" (Vatican I, *Pastor aeternus*, chaps. 1, 2 and 4).

16:23. Jesus rejects St Peter's well-intentioned protestations, giving us to understand the capital importance of accepting the cross if we are to attain salvation (cf. 1 Cor 1:23–25). Shortly before this (Mt 16:17) Jesus had promised Peter: "Blessed are you, Simon"; now he reproves him: "Get behind me, Satan." In the former case Peter's words were inspired by the Holy Spirit, whereas what he says now comes from his own spirit, which he has not yet sloughed off.

16:24. "Divine love, 'poured into our hearts by the Holy Spirit who has been given to us' (Rom 5:5), enables lay people to express concretely in their lives the spirit of the Beatitudes. Following Jesus in his poverty, they feel no depression in want, no pride in plenty; imitating the humble Christ, they are not greedy for vain show (cf. Gal 5:26). They strive to please God rather than men, always ready to abandon everything for Christ (cf. Lk 14:26)

and even to endure persecution in the cause of right (cf. Mt 5:10), having in mind the Lord's saying: 'If any man wants to come after me, let him deny himself and take up his cross and follow me' (Mt 16:24)" (Vatican II, *Apostolicam actuositatem*, 4).

16:25. A Christian cannot ignore these words of Jesus. He has to risk, to gamble, this present life in order to attain eternal life: "How little a life is to offer to God!" (St Josemaría Escrivá, *The Way*, 420).

Our Lord's requirement means that we must renounce our own will in order to identify with the will of God; and so to ensure that, as St John of the Cross comments, we do not follow the way of those many people who "would have God will that which they themselves will, and are fretful at having to will that which he wills, and find it repugnant to accommodate their will to that of God. Hence it happens to them that oftentimes they think that that wherein they find not their own will and pleasure is not the will of God; and that, on the other hand, when they themselves find satisfaction, God is satisfied. Thus they measure God by themselves and not themselves by God" (*Dark Night of the Soul*, book 1, chap. 7, 3).

16:26–27. Christ's words are crystal-clear: every person has to bear in mind

v. Greek *stumbling block*

Ps 62:12
Prov 24:12

he gains the whole world and forfeits his life? Or what shall a man give in return for his life? [27]For the Son of man is to come with his angels in the glory of his Father, and then he will repay every man for what he has done. [28]Truly, I say to you, there are some standing here who will not taste death before they see the Son of man coming in his kingdom."

The Transfiguration

Mk 9:2–13
Lk 5:28–36

2 Pet 1:16–18

17 [1]And after six days Jesus took with him Peter and James and John his brother, and led them up a high mountain apart. [2]And he was transfigured before them, and his face shone like the sun, and his garments became white as light. [3]And behold, there appeared to them Moses and Elijah, talking with him. [4]And

---

the Last Judgment. Salvation, in other words, is something radically personal: "he will repay every man for what he has done" (v. 27).

Man's goal does not consist in accumulating worldly goods; these are only means to an end; man's last end, his ultimate goal, is God himself; he possesses God in advance, as it were, here on earth by means of grace, and possesses him fully and for ever in heaven. Jesus shows the route to take to reach this destination—denying oneself (that is, saying no to ease, comfort, selfishness and attachment to temporal goods) and taking up the cross. For no earthly—impermanent—good can compare with the soul's eternal salvation. As St Thomas expresses it with theological precision, "the least good of grace is superior to the natural good of the entire universe" (*Summa theologiae*, 1–2, 113, 9).

16:28. Here Jesus is referring not to his last coming (which he speaks about in the preceding verse) but to other events which will occur prior to that and which will be a sign of his glorification after death. The coming he speaks of here may refer firstly to his resurrection and his appearances thereafter; it could also refer

to his transfiguration, which is itself a manifestation of his glory. This coming of Christ in his Kingdom might also be seen in the destruction of Jerusalem—a sign of the end of the ancient people of Israel as a form of the Kingdom of God and its substitution by the Church, the new Kingdom.

17:1–13. Realizing that his death will demoralize his disciples, Jesus forewarns them and strengthens their faith. Not content with telling them in advance about his death and resurrection on the third day, he wants two of the three future pillars of the Church (cf. Gal 2:9) to see his transfiguration and thereby glimpse the glory and majesty with which his holy human nature will be endowed in heaven.

The Father's testimony (v. 5), expressed in the same words as he used at Christ's baptism (cf. Mt 3:17), reveals to the three apostles that Jesus Christ is the Son of God, the beloved Son, God himself. To these words—also spoken at Christ's baptism—he adds, "Listen to him", as if to indicate that Jesus is also the supreme prophet foretold by Moses (cf. Deut 18:15–18).

Peter said to Jesus, "Lord, it is well that we are here; if you wish, I will make three booths here, one for you and one for Moses and one for Elijah."* ⁵He was still speaking, when lo, a bright cloud overshadowed them, and a voice from the cloud said, "This is my beloved Son,ʷ with whom I am well pleased; listen to him." ⁶When the disciples heard this, they fell on their faces, and were filled with awe. ⁷But Jesus came and touched them, saying, "Rise, and have no fear." ⁸And when they lifted up their eyes, they saw no one but Jesus only.

⁹And as they were coming down the mountain, Jesus commanded them, "Tell no one the vision, until the Son of man is raised from the dead." ¹⁰And the disciples asked him, "Then why do the scribes say that first Elijah must come?" ¹¹He replied, "Elijah does come, and he is to restore all things; ¹²but I tell you

Deut 18:15

Mal 3:23f

Lk 23:25

17:3. Moses and Elijah are the two most prominent representatives of the Old Testament—the Law and the Prophets. The fact that Christ occupies the central position points up his pre-eminence over them, and the superiority of the New Testament over the Old.

This dazzling glimpse of divine glory is enough to send the apostles into a rapture; so happy are they that Peter cannot contain his desire to prolong this experience.

17:5. In Christ God speaks to all men; through the Church his voice resounds in all ages: "The Church does not cease to listen to his words. She rereads them continually. With the greatest devotion she reconstructs every detail of his life. These words are listened to also by non-Christians. The life of Christ speaks, also, to many who are not capable of repeating with Peter, 'You are the Christ, the Son of the living God' (Mt 16:16). He, the Son of the living God, speaks to people also as Man: it is his life that speaks, his humanity, his fidelity to the truth, his all-embracing love. Furthermore, his death on the Cross speaks—

that is to say the inscrutable depth of his suffering and abandonment. The Church never ceases to relive his death on the Cross and his resurrection, which constitute the content of the Church's daily life [...]. The Church lives his mystery, draws unwearyingly from it and continually seeks ways of bringing this mystery of her Master and Lord to humanity—to the peoples, the nations, the succeeding generations, and every individual human being" (John Paul II, *Redemptor hominis*, 7).

17:10–13. Malachi 4:5 (3:23 in the Hebrew) speaks of the coming of Elijah the prophet before "the great and terrible day of the Lord", the Judgment Day. When Jesus says that Elijah has already come, he is referring to St John the Baptist, whose mission it was to prepare the way for the first coming of the Lord, the same as Elijah will have to do prior to his last coming. The scribes failed to grasp the meaning of the prophecy of Malachi; they thought it referred simply to the coming of the Messiah, the first coming of Christ.

w. Or *my Son, my* (or *the*) *Beloved*

Lk 1:17

that Elijah has already come, and they did not know him, but did to him whatever they pleased. So also the Son of man will suffer at their hands." [13]Then the disciples understood that he was speaking to them of John the Baptist.

Curing of an epileptic boy

Mk 9:14–29
Lk 9:37–42

[14]And when they came to the crowd, a man came up to him and kneeling before him said, [15]"Lord, have mercy on my son, for he is an epileptic and he suffers terribly; for often he falls into the fire, and often into the water. [16]And I brought him to your disciples, and

Deut 32:5
Jn 14:9

they could not heal him." [17]And Jesus answered, "O faithless and perverse generation, how long am I to be with you? How long am I to bear with you? Bring him here to me." [18]And Jesus rebuked him, and the demon came out of him, and the boy was cured instantly. [19]Then the disciples came to Jesus privately and said, "Why could

Lk 17:16
Mk 11:23

we not cast it out?" [20]He said to them, "Because of your little faith. For truly, I say to you, if you have faith as a grain of mustard seed, you will say to this mountain, 'Move hence to yonder place,' and it will move; and nothing will be impossible to you."[x]

Second announcement of the Passion. The temple tax

Mk 9:30–32
Lk 9:43–45
Mt 16:21

[22]As they were gathering[y] in Galilee, Jesus said to them. "The Son of man is to be delivered into the hands of men, [23]and they will

---

17:14–21. This episode of the curing of the boy shows both Christ's omnipotence and the power of prayer full of faith. Because of his deep union with Christ, a Christian shares, through faith, in God's own omnipotence, to such an extent that Jesus actually says on another occasion, "he who believes in me will also do the works that I do; and greater works than these will he do, because I go to the Father" (Jn 14:12).

Our Lord tells the apostles that if they had faith they would be able to work miracles, to move mountains. "Moving mountains" was probably a proverbial saying. God would certainly let a believer move a mountain if that were necessary for his glory and for the edification of one's neighbour; however, Christ's promise is fulfilled every day in a much more exalted way. Some Fathers of the Church (St Jerome, St Augustine) say that "a mountain is moved" every time someone is divinely aided to do something which exceeds man's natural powers. This clearly happens in the work of our sanctification, which the Paraclete effects in our souls when we are docile to him and receive with faith and love the grace given us in the sacraments: we benefit from the sacraments to a greater or lesser degree depending on the dispositions with which we receive them. Sanctification is something much more sublime than moving mountains, and it is something which is happening every day in so many holy souls, even though most people do not notice it.

---

x. Other ancient authorities insert verse 21, *But this kind never comes out except by prayer and fasting*
y. Other ancient authorities read *abode*

kill him, and he will be raised on the third day." And they were greatly distressed.

²⁴When they came to Capernaum, the collectors of the half-shekel tax went up to Peter and said, "Does not your teacher pay the tax?" ²⁵He said, "Yes." And when he came home, Jesus spoke to him first, saying, "What do you think, Simon? From whom do kings of the earth take toll or tribute? From their sons or from others?" ²⁶And when he said, "From others," Jesus said to him, "Then the sons are free. ²⁷However, not to give offence to them, go to the sea and cast a hook, and take the first fish that comes up, and when you open its mouth you will find a shekel; take that and give it to them for me and for yourself."

Ex 30:13

9. THE DISCOURSE ON THE CHURCH

The "little ones" and the Kingdom. On leading others astray. The lost sheep

18 ¹At that time, the disciples came to Jesus, saying, "Who is the greatest in the kingdom of heaven?" ²And calling to

Mk 9:33–47
Lk 9:46–48

The apostles and many saints down the centuries have in fact worked amazing material miracles; but the greatest and most important miracles were, are and will be the miracles of souls dead through sin and ignorance being reborn and developing in the new life of the children of God.

17:20. Here and in the parable of Matthew 13:31–32 the main force of the comparison lies in the fact that a very small seed—the mustard seed—produces a large shrub up to three metres (ten feet) high: even a very small act of genuine faith can produce surprising results.

17:21. See the RSV note and Mk 9:29.

17:24–27. "Half-shekel", or *didrachma*: a coin equal in value to the annual contribution every Jew had to make for the upkeep of the temple—a day's wage of a labourer. The shekel or stater which our Lord refers to in v. 27 was a Greek coin

worth two didrachmas. Jesus uses things great and small to get his teaching across to his disciples. Peter, who is to be the rock on which he will found his Church (Mt 16:18–19), he prepares by letting him see his dramatic transfiguration (17:1–8); now he gives Peter another inkling of his divinity through an apparently unimportant miracle. We should take note of Jesus' teaching method: after his second announcement of his passion, his disciples are downhearted (Mt 17:22–23); here he lifts Peter's spirits with this friendly little miracle.

17:26. This shows how conscientiously our Lord fulfilled his civic duties. Although the half-shekel tax had to do with religion, given the theocratic structure of Israel at the time payment of this tax also constituted a civic obligation.

18:1–35. The teachings of Jesus recorded in chapter 18 of St Matthew are often

Jn 3:3–5   him a child, he put him in the midst of them, ³and said, "Truly, I say to you, unless you turn and become like children, you will never enter the kingdom of heaven. ⁴Whoever humbles himself like this child, he is the greatest in the kingdom of heaven.

called the "discourse on the Church" or "ecclesiastical discourse" because they are a series of instructions on the way in which his Church is to be administered.

The first passage (Mt 18:1–5), addressed to leaders, that is, the future hierarchy of the Church, warns them against natural tendencies to pride and ambition: even though they have positions of government, they must act with humility. In verses 6–10 Jesus emphasizes the fatherly care that pastors of the Church should have for the "little ones"—a term which covers everyone in need of special care for whatever reason (because they are recent converts, or are not well grounded in Church teaching, or are not yet adults, etc.). He makes a special point of warning them about the harm that scandal—leading others to commit sin—can do: Christians' fraternal charity requires that all, and particularly pastors, should avoid doing anything— even anything that in itself is quite legitimate—which could endanger the spiritual health of those who are less robust: God takes special care of the weak and will punish those who harm them.

Our Lord shows similar concern for those who are experiencing spiritual difficulties. Every effort, even an heroic effort, must be made to seek out the "lost sheep" (vv. 12–14). If the Church in general and each Christian in particular should be concerned to spread the Gospel, all the more reason for them to try and see that those who have already embraced the faith do not go astray.

The following passage (vv. 15–18) on fraternal correction has special doctrinal relevance: here Jesus uses the term "the Church" in the sense of a social structure, an actual community, visible and compact, directly dependent on him and his twelve apostles and their successors, who have an all-embracing "power of the keys", a spiritual authority that God himself backs up. Among their powers is that of forgiving or retaining sins, of receiving people into the Church or cutting them off from communion with the Church—a remarkable divine power given by Jesus to the hierarchy and protected by a special kind of divine providence in the form of Jesus' continuous presence in the Church and the Holy Spirit's support of its hierarchical Magisterium.

This is followed by a passage (vv. 19–20) in which Jesus promises to be present whenever a number of Christians come together to pray (v. 20), and teaches the need to forgive any offences committed by one brother against another (vv. 21–22). The chapter ends with the parable of the unforgiving debtor (vv. 23–35), in which our Lord shows what forgiveness involves.

Thus, the whole of chapter 18, the "discourse on the Church", is a survey of the future history of the Church during its earthly stage, and a series of practical rules of conduct for Christians—a kind of complement to the Sermon on the Mount (chaps. 5–7), which is a "magna charta" for the new Kingdom established by Christ.

18:1–6. Clearly the disciples still suffer from human ambition: they want to occupy key positions when Jesus comes to establish his Kingdom on earth (cf. Acts 1:6). To correct their pride, our Lord

5"Whoever receives one such child in my name receives me; Jn 13:20
6but whoever causes one of these little ones who believe in me to Lk 17:1f
sin,ᶻ it would be better for him to have a great millstone fastened
round his neck and to be drowned in the depth of the sea.

---

shows them a child and tells them that if they want to enter the Kingdom of heaven, they must decide to be like children: children are incapable of hating anyone and are totally innocent of vice, particularly of pride, the worst vice of all. They are simple and full of trust.

Humility is one of the main pillars of the Christian life. "If you ask me", St Augustine says, "what is the essential thing in the religion and discipline of Jesus Christ, I shall reply: first humility, second humility and third humility" (*Letters*, 118).

18:3–4. Applying these words to our Lord's virtues, Fray Luis de Granada makes the point that humility is superior to virginity: "If you cannot imitate the virginity of the humble, then imitate the humility of the virgin. Virginity is praiseworthy, but humility is more necessary. The former is recommended to us, the latter is an obligation for us; to the former we are invited, to the latter we are obliged [...]. And so we see that the former is celebrated as a voluntary sacrifice, the latter required as an obligatory sacrifice. Lastly, you can be saved without virginity, but not without humility" (*Suma de la vida cristiana*, book 3, part 2, chap. 10).

18:5. Receiving a child in Jesus' name is the same as receiving Jesus himself. Because children reflect the innocence, purity, simplicity and tenderness of our Lord, "In children and in the sick a soul in love sees him" (St Josemaría Escrivá, *The Way*, 419).

18:6–7. The holy, pained indignation sounding in Jesus' words shows the seriousness of the sin of scandal, which is defined as "something said, done or omitted which leads another person to commit sin" (cf. St Pius X, *Catechism*, 417).

"Millstone": our Lord is referring to a form of punishment used in ancient times, which consisted in throwing a person into the sea with a heavy weight attached to his neck to prevent his body floating to the surface; this was regarded as a particularly ignominious form of death because it was inflicted only on the worst criminals and also because it meant deprival of burial.

Although Jesus affirms that people will cause others to sin, this does not mean that everyone, personally, should not ensure that this does not happen. Therefore, everyone who does cause another to sin is responsible for his action. Here he refers directly to scandal given to children—an action that is particularly malicious given the weakness and innocence of children. The evil of the world as enemy of the soul consists mainly in the harm it does in this way. Its evil maxims and bad example create an environment which draws people away from God, from Christ and from his Church.

The scandal given by those whose function it is to educate others is particularly serious. "If ordinary folk are lukewarm, that is bad; but it can be remedied, and the only one they harm is themselves; but if the teachers are lukewarm, then the Lord's 'Woe to the world'

---

z. Greek *causes ... to stumble*

[7]"Woe to the world for temptations to sin![a] For it is necessary that temptations come, but woe to the man by whom the temptation comes! [8]And if your hand or your foot causes you to sin,[z] cut it off and throw it from you; it is better for you to enter life maimed or lame than with two hands or two feet to be thrown into the eternal fire. [9]And if your eye causes you to sin,[z] pluck it out and throw it from you; it is better for you to enter life with one eye than with two eyes to be thrown into the hell[b]* of fire.

Heb 1:14

[10]"See that you do not despise one of these little ones; for I tell you that in heaven their angels always behold the face of my Father who is in heaven.[c] [12]What do you think? If a man has a hundred sheep, and one of them has gone astray, does he not leave the ninety-nine on the hills and go in search of the one that went

Lk 15:4–7

applies because of the great evil that results from this lukewarmness; this 'woe' threatens those lukewarm teachers who spread their lukewarmness to others and even suffocate their fervour completely" (St Augustine, *Sermons*, 55).

18:8–9. Entering life means entering the Kingdom of heaven. "The fire of hell": eternal punishment, merited by anyone who does not distance himself from what causes sin. Cf. the note on Mt 9:43.

18:8. Jesus is speaking figuratively. His teaching here can guide us in making moral decisions. If something or someone—however much we love them—is liable to cause us to commit sin, we have to stay away from them; it is as simple as that. "If thy right eye scandalize thee, pluck it out and cast it from thee! Your poor heart, that's what scandalizes you! Press it, squeeze it tight in your hands: give it no consolations. And when it asks for them, say to it slowly and with a noble compassion—in confidence, as it were: 'Heart, heart on the Cross, heart on the Cross!'" (St J. Escrivá, *The Way*, 163).

10. Jesus warns that giving scandal to little children is a very serious matter, for they have angels who guard them, who will plead a case before God against those who led them to commit sin.

In this context he speaks of children having guardian angels. However, everyone, adult or child, has a guardian angel. "By God's providence angels have been entrusted with the office of guarding the human race and of accompanying every human being so as to preserve him from any serious dangers [...]. Our heavenly Father has placed over each of us an angel under whose protection and vigilance we are" (St Pius V, *Catechism*, 4, 9, 4).

This means that we should have a trusting relationship with our guardian angel. "Have confidence in your guardian Angel. Treat him as a lifelong friend — that is what he is—and he will render you a thousand services in the ordinary affairs of each day" (*The Way*, 562).

18:11–14. This parable clearly shows our Lord's loving concern for sinners. It expresses in human terms the joy God feels when a wayward child comes back to him.

a. Greek *stumbling blocks* z. Greek *causes ... to stumble* b. Greek *Gehenna* c. Other ancient authorities add verse 11, *For the Son of man came to save the lost*

astray? [13]And if he finds it, truly, I say to you, he rejoices over it more than over the ninety-nine that never went astray. [14]So it is not the will of my[d] Father who is in heaven that one of these little ones should perish.

Fraternal correction. The apostles' authority

[15]"If your brother sins against you, go and tell him his fault, between you and him alone. If he listens to you, you have gained your brother. [16]But if he does not listen, take one or two others along with you, that every word may be confirmed by the evidence of two or three witnesses. [17]If he refuses to listen to them, tell it to the church; and if he refuses to listen even to the church, let him be to you as a Gentile and a tax collector. [18]Truly, I say to you, what-

Lev 19:17
Lk 17:3
Gal 6:1
Deut 19:15

1 Cor 5:13

Mt 16:19
Jn 20:23

Seeing so many souls living away from God, Pope John Paul II comments: "Unfortunately we witness the moral pollution which is devastating humanity, disregarding especially those very little ones about whom Jesus speaks.

"What must we do? We must imitate the Good Shepherd and give ourselves without rest for the salvation of souls. Without forgetting material charity and social justice, we must be convinced that the most sublime charity is spiritual charity, that is, the commitment for the salvation of souls. And souls are saved with prayer and sacrifice. This is the mission of the Church!" (Homily to the Poor Clares of Albano, 14 August 1979).

As the RSV points out, "other ancient authorities add verse 11, *For the Son of man came to save the lost*"—apparently taken from Lk 19:10.

18:15–17. Here our Lord calls on us to work with him for the sanctification of others by means of fraternal correction, which is one of the ways we can do so. He speaks as sternly about the sin of omission as he did about that of scandal (cf. Chrysostom, *Hom. on St Matthew*, 61).

There is an obligation on us to correct others. Our Lord identifies three stages in correction: 1) alone; 2) in the presence of one or two witnesses; and 3) before the Church. The first stage refers to causing scandal and to secret or private sins; here correction should be given privately, just to the person himself, to avoid unnecessarily publicizing a private matter and also to avoid hurting the person and to make it easier for him to mend his ways. If this correction does not have the desired effect, and the matter is a serious one, resort should be had to the second stage—looking for one or two friends, in case they have more influence on him. The last stage is formal judicial correction by reference to the Church authorities. If a sinner does not accept this correction, he should be excommunicated that is, separated from communion with the Church and sacraments.

18:18. This verse needs to be understood in connexion with the authority previously promised to Peter (cf. Mt 16:13–19): it is the hierarchy of the Church that exercises this power given by Christ to Peter, to the

d. Other ancient authorities read *your*

Mk 11:24

Jn 14:23

ever you bind on earth shall be bound in heaven, and whatever you loose on earth shall be loosed in heaven.* [19]Again I say to you, if two of you agree on earth about anything they ask, it shall be done for them by my Father in heaven. [20]For where two or three are gathered in my name, there am I in the midst of them."

Forgiveness of injuries. Parable of the unforgiving servant
[21]Then Peter came up and said to him, "Lord, how often shall my brother sin against me, and I forgive him? As many as seven times?" [22]Jesus said to him, "I do not say to you seven times, but seventy times seven.[e]

Lk 17:4

[23]"Therefore the kingdom of heaven may be compared to a king who wished to settle accounts with his servants. [24]When he began the reckoning, one was brought to him who owed him ten thousand talents;[f] [25]and as he could not pay, his lord ordered him to be sold, with his wife and children and all that he had, and payment to be made. [26]So the servant fell on his knees, imploring him, 'Lord, have patience with me, and I will pay you everything.' [27]And out of pity for him the lord of that servant released him and forgave him the debt. [28]But that same servant, as he went out, came upon one of his fellow servants who owed him a hundred denarii;[g] and seizing him by the throat he said, 'Pay what you

---

apostles and their lawful successors—the Pope and the bishops.

18:19–20. "Ubi caritas et amor, Deus ibi est: where charity and love resides, there God is", the Holy Thursday liturgy entones, drawing its inspiration from the sacred text of 1 Jn 4:12. For it is true that love is inconceivable if there is only one person: it implies the presence of two or more (cf. St Thomas Aquinas, *Comm. on St Matthew*, 18:19–20). And so it is that when Christians meet together in the name of Christ for the purpose of prayer, our Lord is present among them, pleased to listen to the unanimous prayer of his disciples: "All those with one accord devoted themselves to prayer, together with the women and Mary the mother of Jesus" (Acts 1:14). This is why the Church from the very beginning has practised communal prayer (cf. Acts 12:5). There are religious practices—few, short, daily "that have always been lived in Christian families and which I think are marvellous—grace at meals, morning and night prayers, the family rosary (even though nowadays this devotion to our Lady has been criticized by some people). Customs vary from place to place, but I think one should always encourage some acts of piety which the family can do together in a simple and natural fashion" (St Josemaría Escrivá, *Conversations*, 103).

---

e. Or *seventy-seven times* f. A talent was more than fifteen years' wages of a labourer g. The denarius was a day's wage for a labourer

owe.' ²⁹So his fellow servant fell down and besought him, 'Have patience with me, and I will pay you.' ³⁰He refused and went and put him in prison till he should pay his debt. ³¹When his fellow servants saw what had taken place, they were greatly distressed, and they went and reported to their lord all that had taken place. ³²Then his lord summoned him and said to him, 'You wicked servant! I forgave you all that debt because you besought me; ³³and should not you have had mercy on your fellow servant, as I had mercy on you?' ³⁴And in anger his lord delivered him to the jailers,ʰ till he should pay all his debt. ³⁵So also my heavenly Father will do to every one of you, if you do not forgive your brother from your heart.''

Marriage and virginity

19 ¹Now when Jesus had finished these sayings, he went away from Galilee and entered the region of Judea beyond the Jordan; ²and large crowds followed him, and he healed them there.

³And Pharisees came up to him and tested him by asking, "Is it lawful to divorce one's wife for any cause?" ⁴He answered, "Have you not read that he who made them from the beginning made them male and female, ⁵and said, 'For this reason a man shall leave

Mk 10:1–12
Mt 7:28; 11:1;
13:53; 26:1

Gen 1:27

Gen 2:24
Eph 5:31

18:21–35. Peter's question and particularly Jesus' reply prescribe the spirit of understanding and mercy which should govern Christians' behaviour.

In Hebrew the figure of seventy times seven means the same as "always" (cf. Gen 4:24): "Therefore, our Lord did not limit forgiveness to a fixed number, but declared that it must be continuous and forever" (St John Chrysostom, *Hom. on St Matthew*, 6). Here also we can see the contrast between man's ungenerous, calculating approach to forgiveness, and God's infinite mercy. The parable also clearly shows that we are totally in God's debt. A talent was the equivalent of six thousand denarii, and a denarius a working man's daily wage. Ten thousand talents, an enormous sum, gives us an idea of the immense value attaching to the

pardon we receive from God. Overall, the parable teaches that we must always forgive our brothers, and must do so wholeheartedly.

"Force yourself, if necessary, always to forgive those who offend you, from the very first moment. For the greatest injury or offence that you can suffer from them is as nothing compared with what God has pardoned you" (St Josemaría Escrivá, *The Way*, 452).

19:4–5. "Marriage and married love are by nature ordered to the procreation and education of children. Indeed children are the supreme gift of marriage and greatly contribute to the good of the parents themselves. God himself said: 'It is not good that man should be alone' (Gen 2:18), and 'from the beginning (he) made

h. Greek *torturers*

131

his father and mother and be joined to his wife, and the two shall

1 Cor 7:10f   become one'?[i] [6]So they are no longer two but one.[i] What therefore

Deut 24:1   God has joined together, let no man put asunder." [7]They said to
him, "Why then did Moses command one to give a certificate of
divorce, and to put her away?" [8]He said to them, "For your hardness of heart Moses allowed you to divorce your wives, but from

Lk 16:18   the beginning it was not so. [9]And I say to you: whoever divorces his
wife, except for unchastity,[j] and marries another, commits adultery;
and he who marries a divorced woman commits adultery."[k]*

[10]The disciples said to him, "If such is the case of a man with

1 Cor 7:7, 17   his wife, it is not expedient to marry." [11]But he said to them, "Not
all men can receive this precept, but only those to whom it is
given. [12]For there are eunuchs who have been so from birth, and
there are eunuchs who have been made eunuchs by men, and

---

them male and female' (Mt 19:4); wishing to associate them in a special way
with his own creative work, God blessed
man and woman with the words: 'Be
fruitful and multiply' (Gen 1:28). Without intending to underestimate the other
ends of marriage, it must be said that true
married life and the whole structure of
family life which results from it is
directed to disposing the spouses to
cooperate valiantly with the love of the
Creator and Saviour, who through them
will increase and enrich his family from
day to day" (Vatican II, *Gaudium et spes*,
50).

19:9. Our Lord's teaching on the unity
and indissolubility of marriage is the
main theme of this passage, apropos of
which St John Chrysostom comments
that marriage is a lifelong union of man
and woman (cf. *Hom. on St Matthew*,
62). On the meaning of "except for
unchastity", see the note on Mt 5:31–32.

19:11. "Not all men can receive this precept": our Lord is fully aware that the

demands involved in his teaching on
marriage and his recommendation of
celibacy practised out of love of God run
counter to human selfishness. That is
why he says that acceptance of this
teaching is a gift from God.

19:12. Our Lord speaks figuratively
here, referring to those who, out of love
for him, renounce marriage and offer
their lives completely to him. Virginity
embraced for the love of God is one of
the Church's most precious charisms (cf.
1 Cor 7); the lives of those who practise
virginity evoke the state of the blessed in
heaven, who are like the angels (cf. Mt
22:30). This is why the Church's Magisterium teaches that the state of virginity
for the sake of the Kingdom of heaven is
higher than the married state (cf. Council
of Trent, *De Sacram. matr.*, can. 10; cf.
also Pius XII, *Sacra virginitas*). On virginity and celibacy the Second Vatican
Council teaches: "The Church's holiness
is also fostered in a special way by the
manifold counsels which the Lord proposes to his disciples in the Gospel for

---

i. Greek *one flesh*   **j.** Other ancient authorities, after *unchastity*, read *makes her commit adultery*
k. Other ancient authorities omit *and he who marries a divorced woman commits adultery*

there are eunuchs who have made themselves eunuchs for the sake of the kingdom of heaven. He who is able to receive this, let him receive it."*

Jesus blesses the children

¹³Then children were brought to him that he might lay his hands on them and pray. The disciples rebuked the people; ¹⁴but Jesus said, "Let the children come to me, and do not hinder them; for to such belongs the kingdom of heaven." ¹⁵And he laid his hands on them and went away.

Mk 10:13–16
Lk 18:15–17

The rich young man. Christian poverty and renunciation

¹⁶And behold, one came up to him, saying, "Teacher, what good deed must I do, to have eternal life?" ¹⁷And he said to him, "Why

Mk 10:17–31
Lk 18:18–30

them to observe. Towering among these counsels is that precious gift of divine grace given to some by the Father (cf. Mt 19:11; 1 Cor 7:7) to devote themselves to God alone more easily in virginity or celibacy [...]. This perfect continence for love of the Kingdom of heaven has always been held in high esteem by the Church as a sign and stimulus of love, and as a singular source of spiritual fertility in the world" (*Lumen gentium*, 42; cf. *Perfectae caritatis*, 12). And, on celibacy specifically, see Vatican II's *Presbyterorum ordinis*, 16 and *Optatam totius*, 10.

However, both virginity and marriage are necessary for the growth of the Church, and both imply a specific calling from God: "Celibacy is precisely a gift of the Spirit. A similar though different gift is contained in the vocation to true and faithful married love, directed towards procreation according to the flesh, in the very lofty context of the sacrament of Matrimony. It is obvious that this gift is fundamental for the building up of the great community of the Church, the people of God. But if this community wishes to respond fully to its vocation in Jesus Christ, there will also have to be realized in it, in the correct proportion, that other gift, the gift of celibacy 'for the sake of the kingdom of heaven'" (John Paul II, *Letter to all priests*, 8 April 1979).

19:13–14. Once again (see Mt 18:1–6) Jesus shows his special love for children, by drawing them close and blessing them. The Church, also, shows special concern for children by urging the need for Baptism: "That this law extends not only to adults but also to infants and children, and that the Church has received this from Apostolic tradition, is confirmed by the unanimous teaching and authority of the Fathers.

"Besides, it is not to be supposed that Christ the Lord would have withheld the sacrament and grace of Baptism from children, of whom he said: 'Let the little children come to me, and do not hinder them; for to such belongs the kingdom of heaven' whom also he embraced, upon whom he imposed hands, to whom he gave his blessing" (St Pius V, *Catechism*, 2, 2, 32).

19:17. The Vulgate and other translations, supported by a good many Greek

Lk 10:26–28   do you ask me about what is good? One there is who is good. If

Ex 20:12–16   you would enter life, keep the commandments." [18]He said to him,

Deut 5:17–20   "Which?" And Jesus said, "You shall not kill, You shall not commit adultery, You shall not steal, You shall not bear false wit-

Ex 20:12   ness, [19]Honour your father and mother, and, You shall love your

Lev 19:18

Deut 5:16   neighbour as yourself." [20]The young man said to him, "All these I

Lk 12:33   have observed; what do I still lack?" [21]Jesus said to him, "If you would be perfect, go, sell what you possess and give to the poor, and you will have treasure in heaven; and come, follow me."

Ps 62:11   [22]When the young man heard this he went away sorrowful; for he had great possessions.

[23]And Jesus said to his disciples, "Truly, I say to you, it will be hard for a rich man to enter the kingdom of heaven. [24]Again I tell you, it is easier for a camel to go through the eye of a needle than for a rich man to enter the kingdom of God." [25]When the disciples heard this they were greatly astonished, saying, "Who then can be

Gen 18:14   saved?" [26]But Jesus looked at them and said to them, "With men

Job 42:2

Zech 8:6   this is impossible, but with God all things are possible." [27]Then

---

codexes, fill this verse out by saying, "One alone is good, God."

19:20–22. "What do I still lack?" The young man kept the commandments that were necessary for salvation. But there is more. This is why our Lord replies, "if you would be perfect ..." that is to say, if you want to acquire what is still lacking to you. Jesus is giving him an additional calling: "Come, follow me"; he is showing that he wants him to follow him more closely, and therefore he requires him, as he does others (cf. Mt 4:19–22), to give up anything that might hinder his full dedication to the Kingdom of God.

The scene ends rather pathetically: the young man goes away sad. His attachment to his property prevails over Jesus' affectionate invitation. Here is sadness of the kind that stems from cowardice, from failure to respond to God's calling with personal commitment.

In reporting this episode, the evangelists are actually giving us a case-study which describes a situation and formu-

lates a law, a case-study of specific divine vocation to devote oneself to God's service and the service of all men.

This young man has become a symbol of the kind of Christian whose mediocrity and shortsightedness prevent him from turning his life into a generous, fruitful self-giving to the service of God and neighbour. What would this young man have become, had he been generous enough to respond to God's call? A great apostle, surely.

19:24–26. By drawing this comparison Jesus shows that it is simply not possible for people who put their hearts on worldly things to obtain a share in the Kingdom of God. "With God all things are possible": that is, with God's grace man can be brave and generous enough to use wealth to promote the service of God and man. This is why St Matthew, in chapter 5, specifies that the poor *in spirit* are blessed (Mt 5:3).

19:28. "In the new world", in the "regeneration": a reference to the renewal

Peter said in reply, "Lo, we have left everything and followed you. What then shall we have?" [28]Jesus said to them, "Truly, I say to you, in the new world, when the Son of man shall sit on his glorious throne, you who have followed me will also sit on twelve thrones, judging the twelve tribes of Israel. [29]And every one who has left houses or brothers or sisters or father or mother or children or lands, for my name's sake, will receive a hundredfold,[l] and inherit eternal life. [30]But many that are first will be last, and the last first.

Lk 5:11

Lk 22:30
Dan 7:9–18

Heb 10:34

Lk 13:30

Parable of the labourers in the vineyard

20 [1]"For the kingdom of heaven is like a householder who went out early in the morning to hire labourers for his vineyard. [2]After agreeing with the labourers for a denarius[m] a day, he sent them into his vineyard. [3]And going out about the third hour he saw others standing idle in the market place; [4]and to them he said, 'You go into the vineyard too, and whatever is right I will give you.' So they went. [5]Going out again about the sixth hour and

---

of all things which will take place when Jesus Christ comes to judge the living and the dead. The resurrection of the body will be an integral part of this renewal.

The ancient people of God, Israel, was made up of twelve tribes. The new people of God, the Church, to which all men are called, is founded by Jesus Christ on the twelve apostles under the primacy of Peter.

19:29. These graphic remarks should not be explained away. They mean that love for Jesus Christ and his Gospel should come before everything else. What our Lord says here should not be interpreted as conflicting with the will of God himself, the creator and sanctifier of family bonds.

20:1–16. This parable is addressed to the Jewish people, whom God called at an early hour, centuries ago. Now the Gentiles are also being called—with an equal

right to form part of the new people of God, the Church. In both cases it is a matter of a gratuitous, unmerited, invitation; therefore, those who were the "first" to receive the call have no grounds for complaining when God calls the "last" and gives them the same reward—membership of his people. At first sight the labourers of the first hour seem to have a genuine grievance—because they do not realize that to have a job in the Lord's vineyard is a divine gift. Jesus leaves us in no doubt that although he calls us to follow different ways, all receive the same reward—heaven.

20:2. "Denarius": a silver coin bearing an image of Caesar Augustus (Mt 22:19–21).

20:3. The Jewish method of calculating time was different from ours. They divided the whole day into eight parts, four night parts (called "watches") and four

---

l. Other ancient authorities read *manifold*   m. The denarius was a day's wage for a labourer

the ninth hour, he did the same. [6]And about the eleventh hour he went out and found others standing; and he said to them, 'Why do you stand here idle all day?' [7]They said to him, 'Because no one has hired us.' He said to them, 'You go into the vineyard too.' [8]And when evening came, the owner of the vineyard said to his steward, 'Call the labourers and pay them their wages, beginning with the last, up to the first.' [9]And when those hired about the eleventh hour came, each of them received a denarius. [10]Now when the first came, they thought they would receive more; but each of them also received a denarius. [11]And on receiving it they grumbled at the householder, [12]saying, 'These last worked only one hour, and you have made them equal to us who have borne the burden of the day and the scorching heat.' [13]But he replied to one of them, 'Friend, I am doing you no wrong; did you not agree with me for a denarius? [14]Take what belongs to you, and go; I choose to give to this last as I give to you. [15]Am I not allowed to do what I choose with what belongs to me? Or do you begrudge my generosity?'[n] [16]So the last will be first, and the first last."

Rom 9:16, 21

Mt 19:30

day parts (called "hours")—the first, third, sixth and ninth hour.

The first hour began at sunrise and ended around nine o'clock; the third ran to twelve noon; the sixth to three in the afternoon; and the ninth from three to sunset. This meant that the first and ninth hours varied in length, decreasing in autumn and winter and increasing in spring and summer and the reverse happening with the first and fourth watches.

Sometimes intermediate hours were counted—as for example in v. 6 which refers to the eleventh hour, the short period just before sunset, the end of the working day.

20:16. The Vulgate, other translations and a good many Greek codexes add: "For many are called, but few are chosen" (cf. Mt 22:14).

20:18–19. Once again our Lord prophesies to his apostles about his death and

resurrection. The prospect of judging the world (cf. Mt 19:28) might have misled them into thinking in terms of an earthly messianic kingdom, an easy way ahead, leaving no room for the ignominy of the cross.

Christ prepares their minds so that when the testing time comes they will remember that he prophesied his passion and not be totally scandalized by it; he describes his passion in some detail.

Referring to Holy Week, St Josemaría Escrivá writes: "All the things brought to our mind by the different expressions of piety which characterize these days are of course directed to the Resurrection, which is, as St Paul says, the basis of our faith (cf. 1 Cor 15:14). But we should not tread this path too hastily, lest we lose sight of a very simple fact which we might easily overlook. We will not be able to share in our Lord's Resurrection unless we unite ourselves with him in his Passion and Death. If we are to accom-

n. Or *is your eye evil because I am good?*

Third announcement of the Passion

[17]And as Jesus was going up to Jerusalem, he took the twelve disciples aside, and on the way he said to them, [18]"Behold, we are going up to Jerusalem; and the Son of man will be delivered to the chief priests and scribes, and they will condemn him to death, [19]and deliver him to the Gentiles to be mocked and scourged and crucified, and he will be raised on the third day."

Mk 10:32–34
Lk 18:31–33

Mt 16:21;
17:22f

The mother of the sons of Zebedee makes her request

[20]Then the mother of the sons of Zebedee came up to him, with her sons, and kneeling before him she asked him for something. [21]And he said to her, "What do you want?" She said to him, "Command that these two sons of mine may sit, one at your right hand and one at your left, in your kingdom." [22]But Jesus answered, "You do not know what you are asking. Are you able to drink the cup that I am to drink?" They said to him, "We are able." [23]He said to them, "You will drink my cup, but to sit at my right hand and at my left is not mine to grant, but it is for those for whom it has been prepared by my Father." [24]And when the ten heard it they were indig-

Mk 10:34–45
Mt 10:2

Mt 19:28

Jn 18:11

Acts 12:2
Rev 1:9

Lk 22:24–28

---

pany Christ in his glory at the end of Holy Week, we must first enter into his holocaust and be truly united to him, as he lies dead on Calvary" (*Christ Is Passing By*, 95).

20:20. The sons of Zebedee are James the Greater and John. Their mother, Salome, thinking that the earthly reign of the Messiah is about to be established, asks that her sons be given the two foremost positions in it. Christ reproaches them for not grasping the true —spiritual—nature of the Kingdom of heaven and not realizing that government of the Church he is going to found implies service and martyrdom. "If you are working for Christ and imagine that a position of responsibility is anything but a burden, what disillusionment awaits you!" (St Josemaría Escrivá, *The Way*, 950).

20:22. "Drinking the cup" means suffering persecution and martyrdom for following Christ. "We are able": the sons of

Zebedee boldly reply that they can drink the cup; their generous expression evokes what St Paul will write years later: "I can do all things in him who strengthens me" (Phil 4:13).

20:23. "You will drink my cup": James the Greater will die a martyr's death in Jerusalem around the year 44 (cf. Acts 12:2); and John, after suffering imprisonment and the lash in Jerusalem (cf. Acts 4:3; 5:40–41), will spend a long period of exile on the island of Patmos (cf. Rev 1:9).

From what our Lord says here we can take it that positions of authority in the Church should not be the goal of ambition or the subject of human intrigue, but the outcome of a divine calling. Intent on doing the will of his heavenly Father, Christ was not going to allocate positions of authority on the basis of human considerations but, rather, in line with God's plans.

137

nant at the two brothers. ²⁵But Jesus called them to him and said, "You know that the rulers of the Gentiles lord it over them, and their great men exercise authority over them. ²⁶It shall not be so among you; but whoever would be great among you must be your servant, ²⁷and whoever would be first among you must be your slave; ²⁸even as the Son of man came not to be served but to serve, and to give his life as a ransom for many."

Mk 9:35

Lk 22:27
Phil 2:7
1 Tim 2:6

Mk 10:46–52
Lk 18:35–43
Mt 15:22

Curing of the blind men of Jericho

²⁹And as they went out of Jericho, a great crowd followed him. ³⁰And behold, two blind men sitting by the roadside, when they heard that Jesus was passing by, cried out,ᵒ "Have mercy on us, Son of David!" ³¹The crowd rebuked them, telling them to be silent; but they cried out the more, "Lord, have mercy on us, Son of David!" ³²And Jesus stopped and called them, saying, "What do you want me to do for you?" ³³They said to him, "Lord, let our eyes be opened." ³⁴And Jesus in pity touched their eyes, and immediately they received their sight and followed him.

20:26. Vatican II puts a marked emphasis on this *service* which the Church offers to the world and which Christians should show as proof of their Christian identity: "In proclaiming the noble destiny of man and affirming an element of the divine in him, this sacred Synod offers to co-operate unreservedly with mankind in fostering a sense of brotherhood to correspond to this destiny of theirs. The Church is not motivated by an earthly ambition but is interested in one thing only—to carry on the work of Christ under the guidance of the Holy Spirit, for he came into the world to bear witness to the truth, to save and not to judge, to serve and not to be served" (*Gaudium et spes*, 3; cf. *Lumen gentium*, 32; *Ad gentes*, 12; *Unitatis redintegratio*, 7).

20:27–28. Jesus sets himself as an example to be imitated by those who hold authority in the Church. He who is God and Judge of all men (cf. Phil 2:5–11; Jn 5:22–27; Acts 10:42; Mt 28:18) does not impose himself on us: he renders us loving service to the point of giving his life for us (cf. Jn 15:13); that is his way of being the first. St Peter understood him right; he later exhorted priests to tend the flock of God entrusted to them, not domineering over them but being exemplary in their behaviour (cf. 1 Pet 5:1–3); and St Paul also was clear on this *service*: though he was "free from all men", he became the servant of all in order to win all (cf. 1 Cor 9:19ff; 2 Cor 4:5).

Christ's "service" of mankind aims at salvation. The phrase "to give his life as a ransom for many" is in line with the terminology of liturgical sacrificial language. These words were used prophetically in chapter 53 of Isaiah.

Verse 28 also underlines the fact that Christ is a priest, who offers himself as priest and victim on the altar of the cross. The expression "as a ransom for many"

o. Other ancient authorities insert *Lord*

PART THREE

Jesus' ministry in Jerusalem

10. CLEANSING OF THE TEMPLE. CONTROVERSIES

The Messiah enters the Holy City

21 ¹And when they drew near to Jerusalem and came to Bethphage, to the Mount of Olives, then Jesus sent two disciples, ²saying to them, "Go into the village opposite you, and immediately you will find an ass tied, and a colt with her; untie them and bring them to me. ³If any one says anything to you, you shall say, 'The Lord has need of them,' and he will send them immediately." ⁴This took place to fulfil what was spoken by the prophet, saying,

Mk 11:1–10
Lk 19:29–38
Jn 12:12–19

should not be interpreted as implying that God does not will the salvation of all men. "Many", here, is used in contrast with "one" rather than "all": there is only one Saviour, and salvation is offered to all.

20:30–34. These blind men, who seize their opportunity as Christ is passing by, give us a lesson in the kind of boldness and persistence with which we should entreat God to listen to us (cf. commentary on the characteristics of petitionary prayer in note on the Sermon on the Mount: Mt 7:7–8). Chrysostom comments: "Clearly these blind men deserved to be cured: first, because they cried out; and then, because after they received the gift they did not hasten away, the way most people, in their ingratitude, are inclined to do once they have got what they wanted. No, they were not like that: they were both persevering before the gift and grateful after it, for they 'followed him' (*Hom. on St Matthew*, 66).

21:1–5. In his triumphant entry into Jerusalem Jesus reveals himself as the Messiah, as St Matthew and St John (12:14) stress by quoting the prophecy of Zechariah 9:9. Although the Latin translation says "mounted on a [female] ass", the original Hebrew text says "mounted on a [male] ass", and the latter is the text followed in this translation (in the Greek translation of the Septuagint no sex is specified). The other two Synoptic Gospels limit themselves to giving the key fact of Jesus' messianic entry into the Holy City mounted on the colt (Mk 11:2; Lk 19:30). St Matthew sees in the fact that the colt is with the ass a further detail of the prophecy, which refers to the colt being the foal of an ass (that seems to be why the ass is referred to throughout the account, the ass being with the colt, although Jesus was mounted only on the colt).

In the prophecy in Zechariah 9:9 (which in the original Old Testament text is longer than the quotation in Matthew) the future messianic king is described as

Zech 9:9
Is 62:11
5"Tell the daughter of Zion,
Behold, your king is coming to you,
humble, and mounted on an ass,
and on a colt, the foal of an ass."

6The disciples went and did as Jesus had directed them; 7they brought the ass and the colt, and put their garments on them, and 2 Kings 9:13 he sat thereon. 8Most of the crowd spread their garments on the road, and others cut branches from the trees and spread them on Ps 118:25f
2 Sam 14:4 the road. 9And the crowds that went before him and that followed him shouted, "Hosanna to the Son of David! Blessed is he who comes in the name of the Lord! Hosanna in the highest!"* 10And when he entered Jerusalem, all the city was stirred, saying, "Who is this?" 11And the crowds said, "This is the prophet Jesus from Nazareth of Galilee."

Jesus in the temple

Mk 11:11–24
Lk 19:45–48
Jn 2:14–15
12And Jesus entered the temple of Godᵖ and drove out all who sold and bought in the temple, and he overturned the tables of the money-changers and the seats of those who sold pigeons. 13He

---

"humble". The ass, originally a noble mount (cf. Gen 22:3; Ex 4:20; Num 22:21; Jud 5:10), was replaced by the horse in the period of the Israelite monarchy (cf. 1 Kings 4:26; 10:28; etc.). The prophecy, by referring to an ass, shows that the king of peace wins his victory by humility and gentleness, not by force of arms.

The Fathers have read a deeper meaning into this episode. They see the ass as symbolizing Judaism, for long subject to the yoke of the Law, and the foal, on which no one has ridden, as symbolizing the Gentiles. Jesus leads both Jews and Gentiles into the Church, the new Jerusalem.

21:9. The Hebrew word *"Hosanna"*, which the people use to acclaim our Lord, was originally an appeal to God meaning "Save us". Later it was used as a shout of joy, an acclamation, meaning something like "Long live ...". The people are demonstrating their enthusiasm by shout-

ing, "Long live the Son of David!" The phrase "Blessed is he who comes in the name of the Lord" comes from Psalm 118:26 and is a jubilant and appreciative greeting to someone entrusted with a mission from God. The Church takes up these acclamations, incorporating them into the preface of the Mass, to proclaim the kingship of Christ.

21:12–13. Although God is present everywhere and cannot be confined within the walls of temples built by man (Acts 17:24–25), God instructed Moses to build a tabernacle where he would dwell among the Israelites (Ex 25:40). Once the Jewish people were established in Palestine, King Solomon, also in obedience to a divine instruction, built the temple of Jerusalem (1 Kings 6–8), where people went to render public worship to God (Deut 12).

Exodus (23:15) commanded the Israelites not to enter the temple empty-handed, but to bring some victim to be

said to them, "It is written, 'My house shall be called a house of prayer'; but you make it a den of robbers."

[14]And the blind and the lame came to him in the temple, and he healed them. [15]But when the chief priests and the scribes saw the wonderful things that he did, and the children crying out in the temple, "Hosanna to the Son of David!" they were indignant; [16]and they said to him, "Do you hear what these are saying?" And Jesus said to them, "Yes; have you never read,

'Out of the mouth of babes and sucklings
thou hast brought perfect praise'?"

Ps 118:25

Ps 8:2

[17]And leaving them, he went out of the city to Bethany and lodged there.

The cursing of the fig tree

[18]In the morning, as he was returning to the city, he was hungry. [19]And seeing a fig tree by the wayside he went to it, and found nothing on it but leaves only. And he said to it, "May no fruit ever come from you again!" And the fig tree withered at once. [20]When the disciples saw it they marvelled, saying, "How did the fig tree

Lk 13:6

---

sacrificed. To make this easier for people who had to travel a certain distance, a veritable market developed in the temple courtyards with animals being bought and sold for sacrificial purposes. Originally this may have made sense, but seemingly as time went on commercial gain became the dominant purpose of this buying and selling of victims; probably the priests themselves and temple servants benefited from this trade or even operated it. The net result was that the temple looked more like a livestock mart than a place for meeting God.

Moved by zeal for his Father's house (Jn 2:17), Jesus cannot tolerate this deplorable abuse and in holy anger he ejects everyone—to show people the respect and reverence due to the temple as a holy place. We should show much greater respect in the Christian temple—Christian churches—where the eucharis-

tic sacrifice is celebrated and where Jesus Christ, God and Man, is really and truly present, reserved in the tabernacle. For a Christian, proper dress, liturgical gestures and postures, genuflections and reverence to the tabernacle etc. are expressions of the respect due to the Lord in his temple.

21:15–17. The children's acclamations please God and infuriate the proud. This episode fulfils something which Jesus said earlier: "I thank thee, Father, Lord of heaven and earth, that thou hast hidden these things from the wise and understanding and revealed them to babes" (Mt 11:25). Only an attitude of simplicity and humility can grasp the greatness of the King of peace and understand the things of God.

21:18–22. The cursing of the fig tree is a parable in action; Jesus acts in this dra-

---

p. Other ancient authorities omit *of God*

wither at once?" [21]And Jesus answered them, "Truly, I say to you, if you have faith and never doubt, you will not only do what has been done to the fig tree, but even if you say to this mountain, 'Be taken up and cast into the sea,' it will be done. [22]and whatever you ask in prayer, you will receive, if you have faith."

The authority of Jesus is questioned

Mk 11:27–33
Lk 20:1–8
Jn 2:18

[23]And when he entered the temple, the chief priests and the elders of the people came up to him as he was teaching, and said, "By what authority are you doing these things, and who gave you this authority?"* [24]Jesus answered them, "I also will ask you a question; and if you tell me the answer, then I also will tell you

Jn 1:25

by what authority I do these things. [25]The baptism of John, whence was it? From heaven or from men?" And they argued with one another, "If we say, 'From heaven,' he will say to us, 'Why then did you not believe him?' [26]But if we say, 'From men,' we are afraid of the multitude; for all hold that John was a prophet." [27]So they answered Jesus, "We do not know." And he said to them, "Neither will I tell you by what authority I do these things.

---

matic way to show people the power of faith. The disciples marvel not because he curses the fig tree but because it shrivels up instantly.

This is an example of God's omnipotence, which is something we should always keep before our minds. Jesus is explaining the enormous power of faith. A person with faith can do anything; he can do much more difficult things, such as moving a mountain. Jesus goes on to show that one effect of faith is that it makes prayer all-powerful. He also gives us a lesson on genuine and apparent faithfulness in the spiritual life. "I want you to make use of your time. Don't forget the fig tree cursed by our Lord. And it was doing something: sprouting leaves. Like you ... Don't tell me you have excuses. It availed the fig tree little, relates the evangelist, that it was not the season for figs when our Lord came to it to look for them. And barren it remained for ever" (St Josemaría Escrivá, *The Way*, 354).

21:23–27. When the chief priests and elders ask "By what authority are you doing these things?" they are referring both to his teaching and to his self-assured public actions—throwing the traders out of the temple, entering Jerusalem in triumph, allowing the children to acclaim him, curing the sick, etc. What they want him to do is to prove that he has authority to act in this way or to admit openly that he is the Messiah. However, Jesus knows that they are not well-intentioned and he declines to give them a direct answer; he prefers to put a question to them that forces them to make their own attitude clear. He seeks to provoke them into examining their consciences and changing their whole approach.

21:32. St John the Baptist had shown the way to sanctification by proclaiming the imminence of the Kingdom of God and by preaching conversion. The scribes and Pharisees would not believe him, yet they

Parable of the two sons

[28]"What do you think? A man had two sons; and he went to the first and said, 'Son, go and work in the vineyard today.' [29]And he answered, 'I will not'; but afterward he repented and went. [30]And he went to the second and said the same; and he answered, 'I go, sir,' but did not go. [31]Which of the two did the will of his father?" They said, "The first." Jesus said to them, "Truly, I say to you, the tax collectors and the harlots go into the kingdom of God before you. [32]For John came to you in the way of righteousness, and you did not believe him, but the tax collectors and the harlots believed him; and even when you saw it, you did not afterward repent and believe him.

Lk 18:14

Lk 7:29

Parable of the wicked tenants

[33]"Hear another parable.* There was a householder who planted a vineyard, and set a hedge around it, and dug a wine press in it, and built a tower, and let it out to tenants, and went into another country. [34]When the season of fruit drew near, he sent his servants to the tenants, to get his fruit; [35]and the tenants took his servants and beat one, killed another, and stoned another. [36]Again he sent other servants, more than the first; and they did the same to them.

Mk 12:1–12
Lk 20:9–19
Mt 25:14
Is 5:1f

---

boasted of their faithfulness to God's teaching. They were like the son who says "I will go" and then does not go; the tax collectors and prostitutes who repented and corrected the course of their lives will enter the Kingdom before them: they are like the other son who says "I will not", but then does go. Our Lord stresses that penance and conversion can set people on the road to holiness even if they have been living apart from God for a long time.

21:33–46. This very important parable completes the previous one. The parable of the two sons simply identifies the indocility of Israel; that of the wicked tenants focusses on the punishment to come.

Our Lord compares Israel to a choice vineyard, specially fenced, with a watchtower, where a keeper is on the look-out to protect it from thieves and foxes. God has spared no effort to cultivate and embellish his vineyard. The vineyard is in the charge of tenant farmers; the householder is God, and the vineyard, Israel (Is 5:3–5; Jer 2:21; Joel 1:7).

The tenants to whom God has given the care of his people are the priests, scribes and elders. The owner's absence makes it clear that God really did entrust Israel to its leaders; hence their responsibility and the account he demands of them.

The owner used to send his servants from time to time to collect the fruit; this was the mission of the prophets. The second despatch of servants to claim what is owing to the owner—who meet the same fate as the first—refers to the way God's prophets were ill-treated by the kings and priests of Israel (Mt 23:37; Acts 7:42; Heb 11:36–38). Finally he sent his Son to them, thinking that they would have more respect for him; here we can see the difference between Jesus and the prophets, who were servants, not

[37]Afterward he sent his son to them, saying, 'They will respect my son.' [38]But when the tenants saw the son, they said to themselves, 'This is the heir; come, let us kill him and have his inheritance.' [39]And they took him and cast him out of the vineyard, and killed him. [40]When therefore the owner of the vineyard comes, what will he do to those tenants?" [41]They said to him, "He will put those wretches to a miserable death, and let out the vineyard to other tenants who will give him the fruits in their seasons."

Ps 118:22f
Acts 4:11
Rom 9:33
1 Pet 2:6–8

[42]Jesus said to them, "Have you never read in the scriptures:

'The very stone which the builders rejected
has become the head of the corner;
this was the Lord's doing,
and it is marvellous in our eyes'?

Dan 2:34f; 44f

[43]Therefore I tell you, the kingdom of God will be taken away from you and given to a nation producing the fruits of it. [44]And he who falls on this stone will be broken to pieces; but when it falls on any one, it will crush him."[q]

[45]When the chief priests and the Pharisees heard his parables, they perceived that he was speaking about them. [46]But when they tried to arrest him, they feared the multitudes, because they held him to be a prophet.

"the Son": the parable indicates singular, transcendental sonship, expressing the divinity of Jesus Christ.

The malicious purpose of the tenants in murdering the son and heir to keep the inheritance for themselves is the madness of the leaders in expecting to become undisputed masters of Israel by putting Christ to death (Mt 12:14; 26:4). Their ambition blinds them to the punishment that awaits them. Then "they cast him out of the vineyard, and killed him": a reference to Christ's crucifixion, which took place outside the walls of Jerusalem.

Jesus prophesies the punishment God will inflict on the evildoers: he will put them to death and rent the vineyard to others. This is a very significant prophecy. St Peter later repeats it to the Sanhedrin: "this is the stone which was rejected by you builders, but which has become the head of the corner" (Acts 4:11; 1 Pet 2:4). The stone is Jesus of Nazareth, but the architects of Israel, who build up and rule the people, have chosen not to use it in the building. Because of their unfaithfulness the Kingdom of God will be turned over to another people, the Gentiles, who *will* give God the fruit he expects his vineyard to yield (cf. Mt 3:8–10; Gal 6:16).

For the building to be well built, it needs to rest on this stone. Woe to him who trips over it! (cf. Mt 12:30; Lk 2:34), as first Jews and later the enemies of Christ and his Church will discover through bitter experience (cf. Is 8:14–15).

Christians in all ages should see this parable as exhorting them to build faithfully upon Christ and make sure they do not fall into the sin of this Jewish genera-

---

q. Other ancient authorities omit verse 44

Parable of the marriage feast

22 [1]And again Jesus spoke to them in parables, saying, [2]"The kingdom of heaven may be compared to a king who gave a marriage feast for his son, [3]and sent his servants to call those who were invited to the marriage feast; but they would not come. [4]Again he sent other servants, saying, 'Tell those who are invited, Behold, I have made ready my dinner, my oxen and my fat calves are killed, and everything is ready; come to the marriage feast.' [5]But they made light of it and went off, one to his farm, another to his business, [6]while the rest seized his servants, treated them shamefully, and killed them. [7]The king was angry, and he sent his troops and destroyed those murderers and burned their city. [8]Then he said to his servants, 'The wedding is ready, but those invited were not worthy. [9]Go therefore to the thoroughfares, and invite to the marriage feast as many as you find.' [10]And those servants went out into the streets and gathered all whom they found, both bad and good; so the wedding hall was filled with guests.

[11]"But when the king came in to look at the guests, he saw there a man who had no wedding garment;* [12]and he said to him, 'Friend, how did you get in here without a wedding garment?'

Lk 14:16–24
Jn 3:29

---

tion. We should also be filled with hope and a sense of security; for, although the building—*the Church*—at some times seems to be breaking up, its sound construction, with Christ as its cornerstone, is assured.

22:1–14. In this parable Jesus reveals how intensely God the Father desires the salvation of all men—the banquet is the Kingdom of heaven—and the mysterious malice that lies in willingly rejecting the invitation to attend, a malice so vicious that it merits eternal punishment. No human arguments make any sense that go against God's call to conversion and acceptance of faith and its consequences.

The Fathers see in the first invitees the Jewish people: in salvation history God addresses himself first to the Israelites and then to all the Gentiles (Acts 13:46).

Indifference and hostility cause the Israelites to reject God's loving call and therefore to suffer condemnation. But the Gentiles also need to respond faithfully to the call they have received; otherwise they will suffer the fate of being cast "into outer darkness".

"The marriage", says St Gregory the Great (*In Evangelia homiliae*, 36) "is the wedding of Christ and his Church, and the garment is the virtue of charity: a person who goes into the feast without a wedding garment is someone who believes in the Church but does not have charity."

The wedding garment signifies the dispositions a person needs for entering the Kingdom of heaven. Even though he may belong to the Church, if he does not have these dispositions he will be condemned on the day when God judges all mankind. These dispositions essentially mean responding to grace.

And he was speechless. [13]Then the king said to the attendants, 'Bind him hand and foot, and cast him into the outer darkness; there men will weep and gnash their teeth.' [14]For many are called, but few are chosen."

Paying tax to Caesar

Mk 12:13–17
Lk 20:20–26
Jn 8:6

Mk 3:6
Jn 3:2

[15]Then the Pharisees went and took counsel how to entangle him in his talk. [16]And they sent their disciples to him, along with the Herodians, saying, "Teacher, we know that you are true, and teach the way of God truthfully, and care for no man; for you do not regard the position of men. [17]Tell us, then, what you think. Is it lawful to pay taxes to Caesar, or not?" [18]But Jesus, aware of their malice, said, "Why put me to the test, you hypocrites? [19]Show me the money for the tax." And they brought him a coin.[r] [20]And Jesus

Rom 13:7

said to them, "Whose likeness and inscription is this?" [21]They said, "Caesar's." Then he said to them, "Render therefore to

---

22:13. Vatican II reminds us of the doctrine of the "last things", one aspect of which is covered in this verse. Referring to the eschatological dimension of the Church, the Council recalls our Lord's warning about being on the watch against the wiles of the devil, in order to resist in the evil day (cf. Eph 6:11–13). "Since we know neither the day nor the hour, we should follow the advice of the Lord and watch constantly so that, when the single course of our earthly life is completed (cf. Heb 9:27), we may merit to enter with him into the marriage feast and be numbered among the blessed (cf. Mt 25:31–46) and not, like the wicked and slothful servants (cf. Mt 25:26), be ordered to depart into the eternal fire (cf. Mt 25:41), into the outer darkness where 'men will weep and gnash their teeth' " (*Lumen gentium*, 48).

22:14. These words in no way conflict with God's will that all should be saved (cf. 1 Tim 2:4). In his love for men, Christ patiently seeks the conversion of

every single soul, going as far as to die on the cross (cf. Mt 23:37; Lk 15:4–7). St Paul teaches this when he says that Christ loved us and "gave himself up for us, a fragrant offering and sacrifice to God" (Eph 5:2). Each of us can assert with the apostle that Christ "loved me and gave himself for me" (Gal 2:20). However, God in his infinite wisdom respects man's freedom: man is free to reject grace (cf. Mt 7:13–14).

22:15–21. The Pharisees and Herodians join forces to plot against Jesus. The Herodians were supporters of the regime of Herod and his dynasty. They were quite well disposed to Roman rule and, as far as religious matters were concerned, they held the same kind of materialistic ideas as the Sadducees. The Pharisees were zealous keepers of the Law; they were anti-Roman and regarded the Herods as usurpers. It is difficult to imagine any two groups more at odds with each other: their amazing pact shows how much they hated Jesus.

---

r. Greek *a denarius*

Caesar the things that are Caesar's, and to God the things that are God's." [22]When they heard it, they marvelled; and they left him and went away.

Jn 8:9

The resurrection of the dead

[23]The same day Sadducees came to him, who say that there is no resurrection; and they asked him a question, [24]saying, "Teacher, Moses said, 'If a man dies, having no children, his brother must marry the widow, and raise up children for his brother.' [25]Now there were seven brothers among us; the first married, and died, and having no children left his wife to his brother. [26]So too the second and third, down to the seventh. [27]After them all, the woman died. [28]In the resurrection, therefore, to which of the seven will she be wife? For they all had her."

Mk 12:18–27
Lk 20:27–40
Acts 23:6, 8
Gen 38:8
Deut 25:5f

Had Jesus replied that it was lawful to pay taxes to Caesar, the Pharisees could have discredited him in the eyes of the people, who were very nationalistic; if he said it was unlawful, the Herodians would have been able to denounce him to the Roman authorities.

Our Lord's answer is at once so profound that they fail to grasp its meaning, and it is also faithful to his preaching about the Kingdom of God: give Caesar what is his due, but no more, because God must assuredly be given what *he* has a right to (the other side of the question, which they omitted to put). God and Caesar are on two quite different levels, because for an Israelite God transcends all human categories. What has Caesar a right to receive? Taxes, which are necessary for legitimate state expenses. What must God be given? Obviously, obedience to *all* his commandments—which implies personal love and commitment. Jesus' reply goes beyond the human horizons of these temptors, far beyond the simple yes or no they wanted to draw out of him.

The teaching of Jesus transcends any kind of political approach, and if the faithful, using the freedom that is theirs, chose one particular method of solving temporal questions, they "ought to remember that in those cases no one is permitted to identify the authority of the Church exclusively with his own opinion" (Vatican II, *Gaudium et spes*, 43).

Jesus' words show that he recognized civil authority and its rights, but he made it quite clear that the superior rights of God must be respected (cf. Vatican II, *Dignitatis humanae*, 11), and pointed out that it is part of God's will that we faithfully fulfil our civic duties (cf. Rom 13:1–7).

22:23–33. The Sadducees argue against belief in the resurrection of the dead on the basis of the levirate law, a Jewish law which laid down that when a married man died without issue, one of his brothers, according to a fixed order, should marry his widow and the first son of that union be given the dead man's name. By outlining an extreme case the Sadducees make the law and belief in resurrection look ridiculous. In his reply Jesus shows up the frivolity of their objections and asserts the truth of the resurrection of the dead.

Ex 3:6

[29]But Jesus answered them, "You are wrong, because you know neither the scriptures nor the power of God. [30]For in the resurrection they neither marry nor are given in marriage, but are like angels[s] in heaven. [31]And as for the resurrection of the dead, have you not read what was said to you by God, [32]'I am the God of Abraham, and the God of Isaac, and the God of Jacob'? He is not God of the dead, but of the living." [33]And when the crowd heard it, they were astonished at his teaching.

The greatest commandment of all

Mk 12:28–31
Lk 10:25–28

[34]But when the Pharisees heard that he had silenced the Sadducees, they came together. [35]And one of them, a lawyer, asked

---

22:30. Jesus explains quite unequivocally that the blessed have transcended the natural condition of man and the institution of marriage therefore no longer has any raison d'etre in heaven. The primary aim of marriage—the procreation and education of children—no longer applies because once immortality is reached there is no need for procreation to renew the human race (cf. St Thomas Aquinas, *Comm. on St Matthew*, 22:30). Similarly, mutual help—another aim of marriage—is no longer necessary, because the blessed enjoy an eternal and total happiness by possessing God.

22:34–40. In reply to the question, our Lord points out that the whole law can be condensed into two commandments: the first and more important consists in unconditional love of God; the second is a consequence and result of the first, because when man is loved, St Thomas says, God is loved, for man is the image of God (cf. ibid., 22:4).

A person who genuinely loves God also loves his fellows because he realizes that they are his brothers and sisters, children of the same Father, redeemed by the same blood of our Lord Jesus Christ: "this commandment we have from him, that he

who loves God should love his brother also" (1 Jn 4:21). However, if we love man for man's sake without reference to God, this love will become an obstacle in the way of keeping the first commandment, and then it is no longer genuine love of our neighbour. But love of our neighbour for God's sake is clear proof that we love God: "If anyone says, 'I love God', and hates his brother, he is a liar" (1 Jn 4:20).

"You shall love your neighbour as yourself ": here our Lord establishes as the guideline for our love of neighbour the love each of us has for himself; both love of others and love of self are based on love of God. Hence, in some cases it can happen that God requires us to put our neighbour's need before our own; in others, not: it depends on what value, in the light of God's love, needs to be put on the spiritual and material factors involved.

Obviously spiritual goods take absolute precedence over material ones, even over life itself. Therefore, spiritual goods, be they our own or our neighbour's, must be the first to be safeguarded. If the spiritual good in question is the supreme one of the salvation of the soul, no one is justified in putting his own soul into certain danger of being condemned in order to save another,

---

s. Other ancient authorities add *of God*

him a question, to test him. [36]"Teacher, which is the great com-   Deut 6:5
mandment in the law?" [37]And he said to him, "You shall love the
Lord your God with all your heart, and with all your soul, and
with all your mind. [38]This is the great and first commandment.
[39]And a second is like it, You shall love your neighbour as your-   Lev 19:18
self. [40]On these two commandments depend all the law and the   Rom 13:10
prophets."   Gal 4:14

The divinity of the Messiah

[41]Now while the Pharisees were gathered together, Jesus asked   Mk 12:25–37
them a question, [42]saying, "What do you think of the Christ?   Lk 20:41–44
Whose son is he?" They said to him, "The son of David." [43]He   Jn 7:42

---

because given human freedom we can never be absolutely sure what personal choice another person may make: this is the situation in the parable (cf. Mt 25:1–13), where the wise virgins refuse to give oil to the foolish ones; similarly St Paul says that he would wish himself to be rejected if that could save his brothers (cf. Rom 9:3)—an unreal theoretical situation. However, what is quite clear is that we have to do all we can to save our brothers, conscious that, if someone helps to bring a sinner back to the way, he will save himself from eternal death and cover a multitude of his own sins (Jas 5:20). From all this we can deduce that self-love of the right kind, based on God's love for man, necessarily involves forgetting oneself in order to love God and our neighbour for God.

22:37–38. The commandment of love is the most important commandment because by obeying it man attains his own perfection (cf. Col 3:14). "The more a soul loves," St John of the Cross writes, "the more perfect is it in that which it loves; therefore this soul that is now perfect is wholly love, if it may thus be expressed, and all its actions are love and it employs all its faculties and possessions in loving, giving all that it has, like the wise mer-

chant, for this treasure of love which it has found hidden in God [...]. For, even as the bee extracts from all plants the honey that is in them, and has no use for them for aught else save for that purpose, even so the soul with great facility extracts the sweetness of love that is in all the things that pass through it; it loves God in each of them, whether pleasant or unpleasant; and being, as it is, informed and protected by love, it has neither feeling nor taste nor knowledge of such things, for, as we have said, the soul knows naught but love, and its pleasure in all things and occupations is ever, as we have said, the delight of the love of God" (*Spiritual Canticle*, stanza 27, 8).

22:41–46. God promised King David that one of his descendants would reign forever (2 Sam 7:12ff); this was obviously a reference to the Messiah, and was interpreted as such by all Jewish tradition, which gave the Messiah the title of "Son of David". In Jesus' time this messianic title was understood in a very nationalistic sense: the Jews were expecting an earthly king, a descendant of David, who would free them from Roman rule. In this passage Jesus shows the Pharisees that the Messiah has a higher origin: he is not only "Son of David"; his nature is

said to them, "How is it then that David, inspired by the Spirit,[t] calls him Lord, saying,

Ps 110:1
Acts 2:34f

[44]'The Lord said to my Lord,
Sit at my right hand,
till I put thy enemies under thy feet'?

[45]If David thus calls him Lord, how is he his son?" [46]And no one was able to answer him a word, nor from that day did any one dare to ask him any more questions.

Jesus berates the scribes and Pharisees

Mk 12:38–40
Lk 20:45–47;
11:39–52

Mal 2:7f

23 [1]Then said Jesus to the crowds and to his disciples, [2]"The scribes and the Pharisees sit on Moses' seat; [3]so practise and observe whatever they tell you, but not what they do; for they

---

more exalted than that, for he is the Son of God and transcends the purely earthly level. The reference to Psalm 110:1 which Jesus uses in his argument explains that the Messiah is God: which is why David calls him Lord—and why he is seated at the right hand of God, his equal in power, majesty and glory (cf. Acts 33–36; 1 Cor 6:25).

23:1–39. Throughout this chapter Jesus severely criticizes the scribes and Pharisees and demonstrates the sorrow and compassion he feels towards the ordinary mass of the people, who have been ill-used, "harassed and helpless, like sheep without a shepherd" (Mt 9:36). His address may be divided into three parts: in the first (vv. 1–12) he identifies their principal vices and corrupt practices; in the second (vv. 13–36) he confronts them and speaks his famous "woes", which in effect are the reverse of the beatitudes he preached in chapter 5: no one can enter the Kingdom of heaven—no one can escape condemnation to the flames—unless he changes his attitude and behaviour; in the third part (vv. 37–39) he weeps over Jerusalem, so grieved is he

by the evils into which the blind pride and hardheartedness of the scribes and Pharisees have misled the people.

23:2–3. Moses passed on to the people the Law received from God. The scribes, who for the most part sided with the Pharisees, had the function of educating the people in the Law of Moses; that is why they were said to "sit on Moses' seat". Our Lord recognized that the scribes and Pharisees did have authority to teach the Law; but he warns the people and his disciples to be sure to distinguish the Law as read out and taught in the synagogues from the practical interpretations of the Law to be seen in their leaders' lifestyles. Some years later, St Paul—a Pharisee like his father before him—faced his former colleagues with exactly the same kind of accusations as Jesus makes here: "You then who teach others, will you not teach yourself? While you preach against stealing, do you steal? You who say that one must not commit adultery, do you commit adultery? You who abhor idols, do you rob temples? You who boast in the law, do you dishonour God by breaking the law?

t. Or *David in the Spirit*

preach, but do not practise. ⁴They bind heavy burdens, hard to bear,ᵘ and lay them on men's shoulders; but they themselves will not move them with their finger. ⁵They do all their deeds to be seen by men; for they make their phylacteries* broad and their fringes long, ⁶and they love the place of honour at feasts and the best seats in the synagogues, ⁷and salutations in the market places, and being called rabbi by men. ⁸But you are not to be called rabbi, for you have one teacher, and you are all brethren. ⁹And call no man your father on earth, for you have one Father, who is in heaven.* ¹⁰Neither be called masters, for you have one master, the Christ. ¹¹He who is greatest among you shall be your servant; ¹²whoever exalts himself will be humbled, and whoever humbles himself will be exalted.

Ex 13:9
Num 15:38f

Lk 14:7
Jn 5:44

Prov 29:23
Job 22:29
Ezek 21:26
Lk 18:14
1 Pet 5:5

For, as it is written, 'The name of God is blasphemed among the Gentiles because of you' " (Rom 2:21–24).

23:5. "Phylacteries": belts or bands carrying quotations from Holy Scripture which the Jews used to wear fastened to their arms or foreheads. To mark themselves out as more religiously observant than others, the Pharisees used to wear broader phylacteries. The fringes were light-blue stripes on the hems of cloaks; the Pharisees ostentatiously wore broader fringes.

23:8–10. Jesus comes to teach the Truth; in fact, he is the Truth (cf. Jn 14:6). As a teacher, therefore, he is absolutely unique and unparalleled. "The whole of Christ's life was a continual teaching: his silences, his miracles, his gestures, his prayer, his love for people, his special affection for the little and the poor, his acceptance of the total sacrifice on the cross for the redemption of the world, and his resurrection are the actualization of his word and the fulfilment of revelation. Hence for Christians the crucifix is one of the most sublime and popular images of Christ the Teacher.

"These considerations are in line with the great traditions of the Church and they all strengthen our fervour with regard to Christ, the Teacher who reveals God to man and man to himself, the Teacher who saves, sanctifies and guides, who lives, who speaks, rouses, moves, redresses, judges, forgives, and goes with us day by day on the path of history, the Teacher who comes and will come in glory" (John Paul II, *Catechesi tradendae*, 9).

23:11. The Pharisees were greedy for honour and recognition: our Lord insists that every form of authority, particularly in the context of religion, should be exercised as a form of service of others; it must not be used to indulge personal vanity or greed. "He who is greatest among you shall be your servant".

23:12. A spirit of pride and ambition is incompatible with being a disciple of Christ. Here our Lord stresses the need for true humility, for anyone who is to follow him. The verbs "will be humbled", "will be exalted" have "God" as their active agent. Along the same lines, St James preaches that "God opposes the proud, but gives

u. Other ancient authorities omit *hard to bear*

151

¹³"But woe to you, scribes and Pharisees, hypocrites! because you shut the kingdom of heaven against men; for you neither enter yourselves, nor allow those who would enter to go in.ᵛ ¹⁵Woe to you, scribes and Pharisees, hypocrites! for you traverse sea and land to make a single proselyte, and when he becomes a proselyte, you make him twice as much a child of hellʷ as yourselves.

¹⁶"Woe to you, blind guides, who say, 'If any one swears by the temple, it is nothing; but if any one swears by the gold of the temple, he is bound by his oath.' ¹⁷You blind fools! For which is greater, the gold or the temple that has made the gold sacred? ¹⁸And you say, 'If any one swears by the altar, it is nothing; but if any one swears by the gift that is on the altar, he is bound by his oath.' ¹⁹You blind men! For which is greater, the gift or the altar that makes the gift sacred? ²⁰So he who swears by the altar, swears

Ezek 29:37

---

grace to the humble" (Jas 4:6). And in the *Magnificat*, the Blessed Virgin explains that the Lord "has put down the mighty from their thrones, and exalted those of low degree [the humble]" (Lk 1:52).

23:13. Now comes our Lord's invective against the behaviour of the scribes and Pharisees: his "woes" condemn their past conduct and threaten them with punishment if they do not repent and mend their ways.

23:14. See the RSV note below. Our Lord is not reproaching them for praying long prayers but for their hypocrisy and cupidity. By going in for a lot of external religious practices, the Pharisees wanted to be recognized as devout men and then trade on that reputation particularly with vulnerable people. Widows, for example, would ask them to say prayers; the Pharisees in turn would ask for alms. What Jesus means here is that prayer should always come from an upright heart and a generous spirit. See the notes on Mt 6:5–8.

23:15. "Proselyte": a pagan convert to Judaism. The root of the word means "he who comes", he who—coming from idolatry—joins the chosen people in response to a calling from God. The Pharisees spared no effort to gain converts. Our Lord reproaches them not for this, but because they were concerned only about human success, their motivation being vainglory.

The sad thing about these proselytes was that, after receiving the light of Old Testament revelation, they remained under the influence of scribes and Pharisees, who passed on to them their own narrow outlook.

23:22. Our Lord's teaching about taking oaths is given in the Sermon on the Mount (Mt 5:33–37). Jesus does away with the nitpicking casuistry of the Pharisees by focussing directly on the uprightness of the intention of the oath-taker and by stressing the respect due to God's majesty and dignity. What Jesus wants is a pure heart, with no element of deceit. Our Lord

---

v. Other authorities add here (or after verse 12) verse 14, *Woe to you, scribes and Pharisees, hypocrites! for you devour widows' houses and for a pretence you make long prayers; therefore you will receive the greater condemnation* w. Greek *Gehenna*

by it and by everything on it; [21]and he who swears by the temple, swears by it and by him who dwells in it; [22]and he who swears by heaven, swears by the throne of God and by him who sits upon it.

[23]"Woe to you, scribes and Pharisees, hypocrites! for you tithe mint and dill and cummin, and have neglected the weightier matters of the law, justice and mercy and faith; these you ought to have done, without neglecting the others. [24]You blind guides, straining out a gnat and swallowing a camel!

[25]"Woe to you, scribes and Pharisees, hypocrites! for you cleanse the outside of the cup and of the plate, but inside they are full of extortion and rapacity. [26]You blind Pharisee! first cleanse the inside of the cup and of the plate, that the outside also may be clean.

[27]"Woe to you, scribes and Pharisees, hypocrites! for you are like whitewashed tombs, which outwardly appear beautiful, but within they are full of dead men's bones and all uncleanness. [28]So

Lev 27:30
Mic 6:8

Mk 7:4

Tit 1:15
Jn 9:40

Acts 23:2

---

particularly reproves any tendency to undermine the content of an oath, as the doctors of the Law tended to do, thereby failing to respect holy things and especially the holy name of God. He therefore draws attention to the commandment of the Law which says, "You shall not take the name of the Lord your God in vain" (Ex 20:7; Lev 19:12; Deut 5:11).

23:23. Mint, dill (aniseed) and cummin were herbs the Jews used in cooking or to perfume rooms. They were such insignificant items that they were not covered by the Mosaic precept on paying tithes (Lev 27:30–33; Deut 14:22ff); the precept did not apply to domestic animals and the more common agricultural products such as wheat, wine and olive oil. However, the Pharisees, being so intent on showing their scrupulous observance of the Law, paid tithes even of these herbs. Our Lord does not despise or reject the Law; he is simply telling people to get their priorities right: there is no point in attending to secondary details if one is neglecting what is really basic and important—justice, mercy and faith.

23:24. The Pharisees were so scrupulous about not swallowing any insect which the Law declared to be unclean that they went as far as to filter drinks through a linen cloth. Our Lord criticizes them for being so inconsistent—straining mosquitos, being so scrupulous about little things, yet quite happily "swallowing a camel", committing serious sins.

23:25–26. After reproaching the Pharisees for their hypocrisy in religious practice, our Lord now goes on to indict their twofacedness in matters of morality. The Jews used to perform elaborate washings of plates, cups and other tableware, in line with the regulations on legal cleansing (cf. Mk 7:1–4).

The example he chooses suggests a deeper level of meaning—concern for that moral purity which should characterize man's interior life. What is of prime importance is cleanness of heart, an upright intention, consistency between what one says and what one does, etc.

23:27–28. The Jews used to whitewash tombs annually, shortly before the feast of the Passover. The whitewash made the

153

Lk 16:15 you also outwardly appear righteous to men, but within you are full of hypocrisy and iniquity.

²⁹"Woe to you, scribes and Pharisees, hypocrites! for you build the tombs of the prophets and adorn the monuments of the righteous, ³⁰saying, 'If we had lived in the days of our fathers, we would not have taken part with them in shedding the blood of the prophets.' ³¹Thus you witness against yourselves, that you are sons of those who murdered the prophets. ³²Fill up, then, the measure of your fathers. ³³You serpents, you brood of vipers, how are you to escape being sentenced to hell?ʷ ³⁴Therefore I send you prophets and wise men and scribes, some of whom you will kill and crucify, and some you will scourge in your synagogues and persecute from town to town, ³⁵that upon you may come all the righteous blood shed on earth, from the blood of innocent Abel to the blood of Zechariah the son of Barachiah, whom you murdered between the sanctuary and the altar. ³⁶Truly, I say to you, all this will come upon this generation.

Acts 7:52

1 Thess 2:15

Gen 4:8
2 Chron 24:20f
Mt 27:25

---

tombs more visible and helped to avoid people brushing against them, which would have meant incurring legal uncleanness for seven days (Num 19:16; cf. Lk 11:44). In the sunlight, these tombs sparkled radiantly white, but inside they still held corruption.

23:29–32. Our Lord shows them that they are cut from the same cloth as their ancestors—not because they erect mausoleums in honour of prophets and just men but because they are guilty of the same sin as those who killed the prophets. Hence their hypocrisy, which makes them even worse than their fathers. With pained irony Jesus tells them that they are compounding the sins of their ancestors.

Clearly this is referring to his passion and death: if the ancients killed the prophets, by causing him to suffer and die our Lord's contemporaries will be still more cruel.

23:34. The New Testament does in fact refer to prophets (cf. 1 Cor 12:28; Acts 13:1), wise men (cf. 1 Cor 2:6; Mt 13:52) and teachers (cf. Acts 13:1; 1 Cor 12:28), because the people in question are indeed full of the Holy Spirit and teach in Christ's name. The history of the Church shows that what Jesus says here came true, for it was in the synagogue that the first persecutions of the Christians occurred.

23:35. This Zechariah was different from the last but one of the main prophets. Apparently Jesus is referring to the Zechariah who suffered death by stoning during the reign of King Joash (2 Chron 24:16–22). "Between the sanctuary and the altar": within the sacred precincts, marked off by a wall, was the building which may be called the temple proper, in front of which was the great altar of holocausts.

23:37–39. Jesus' moving remarks seem almost to sum up the entire history of salvation and are a testimony to his divinity. Who if not God was the source of all these acts of mercy which mark the stages of the history of Israel? The image of

w. Greek *Gehenna*

Jerusalem admonished

[37]"O Jerusalem, Jerusalem, killing the prophets and stoning those who are sent to you! How often would I have gathered your children together as a hen gathers her brood under her wings, and you would not! [38]Behold, your house is forsaken and desolate.[x] [39]For I tell you, you will not see me again, until you say, 'Blessed is he who comes in the name of the Lord.' "

Lk 13:3f
Acts 7:59
1 Thess 2:15

Jer 22:5; 12:7
1 Kings 9:7f
Mt 21:9
Ps 118:26

11. THE ESCHATOLOGICAL DISCOURSE

Announcement of the destruction of the temple

24 [1]Jesus left the temple and was going away, when his disciples came to point out to him the buildings of the temple.* [2]But he answered them, "You see all these, do you not? Truly, I say to you, there will not be left here one stone upon another, that will not be thrown down."

Mk 13
Lk 21:5–36

Lk 19:44

---

being protected by wings, which occurs often in the Old Testament, refers to God's love and protection of his people. It is to be found in the prophets, in the canticle of Moses (cf. Deut 32:11), and in many psalms (cf. 17:8; 36:8; 57:2; 61:5; 63:8). "And you would not": the Kingdom of God has been preached to them unremittingly for centuries by the prophets; in these last few years by Jesus himself, the Word of God made man. But the "Holy City" has resisted all the unique graces offered it. Jerusalem should serve as a warning to every Christian: the freedom God has given us by creating us in his image and likeness means that we have this terrible capacity to reject him. A Christian's life is a continuous series of conversions—repeated instances of repentance, of turning to God, who, loving Father that he is, is ever ready to forgive.

24:1. In this discourse in which our Lord tells us about the last things, three prophecies seem to be interwoven—the destruction of Jerusalem (by the armies of

the Emperor Titus in the year 70); the end of the world; and the last coming of Christ. Our Lord invites us to be watchful and pray, as we await these three events.

The headings and side headings added into the Gospel text may be of some help in working out what Jesus is referring to at different stages in the discourse. It is quite easy to confuse the signs and times of the destruction of Jerusalem and those of the end of the world and the last coming—which is not all that surprising, given that the destruction of Jerusalem itself symbolizes the end of the world. Our Lord is speaking here very much in the style and language used by the prophets, who announced future events without specifying the order in which they would happen and who used a profusion of images and symbols. Every prophecy about the future seems quite obscure at first but as the events unfold everything fits into place. The Old Testament prophecies were not well understood until they were fulfilled during Christ's first coming; and the New Testament prophecies will

---

x. Other ancient authorities omit *and desolate*

The beginning of tribulations. Persecution on account of the Gospel

Jn 5:43
Acts 5:36f
1 Jn 2:18
Dan 2:28

³As he sat on the Mount of Olives, the disciples came to him privately, saying, "Tell us, when will this be, and what will be the sign of your coming and of the close of the age?" ⁴And Jesus answered them, "Take heed that no one leads you astray. ⁵For many will come in my name, saying, 'I am the Christ,' and they will lead many astray. ⁶ And you will hear of wars and rumours of wars; see that you are not alarmed; for this must take place, but the end is not yet. ⁷For nation will rise against nation, and kingdom against kingdom, and there will be famines and earthquakes in various places: ⁸all this is but the beginning of the sufferings.

Is 19:2
2 Chron 15:6
Mt 10:17–22
Jn 16:2
Dan 11:41
1 Jn 4:1

2 Thess 2:10
2 Tim 3:1–5
Mt 10:22
Rev 13:10

⁹"Then they will deliver you up to tribulation, and put you to death; and you will be hated by all nations for my name's sake. ¹⁰And then many will fall away,ʸ and betray one another, and hate one another. ¹¹And many false prophets will arise and lead many astray. ¹²And because wickedness is multiplied, most men's love will grow cold. ¹³But he who endures to the end will be saved. ¹⁴And this gospel of the kingdom will be preached throughout the

---

not become clear until his second coming. The notes which follow should be read against this background.

24:3. This dramatic prophecy makes such an impression on Christ's disciples that they want to know when it will happen; they see the end of the temple and the end of the world as coinciding (as yet the Holy Spirit has not yet come; he will make many things plain to them: cf. Jn 14:26).

24:4–14. Our Lord says that between then and the end of the world, the Gospel will be preached to every creature. In the intervening period, the Church will experience all kinds of tribulations. These are not signs of the end of the world; they are simply the normal context in which Christian preaching takes place.

24:15. "The desolating sacrilege": Jesus is referring to a prophecy in Daniel (Dan 9:27; 11:31; 12:11) where the prophet

foretold that the king (Antiochus IV) would occupy the temple and erect images of false gods on the altar of holocausts. This came to pass, and the idol was set up on the altar—a sign of "abomination" (idolatry) and desolation. Our Lord applies this episode in the history of Israel to the future destruction of Jerusalem—asking people ("let the reader understand") to pay more heed to the text in Daniel. Jesus tells them that a new abomination will occur, ruining the temple to make way for idolatrous worship—as happened in AD 70, when the Roman armies destroyed and profaned the temple, and later under Hadrian, who ordered the erection of a statue of Jupiter on the ruins.

"Having spoken of the ills that were to overtake the city, and of the trials of the apostles, and having said that they should remain unsubdued, and should conquer the whole world, he mentions again the Jews' calamities, showing that when the one [the Church] should be glorious,

y. Or *stumble*

whole world, as a testimony to all nations; and then the end will come.

The great tribulation

¹⁵"So when you see the desolating sacrilege spoken of by the prophet Daniel, standing in the holy place (let the reader understand), ¹⁶then let those who are in Judea flee to the mountains; ¹⁷let him who is on the housetop not go down to take what is in his house; ¹⁸and let him who is in the field not turn back to take his mantle. ¹⁹And alas for those who are with child and for those who give suck in those days! ²⁰Pray that your flight may not be in winter or on a sabbath. ²¹For then there will be great tribulation, such as has not been from the beginning of the world until now, no, and never will be. ²²And if those days had not been shortened, no human being would be saved; but for the sake of the elect those days will be shortened. ²³Then if any one says to you, 'Lo, here is the Christ!' or 'There he is!' do not believe it. ²⁴For false Christs and false prophets will arise and show great signs and wonders, so

Dan 9:27;
12:11

Lk 17:31

Acts 1:12
Dan 12:1
Joel 2:2

Deut 13:1–3
2 Thess 2:8f

---

having taught the whole world, the other [Israel] should suffer calamity" (St John Chrysostom, *Hom. on St Matthew*, 76).

24:15–20. People really did have to flee to escape the Romans (cf. Lk 21:20–21): the Christians had to leave the plains of Judea to take refuge in mountain caves. Many fled into present-day Transjordan (cf. Eusebius, *Ecclesiastical History*, 3, 5). Palestinian houses used to have a ladder directly from the terrace to the outside. On the sabbath, one was not allowed to walk more than two thousand paces—a little more than a kilometre (less than one mile).

Flavius Josephus, a contemporary Jewish historian, says that one million, one hundred thousand people died during the siege of Jerusalem in the year 70 (cf. *The Jewish War*, 6, 420)—which gives some idea of the scale of these events. The siege began when the city was full of pilgrims from all over the world, who had come to celebrate the Passover; therefore, Flavius Josephus' figure may not be all that far off the truth.

24:22. What salvation is our Lord referring to here? First, physical safety: if God in his mercy had not come to the rescue everyone would have died. Second, eternal salvation: this test will be so severe that God will have to cut the time short to avoid the elect being overcome by temptation, to ensure their salvation. We should bear in mind that tribulation has a physical dimension (earthquakes, upheavals, wars) and a spiritual one (false prophets, heresies, etc.).

24:23–28. Interwoven with the prophecy of the destruction of Jerusalem comes Jesus' announcement of his second coming. He uses mysterious words, whose meaning is obscure. Many events he speaks of in a very general way; they remain mere shadows.

The main thing we should do is grow in trust of Jesus and his teaching—"Lo, I have told you beforehand" (v. 25), as he has just said—and persevere until the end.

The same pattern as in vv. 4–13: between the fall of Jerusalem and the end

as to lead astray, if possible, even the elect. [25]Lo, I have told you
beforehand. [26]So, if they say to you, 'Lo, he is in the wilderness,'
do not go out; if they say, 'Lo, he is in the inner rooms,' do not
believe it. [27]For as the lightning comes from the east and shines as
far as the west, so will be the coming of the Son of man.
[28]Wherever the body is, there the eagles[z] will be gathered together.

Lk 17:23–24
Job 39:30
Heb 1:18
Lk 17:37

Is 13:10; 34:4
2 Pet 3:10

The coming of the Son of man

[29]"Immediately after the tribulation of those days the sun will be
darkened, and the moon will not give its light, and the stars will fall
from heaven, and the powers of the heavens will be shaken; [30]then
will appear the sign of the Son of man in heaven, and then all the
tribes of the earth will mourn, and they will see the Son of man
coming on the clouds of heaven with power and great glory; [31]and he

Rev 1:7
Mt 26:64
Dan 7:13f
Zech 12:10ff
Rev 19:11

---

of the world, Christians will experience
suffering time and time again—persecution, false prophets, false messiahs who
will lead others to perdition (vv. 23–24).
Verse 28 is difficult to interpret; it looks
like a proverb based on the speed with
which birds of prey swoop down on their
quarry. There may be a suggestion that at
Christ's second coming all mankind will
gather round him—good and bad, living
and dead, all irresistibly attracted to
Christ in triumph, some drawn by love,
others forced by justice. St Paul has
described the force of attraction in the
Son of man when he says that the just
"will be caught up ... in the clouds to
meet the Lord in the air" (1 Thess 4:17).

24:29. Nature itself will tremble in the
presence of this supreme Judge when he
appears vested in all his power.

24:30. "The sign of the Son of man" has
been traditionally interpreted as the cross
in glory, which will shine like the sun (cf.
St John Chrysostom, *Hom. on St Matthew*,
76). The liturgy of the cross contains the
same interpretation: "this sign will appear
in the heavens, when the Lord comes to

judge". This instrument of our Lord's passion will be a sign of condemnation for
those who have despised it, and of joy for
those who have borne a share of it.

24:32–35. Seeing in the destruction of
Jerusalem a symbol of the end of the
world, St John Chrysostom applies to it
this parable of the fig tree: "Here he also
foretells a spiritual spring and a calm
which, after the storm of the present life,
the righteous will experience; whereas
for sinners there will be a winter after the
spring they have had [...]. But this was
not the only reason why he put before
them the parable of the fig tree, to tell
them of the interval before his coming;
he wanted to show them that his word
would assuredly come true. As sure as
the coming of spring is the coming of the
Son of man" (ibid., 77).

"This generation": this verse is a
clear example of what we say in the note
on Mt 24:1 about the destruction of
Jerusalem. "This
generation" refers firstly to the people
alive at the time of the destruction of
Jerusalem. But, since that event is symbolic of the end of the world, we can say

z. Or *vultures*

will send out his angels with a loud trumpet call, and they will gather his elect from the four winds, from one end of heaven to the other.

1 Cor 15:52
1 Thess 4:16
Rev 8:1f
Is 27:13

The end will surely come. The lesson of the fig tree

[32]"From the fig tree learn its lesson: as soon as its branch becomes tender and puts forth its leaves, you know that summer is near. [33]So also, when you see all these things, you know that he is near, at the very gates. [34]Truly, I say to you, this generation will not pass away till all these things take place. [35]Heaven and earth will pass away, but my words will not pass away.

Deut 30:4

The time of the second coming of Christ

[36]"But of that day and hour no one knows, not even the angels of heaven, nor the Son,[a] but the Father only. [37]As were the days of

1 Thess 5:1f
Gen 6:11–13
Lk 17:26f

---

with St John Chrysostom that "the Lord was speaking not only of the generation then living, but also of the generation of the believers; for he knows that a generation is distinguished not only by time but also by its mode of religious worship and practice: this is what the Psalmist means when he says that 'such is the generation of those who seek him'(Ps 24:6)" (ibid.).

24:35. This is further confirmation that the prophecies he has just made will be fulfilled; it is as if he were saying: it is easier for heaven and earth, which seem so stable, to disappear, than for my words not to come true. Also he is making a formal statement about the value attaching to God's word: "heaven and earth, since they are created things, are not necessarily unchangeable: it is possible for them to cease to exist; whereas, Christ's words, which originate in eternity, have such power and force that they will last forever"(St Hilary, *In Matth.*, 26).

24:36. Every revelation about the end of the world is clothed in mystery; Jesus, being God, knows every detail of the plan

of salvation but he refrains from revealing the date of the Last Judgment. Why? To ensure that his apostles and disciples stay on the alert, and to underline the transcendence of this mysterious design. This phrase carries echoes of Jesus' reply to the sons of Zebedee: "to sit at my right hand and at my left is not mine to grant, but it is for those for whom it has been prepared by my Father" (Mt 20:23)—not because he does not know the details, but because it is not for him to reveal them.

"That day": the way the Bible usually refers to the day when God will judge all men (cf. Amos 2:26; 8:9, 12; Is 2:20; Mic 2:4; Mal 3:19; Mt 7:22; Mk 13:32; Lk 10:12; 2 Tim 1:12; etc.).

24:37–39. In a few strokes our Lord sketches man's perennial insensitivity and carelessness towards the things of God. Man thinks it is more important to eat and drink, to find a husband or wife; but if that is his attitude he is forgetting about the most important thing—eternal life. Our Lord also foretells that the end of the world will be like the great flood; the Son of man's second coming will happen

---

a. Other ancient authorities omit *nor the Son*

2 Pet 3:5f
Gen 7:7

Noah, so will be the coming of the Son of man. [38]For as in those days before the flood they were eating and drinking, marrying and giving in marriage, until the day when Noah entered the ark, [39]and they did not know until the flood came and swept them all away,

Lk 17:35f

so will be the coming of the Son of man. [40]Then two men will be in the field; one is taken and one is left. [41]Two women will be grinding at the mill; one is taken and one is left. [42]Watch therefore,

Lk 12:39–46

for you do not know on what day your Lord is coming. [43]But know this, that if the householder had known in what part of the night the thief was coming, he would have watched and would not

Rev 16:15

have let his house be broken into. [44]Therefore you also must be ready; for the Son of man is coming at an hour you do not expect.

Parable of the faithful servant

[45]"Who then is the faithful and wise servant, whom his master has set over his household, to give them their food at the proper time? [46]Blessed is that servant whom his master when he comes will find so doing. [47]Truly, I say to you, he will set him over all his

Eccles 8:11

possessions. [48]But if that wicked servant says to himself, 'My master is delayed,' [49]and begins to beat his fellow servants, and eats and drinks with the drunken, [50]the master of that servant will come on a day when he does not expect him and at an hour he does not know, [51]and will punish[b] him, and put him with the hypocrites; there men will weep and gnash their teeth.

---

unexpectedly, taking people by surprise, whether they are doing good or evil.

24:40. It is in the context of the ordinary affairs of life—farmwork, housework etc.—that God calls man, and man responds: that is where his eternal happiness or eternal punishment is decided. To be saved, one does not need to meet any special conditions, or to be in a special position in life: one simply has to be faithful to the Lord in the middle of ordinary everyday affairs.

24:42. Jesus himself draws from this revelation about the future the practical moral that a Christian needs to be on the watch,

living each day as if it were his last. The important thing is not to be speculating about when these events will happen and what form they will take, but to live in such a way that they find us in the state of grace.

24:51. "And will punish him [or, cut him in pieces]": this can be understood as a metaphor for "will cast him away". "Weeping and gnashing of teeth": the pains of hell.

25:1–46. The whole of chapter 25 is a practical application of the teaching contained in chapter 24. With these parables of the wise and foolish virgins and of the talents, and his teaching on the Last

b. Or *cut him in pieces*

Parable of the wise and foolish maidens

25 [1]"Then the kingdom of heaven shall be compared to ten maidens who took their lamps and went to meet the bridegroom.[c] [2]Five of them were foolish, and five were wise. [3]For when the foolish took their lamps, they took no oil with them; [4]but the wise took flasks of oil with their lamps. [5]As the bridegroom was delayed, they all slumbered and slept. [6]But at midnight there was a cry, 'Behold, the bridegroom! Come out to meet him.' [7]Then all those maidens rose and trimmed their lamps. [8]And the foolish said to the wise, 'Give us some of your oil, for our lamps are going out.' [9]But the wise replied, 'Perhaps there will not be enough for us and for you; go rather to the dealers and buy for yourselves.' [10]And while they went to buy, the bridegroom came, and those who were ready went in with him to the marriage feast; and the door was shut. [11]Afterward the other maidens came also, saying, 'Lord, lord, open to us.' [12]But he replied, 'Truly, I say to you, I do not know you.' [13]Watch therefore, for you know neither the day nor the hour.

Lk 12:35f
Rev 19:7

Lk 13:25–27

Parable of the talents

[14]"For it will be as when a man going on a journey called his servants and entrusted to them his property; [15]to one he gave five tal-

Lk 19:12–27

Judgment, our Lord is again emphasizing the need for vigilance (cf. the note on Mt 24:42). In this sense, chapter 25 makes chapter 24 more intelligible.

25:1–13. The main lesson of this parable has to do with the need to be on the alert: in practice, this means having the light of faith, which is kept alive with the oil of charity. Jewish weddings were held in the house of the bride's father. The virgins are young unmarried girls, bridesmaids who are in the bride's house waiting for the bridegroom to arrive. The parable centres on the attitude one should adopt up to the time when the bridegroom comes. In other words, it is not enough to know that one is "inside" the Kingdom, the Church: one has to be on the watch and be preparing for Christ's coming by doing good works.

This vigilance should be continuous and unflagging, because the devil is forever after us, prowling around "like a roaring lion, seeking someone to devour" (1 Pet 5:8). "Watch with the heart, watch with faith, watch with love, watch with charity, watch with good works [...]; make ready the lamps, make sure they do not go out [...], renew them with the inner oil of an upright conscience; then shall the Bridegroom enfold you in the embrace of his love and bring you into his banquet room, where your lamp can never be extinguished" (St Augustine, *Sermons*, 93).

25:14–30. A talent was not any kind of coin but a measure of value worth about fifty kilos (one hundred pounds) of silver.

In this parable the main message is the need to respond to grace by making a gen-

c. Other ancient authorities add *and the bride*

Rom 12:6

ents,[d] to another two, to another one, to each according to his ability. Then he went away. [16]He who had received the five talents went at once and traded with them; and he made five talents more. [17]So also, he who had the two talents made two talents more. [18]But he who had received the one talent went and dug in the ground and hid his master's money. [19]Now after a long time the master of those servants came and settled accounts with them. [20]And he who received the five talents came forward, bringing five talents more, saying, 'Master, you delivered to me five talents; here I have made five talents more.' [21]His master said to him, 'Well done, good and

Lk 16:10
Heb 12:2

faithful servant; you have been faithful over a little, I will set you over much; enter into the joy of your master.' [22]And he also who had the two talents came forward, saying, 'Master, you delivered to me two talents; here I have made two talents more.' [23]His master said to him, 'Well done, good and faithful servant; you have been faithful over a little, I will set you over much; enter into the joy of your master.' [24]He also who had received the one talent came forward, saying, 'Master, I knew you to be a hard man, reaping where you did not sow, and gathering where you did not winnow; [25]so I was afraid, and I went and hid your talent in the ground. Here you have what is yours.' [26]But his master answered him, 'You wicked and slothful servant! You knew that I reap where I have not sowed, and gather where I have not winnowed?

uine effort right through one's life. All the gifts of nature and grace which God has given us should yield a profit. It does not matter how many gifts we have received; what matters is our generosity in putting them to good use. A person's Christian calling should not lie hidden and barren: it should be outgoing, apostolic and self-sacrificial. "Don't lose your effectiveness; instead, trample on your selfishness. You think your life is for yourself? Your life is for God, for the good of all men, through your love for our Lord. Your buried talent, dig it up again! Make it yield" (St Josemaría Escrivá, *Friends of God*, 47).

An ordinary Christian cannot fail to notice that Jesus chose to outline his teaching in response to grace by using the simile of men at work. Here we have a reminder that the Christian normally lives out his vocation in the context of ordinary, everyday affairs. "There is just one life, made of flesh and spirit. And it is this life which has to become, in both soul and body, holy and filled with God. We discover the invisible God in the most visible and material things. There is no other way. Either we learn to find our Lord in ordinary, everyday life, or else we shall never find him" (St Josemaría Escrivá, *Conversations*, 114).

25:31–46. The three parables (Mt 24:42–51; 25:1–13; and 25:14–30) are completed by the announcement of a rigorous last judgment, a last act in a

d. A talent was more than fifteen years' wages of a labourer

27Then you ought to have invested my money with the bankers, and at my coming I should have received what was my own with interest. 28So take the talent from him, and give it to him who has the ten talents. 29For to every one who has will more be given, and he will have abundance; but from him who has not, even what he has will be taken away.* 30And cast the worthless servant into the outer darkness; there men will weep and gnash their teeth.'

The Last Judgment

31"When the Son of man comes in his glory, and all the angels with him, then he will sit on his glorious throne. 32Before him will be gathered all the nations, and he will separate them one from another as a shepherd separates the sheep from the goats, 33and he will place the sheep at his right hand, but the goats at the left. 34Then the King will say to those at his right hand, 'Come, O blessed of my Father, inherit the kingdom prepared for you from the foundation of the world; 35for I was hungry and you gave me food, I was thirsty and you gave me drink, I was a stranger and you welcomed me, 36I was naked and you clothed me, I was sick and you visited me, I was in prison and you came to me.' 37Then the righteous will answer him, 'Lord, when did we see thee hungry and feed thee, or thirsty and give thee drink? 38And when

Zech 14:5
Rev 20:11–33
Rom 14:10

Ezek 34:17

Is 58:7

---

drama, in which all matters of justice are resolved. Christian tradition calls it the Last Judgment, to distinguish it from the "Particular Judgment" which everyone undergoes immediately after death. The sentence pronounced at the end of time will simply be a public, formal confirmation of that already passed on the good and the evil, the elect and the reprobate.

In this passage we can discover some basic truths of faith: 1) that there will be a last judgment at the end of time; 2) the way Christ identifies himself with everyone in need—the hungry, the thirsty, the naked, the sick, the imprisoned; and 3) confirmation that the sinful will experience an eternal punishment, and the just an eternal reward.

25:31–33. In the Prophets and in the Book of Revelation the Messiah is depicted on a

throne, like a judge. This is how Jesus will come at the end of the world, to judge the living and the dead. The Last Judgment is a truth spelt out in the very earliest credal statements of the Church and a dogma of faith solemnly defined by Benedict XII in the Constitution *Benedictus Deus* (29 January 1336).

25:35–46. All the various things listed in this passage (giving people food and drink, clothing them, visiting them) become works of Christian charity when the person doing them sees Christ in these "least" of his brethren.

Here we can see the seriousness of sins of omission. Failure to do something which one should do means leaving Christ unattended.

"We must learn to recognize Christ when he comes out to meet us in our

did we see thee a stranger and welcome thee, or naked and clothe thee? [39]And when did we see thee sick or in prison and visit thee?'

Prov 19:17
Heb 2:11
[40]And the King will answer them, 'Truly I say to you, as you did it to one of the least of my brethren, you did it to me.' [41]Then he
Mt 7:23
Rev 20:10, 15
will say to those at his left hand, 'Depart from me, you cursed, into the eternal fire prepared for the devil and his angels; [42]for I was hungry and you gave me no food; I was thirsty and you gave me no drink, [43]I was a stranger and you did not welcome me, naked and you did not clothe me, sick and in prison and you did not visit me.' [44]Then they also will answer, 'Lord, when did we see thee hungry or thirsty or a stranger or naked or sick or in prison, and did not minister to thee?' [45]Then he will answer them, 'Truly, I say to you, as you did it not to one of the least of these,
Jn 5:29
Dan 12:2
you did it not to me.' [46]And they will go away into eternal punishment, but the righteous into eternal life."

---

brothers, the people around us. No human life is ever isolated. It is bound up with other lives. No man or woman is a single verse; we all make up one divine poem which God writes with the cooperation of our freedom" (St Josemaría Escrivá, *Christ Is Passing By*, 111).

We will be judged on the degree and quality of our love (cf. St John of the Cross, *Spiritual Sentences and Maxims*, 57). Our Lord will ask us to account not only for the evil we have done but also for the good we have omitted. We can see that sins of omission are a very serious matter and that the basis of love of neighbour is Christ's presence in the least of our brothers and sisters.

St Teresa of Avila writes: "Here the Lord asks only two things of us: love for his Majesty and love for our neighbour. It is for these two virtues that we must strive, and if we attain them perfectly we are doing his will [...]. The surest sign that we are keeping these two commandments is, I think, that we should really be loving our neighbour; for we cannot be sure if we are loving God, although we may have good reasons for believing that we are, but we can know quite well if we

are loving our neighbour. And be certain that, the farther advanced you find you are in this, the greater the love you will have for God; for so dearly does his Majesty love us that he will reward our love for our neighbour by increasing the love which we bear to himself, and that in a thousand ways: this I cannot doubt" (*Interior Castle*, 5, 3).

This parable clearly shows that Christianity cannot be reduced to a kind of agency for "doing good". Service of our neighbour acquires supernatural value when it is done out of love for Christ, when we see Christ in the person in need. This is why St Paul asserts that "if I give away all I have ... but have not love, I gain nothing" (1 Cor 13:3). Any interpretation of Jesus' teaching on the Last Judgment would be wide of the mark if it gave it a materialistic meaning or confused mere philanthrophy with genuine Christian charity.

25:40–45. In describing the exigencies of Christian charity which gives meaning to "social aid", the Second Vatican Council says: "Wishing to come down to topics that are practical and of some urgency, the

12. THE PASSION, DEATH AND RESURRECTION OF JESUS

Last announcement of the Passion. The conspiracy against Jesus

26 [1]When Jesus had finished all these sayings, he said to his disciples, [2]"You know that after two days the Passover is coming, and the Son of man will be delivered up to be crucified."

Mk 14:1f
Lk 22:1f
Mk 20:18

[3]Then the chief priests and the elders of the people gathered in the palace of the high priest, who was called Caiaphas, [4]and took counsel together in order to arrest Jesus by stealth and kill him.

Council lays stress on respect for the human person: everyone should look upon his neighbour (without any exception) as another self, bearing in mind, above all, his life and the means necessary for living it in a dignified way 'lest he follow the example of the rich man who ignored Lazarus, the poor man' (cf. Lk 16:18–31).

"Today there is an inescapable duty to make ourselves the neighbour of every man, no matter who he is, and if we meet him, to come to his aid in a positive way, whether he is an aged person abandoned by all, a foreign worker despised without reason, a refugee, an illegitimate child wrongly suffering for a sin he did not commit, or a starving human being who awakens our conscience by calling to mind the words of Christ: 'As you did it to one of the least of these my brethren, you did it to me'" (*Gaudium et spes*, 27).

25:46. The eternal punishment of the reprobate and the eternal reward of the elect are a dogma of faith solemnly defined by the Magisterium of the Church in the Fourth Lateran Council (1215): "He [Christ] will come at the end of the world; he will judge the living and the dead; and he will reward all, both the lost and the elect, according to their works. And all these will rise with their own bodies which they now have so that they may receive according to their works, whether good or bad; the wicked, a perpetual punishment with the devil; the good, eternal glory with Christ."

26:1. The Gospel account of the Passion (Mt 26 and 27 and par.) is far more detailed than that of any other event in Christ's life—which is not surprising because the passion and death of our Lord are the culmination of his life on earth and his work of redemption; they constitute the sacrifice which he offers to God the Father to atone for our sins. Moreover, the terrible suffering he undergoes vividly demonstrates his infinite love for each and every one of us, and the gravity of our sins.

26:2. The Passover was the principal national festival, held to commemorate the liberation of Israel from slavery in Egypt and the protection Yahweh gave the Israelites when he castigated the Egyptians by causing their first born to die (cf. Ex 12). For a long time the festival was celebrated within the confines of the home, the essential ceremonies being the sacrifice of an unblemished lamb, whose blood was then smeared on the jambs and lintel of the front door of the house, and a thanksgiving meal. In our Lord's time the sacrifice was carried out

⁵But they said, "Not during the feast, lest there be a tumult among the people."

The anointing at Bethany. Judas betrays Jesus

Mk 14:3–9
Lk 7:36–50
Jn 12:18

⁶Now when Jesus was at Bethany in the house of Simon the leper, ⁷a woman came up to him with an alabaster jar of very expensive ointment, and she poured it on his head, as he sat at table. ⁸But when the disciples saw it, they were indignant saying, "Why this waste? ⁹For this ointment might have been sold for a large sum,

Lk 11:7

and given to the poor." ¹⁰But Jesus, aware of this, said to them, "Why do you trouble the woman? For she has done a beautiful

Deut 15:11

thing to me. ¹¹For you always have the poor with you, but you will not always have me. ¹²In pouring this ointment on my body she has done it to prepare me for burial. ¹³Truly, I say to you, wherever this gospel is preached in the whole world, what she has done

Mk 14:10f
Lk 22:3–6
Jn 11:57
Zech 11:12

will be told in memory of her."

¹⁴Then one of the twelve, who was called Judas Iscariot, went to the chief priests ¹⁵and said, "What will you give me if I deliver

---

in the temple of Jerusalem, while the meal took place in private houses, with the whole family attending.

Christ uses this to provide the setting for the new Passover, in which he himself will be the spotless lamb who will set all men free from the slavery of sin by shedding his blood on the cross.

26:3–5. This describes the rulers' final plot to do away with Jesus. The crime they are planning will provide the vehicle for Christ to fulfil to the very end his Father's plan of redemption (cf. Lk 24:26–27; Acts 2:23). This passage also shows that it was not the whole Jewish nation that plotted the death of the Lord, but only its leaders.

26:6. Bethany, where Lazarus and his sisters lived, was a small town to the east of the Mount of Olives, on the way from Jerusalem to Jericho. It is different from the other town of the same name where John the Baptist baptized people (cf. Jn 1:28).

26:8–11. The disciples criticize the generosity of this woman because they fail to understand the true meaning of poverty. They see her action as a waste of money—for, as St John tells us (12:5), the perfume cost more than three hundred denarii—that is, a labourer's annual earnings. They do not yet realize the love which motivated the woman's actions.

"The woman in the house of Simon the leper in Bethany, who anoints the Master's head with precious ointment, reminds us of our duty to be generous in the worship of God.

"All beauty, richness and majesty seem little to me. And against those who attack the richness of sacred vessels, of vestments and altars, stands the praise given by Jesus: *'opus enim bonum operata est in me*: she has acted well towards me'" (St Josemaría Escrivá, *The Way*, 527). See the note on Mt 21:12–13.

26:12. Wealthier Jews had bodies embalmed before burial, using rich ointments and perfumes. This woman is

him to you?" And they paid him thirty pieces of silver. [16]And from
that moment he sought an opportunity to betray him.

1 Tim 6:9f

Preparations for the Last Supper and announcement of Judas' treachery

[17]Now on the first day of Unleavened Bread the disciples came to
Jesus, saying, "Where will you have us prepare for you to eat the
passover?"* [18]He said, "Go into the city to such a one, and say to
him, 'The Teacher says, My time is at hand; I will keep the
passover at your house with my disciples.'" [19]And the disciples
did as Jesus had directed them, and they prepared the passover.

Mk 14:12–16
Lk 22:7–13
Ex 12:18–20

[20]When it was evening, he sat at table with the twelve disciples;[e] [21]and as they were eating, he said, "Truly, I say to you, one
of you will betray me." [22]And they were very sorrowful, and
began to say to him one after another, "Is it I, Lord?" [23]He
answered, "He who has dipped his hand in the dish with me, will
betray me. [24]The Son of man goes as it is written of him, but woe
to that man by whom the Son of man is betrayed! It would have

Mk 14:17–26
Lk 22:14–23
Jn 13:21–26

---

anticipating our Lord's death. She saw her action as a generous gesture and a recognition of Jesus' dignity; additionally it becomes a prophetic sign of his redemptive death.

26:15. It is disconcerting and sobering to realize that Judas Iscariot actually went as far as to sell the man whom he had believed to be the Messiah and who had called him to be one of the apostles. Thirty shekels or pieces of silver were the price of a slave (cf. Ex 21:32), the same value as Judas put on his Master.

26:17. This unleavened bread, azymes, took the form of loaves which had to be eaten over a seven-day period, in com-memoration of the unleavened bread which the Israelites had to take with them in their hurry to leave Egypt (cf. Ex 12:34). In Jesus' time the passover supper was celebrated on the first day of the week of the Unleavened Bread.

26:18. Although the reference is to an unnamed person, probably our Lord gave the person's actual name. In any event, from what other evangelists tell us (Mk 14:13; Lk 22:10), Jesus gave the disci-ples enough information to enable them to find the house.

26:22. Although the glorious events of Easter have yet to occur (which will teach the apostles much more about Jesus), their faith has been steadily forti-fied and deepened in the course of Jesus' public ministry (cf. Jn 2:11; 6:68–69) through their contact with him and the divine grace they have been given (cf. Mt 16:17). At this point they are quite con-vinced that our Lord knows their internal attitudes and how they are going to act: each asks in a concerned way whether he will prove to be loyal in the time ahead.

26:24. Jesus is referring to the fact that he will give himself up freely to suffering

e. Other authorities omit *disciples*

been better for that man if he had not been born." [25]Judas, who betrayed him, said, "Is it I, Master?"[f] He said to him, "You have said so."

The institution of the Eucharist

1 Cor
11:23–25

[26]Now as they were eating,* Jesus took bread, and blessed, and broke it, and gave it to the disciples and said, "Take, eat; this is my body." [27]And he took a cup, and when he had given thanks he gave it to them, saying, "Drink of it, all of you; [28]for this is my

and death. In so doing he would fulfil the will of God, as proclaimed centuries before (cf. Ps 41:10; Is 53:7). Although our Lord goes to his death voluntarily, this does not reduce the seriousness of Judas' treachery.

26:25. This advance indication that Judas is the traitor is not noticed by the other apostles (cf. Jn 13:26–29).

26:26–29. This short scene, covered also in Mk 14:22–25, Lk 22:19–20 and 1 Cor 11:23–26, contains the essential truths of faith about the sublime mystery of the Eucharist—1) the institution of this sacrament and Jesus' real presence in it; 2) the institution of the Christian priesthood; and 3) the Eucharist, the sacrifice of the New Testament or the Mass.

1) In the first place, we can see the institution of the Eucharist by Jesus Christ, when he says, "This is my body ... , this is my blood ...". What up to this point was nothing but unleavened bread and wine, now—through the words and by the will of Jesus Christ, true God and true Man—becomes the true body and true blood of the Saviour. His words, which have such a realism about them, cannot be interpreted as being merely symbolic or explained in a way which obscures the mysterious fact that Christ is really present in the Eucharist: all we can

do is humbly subscribe to the faith "which the Catholic Church has always held and which she will hold until the end of the world" (Council of Trent, *De SS. Eucharistia*). Paul VI expresses this faith in these words in his encyclical letter *Mysterium fidei*, 5: "The continuous teaching of the Catholic Church, the traditions delivered to catechumens, the perception of the Christian people, the doctrine defined by the Council of Trent, and the very words of Christ as he instituted the most holy Eucharist, all insist that we profess: 'The Eucharist is the flesh of our Saviour Jesus Christ; the flesh which suffered for our sins and which the Father, of his kindness, brought to life.' To these words of St Ignatius of Antioch may be added the statement addressed to the people by Theodore of Mopsuestia, a faithful witness of the Church's belief on this subject: 'The Lord did not say: "This is the symbol of my body and this the symbol of my blood." He said: "This is my body and my blood".' "

This sacrament, which not only has the power to sanctify but actually contains the very Author of holiness, was instituted by Jesus Christ to be spiritual nourishment of the soul, to strengthen it in its struggle to attain salvation. The Church teaches that it also confers pardon of venial sins and helps the Christian not

f. Or *Rabbi*

blood of the[g] covenant, which is poured out for many for the for-giveness of sins. [29]I tell you I shall not drink again of this fruit of the vine until that day when I drink it new with you in my Father's kingdom."

Ex 24:8
Jer 31:31
Zech 9:11

The disciples' desertion foretold

[30]And when they had sung a hymn, they went out to the Mount of Olives. [31]Then Jesus said to them, "You will all fall away because of me this night; for it is written, 'I will strike the shepherd, and the

Ps 113–118
Lk 22:39
Jn 18:1
Mk 14:27–31
Lk 22:31–34
Zech 13:7
Jn 16:32

---

to fall into mortal sin: it unites us to God and thereby is a pledge of future glory.

2) In instituting the Blessed Eucharist our Lord laid down that it should be repeated until the end of time (cf. 1 Cor 11:24–25; Lk 22:19) by giving the apos-tles the power to perform it. From this passage, and the accounts in St Paul and St Luke (loc. cit.), we can see that Christ also instituted the priesthood, giving the apostles the power to confect the Eucharist, a power which they in turn passed on to their successors. This making of the Eucharist takes place at Mass when the priest, with the intention of doing what the Church does, says Christ's words of consecration over the bread and the wine. At this very moment, "a change takes place in which the whole substance of bread is changed into the substance of the body of Christ our Lord and the whole substance of the wine into the substance of his blood" (*De SS. Eucharistia*). This amazing change is given the name of "transubstantiation". Through transubstantiation the unleav-ened bread and the fruit of the vine dis-appear, becoming the body, blood, soul and divinity of Jesus Christ. Christ's real presence is to be found also in any little particles which become detached from the host, or the smallest drop from the chalice, after the consecration. It contin-ues when the sacred species are reserved in the tabernacle, as long as the appear-ances (of bread and wine) last.

3) At the Last Supper, Christ—miraculously, in an unbloody manner—brought forward his passion and death. Every Mass celebrated from then on renews the sacrifice of our Saviour on the cross—Jesus once again giving his body and blood, offering himself to God the Father as a sacrifice on man's behalf, as he did on Calvary—with this clear differ-ence: on the cross he gave himself shed-ding his blood, whereas on the altar he does so in an unbloody manner. "He, then, our Lord and our God, was once and for all to offer himself by his death on the altar of the cross to God the Father, to accomplish for them an ever-lasting redemption. But death was not to end his priesthood. And so, at the Last Supper, [...] in order to leave for his beloved spouse, the Church, a sacrifice that was visible, [...] he offered his body and blood under the species of bread and wine to God the Father and he gave his body and blood under the same species to the apostles to receive, making them priests of the New Testament at that time. This sacrifice was to represent the bloody sacrifice which he accomplished on the cross once and for all" (Council of Trent, *De SS. Missae sacrificio*, chap. 1).

The expression "which is poured out for many for the forgiveness of sins"

---

g. Other ancient authorities insert *new*

sheep of the flock will be scattered.' [32]But after I am raised up, I will
go before you to Galilee." [33]Peter declared to him, "Though they all
fall away because of you, I will never fall away." [34]Jesus said to him,
"Truly, I say to you, this very night, before the cock crows, you will
deny me three times." [35]Peter said to him, "Even if I must die with
you, I will not deny you." And so did all the disciples.

Jn 13:38

Gethsemane—the agony in the garden

Mk 14:32-42
Lk 22:40-46
Heb 5:7
Ps 43:5
Jn 12:27
Jn 18:11
Heb 5:8

[36]Then Jesus went with them to a place called Gethsemane, and he
said to his disciples, "Sit here, while I go yonder and pray." [37]And
taking with him Peter and the two sons of Zebedee, he began to be
sorrowful and troubled. [38]Then he said to them, "My soul is very
sorrowful, even to death; remain here, and watch[h] with me." [39]And
going a little farther he fell on his face and prayed, "My Father, if
it be possible, let this cup pass from me; nevertheless, not as I will,
but as thou wilt." [40]And he came to the disciples and found them
sleeping; and he said to Peter, "So, could you not watch[h] with me

means the same as "which is poured out
for all" (cf. the note on Mt 20:27–28).
Here we have the fulfilment of the prophecies of Isaiah (chap. 53), which spoke of
the atoning death of Christ for all men.
Only Christ's sacrifice is capable of atoning to the Father; the Mass has this power
because it is that very sacrifice: "The
priest offers the Holy Sacrifice *in persona
Christi*; this means more than offering 'in
the name of' or 'in the place of' Christ. *In
persona* means in specific sacramental
identification with the eternal High Priest,
who is the Author and principal Subject of
this sacrifice of his, a sacrifice in which, in
truth, nobody can take his place. Only
he—only Christ—was able and is always
able to be the true and effective 'expiation
for our sins and ... for the sins of the
whole world' (1 Jn 2:2; cf. 4:10)" (John
Paul II, *Letter to all bishops*, on the
Eucharist, 24 November 1980).

Finally, we should notice that this
sublime sacrament should be received
with proper dispositions of soul and

body—in the state of grace, in a spirit of
adoration, respect and recollection, for it
is God himself whom one is receiving.
"Let a man examine himself, and so eat
of the bread and drink of the cup. For
anyone who eats and drinks without discerning the body eats and drinks judgment upon himself" (1 Cor 11:28–29).

26:30–35. At the celebration of the Passover, Psalms 113–118 were recited: this
is what the reference to the "hymn"
means. Our Lord knows what is going to
happen—the main events (his death and
resurrection) and the lesser ones (such as
Peter's denials).

Peter becomes so afraid that he
denies his Master three times—a fall
which Jesus allowed to happen in order
to teach him humility. "Here we learn a
great truth: that a man's resolution is not
sufficient unless he relies on the help of
God" (St John Chrysostom, *Hom. on St
Matthew*, 83).

h. Or *keep awake*

one hour? [41]Watch[h] and pray that you may not enter into temptation; the spirit indeed is willing, but the flesh is weak." [42]Again, for
the second time, he went away and prayed, "My Father, if this
cannot pass unless I drink it, thy will be done." [43]And again he
came and found them sleeping, for their eyes were heavy. [44]So,
leaving them again, he went away and prayed for the third time,
saying the same words. [45]Then he came to the disciples and said to
them, "Are you still sleeping and taking your rest? Behold, the
hour is at hand, and the Son of man is betrayed into the hands of
sinners. [46]Rise, let us be going; see, my betrayer is at hand."

Heb 2:14; 4:15

2 Cor 12:8
2 Sam 24:14

Jn 14:31

Arrest of Jesus

[47]While he was still speaking, Judas came, one of the twelve, and
with him a great crowd with swords and clubs, from the chief
priests and the elders of the people. [48]Now the betrayer had given
them a sign, saying, "The one I shall kiss is the man; seize him."
[49]And he came up to Jesus at once and said, "Hail, Master!"[i] And

Mk 14:43–50
Lk 22:47–53
Jn 18:3–12

26:36–46. Here our Lord allows us to
glimpse the full reality and exquisite sensitivity of his human nature. Strictly
speaking, Christ, because he had complete
self-control, could have avoided showing
these limitations. However, by letting
them express themselves, we are better
able to understand the mystery of his genuine humanness—and to that extent, better
able to imitate it. After tempting Jesus in
the wilderness, the devil "departed from
him until an opportune time" (Lk 4:13).
Now, with the passion, he attacks again,
using the flesh's natural repugnance to
suffering; this is his hour "and the power
of darkness" (Lk 22:53).

"Remain here": as if he did not want
them to be depressed by seeing his
agony; and "watch with me": to keep him
company and to prepare themselves by
prayer for the temptations that will
follow. He goes a little farther away—
about a stone's throw, St Luke tells us
(22:41). Because there was a full moon,
the apostles may have been able to see

Jesus; they may also have heard some
words of his prayers; but that could
hardly explain how they were able to
report this scene in such detail. It is more
likely that our Lord, after his resurrection, told his disciples about his agony
(cf. Acts 1:3), as he must also have told
them about the time he was tempted in
the wilderness (Mt 4:1).

26:47–56. Jesus again demonstrates that
he is giving himself up of his own free
will. He could have asked his Father to
send angels to defend him, but he does
not do so. He knows why this is all happening and he wants to make it quite
clear that in the last analysis it is not
force which puts him to death but his
own love and his desire to fulfil his
Father's will. His opponents fail to grasp
Jesus' supernatural way of doing things;
he had done his best to teach them but
their hardness of heart came in the way
and prevented them from accepting his
teaching.

---

i. Or *Rabbi*   **j.** Or *do that for which you have come*

he kissed him. [50]Jesus said to him, "Friend, why are you here?"[j] Then they came up and laid hands on Jesus and seized him. [51]And behold, one of those who were with Jesus stretched out his hand and drew his sword, and struck the slave of the high priest, and cut off his ear.* [52]Then Jesus said to him, "Put your sword back into its place; for all who take the sword will perish by the sword. [53]Do you think that I cannot appeal to my Father, and he will at once send me more than twelve legions of angels? [54]But how then should the scriptures be fulfilled, that it must be so?" [55]At that hour Jesus said to the crowds, "Have you come out as against a robber, with swords and clubs to capture me? Day after day I sat in the temple teaching, and you did not seize me. [56]But all this has taken place, that the scriptures of the prophets might be fulfilled." Then all the disciples forsook him and fled.

Gen 9:6
Rev 13:10

Jesus before the chief priests

Mk 14:53–72
Lk 22:54–27
Jn 18:12–27

[57]Then those who had seized Jesus led him to Caiaphas the high priest, where the scribes and the elders had gathered. [58]But Peter followed him at a distance, as far as the courtyard of the high priest, and going inside he sat with the guards to see the end. [59]Now the chief priests and the whole council sought false testimony against Jesus that they might put him to death,* [60]but they found none, though many false witnesses came forward. At last two came forward [61]and said, "This fellow said, 'I am able to destroy the temple of God, and to build it in three days.'" [62]And the high priest stood up and said, "Have you no answer to make?

Jn 2:19–21

26:50. To effect his betrayal Judas uses a sign of friendship and trust. Although he knows what Judas is about, Jesus treats him with great gentleness: he gives him a chance to open his heart and repent. This shows us that we should respect even people who harm us and should treat them with a refined charity.

26:61. As we know from St John's Gospel (2:19), Jesus had said, "Destroy this temple, and in three days I will raise it up", referring to the destruction of his own body, that is, his death and resurrection. They misunderstood him (Jn 2:20), thinking he referred to the temple of Jerusalem.

26:69. The houses of well-to-do Jews had a front lobby or porter's office; going through the lobby one came into a patio and by crossing the patio one could enter the rooms proper. Peter goes through the lobby but he is afraid to follow the mill of people around Jesus, so he stays in the patio, with the servants.

26:70–75. When they went to arrest Jesus in the Garden of Olives, Peter set about defending him and, sword in hand, he struck at the head of the first to lay a hand on his Master, but he only succeeded in cutting off his ear. Our Lord's reaction ("Put your sword back into its place": Mt 26:52) disconcerts Peter. His

What is it that these men testify against you?" [63]But Jesus was silent. And the high priest said to him, "I adjure you by the living God, tell us if you are the Christ, the Son of God." [64]Jesus said to him, "You have said so. But I tell you, hereafter you will see the Son of man seated at the right hand of Power, and coming on the clouds of heaven." [65]Then the high priest tore his robes, and said, "He has uttered blasphemy. Why do we still need witnesses? You have now heard his blasphemy.* [66]What is your judgment?" They answered, "He deserves death." [67]Then they spat in his face, and struck him; and some slapped him, [68]saying, "Prophesy to us, you Christ! Who is it that struck you?"

Ps 110:1;
68:35
Mt 16:27;
24:30
Dan 7:13
Acts 7:56
Jn 10:33
Mk 16:19

Jn 19:7
Lev 24:16
Is 50:6

Peter's denials

[69]Now Peter was sitting outside in the courtyard. And a maid came up to him, and said, "You also were with Jesus the Galilean." [70]But he denied it before them all, saying, "I do not know what you mean." [71]And when he went out to the porch, another maid saw him, and she said to the bystanders, "This man was with Jesus of Nazareth." [72]And again he denied it with an oath, "I do not know the man." [73]After a little while the bystanders came up and said to Peter, "Certainly you are also one of them, for your accent betrays you." [74]Then he began to invoke a curse on himself and to swear, "I do not know the man." And immediately the cock crowed. [75]And Peter remembered the saying of Jesus, "Before the cock crows, you will deny me three times." And he went out and wept bitterly.

Jn 8:55

---

faith is not in doubt—Jesus himself had praised him above the other apostles (Mt 16:17)—but it is still too human and needs a profound purification. On Jesus' arrest, all the disciples flee in disarray; thereby the prophecy is fulfilled which says "Strike the shepherd, that the sheep may be scattered" (Zech 13:7). However, Peter keeps following our Lord, though at a distance (Mt 26:58); he is quite demoralized and disconcerted yet brave enough to enter Caiaphas' house, where Malchus, the man whose ear he cut off, works (Jn 18:10–11).

Peter's faith is put to the supreme test. A few hours before Jesus' arrest Peter had assured him, "Lord, I am ready to go with you to prison and to death" (Lk 22:33); and now, as Jesus predicted, he three times denies that he ever knew him. In the midst of his confusion, our Lord's serene glance reinforces his faith (Lk 22:61) and Peter's tears purify it. What our Lord had said a few hours earlier, in the intimacy of the Last Supper, has come true: "Simon, Simon, behold, Satan demanded to have you, that he might sift you like wheat, but I have prayed for you that your faith may not fail; and when you have turned again, strengthen your brethren" (Lk 22:31–32).

Peter has committed a grave sin, but his repentance also is deep. His faith, now put to the test, will become the basis

Jesus is brought before Pilate

Mk 15:1
Lk 22:66
Jn 18:28

Lk 23:1
Jn 18:31f

27 [1]When morning came, all the chief priests and the elders of the people took counsel against Jesus to put him to death; [2]and they bound him and led him away and delivered him to Pilate the governor.

Judas' despair and death

[3]When Judas, his betrayer, saw that he was condemned, he repented and brought back the thirty pieces of silver to the chief priests and the elders, [4]saying, "I have sinned in betraying innocent blood." They said, "What is that to us? See to it yourself."

Acts 1:18
2 Sam 17:23
Mk 12:41

[5]And throwing down the pieces of silver in the temple, he departed; and he went and hanged himself. [6]But the chief priests, taking the pieces of silver, said, "It is not lawful to put them into the treasury, since they are blood money." [7]So they took counsel, and bought with them the potter's field, to bury strangers in.

Acts 1:19
Zech 11:12f
Jer 32:6–9

[8]Therefore that field has been called the Field of Blood to this day. [9]Then was fulfilled what had been spoken by the prophet Jeremiah, saying, "And they took the thirty pieces of silver, the price of him on whom a price had been set by some of the sons of Israel, [10]and they gave them for the potter's field, as the Lord directed me."

---

on which Christ will build his Church (Mt 16:18).

As regards our own lives we should remember that no matter how low we may have fallen, God in his mercy, which is infinite, is ever ready to forgive us, because he does not despise a broken and contrite heart (Ps 51:19). If we sincerely repent, God will use us, sinners though we be, as his faithful instruments.

27:2. During this period the governor or procurator was the senior official in Judea. Although he was subordinate to the Roman legate in Syria, he had the *ius gladii*, the authority to condemn a criminal to death—which was why the Jewish leaders brought Jesus before Pilate: they were seeking a public sentence of death, to counteract Jesus' reputation and erase his teaching from people's minds.

27:3–5. Judas' remorse does not lead

him to repent his sins and be converted; he cannot bring himself to turn trustingly to God and be forgiven. He despairs, mistrusting God's infinite mercy, and takes his own life.

27:6. Once again the chief priests and elders show their hypocrisy. They behave inconsistently: they worry about exact fulfilment of a precept of the Law—not to put into the temple treasury money resulting from an evil action—yet they themselves have instigated that action.

27:9. By recalling the prophecy of Jeremiah (cf. Jer 18:2; 19:1; 32:6–15) and completing it with that of Zechariah (Zech 11:12–13), the Gospel shows that this incident was foreseen by God.

27:14. The evangelist possibly wishes to indicate that this silence was foretold in

Jesus' trial before Pilate

[11]Now Jesus stood before the governor; and the governor asked him, "Are you the King of the Jews?" Jesus said to him, "You have said so." [12]But when he was accused by the chief priests and elders, he made no answer. [13]Then Pilate said to him, "Do you not hear how many things they testify against you?" [14]But he gave him no answer, not even to a single charge; so that the governor wondered greatly.

[15]Now at the feast the governor was accustomed to release for the crowd any one prisoner whom they wanted. [16]And they had then a notorious prisoner, called Barabbas.[k] [17]So when they had gathered, Pilate said to them, "Whom do you want me to release for you, Barabbas[k] or Jesus who is called Christ?" [18]For he knew that it was out of envy that they had delivered him up. [19]Besides, while he was sitting on the judgment seat, his wife sent word to him, "Have nothing to do with that righteous man, for I have suffered much over him today in a dream." [20]Now the chief priests and the elders persuaded the people to ask for Barabbas and destroy Jesus. [21]The governor again said to them, "Which of the two do you want me to release for you?" And they said, "Barabbas." [22]Pilate said to them, "Then what shall I do with Jesus who is called Christ?" They all said, "Let him be crucified." [23]And he said, "Why, what evil has he done?" But they shouted all the more, "Let him be crucified."

Margin references:
Mk 15:2–5
Lk 23:2f
Jn 18:29–38
Mt 26:63
Is 53:7

Jn 19:9

Mk 15:6–15
Lk 23:13–25
Jn 18:29–19:1

Mt 31:38
Jn 11:47f;
12:19

Acts 7:9

---

the Old Testament when Isaiah 53:7 speaks of his being "afflicted, yet he opened not his mouth; like a lamb that is led to the slaughter, and like a sheep that before its shearers is dumb."

Sometimes the right thing for a Christian to do is to remain silent, bearing out what Isaiah says elsewhere: "in quietness and in trust shall be your strength" (Is 30:15).

" 'Jesus remained silent. *Jesus autem tacebat.*' Why do you speak, to console yourself or to excuse yourself? Say nothing. Seek joy in contempt; you will always receive less than you deserve. Can you, by any chance, ask: '*Quid enim mali feci?* What evil have I done?' " (St Josemaría Escrivá, *The Way*, 671).

27:18. The chief priests and elders had seen how the crowd followed Jesus. This caused them to be envious of him, an envy which grew into a hatred that sought his death (Jn 11:47).

St Thomas observes that just as at the beginning it was envy that caused man's death (Wis 2:24), so it was envy that condemned Christ (cf. *Comm. on St Matthew*, 27:18).

Envy is indeed one of the causes of hatred (Gen 37:8). "So put away all malice and all guile and insincerity and envy and all slander" (1 Pet 2:1).

27:23. "It is hard to read that question of Pilate's in the holy Gospel: 'Whom do you wish to me to release to you, Barabbas or Jesus, who is called Christ?' But it is

---

k. Other ancient authorities read *Jesus Barabbas*

Deut 21:6

²⁴So when Pilate saw that he was gaining nothing, but rather that a riot was beginning, he took water and washed his hands before the crowd, saying, "I am innocent of this righteous man's

Acts 5:28
Mt 23:35

blood;¹ see to it yourselves." ²⁵And all the people answered, "His blood be on us and on our children!" ²⁶Then he released for them Barabbas, and having scourged Jesus, delivered him to be crucified.

The crowning with thorns

Mk 15:16–19
Jn 19:2f

²⁷Then the soldiers of the governor took Jesus into the praetorium, and they gathered the whole battalion before him. ²⁸And they

more painful to hear the answer: 'Barabbas!' And more terrible still when I realize that very often by going astray I too have said 'Barabbas' and added 'Christ? … *Crucifige eum!* Crucify him!' " (St Josemaría Escrivá, *The Way*, 296).

27:24. Pilate tries publicly to justify his lack of courage, even though he has all the material necessary for giving an honest verdict. His cowardice, which he disguises by this external gesture, ends up condemning Christ to death.

27:26–50. Meditation on the passion of our Lord has made many saints in the course of Church history. Few things are of more benefit to a Christian than contemplation—slow and devout, to the point of being amazed—of the saving events surrounding the death of the Son of God made man. Our mind and heart will be overwhelmed to see the suffering of him who created the angels, men, heaven and earth; who is the Lord of all creation; the Almighty who humbles himself to this extent (something quite unimaginable, were it not that it happened). He suffers in this way because of sin—the original sin of our first parents, the personal sins of all men, of those who have gone before us and those who will come after us, and each one's own sins. Christ's terrible sufferings

spell out for us, as nothing else can, the infinite gravity of sin, which has called for the death of God himself made man; moreover, this physical and moral suffering which Jesus undergoes is also the most eloquent proof of his love for the Father, which seeks to atone to him for man's incredible rebellion by the punishment inflicted on his own innocent humanity; and of his love for mankind, his brothers and sisters; he suffers what we deserve to suffer in just punishment for our sins. Our Lord's desire to atone was so great that there was no part of his body that he did not permit to be inflicted with pain—his hands and feet pierced by the nails; his head torn by the crown of thorns; his face battered and spat upon; his back pitted by the terrible scourging he received; his chest pierced by the lance; finally, his arms and legs utterly exhausted by such pain and weariness that he dies. His spirit, also, is saturated with suffering—the pain caused by his being abandoned and betrayed by his disciples, the hatred his own people turn on him, the jeers and brutality of the Gentiles, the mysterious way his divinity permits his soul to suffer.

Only one thing can explain why Christ undergoes this redemptive passion—love, immense, infinite, indescribable love. As he himself taught, the entire Law of God and the Prophets are sum-

l. Other ancient authorities omit *righteous* or *man's*

stripped him and put a scarlet robe upon him, [29]and plaiting a crown of thorns they put it on his head, and put a reed in his right hand. And kneeling before him they mocked him, saying, "Hail, King of the Jews!" [30]And they spat upon him, and took the reed and struck him on the head. [31]And when they had mocked him, they stripped him of the robe, and put his own clothes on him, and led him away to crucify him.

Is 50:6

Mk 15:20–41
Lk 23:26,
33–49
Jn 19:16–30

The crucifixion and death of Jesus

[32]As they were marching out, they came upon a man of Cyrene, Simon by name; this man they compelled to carry his cross. [33]And

---

med up in the divine comandment of love (cf. Mt 22:36–40).

The four evangelists have filled many pages with their account of the sufferings of our Lord. Contemplation of Jesus' passion, identification with the suffering Christ, should play a key role in the life of every Christian, if he is to share later in the resurrection of his Lord: "Don't hinder the work of the Paraclete: seek union with Christ, so as to be purified, and feel with him the insults, the spits, and the blows, and the thorns, and the weight of the cross ... , and the nails tearing through your flesh, and the agony of a forsaken death.

"And enter through our Lord's open side until you find sure refuge there in his wounded Heart" (St Josemaría Escrivá, *The Way*, 58).

27:27. A cohort, or battalion, consisted of some 625 soldiers. In Jesus' time there was always a cohort garrisoned in Jerusalem, quartered in the Antonia Tower, adjoining the temple. This reported to the governor and was recruited from non-Jewish inhabitants of the region.

27:28–31. The Gospel describes very soberly how Jesus puts up no resistance to being beaten and ridiculed; the facts are allowed to speak for themselves. He takes upon himself, out of love for the

Father and for us, the punishment we deserve to suffer for our sins. This should make us very grateful and, at the same time, cause us to have sorrow for sin, to desire to suffer in silence at Jesus' side and atone for our sins and those of others: Lord, I want never to sin again; but you must help me to stay true to you.

27:32. Seeing how much Jesus has suffered, the soldiers realize that he is incapable of carrying the cross on his own as far as the top of Golgotha. There he is, in the centre of the crowd, with not a friend in sight. Where are all the people who benefitted from his preaching and healing and miracles? None of them is there to help him. He had said, "If any man would come after me, let him deny himself and take up his cross and follow me" (Mt 16:24). But cowardice and fear have taken over. The soldiers resort to laying hold of a stranger and forcing him to carry the cross. Our Lord will reward this favour done to him: God's grace will come down on "Simon of Cyrene, ... the father of Alexander and Rufus" (Mk 15:21), who will soon be prominent members of the early Church. The experience of pain proves to be the best route to Christian discipleship.

Christ's disciples must try to ensure that cowardice does not undermine their

Ps 69:21
Ps 22:18

Ps 22:7;
109:25

Mt 26:61
Jn 2:19

when they came to a place called Golgotha (which means the place of a skull), ³⁴they offered him wine to drink, mingled with gall; but when he tasted it, he would not drink it. ³⁵And when they had crucified him, they divided his garments among them by casting lots; ³⁶then they sat down and kept watch over him there. ³⁷And over his head they put the charge against him, which read, "This is Jesus the King of the Jews." ³⁸Then two robbers were crucified with him, one on the right and one on the left. ³⁹And those who passed by derided him, wagging their heads ⁴⁰and saying, "You who would destroy the temple and build it in three days, save yourself! If you are the Son of God, come down from the cross." ⁴¹So also the chief priests, with the scribes and elders, mocked him, saying, ⁴²"He saved others; he cannot save himself.

---

commitment: "See how lovingly he embraces the Cross. Learn from him. Jesus carries the Cross for you: you … carry it for Jesus. But don't drag the Cross … Carry it squarely on your shoulder, because your Cross, if you carry it like that, will not be just any Cross.… It will be the Holy Cross. Don't carry your Cross with resignation: resignation is not a generous word. Love the Cross. When you really love it, your Cross will be … a Cross without a Cross" (St J. Escrivá, *Holy Rosary*, fourth sorrowful mystery).

27:33. On the outskirts of Jerusalem there was a little hill called "Golgotha", or "the place of a skull", as the evangelist expressly states. It was used as a site for executing criminals. The name "Golgotha" comes from a transcription of an Aramaic word meaning "head". The name "Calvary" comes from a Latin word with the same meaning.

27:34. They offered Jesus a drink consisting of a mixture of wine, honey and myrrh (cf. Mk 15:23); this was usually given to people condemned to death, as a narcotic to lessen the pain. Our Lord chooses not to take it, because he wants to suffer the full rigour of his passion.

"Let us drink to the last drop the chalice of pain in this poor present life. What does it matter to suffer for ten years, twenty, fifty … if afterwards there is heaven forever, forever … forever? And, above all—rather than because of the reward, *propter retributionem*—what does suffering matter if we suffer to console, to please God our Father, in a spirit of reparation, united to him on his cross; in a word: if we suffer for Love? …" (St Josemaría Escrivá, *The Way*, 182).

27:35. Some manuscripts add to this verse the following words taken from John 19:24: "This was to fulfil the scripture, 'They parted my garments among them, and for my clothing they cast lots'" (cf. Ps 22:18).

27:45. Approximately from twelve midday to three o'clock in the afternoon. See the note on Mt 20:3.

27:46. Words from Psalm 22:1, which our Lord uses to show the physical and moral pain he is suffering. In no sense should these words be taken as a complaint against God's plans. "Suffering does not consist in not feeling since that is proper to those who have no feelings;

He is the King of Israel; let him come down now from the cross, and we will believe in him. [43]He trusts in God, let God deliver him now, if he desires him; for he said, 'I am the Son of God.'" [44]And the robbers who were crucified with him also reviled him in the same way.

[45]Now from the sixth hour there was darkness over all the land[m] until the ninth hour. [46]And about the ninth hour Jesus cried with a loud voice, "Eli, Eli, lama sabachthani?" that is, "My God, my God, why hast thou forsaken me?"* [47]And some of the bystanders hearing it said, "This man is calling Elijah." [48]And one of them at once ran and took a sponge, filled it with vinegar, and put it on a reed, and gave it to him to drink. [49]But the others said, "Wait, let us see whether Elijah will come to save him."[n] [50]And Jesus cried again with a loud voice and yielded up his spirit.

Ps 22:8
Wis 2:13, 18–20

Ps 22:1

Ps 69:21

nor does it lie in not showing that one feels pain: rather, suffering means that in spite of pain one does not set aside the law or obedience to God. For feeling is natural to the flesh, which is not like bronze; and so reason does not remove it, because reason gives to everything what its nature demands; and our sensitivity is very soft and tender; when it is wounded it of necessity feels, and when it feels it has to cry out" (Fray Luis de León, *Exposición del Libro de Job*).

In his agony in the garden (cf. note on Mt 26:36–46), Jesus experienced a kind of anticipation of the pain and abandonment he feels at this point in his passion. In the context of the mystery of Jesus Christ, God-and-Man, we should notice how his humanity—body and soul—suffers without his divinity assuaging that suffering, as it could have done. "Here before the cross, we should have sorrow for our sins and for those of all men, for they are responsible for Jesus' death. We should have faith to penetrate deep into this sublime truth which surpasses our understanding and to fill ourselves with amazement at God's love.

And we should pray so that Christ's life and death may become the model and motivation for our own life and self-giving. Only thus will we earn the name of conquerors: for the risen Christ will conquer in us, and death will be changed into life" (St Josemaría Escrivá, *Christ Is Passing By*, 101).

27:50. The phrase "yielded up his spirit" (literally, "released, exhaled") is a way of saying that Christ really died; like any other man, his death meant the separation of soul and body. The fact that he genuinely did die—something that everyone, even his enemies, acknowledged— will show that his resurrection was a real resurrection, a miraculous, divine fact.

This is the climax of Christ's surrender to the will of the Father. Here he accomplishes the salvation of mankind (Mt 26:27–28; Mk 10:45; Heb 9:14) and gives us the greatest proof of God's love for us (Jn 3:16). The saints usually explain the expiatory value of Christ's sacrifice by underlining that he voluntarily "yielded up his spirit". "Our Saviour's death was a sacrifice of holocaust which

m. Or *earth* **n.** Other ancient authorities insert *And another took a spear and pierced his side, and out came water and blood*

Ex 26:31
Heb 10:19f

⁵¹And behold, the curtain of the temple was torn in two, from top to bottom; and the earth shook, and the rocks were split; ⁵²the tombs also were opened, and many bodies of the saints who had

Acts 26:23
Dan 12:2

fallen asleep were raised, ⁵³and coming out of the tombs after his resurrection they went into the holy city and appeared to many. ⁵⁴When the centurion and those who were with him, keeping watch over Jesus, saw the earthquake and what took place, they were filled with awe, and said, "Truly this was the Son[x] of God!"

Lk 8:2f

⁵⁵There were also many women there, looking on from afar, who had followed Jesus from Galilee, ministering to him; ⁵⁶among whom were Mary Magdalene, and Mary the mother of James and Joseph, and the mother of the sons of Zebedee.

The burial of Jesus

Mk 15:42–47
Lk 23:50–55
Jn 19:38–42
Ex 34:25

⁵⁷When it was evening, there came a rich man from Arimathea, named Joseph, who also was a disciple of Jesus. ⁵⁸He went to Pilate and asked for the body of Jesus. Then Pilate ordered it to be

---

he himself offered to his Father for our redemption; for though the pains and sufferings of his passion were so great and violent that anyone else would have died of them, Jesus would not have died of them unless he so chose and unless the fire of his infinite charity had consumed his life. He was, then, himself the sacrificer who offered himself to the Father and immolated himself, dying in love, to love, by love, for love and of love" (St Francis de Sales, *Treatise on the Love of God*, book 10, chap. 17). This fidelity of Christ to the point of dying should be a permanent encouragement to us to persevere until the end, conscious of the fact that only he who is true until death will receive the crown of life (cf. Rev 2:10).

27:51–53. The rending of the temple veil indicates that the way to God the Father has been opened up to all men (cf. Heb 9:15) and that the New Covenant, sealed with the blood of Christ, has begun to operate. The other portents which attend

Jesus' death are signs of the divine character of that event: it was not just one more man who was dying, but the Son of God.

27:52–53. These events are undoubtedly difficult to understand. No explanation should say what the text does not say. Nor does any other part of Holy Scripture, or the Magisterium of the Church, help to clarify what actually happened.

The great Church writers have suggested three possible explanations. First: that it was not a matter of resurrections in the strict sense, but of apparitions of these dead people. Second: they would have been dead people who arose in the way Lazarus did, and then died again. Third: their resurrection would have been definitive, that is glorious, in this way anticipating the final universal resurrection of the dead.

The first explanation does not seem to be very faithful to the text, which does use the words "were raised" (*surrexerunt*). The third is difficult to recon-

x. Or *a son*

180

given to him. [59]And Joseph took the body, and wrapped it in a clean linen shroud, [60]and laid it in his own new tomb, which he had hewn in the rock; and he rolled a great stone to the door of the tomb, and departed. [61]Mary Magdalene and the other Mary were there, sitting opposite the sepulchre.

Is 53:9

[62]Next day, that is, after the day of Preparation, the chief priests and the Pharisees gathered before Pilate [63]and said, "Sir, we remember how that imposter said, while he was still alive, 'After three days I will rise again.' [64]Therefore order the sepulchre to be made secure until the third day, lest his disciples go and steal him away, and tell the people, 'He has risen from the dead,' and the last fraud will be worse than the first." [65]Pilate said to them, 'You have a guard[o] of soldiers; go, make it as secure as you can."[p] [66]So they went and made the sepulchre secure by sealing the stone and setting a guard.*

2 Cor 6:8

Dan 6:18

---

cile with the clear assertion of Scripture that Christ was the first-born from the dead (cf. 1 Cor 15:20; Col 1:18). St Augustine, St Jerome and St Thomas are inclined towards the second explanation because they feel it fits in best with the sacred text and does not present the theological difficulties which the third does (cf. *Summa theologiae*, 3, 53, 3). It is also in keeping with the solution proposed by the *St Pius V Catechism*, 1, 6, 9.

27:55–56. The presence of the holy women beside Christ on the cross gives an example of stoutheartedness to all Christians.

"Woman is stronger than man, and more faithful, in the hour of suffering: Mary Magdalene and Mary Cleophas and Salome! With a group of valiant women like these, closely united to our Lady of Sorrows, what work for souls could be done in the world!" (St Josemaría Escrivá, *The Way*, 982).

27:60. It was customary for well-to-do Jews to build tombs for themselves on their own property. Most of these tombs were excavated out of rock, in the form

of a cavern; they would have had a small hall or vestibule leading to the tomb proper. At the end of the hall, which would only have been a few metres long, a very low doorway gave access to the burial chamber. The first entrance door, which was at ground level, was closed off by a huge stone which could be rolled (it was called a "gobel"), fitted into a groove to make rolling easier.

27:62. The Day of Preparation (the Greek word *parasceve* means "preparation") was the day prior to the sabbath (cf. Lk 23:54). It got its name from the fact that it was the day when everything needed for the sabbath was prepared, the sabbath being a day of rest, consecrated to God, on which no work was permitted.

27:66. All these preventive measures (sealing the entrance to the tomb, placing the guard there, etc.)—measures taken by Christ's enemies—became factors which helped people believe in his resurrection.

28:1–15. The resurrection of Jesus, which

o. Or *take a guard* p. Greek *know*

Jesus rises from the dead and appears to the women

Mk 16:1–10
Lk 24:1–10
Jn 20:1–18
Mt 27:61

Acts 1:10

Acts 2:36
Mt 26:32

28 * ¹Now after the sabbath, toward the dawn of the first day of the week, Mary Magdalene and the other Mary went to see the sepulchre. ²And behold, there was a great earthquake; for an angel of the Lord descended from heaven and came and rolled back the stone, and sat upon it. ³His appearance was like lightning, and his raiment white as snow. ⁴And for fear of him the guards trembled and became like dead men. ⁵But the angel said to the women. "Do not be afraid; for I know that you seek Jesus who was crucified. ⁶He is not here; for he has risen, as he said. Come, see the place where heq lay. ⁷Then go quickly and tell his disciples that he has risen from the dead, and behold, he is going before you to Galilee; there you will see him. Lo, I have told you." ⁸So they departed quickly from the tomb with fear and great joy, and

happened in the early hours of the Sunday morning, is a fact which all the evangelists state clearly and unequivocally. Some holy women discover to their surprise that the tomb is open. On entering the hall (cf. Mk 16:5–6), they see an angel who says to them, "He is not here; for he has risen, as he said." The guards who were on duty when the angel rolled back the stone go to the city and report what has happened to the chief priests. These, because of the urgency of the matter, decide to bribe the guards; they give them a considerable sum of money on condition that they spread the word that his disciples came at night and stole the body of Jesus when they were asleep. "Wretched craftiness," says St Augustine, "do you give us witnesses who were asleep? It is you who are really asleep if this is the only kind of explanation you have to offer!" (*Enarrationes in Psalmos*, 63, 15). The apostles, who a couple of days before fled in fear, will, now that they have seen him and have eaten and drunk with him, become tireless preachers of this great event: "This Jesus", they will say, "God raised up, and of that we

are all witnesses" (Acts 2:32).

Just as he foretold he would go up to Jerusalem and be delivered to the leaders of the Jews and put to death, he also prophesied that he would rise from the dead (Mt 20:17–19; Mk 10:32–34; Lk 18:31–34). By his resurrection he completes the sign he promised to give unbelievers to show his divinity (Mt 12:40).

The resurrection of Christ is one of the basic dogmas of the Catholic faith. In fact, St Paul says, "If Christ has not been raised, then our preaching is in vain and your faith is in vain" (1 Cor 15:14); and, to prove his assertion that Christ rose, he tells us "that he appeared to Cephas, then to the Twelve. Then he appeared to more than five hundred brethren at one time, most of whom are still alive, though some have fallen asleep. Then he appeared to James, then to all the apostles. Last of all, as to one untimely born, he appeared also to me" (1 Cor 15:5–8). The creeds state that Jesus rose from the dead on the third day (*Nicene Creed*), by his own power (Ninth Council of Toledo, *De Redemptione*), by a true resurrection of the flesh (*Creed* of St Leo IX), reunit-

q. Other ancient authorities read *the Lord*

ran to tell his disciples. [9]And behold, Jesus met them and said, "Hail!" And they came up and took hold of his feet and worshipped him. [10]Then Jesus said to them, "Do not be afraid; go and tell my brethren to go to Galilee; and there they will see me."

Heb 2:11
Gen 45:4;
50:19

The soldiers are bribed

[11]While they were going, behold, some of the guard went into the city and told the chief priests all that had taken place. [12]And when they had assembled with the elders and taken counsel, they gave a sum of money to the soldiers [13]and said, "Tell people, 'His disciples came by night and stole him away while we were asleep.' [14]And if this comes to the governor's ears, we will satisfy him and keep you out of trouble." [15]So they took the money and did as they were directed; and this story has been spread among the Jews to this day.

---

ing his soul with his body (Innocent III, *Eius exemplo*), and that this fact of the resurrection is historically proven and provable (St Pius X, *Lamentabili*).

"By the word 'resurrection' we are not merely to understand that Christ was raised from the dead ... but that he rose by his own power and virtue, a singular prerogative peculiar to him alone. Our Lord confirmed this by the divine testimony of his own mouth when he said: 'I lay down my life, that I may take it again.[...] I have power to lay it down: and I have power to take it up again' (Jn 10:17–18). To the Jews he also said, in corroboration of his doctrine: 'Destroy this temple, and in three days I will raise it up' (Jn 2:19–20) [...]. We sometimes, it is true, read in Scripture that he was raised by the Father (cf. Acts 2:24; Rom 8:11); but this refers to him as man, just as those passages on the other hand, which say that he rose by his own power, relate to him as God" (St Pius V, *Catechism*, 1, 6, 8).

Christ's resurrection was not a return to his previous earthly existence; it was a "glorious" resurrection, that is to say, attaining the full development of human life—immortal, freed from all limitations of space and time. As a result of the resurrection, Christ's body now shares in the glory which his soul had from the beginning. Here lies the unique nature of the historical fact of the resurrection. He could be seen not by anyone but only by those to whom he granted that grace, to enable them to be witnesses of this resurrection, and to enable others to believe in him by accepting the testimony of the seers.

Christ's resurrection was something necessary for the completion of the work of our redemption. For, Jesus Christ through his death freed us from sins; but by his resurrection he restored to us all that we had lost through sin and, moreover, opened for us the gates of eternal life (cf. Rom 4:25). Also, the fact that he rose from the dead by his own power is a definitive proof that he is the Son of God, and therefore his resurrection fully confirms our faith in his divinity.

The resurrection of Christ, as has been pointed out, is the most sublime truth of our faith. That is why St Augustine exclaims: "It is no great thing to believe that Christ died; for this is something that is also believed by pagans and Jews and by all the wicked: everyone believes that he died. The Christians' faith is in Christ's resurrection; this is

Appearance in Galilee. The mission to the world

[16]Now the eleven disciples went to Galilee, to the mountain to which Jesus had directed them. [17]And when they saw him they worshipped him; but some doubted. [18]And Jesus came and said to them, "All authority in heaven and on earth has been given to me. [19]Go therefore and make disciples of all nations, baptizing them in

Eph 1:20–22
Dan 7:14
Mk 16:15f

---

what we hold to be a great thing—to believe that he rose" (*Enarrationes in Psalmos*, 120).

The mystery of the Redemption wrought by Christ, which embraces his death and resurrection, is applied to every man and woman through Baptism and the other sacraments, by means of which the believer is as it were immersed in Christ and in his death, that is to say, in a mystical way he becomes part of Christ, he dies and rises with Christ: "We were buried therefore with him by baptism unto death, so that as Christ was raised from the dead by the glory of the Father, we too might walk in newness of life" (Rom 6:4).

An ardent desire to seek the things of God and an interior taste for the things that are above (cf. Col 3:1–3) are signs of our resurrection with Christ.

28:16–20. This short passage, which brings to a close the Gospel of St Matthew, is of great importance. Seeing the risen Christ, the disciples adore him, worshipping him as God. This shows that at last they are fully conscious of what, from much earlier on, they felt in their heart and confessed by their words—that their Master is the Messiah, the Son of God (cf. Mt 16:18; Jn 1:49). They are overcome by amazement and joy at the wonder their eyes behold: it seems almost impossible, were he not before their very eyes. Yet he is completely real, so their fearful amazement gives way to adoration. The Master addresses them with the majesty proper to God: "All authority in heaven and on earth has been

given to me." Omnipotence, an attribute belonging exclusively to God, belongs to him: he is confirming the faith of his worshippers; and he is also telling them that the authority which he is going to give them to equip them to carry out their mission to the whole world, derives from his own divine authority.

On hearing him speak these words, we should bear in mind that the authority of the Church, which is given it for the salvation of mankind, comes directly from Jesus Christ, and that this authority, in the sphere of faith and morals, is above any other authority on earth.

The apostles present on this occasion, and after them their lawful successors, receive the charge of teaching all nations what Jesus taught by word and work: he is the only path that leads to God. The Church, and in it all Christian faithful, has the duty to proclaim until the end of time, by word and example, the faith that she has received. This mission belongs especially to the successors of the apostles, for on them devolves the power to teach with authority, "for, before Christ ascended to his Father after his resurrection, he [...] entrusted them with the mission and power to proclaim to mankind what they had heard, what they had seen with their eyes, what they had looked upon and touched with their hands, concerning the Word of Life (1 Jn 1:1). He also entrusted them with the mission and power to explain with authority what he had taught them, his words and actions, his signs and commandments. And he gave them the Spirit

the name of the Father and of the Son and of the Holy Spirit,
²⁰teaching them to observe all that I have commanded you; and lo,   Jn 14:23
I am with you always, to the close of the age."

---

to fulfil their mission" (John Paul II, *Catechesi tradendae*, 1). Therefore, the teachings of the Pope and of the bishops united in communion with him should always be accepted by everyone with assent and obedience.

Here Christ also passes on to the apostles and their successors the power to baptize, that is, to receive people into the Church, thereby opening up to them the way to personal salvation.

The mission which the Church is definitively given here at the end of St Matthew's Gospel is one of continuing the work of Christ—teaching men and women the truths concerning God and the duty incumbent on them to identify with these truths, to make them their own by having constant recourse to the grace of the sacraments. This mission will endure until the end of time and, to enable the Church to do this work, the risen Christ promises to stay with it and never leave it. When Holy Scripture says that God is with someone, this means that that person will be successful in everything he undertakes. Therefore, the Church, helped in this way by the presence of its divine Founder, can be confident of never failing to fulfil its mission down the centuries until the end of time.

New Vulgate Text

EVANGELIUM SECUNDUM MATTHAEUM

[1] ¹Liber generationis Iesu Christi filii David filii Abraham. ²Abraham genuit Isaac, Isaac autem genuit Iacob, Iacob autem genuit Iudam et fratres eius, ³Iudas autem genuit Phares et Zara de Thamar, Phares autem genuit Esrom, Esrom autem genuit Aram, ⁴Aram autem genuit Aminadab, Aminadab autem genuit Naasson, Naasson autem genuit Salmon, ⁵Salmon autem genuit Booz de Rahab, Booz autem genuit Obed ex Ruth, Obed autem genuit Iesse, ⁶Iesse autem genuit David regem. David autem genuit Salomonem ex ea, quae fuit Uriae, ⁷Salomon autem genuit Roboam, Roboam autem genuit Abiam, Abia autem genuit Asa, ⁸Asa autem genuit Iosaphat, Iosaphat autem genuit Ioram, Ioram autem genuit Oziam, ⁹Ozias autem genuit Ioatham, Ioatham autem genuit Achaz, Achaz autem genuit Ezechiam, ¹⁰Ezechias autem genuit Manassen, Manasses autem genuit Amon, Amon autem genuit Iosiam, ¹¹Iosias autem genuit Iechoniam et fratres eius in transmigratione Babylonis. ¹²Et post transmigrationem Babylonis Iechonias genuit Salathiel, Salathiel autem genuit Zorobabel, ¹³Zorobabel autem genuit Abiud, Abiud autem genuit Eliachim, Eliachim autem genuit Azor, ¹⁴Azor autem genuit Sadoc, Sadoc autem genuit Achim, Achim autem genuit Eliud, ¹⁵Eliud autem genuit Eleazar, Eleazar autem genuit Matthan, Matthan autem genuit Iacob, ¹⁶Iacob autem genuit Ioseph virum Mariae, de qua natus est Iesus, qui vocatur Christus. ¹⁷Omnes ergo generationes ab Abraham usque ad David generationes quattuordecim; et a David usque ad transmigrationem Babylonis generationes quattuordecim; et a transmigratione Babylonis usque ad Christum generationes quattuordecim. ¹⁸Iesu Christi autem generatio sic erat. Cum esset desponsata mater eius Maria Ioseph, antequam convenirent inventa est in utero habens de Spiritu Sancto. ¹⁹Ioseph autem vir eius, cum esset iustus et nollet eam traducere, voluit occulte dimittere eam. ²⁰Haec autem eo cogitante, ecce angelus Domini in somnis apparuit ei dicens: «Ioseph fili David, noli timere accipere Mariam coniugem tuam. Quod enim in ea natum est, de Spiritu Sancto est; ²¹pariet autem filium, et vocabis nomen eius Iesum: ipse enim salvum faciet populum suum a peccatis eorum». ²²Hoc autem totum factum est, ut adimpleretur id, quod dictum est a Domino per prophetam dicentem: ²³«*Ecce, virgo in utero habebit et pariet filium, et vocabunt nomen eius Emmanuel*», quod est interpretatum *Nobiscum Deus*. ²⁴Exsurgens autem Ioseph a somno fecit, sicut praecepit ei angelus Domini, et accepit coniugem suam; ²⁵et non cognoscebat eam, donec peperit filium, et vocavit nomen eius Iesum.   [2] ¹Cum autem natus esset Iesus in Bethlehem Iudaeae in diebus Herodis regis, ecce Magi ab oriente venerunt Hierosolymam, ²dicentes: «Ubi est, qui natus est, rex Iudaeorum? Vidimus enim stellam eius in oriente et venimus adorare eum». ³Audiens autem Herodes rex turbatus est et omnis Hierosolyma cum illo; ⁴et congregans omnes principes sacerdotum et scribas populi, sciscitabatur ab eis ubi Christus nasceretur. ⁵At illi dixerunt ei: «In Bethlehem Iudaeae. Sic enim scriptum est per prophetam: ⁶"*Et tu, Bethlehem* terra Iudae, / nequaquam *minima es in principibus Iudae*; / *ex te enim exiet dux,* / *qui reget populum meum Israel*"». ⁷Tunc Herodes, clam vocatis Magis, diligenter didicit ab eis tempus stellae, quae apparuit eis, ⁸et mittens illos in Bethlehem dixit: «Ite et interrogate diligenter de puero; et cum inveneritis renuntiate mihi, ut et ego veniens adorem eum». ⁹Qui cum audissent regem, abierunt. Et ecce stella, quam viderant in oriente, antecedebat eos, usque dum veniens staret supra, ubi erat puer. ¹⁰Videntes autem stellam gavisi sunt gaudio magno valde. ¹¹Et intrantes domum viderunt puerum cum Maria matre eius, et procidentes adoraverunt eum; et apertis thesauris suis, obtulerunt ei munera, aurum et tus et myrrham. ¹²Et responso accepto in somnis, ne redirent ad Herodem, per aliam viam reversi sunt in regionem suam. ¹³Qui cum recessissent, ecce angelus Domini apparet in somnis Ioseph dicens: «Surge et accipe puerum et matrem eius et fuge in Aegyptum et esto ibi, usque dum dicam tibi; futurum est enim ut Herodes quaerat puerum ad perdendum eum». ¹⁴Qui consurgens accepit puerum et matrem eius nocte et recessit in Aegyptum ¹⁵et erat ibi usque ad obitum Herodis, ut adimpleretur, quod dictum est a Domino per prophetam dicentem: «*Ex Aegypto vocavi filium meum*». ¹⁶Tunc Herodes videns quoniam illusus esset a Magis, iratus est

valde et mittens occidit omnes pueros, qui erant in Bethlehem et in omnibus finibus eius, a bimatu et infra, secundum tempus, quod exquisierat a Magis. [17]Tunc adimpletum est, quod dictum est per Ieremiam prophetam dicentem: [18]«*Vox in Rama audita est, / ploratus et ululatus multus: / Rachel plorans filios suos, / et noluit consolari, quia non sunt*». [19]Defuncto autem Herode, ecce apparet angelus Domini in somnis Ioseph in Aegypto [20]dicens: «Surge et accipe puerum et matrem eius et vade in terram Israel; defuncti sunt enim, qui quaerebant animam pueri». [21]Qui surgens accepit puerum et matrem eius et venit in terram Israel. [22]Audiens autem quia Archelaus regnaret in Iudaea pro Herode patre suo, timuit illuc ire; et admonitus in somnis, secessit in partes Galilaeae [23]et veniens habitavit in civitate, quae vocatur Nazareth, ut adimpleretur, quod dictum est per Prophetas: «Nazaraeus vocabitur». [3] [1]In diebus autem illis venit Ioannes Baptista praedicans in deserto Iudaeae [2]et dicens: «Paenitentiam agite; appropinquavit enim regnum caelorum». [3]Hic est enim, qui dictus est per Isaiam prophetam dicentem: «*Vox clamantis in deserto: / "Parate viam Domini, / rectas facite semitas eius!"*». [4]Ipse autem Ioannes habebat vestimentum de pilis cameli et zonam pelliceam circa lumbos suos; esca autem eius erat locustae et mel silvestre. [5]Tunc exibat ad eum Hierosolyma et omnis Iudaea et omnis regio circa Iordanem, [6]et baptizabantur in Iordane flumine ab eo, confitentes peccata sua. [7]Videns autem multos pharisaeorum et sadducaeorum venientes ad baptismum suum, dixit eis: «Progenies viperarum, quis demonstravit vobis fugere a futura ira? [8]Facite ergo fructum dignum paenitentiae [9]et ne velitis dicere intra vos: "Patrem habemus Abraham"; dico enim vobis quoniam potest Deus de lapidibus istis suscitare Abrahae filios. [10]Iam enim securis ad radicem arborum posita est; omnis ergo arbor, quae non facit fructum bonum, exciditur et in ignem mittitur. [11]Ego quidem vos baptizo in aqua in paenitentiam; qui autem post me venturus est, fortior me est, cuius non sum dignus calceamenta portare; ipse vos baptizabit in Spiritu Sancto et igni, [12]cuius ventilabrum in manu sua, et permundabit aream suam et congregabit triticum suum in horreum, paleas autem comburet igni inexstinguibili». [13]Tunc venit Iesus a Galilaea in Iordanem ad Ioannem, ut baptizaretur ab eo. [14]Ioannes autem prohibebat eum dicens: «Ego a te debeo baptizari, et tu venis ad me?». [15]Respondens autem Iesus dixit ei: «Sine modo, sic enim decet nos implere omnem iustitiam». Tunc dimittit eum. [16]Baptizatus autem Iesus, confestim ascendit de aqua; et ecce aperti sunt ei caeli, et vidit Spiritum Dei descendentem sicut columbam et venientem super se. [17]Et ecce vox de caelis dicens: «Hic est Filius meus dilectus, in quo mihi complacui». [4] [1]Tunc Iesus ductus est in desertum a Spiritu, ut tentaretur a Diabolo. [2]Et cum ieiunasset quadraginta diebus et quadraginta noctibus, postea esuriit. [3]Et accedens tentator dixit ei: «Si Filius Dei es, dic, ut lapides isti panes fiant». [4]Qui respondens dixit: «Scriptum est: / "*Non in pane solo vivet homo, / sed in omni verbo, quod procedit de ore Dei*"». [5]Tunc assumit eum Diabolus in sanctam civitatem et statuit eum supra pinnaculum templi [6]et dicit ei: «Si Filius Dei es, mitte te deorsum. Scriptum est enim: "*Angelis suis mandabit de te, / et in manibus tollent te, / ne forte offendas ad lapidem pedem tuum*"». [7]Ait illi Iesus: «Rursum scriptum est: "*Non tentabis Dominum Deum tuum*"». [8]Iterum assumit eum Diabolus in montem excelsum valde et ostendit ei omnia regna mundi et gloriam eorum [9]et dicit illi: «Haec tibi omnia dabo, si cadens adoraveris me». [10]Tunc dicit ei Iesus: «Vade, Satanas! Scriptum est enim: / "*Dominum Deum tuum adorabis / et illi soli servies*"». [11]Tunc reliquit eum Diabolus, et ecce angeli accesserunt et ministrabant ei. [12]Cum autem audisset quod Ioannes traditus esset, secessit in Galilaeam. [13]Et relicta Nazareth, venit et habitavit in Capharnaum maritimam [14]in finibus Zabulon et Nephthali, ut impleretur, quod dictum est per Isaiam prophetam dicentem: [15]«*Terra Zabulon et terra Nephthali, / ad viam maris, trans Iordanem, / Galilaea gentium; / [16]populus, qui sedebat in tenebris, / lucem vidit magnam, / et sedentibus in regione et umbra mortis / lux orta est eis*». [17]Exinde coepit Iesus praedicare et dicere: «Paenitentiam agite; appropinquavit enim regnum caelorum». [18]Ambulans autem iuxta mare Galilaeae, vidit duos fratres, Simonem, qui vocatur Petrus, et Andream fratrem eius, mittentes rete in mare; erant enim piscatores. [19]Et ait illis: «Venite post me, et faciam vos piscatores hominum». [20]At illi continuo, relictis retibus, secuti sunt eum. [21]Et procedens inde vidit alios duos fratres, Iacobum Zebedaei et Ioannem fratrem eius, in navi cum Zebedaeo patre eorum reficientes retia sua, et vocavit eos. [22]Illi autem statim, relicta navi et patre suo, secuti sunt eum. [23]Et circumibat Iesus totam Galilaeam, docens in synagogis eorum et praedicans evangelium regni et sanans omnem languorem et omnem infirmitatem in populo. [24]Et abiit opinio eius in totam Syriam; et obtulerunt ei omnes male habentes, variis languoribus et tormentis comprehensos, et qui daemonia habebant, et lunaticos et paralyticos, et curavit eos. [25]Et secutae sunt eum turbae multae de Galilaea et Decapoli et Hierosolymis et Iudaea et de trans Iordanem. [5] [1]Videns autem turbas, ascendit in montem; et cum sedisset, accesserunt ad eum discipuli eius; [2]et aperiens os suum docebat eos dicens: [3]«Beati pauperes spiritu, quoniam ipsorum est regnum caelorum. [4]Beati, qui lugent, quoniam ipsi consolabuntur. [5]Beati mites, quoniam ipsi possidebunt terram. [6]Beati, qui esuriunt et sitiunt iustitiam, quoniam ipsi saturabuntur. [7]Beati misericordes, quia ipsi misericordiam consequentur. [8]Beati mundo corde, quoniam ipsi Deum videbunt. [9]Beati pacifici, quoniam filii Dei vocabuntur. [10]Beati, qui persecutionem patiuntur propter iustitiam, quoniam ipsorum est regnum caelorum. [11]Beati estis cum maledixerint vobis et persecuti vos fuerint et dixerint omne malum adversum vos, mentientes, propter me. [12]Gaudete et exsultate, quoniam merces vestra copiosa est in caelis; sic enim persecuti sunt prophetas, qui fuerunt ante vos. [13]Vos estis sal terrae; quod si sal evanuerit, in quo salietur? Ad nihilum valet ultra, nisi ut mittatur foras et conculcetur ab hominibus. [14]Vos estis lux mundi. Non potest civitas abscondi supra montem posita; [15]neque accendunt lucernam et ponunt eam sub modio, sed super candelabrum, ut luceat omnibus, qui in domo sunt. [16]Sic luceat lux vestra coram hominibus, ut videant vestra bona opera et glorificent Patrem vestrum, qui in caelis est. [17]Nolite putare quoniam veni solvere Legem aut Prophetas; non veni solvere, sed adimplere. [18]Amen quippe dico vobis: Donec transeat caelum et terra, iota unum aut unus apex non praeteribit a Lege, donec omnia fiant. [19]Qui ergo solverit unum de mandatis istis minimis et docuerit sic homines, minimus vocabitur in regno caelorum; qui autem fecerit et docuerit, hic magnus vocabitur in regno caelorum. [20]Dico enim vobis: Nisi abundaverit iustitia vestra plus quam scribarum et pharisaeorum, non intrabitis in regnum caelorum. [21]Audistis quia dictum est antiquis: *"Non occides*; qui autem occiderit, reus erit iudicio". [22]Ego autem dico vobis: Omnis, qui irascitur fratri suo, reus erit iudicio; qui autem dixerit fratri suo: "Racha", reus erit concilio; qui autem dixerit: "Fatue", reus erit gehennae ignis. [23]Si ergo offeres munus tuum ad altare, et ibi recordatus fueris quia frater tuus habet aliquid adversum te, [24]relinque ibi munus tuum ante altare et vade prius, reconciliare fratri tuo et tunc veniens offer munus tuum. [25]Esto consentiens adversario tuo cito, dum es in via cum eo, ne forte tradat te adversarius iudici, et iudex tradat te ministro, et in carcerem mittaris. [26]Amen dico tibi: Non exies inde, donec reddas novissimum quadrantem. [27]Audistis quia dictum est: *"Non moechaberis"*. [28]Ego autem dico vobis: Omnis, qui viderit mulierem ad concupiscendum eam, iam moechatus est eam in corde suo. [29]Quod si oculus tuus dexter scandalizat te, erue eum et proice abs te; expedit enim tibi, ut pereat unum membrorum tuorum, quam totum corpus tuum mittatur in gehennam. [30]Et si dextera manus tua scandalizat te, abscide eam et proice abs te; expedit enim tibi, ut pereat unum membrorum tuorum, quam totum corpus tuum abeat in gehennam. [31]Dictum est autem: *"Quicumque dimiserit uxorem suam, det illi libellum repudii"*. [32]Ego autem dico vobis: Omnis, qui dimiserit uxorem suam, excepta fornicationis causa, facit eam moechari; et, qui dimissam duxerit, adulterat. [33]Iterum audistis quia dictum est antiquis: *"Non periurabis*; reddes autem *Domino iuramenta tua"*. [34]Ego autem dico vobis: Non iurare omnino, neque per *caelum*, quia *thronus Dei est*, [35]neque per *terram*, quia *scabellum est pedum eius*, neque per Hierosolymam, quia *civitas* est *magni Regis*; [36]neque per caput tuum iuraveris, quia non potes unum capillum album facere aut nigrum. [37]Sit autem sermo vester: "Est, est", "Non, non"; quod autem his abundantius est, a Malo est. [38]Audistis quia dictum est: *"Oculum pro oculo* et *dentem pro dente"*. [39]Ego autem dico vobis: Non resistere malo; sed si quis te percusserit in dextera maxilla tua, praebe illi et alteram; [40]et ei, qui vult tecum iudicio contendere et tunicam tuam tollere, remitte ei et pallium; [41]et quicumque te angariaverit mille passus, vade cum illo duo. [42]Qui petit a te, da ei; et volenti mutuari a te, ne avertaris. [43]Audistis quia dictum est: *"Diliges proximum tuum* et odio habebis inimicum tuum". [44]Ego autem dico vobis: Diligite inimicos vestros et orate pro persequentibus vos, [45]ut sitis filii Patris vestri, qui in caelis est, quia solem suum oriri facit super malos et bonos et pluit super iustos et iniustos. [46]Si enim dilexeritis eos, qui vos diligunt, quam mercedem habetis? Nonne et publicani hoc faciunt? [47]Et si salutaveritis fratres vestros tantum, quid amplius facitis? Nonne et ethnici hoc faciunt? [48]Estote ergo vos perfecti, sicut Pater vester caelestis perfectus est.   **[6]** [1]Attendite, ne iustitiam vestram faciatis coram hominibus, ut videamini ab eis; alioquin mercedem non habetis apud Patrem vestrum, qui in caelis est.[2]Cum ergo facies eleemosynam, noli tuba canere ante te, sicut hypocritae faciunt in synagogis et in vicis, ut honorificentur ab hominibus. Amen dico vobis: Receperunt mercedem suam. [3]Te autem faciente eleemosynam, nesciat sinistra tua quid faciat dextera tua, [4]ut sit eleemosyna tua in abscondito, et Pater tuus, qui videt in abscondito, reddet tibi. [5]Et cum oratis, non eritis sicut hypocritae, qui amant in synagogis et in angulis platearum stantes orare, ut videantur ab hominibus. Amen dico vobis: Receperunt mercedem suam. [6]Tu autem cum orabis, intra in cubiculum tuum et, clauso ostio tuo, ora Patrem tuum, qui est in abscondito; et Pater tuus, qui videt in abscondito, reddet tibi. [7]Orantes autem nolite multum loqui sicut ethnici: putant enim quia in multiloquio suo exaudiantur. [8]Nolite ergo assimilari eis; scit enim Pater vester, quibus opus sit vobis, antequam petatis eum. [9]Sic ergo vos orabitis: Pater noster, qui es in caelis, / sanctificetur nomen tuum, / [10]adveniat regnum tuum, / fiat voluntas tua, / sicut in caelo, et in terra. / [11]Panem nostrum supersubstantialem da nobis hodie; / [12]et dimitte nobis debita nostra, / sicut et nos dimittimus debitoribus nostris; / [13]et ne inducas nos in tentationem, / sed libera nos a Malo. [14]Si enim dimiseritis hominibus peccata eorum, dimittet et vobis Pater vester caelestis; [15]si autem non dimiseritis hominibus, nec Pater vester dimittet peccata vestra. [16]Cum autem ieiunatis, nolite fieri sicut hypocritae tristes; demoliuntur enim facies suas, ut pareant hominibus ieiunantes. Amen dico vobis: Receperunt mercedem suam. [17]Tu autem cum ieiunas, unge caput tuum et faciem tuam lava, [18]ne videaris hominibus ieiunans sed Patri tuo, qui est in abscondito; et Pater tuus, qui videt in abscondito, reddet tibi. [19]Nolite thesaurizare vobis thesauros in terra, ubi aerugo et tinea demolitur, et ubi fures effodiunt et furantur; [20]thesaurizate autem vobis thesauros in caelo, ubi neque aerugo neque tinea demolitur, et ubi fures non effodiunt nec furantur; [21]ubi enim est thesaurus tuus, ibi erit et cor tuum. [22]Lucerna corporis est oculus. Si ergo fuerit oculus tuus simplex, totum corpus tuum lucidum erit; [23]si autem oculus tuus nequam fuerit, totum corpus tuum tenebrosum erit. Si ergo lumen, quod in te est, tenebrae sunt, tenebrae quantae erunt! [24]Nemo potest duobus dominis servire: aut enim unum odio habebit et alterum diliget aut unum sustinebit et alterum contemnet; non potestis Deo servire et mammonae. [25]Ideo dico vobis: Ne solliciti sitis animae vestrae quid manducetis, neque corpori vestro quid induamini. Nonne anima plus est quam esca, et corpus quam vestimentum? [26]Respicite volatilia caeli, quoniam non serunt neque metunt neque congregant in horrea, et Pater vester caelestis pascit illa. Nonne vos magis pluris estis illis? [27]Quis autem vestrum cogitans potest adicere ad aetatem suam cubitum unum? [28]Et de vestimento quid solliciti estis? Considerate lilia agri quomodo crescunt: non laborant neque nent. [29]Dico autem vobis quoniam nec Salomon in omni gloria sua coopertus est sicut unum ex istis. [30]Si autem fenum agri, quod hodie est et cras in clibanum mittitur, Deus sic vestit, quanto magis vos, modicae fidei? [31]Nolite ergo solliciti esse dicentes: "Quid manducabimus?", aut: "Quid bibemus?", aut: "Quo operiemur?". [32]Haec enim omnia gentes inquirunt; scit enim Pater vester caelestis quia his omnibus indigetis. [33]Quaerite autem primum regnum Dei et iustitiam eius, et haec omnia adicientur vobis. [34]Nolite ergo esse solliciti in crastinum; crastinus enim dies sollicitus erit sibi ipse. Sufficit diei malitia sua. [7] [1]Nolite iudicare, ut non iudicemini; [2]in quo enim iudicio iudicaveritis, iudicabimini, et in qua mensura mensi fueritis, metietur vobis. [3]Quid autem vides festucam in oculo fratris tui, et trabem in oculo tuo non vides? [4]Aut quomodo dices fratri tuo: 'Sine, eiciam festucam de oculo tuo', et ecce trabes est in oculo tuo? [5]Hypocrita, eice primum trabem de oculo tuo, et tunc videbis eicere festucam de oculo fratris tui. [6]Nolite dare sanctum canibus, neque mittatis margaritas vestras ante porcos, ne forte conculcent eas pedibus suis et conversi dirumpant vos. [7]Petite, et dabitur vobis; quaerite et invenietis; pulsate, et aperietur vobis. [8]Omnis enim qui petit, accipit; et, qui quaerit, invenit; et pulsanti aperietur. [9]Aut quis est ex vobis homo, quem si petierit filius suus panem, numquid lapidem porriget ei? [10]Aut si piscem petierit, numquid serpentem porriget ei? [11]Si ergo vos, cum sitis mali, nostis dona bona dare filiis vestris, quanto magis Pater vester, qui in caelis est, dabit bona petentibus se. [12]Omnia ergo, quaecumque vultis ut faciant vobis homines, ita et vos facite eis; haec est enim Lex et Prophetae. [13]Intrate per angustam portam, quia lata porta et spatiosa via, quae ducit ad perditionem, et multi sunt, qui intrant per eam; [14]quam angusta porta et arta via, quae ducit ad vitam, et pauci sunt, qui inveniunt eam! [15]Attendite a falsis prophetis, qui veniunt ad vos in vestimentis ovium, intrinsecus autem sunt lupi rapaces. [16]A fructibus eorum cognoscetis eos: numquid colligunt de spinis uvas aut de tribulis ficus? [17]Sic omnis arbor bona fructus bonos facit, mala autem arbor fructus malos facit: [18]non potest arbor bona fructus malos facere, neque arbor mala fructus bonos facere. [19]Omnis arbor, quae non facit fructum bonum, exciditur et in ignem mittitur. [20]Igitur ex fructibus eorum cognoscetis eos. [21]Non omnis, qui dicit mihi: "Domine Domine", intrabit in regnum caelorum, sed qui facit voluntatem Patris mei, qui in caelis est. [22]Multi dicent mihi in illa die: "Domine, Domine, nonne in tuo nomine prophetavimus, et in tuo nomine daemonia eiecimus, et in tuo nomine virtutes multas fecimus?". [23]Et tunc confitebor illis: Numquam novi vos; discedite a me, qui operamini iniquitatem. [24]Omnis ergo, qui audit verba mea haec et facit ea, assimilabitur viro sapienti, qui aedificavit domum suam supra petram. [25]Et descendit pluvia, et venerunt flumina, et flaverunt venti et irruerunt in domum illam, et non cecidit; fundata enim erat supra petram. [26]Et omnis, qui audit verba mea haec et non facit ea, similis erit viro stulto, qui aedificavit domum suam supra arenam. [27]Et descendit pluvia, et venerunt flumina, et flaverunt venti et irruerunt in domum illam, et cecidit, et fuit ruina eius magna». [28]Et factum est cum consummasset Iesus verba haec, admirabantur turbae super doctrinam eius; [29]erat enim docens eos sicut potestatem habens et non sicut scribae eorum. [8] [1]Cum autem descendisset de monte, secutae sunt eum turbae multae. [2]Et ecce leprosus veniens adorabat eum dicens: «Domine, si vis, potes me mundare». [3]Et extendens manum, tetigit eum dicens: «Volo, mundare!»; et confestim mundata est lepra eius. [4]Et ait illi Iesus: «Vide, nemini dixeris; sed vade, ostende te sacerdoti et offer munus, quod praecepit Moyses, in testimonium illis». [5]Cum autem introisset Capharnaum, accessit ad eum centurio rogans eum [6]et dicens: «Domine, puer meus iacet in domo paralyticus et male torquetur». [7]Et ait illi: «Ego veniam et curabo eum». [8]Et respondens centurio ait: «Domine, non sum dignus, ut intres sub tectum meum, sed tantum dic verbo, et sanabitur puer meus. [9]Nam et ego homo sum sub potestate, habens sub me milites, et dico huic: "Vade", et vadit; et alii: "Veni", et venit; et servo meo: "Fac hoc", et facit». [10]Audiens autem Iesus, miratus est et sequentibus se dixit: «Amen dico vobis: Apud nullum inveni tantam fidem in Israel! [11]Dico autem vobis quod multi ab oriente et occidente venient et recumbent cum Abraham et Isaac et Iacob in regno caelorum; [12]filii autem regni eicientur in tenebras exteriores: ibi erit fletus et stridor dentium». [13]Et dixit Iesus centurioni: «Vade; sicut credidisti fiat tibi». Et sanatus est puer in hora illa. [14]Et cum venisset Iesus in domum Petri, vidit socrum eius iacentem et febricitantem; [15]et tetigit manum eius, et dimisit eam febris; et surrexit et ministrabat ei. [16]Vespere autem facto, obtulerunt ei multos daemonia habentes; et eiciebat spiritus verbo et omnes male habentes curavit, [17]ut adimpleretur, quod dictum est per Isaiam prophetam dicentem: *Ipse infirmitates nostras accepit* / *et aegrotationes portavit*». [18]Videns autem Iesus turbas multas circum se, iussit ire trans fretum. [19]Et accedens unus scriba ait illi: «Magister, sequar te quocumque ieris». [20]Et dicit ei Iesus: «Vulpes foveas habent et volucres caeli tabernacula, Filius autem hominis non habet, ubi caput reclinet». [21]Alius autem de discipulis eius ait illi: «Domine, permitte me primum ire et sepelire patrem meum». [22]Iesus autem ait illi: «Sequere me et dimitte mortuos sepelire mortuos suos». [23]Et ascendente eo in naviculam, secuti sunt eum discipuli eius. [24]Et ecce motus magnus factus est in mari, ita ut navicula operiretur fluctibus; ipse vero dormiebat. [25]Et accesserunt et suscitaverunt eum dicentes: «Domine, salva nos, perimus!». [26]Et dicit eis: «Quid timidi estis, modicae fidei?». Tunc surgens increpavit ventis et mari, et facta est tranquillitas magna. [27]Porro homines mirati sunt dicentes: «Qualis est hic, quia et venti et mare oboediunt ei?». [28]Et cum venisset trans fretum in regionem Gadarenorum, occurrerunt ei duo habentes daemonia, de monumentis exeuntes, saevi nimis, ita ut nemo posset transire per viam illam. [29]Et ecce clamaverunt dicentes: «Quid nobis et tibi, Fili Dei? Venisti huc ante tempus torquere nos?». [30]Erat autem longe ab illis grex porcorum multorum pascens. [31]Daemones autem rogabant eum dicentes: «Si eicis nos, mitte nos in gregem porcorum». [32]Et ait illis: «Ite». Et illi exeuntes abierunt in porcos; et ecce impetu abiit totus grex per praeceps in mare, et mortui sunt in aquis. [33]Pastores autem fugerunt et venientes in civitatem nuntiaverunt omnia et de his, qui daemonia habuerant. [34]Et ecce tota civitas exiit obviam Iesu, et viso eo rogabant, ut transiret a finibus eorum.   [9] [1]Et ascendens in naviculam transfretavit et venit in civitatem suam. [2]Et ecce offerebant ei paralyticum iacentem in lecto. Et videns Iesus fidem illorum, dixit paralytico: «Confide, fili; remittuntur peccata tua». [3]Et ecce quidam de scribis dixerunt intra se: «Hic blasphemat». [4]Et cum vidisset Iesus cogitationes eorum, dixit: «Ut quid cogitatis mala in cordibus vestris? [5]Quid enim est facilius, dicere: "Dimittuntur peccata tua", aut dicere: "Surge et ambula"? [6]Ut sciatis autem quoniam Filius hominis habet potestatem in terra dimittendi peccata — tunc ait paralytico—: Surge, tolle lectum tuum et vade in domum tuam». [7]Et surrexit et abiit in domum suam. [8]Videntes autem turbae timuerunt et glorificaverunt Deum, qui dedit potestatem talem hominibus. [9]Et cum transiret inde Iesus, vidit hominem sedentem in teloneo, Matthaeum nomine, et ait illi: «Sequere me». Et surgens secutus est eum. [10]Et factum est, discumbente eo in domo, ecce multi publicani et peccatores venientes simul discumbebant cum Iesu et discipulis eius. [11]Et videntes pharisaei dicebant discipulis eius: «Quare cum publicanis et peccatoribus manducat magister vester?». [12]At ille audiens ait: «Non est opus valentibus medico sed male habentibus. [13]Euntes autem discite quid est: *"Misericordiam volo et non sacrificium"*. Non enim veni vocare iustos, sed peccatores». [14]Tunc accedunt ad eum discipuli Ioannis dicentes: «Quare nos et pharisaei ieiunamus frequenter, discipuli autem tui non ieiunant?». [15]Et ait illis Iesus: «Numquid possunt convivae nuptiarum lugere, quamdiu cum illis est sponsus? Venient autem dies, cum auferetur ab eis sponsus, et tunc ieiunabunt. [16]Nemo autem immittit commissuram panni rudis in vestimentum vetus; tollit enim supplementum eius a vestimento, et peior scissura fit. [17]Neque mittunt vinum novum in utres veteres, alioquin rumpuntur utres, et vinum effunditur, et utres pereunt; sed vinum novum in utres novos mittunt, et ambo conservantur». [18]Haec illo loquente ad eos, ecce princeps unus accessit et adorabat eum dicens: «Filia mea modo defuncta est; sed veni, impone manum tuam super eam, et vivet». [19]Et surgens Iesus sequebatur eum et discipuli eius. [20]Et ecce mulier, quae sanguinis fluxum patiebatur duodecim annis, accessit retro et tetigit fimbriam vestimenti eius. [21]Dicebat enim intra se: «Si tetigero tantum vestimentum eius, salva ero». [22]At Iesus conversus et videns eam dixit: «Confide, filia; fides tua te salvam fecit». Et salva facta est mulier ex illa hora. [23]Et cum venisset Iesus in domum principis et vidisset tibicines et turbam tumultuantem, [24]dicebat: «Recedite; non est enim mortua puella, sed dormit». Et deridebant eum. [25]At cum eiecta esset turba, intravit et tenuit manum eius, et surrexit puella. [26]Et exiit fama haec in universam terram illam. [27]Et transeunte inde Iesu, secuti sunt eum duo caeci clamantes et dicentes: «Miserere nostri, fili David!». [28]Cum autem venisset domum, accesserunt ad eum caeci, et dicit eis Iesus: «Creditis quia possum hoc facere?». Dicunt ei: «Utique, Domine». [29]Tunc tetigit oculos eorum dicens: «Secundum fidem vestram fiat vobis». [30]Et aperti sunt oculi illorum. Et comminatus est illis Iesus dicens: «Videte, ne quis sciat». [31]Illi autem exeuntes diffamaverunt eum in universa terra illa. [32]Egressis autem illis, ecce obtulerunt ei hominem mutum, daemonium habentem. [33]Et eiecto daemone, locutus est mutus. Et miratae sunt turbae dicentes: «Numquam apparuit sic in Israel!». [34]Pharisaei autem dicebant: «In principe daemoniorum eicit daemones». [35]Et circumibat Iesus civitates omnes et castella, docens in synagogis eorum et praedicans evangelium regni et curans omnem languorem et omnem infirmitatem. [36]Videns autem turbas, misertus est eis quia erant vexati et iacentes sicut oves non habentes pastorem. [37]Tunc dicit discipulis suis: «Messis quidem multa, operarii autem pauci; [38]rogate ergo Dominum messis, ut mittat operarios in messem suam». **[10]** [1]Et convocatis Duodecim discipulis suis, dedit illis potestatem spirituum immundorum, ut eicerent eos et curarent omnem languorem et omnem infirmitatem. [2]Duodecim autem apostolorum nomina sunt haec: primus Simon, qui dicitur Petrus, et Andreas frater eius, et Iacobus Zebedaei et Ioannes frater eius, [3]Philippus et Bartholomaeus, Thomas et Matthaeus publicanus, Iacobus Alphaei et Thaddaeus, [4]Simon Chananaeus et Iudas Iscariotes, qui et tradidit eum. [5]Hos Duodecim misit Iesus praecipiens eis et dicens: «In viam gentium ne abieritis et in civitates Samaritanorum ne intraveritis; [6]sed potius ite ad oves, quae perierunt domus Israel. [7]Euntes autem praedicate dicentes: «Appropinquavit regnum caelorum. [8]Infirmos curate, mortuos suscitate, leprosos mundate, daemones eicite; gratis accepistis, gratis date. [9]Nolite possidere aurum neque argentum neque pecuniam in zonis vestris, [10]non peram in via neque duas tunicas neque calceamenta neque virgam; dignus enim est operarius cibo suo. [11]In quamcumque civitatem aut castellum intraveritis, interrogate quis in ea dignus sit; et ibi manete donec exeatis. [12]Intrantes autem in domum, salutate eam; [13]et siquidem fuerit domus digna, veniat pax vestra super eam; si autem non fuerit digna, pax vestra ad vos revertatur. [14]Et quicumque non receperit vos neque audierit sermones vestros, exeuntes foras de domo vel de civitate illa, excutite pulverem de pedibus vestris. [15]Amen dico vobis: Tolerabilius erit terrae Sodomorum et Gomorraeorum in die iudicii quam illi civitati. [16]Ecce ego mitto vos sicut oves in medio luporum; estote ergo prudentes sicut serpentes et simplices sicut columbae. [17]Cavete autem ab hominibus; tradent enim vos in conciliis, et in synagogis suis flagellabunt vos; [18]et ad praesides et ad reges ducemini propter me in testimonium illis et gentibus. [19]Cum autem tradent vos, nolite cogitare quomodo aut quid loquamini; dabitur enim vobis in illa hora quid loquamini. [20]Non enim vos estis, qui loquimini, sed Spiritus Patris vestri, qui loquitur in vobis. [21]Tradet autem frater fratrem in mortem, et pater filium; et insurgent filii in parentes et morte eos afficient. [22]Et eritis odio omnibus propter nomen meum; qui autem perseveraverit in finem, hic salvus erit. [23]Cum autem persequentur vos in civitate ista, fugite in aliam; amen enim dico vobis: Non consummabitis civitates Israel, donec veniat Filius hominis. [24]Non est discipulus super magistrum nec servus super dominum suum. [25]Sufficit discipulo, ut sit sicut magister eius, et servus sicut dominus eius. Si patrem familias Beelzebul vocaverunt, quanto magis domesticos eius! [26] Ne ergo timueritis eos. Nihil enim est opertum, quod non revelabitur, et occultum, quod non scietur. [27]Quod dico vobis in tenebris, dicite in lumine; et quod in aure auditis, praedicate super tecta. [28]Et nolite timere eos, qui occidunt corpus, animam autem non possunt occidere; sed potius eum timete, qui potest et animam et corpus perdere in gehenna. [29]Nonne duo passeres asse veneunt? Et unus ex illis non cadet super terram sine Patre vestro. [30]Vestri autem et capilli capitis omnes numerati sunt. [31]Nolite ergo timere; multis passeribus meliores estis vos. [32]Omnis ergo qui confitebitur me coram hominibus, confitebor et ego eum coram Patre meo, qui est in caelis; [33]qui autem negaverit me coram hominibus, negabo et ego eum coram Patre meo, qui est in caelis. [34]Nolite arbitrari quia venerim mittere pacem in terram; non veni pacem mittere sed gladium. [35]Veni enim separare hominem *adversus patrem suum / et filiam adversus matrem suam / et nurum adversus socrum suam: /* [36]et *inimici hominis domestici eius.* [37]Qui amat patrem aut matrem plus quam me, non est me dignus; et, qui amat filium aut filiam super me, non est me dignus; [38]et, qui non accipit crucem suam et sequitur me, non est me dignus. [39]Qui invenerit animam suam, perdet illam; et, qui perdiderit animam suam propter me, inveniet eam. [40]Qui recipit vos, me recipit; et, qui me recipit, recipit eum, qui me misit. [41]Qui recipit prophetam in nomine prophetae, mercedem prophetae accipiet; et, qui recipit iustum in nomine iusti, mercedem iusti accipiet. [42]Et, quicumque potum dederit uni ex minimis istis calicem aquae frigidae tantum in nomine discipuli, amen dico vobis: Non perdet mercedem suam». **[11]** [1]Et factum est cum consummasset Iesus praecipiens Duodecim discipulis suis, transiit inde, ut doceret et praedicaret in civitatibus eorum. [2]Ioannes autem, cum audisset in vinculis opera Christi, mittens per discipulos suos [3]ait illi: «Tu es qui venturus es, an alium exspectamus?». [4]Et respondens Iesus ait illis: «Euntes renuntiate Ioanni, quae auditis et videtis: [5]*caeci vident* et claudi ambulant, leprosi mundantur et surdi audiunt et mortui resurgunt et *pauperes evangelizantur;* [6]et beatus est, qui non fuerit scandalizatus in me». [7]Illis autem abeuntibus, coepit Iesus dicere ad turbas de Ioanne:

«Quid existis in desertum videre? Arundinem vento agitatam? [8]Sed quid existis videre? Hominem mollibus vestitum? Ecce, qui mollibus vestiuntur, in domibus regum sunt. [9]Sed quid existis videre? Prophetam? Etiam, dico vobis, et plus quam prophetam. [10]Hic est, de quo scriptum est: *"Ecce ego mitto angelum meum ante faciem tuam, / qui praeparabit viam* tuam *ante* te". [11]Amen dico vobis: Non surrexit inter natos mulierum maior Ioanne Baptista; qui autem minor est in regno caelorum, maior est illo. [12]A diebus autem Ioannis Baptistae usque nunc regnum caelorum vim patitur, et violenti rapiunt illud. [13]Omnes enim Prophetae et Lex usque ad Ioannem prophetaverunt; [14]et si vultis recipere, ipse est Elias, qui venturus est. [15]Qui habet aures, audiat. [16]Cui autem similem aestimabo generationem istam? Similis est pueris sedentibus in foro, qui clamantes coaequalibus [17]dicunt: "Cecinimus vobis, et non saltastis; / lamentavimus, et non planxistis". [18]Venit enim Ioannes neque manducans neque bibens, et dicunt: "Daemonium habet!"; [19]venit Filius hominis manducans et bibens, et dicunt: "Ecce homo vorax et potator vini, publicanorum amicus et peccatorum!". Et iustificata est sapientia ab operibus suis».
[20]Tunc coepit exprobrare civitatibus, in quibus factae sunt plurimae virtutes eius, quia non egissent paenitentiam: [21]«Vae tibi, Chorazin! Vae tibi, Bethsaida! Quia si in Tyro et Sidone factae essent virtutes, quae factae sunt in vobis, olim in cilicio et cinere paenitentiam egissent. [22]Verumtamen dico vobis: Tyro et Sidoni remissius erit in die iudicii quam vobis. [23]Et tu, Capharnaum, numquid *usque in caelum exaltaberis? Usque in infernum descendes!* Quia si in Sodomis factae fuissent virtutes, quae factae sunt in te, mansissent usque in hunc diem. [24]Verumtamen dico vobis: Terrae Sodomorum remissius erit in die iudicii quam tibi». [25]In illo tempore respondens Iesus dixit: «Confiteor tibi, Pater, Domine caeli et terrae, quia abscondisti haec a sapientibus et prudentibus et revelasti ea parvulis. [26]Ita, Pater, quoniam sic fuit placitum ante te. [27]Omnia mihi tradita sunt a Patre meo; et nemo novit Filium nisi Pater, neque Patrem quis novit nisi Filius et cui voluerit Filius revelare. [28]Venite ad me, omnes, qui laboratis et onerati estis, et ego reficiam vos. [29]Tollite iugum meum super vos et discite a me, quia mitis sum et humilis corde, et invenietis requiem animabus vestris. [30]Iugum enim meum suave et onus meum leve est». **[12]** [1]In illo tempore abiit Iesus sabbatis per sata; discipuli autem eius esurierunt et coeperunt vellere spicas et manducare. [2]Pharisaei autem videntes dixerunt ei: «Ecce discipuli tui faciunt, quod non licet facere sabbato». [3]At ille dixit eis: «Non legistis quid fecerit David, quando esuriit, et qui cum eo erant? [4]Quomodo intravit in domum Dei et panes propositionis comedit, quod non licebat ei edere neque his, qui cum eo erant, nisi solis sacerdotibus? [5]Aut non legistis in Lege quia sabbatis sacerdotes in templo sabbatum violant et sine crimine sunt? [6]Dico autem vobis quia templo maior est hic. [7]Si autem sciretis quid est: *"Misericordiam volo et non sacrificium"*, numquam condemnassetis innocentes. [8]Dominus est enim Filius hominis sabbati». [9]Et cum inde transisset, venit in synagogam eorum; [10]et ecce homo manum habens aridam. Et interrogabant eum dicentes: «Licet sabbatis curare?», ut accusarent eum. [11]Ipse autem dixit illis: «Quis erit ex vobis homo, qui habeat ovem unam et, si ceciderit haec sabbatis in foveam, nonne tenebit et levabit eam? [12]Quanto igitur melior est homo ove! Itaque licet sabbatis bene facere». [13]Tunc ait homini: «Extende manum tuam». Et extendit, et restituta est sana sicut altera. [14]Exeuntes autem pharisaei consilium faciebant adversus eum, quomodo eum perderent. [15]Iesus autem sciens secessit inde. Et secuti sunt eum multi, et curavit eos omnes [16]et comminatus est eis, ne manifestum eum facerent, [17]ut adimpleretur, quod dictum est per Isaiam prophetam dicentem: [18]«*Ecce puer meus, quem elegi, / dilectus meus, in quo bene placuit animae meae; / ponam Spiritum meum super eum, / et iudicium gentibus nuntiabit. / [19] Non contendet neque clamabit, / neque audiet aliquis in plateis vocem eius. / [20]Arundinem quassatam non confringet / et linum fumigans non exstinguet, / donec eiciat ad victoriam iudicium; / [21]et in nomine eius gentes sperabunt*». [22]Tunc oblatus est ei daemonium habens, caecus et mutus, et curavit eum, ita ut mutus loqueretur et videret. [23]Et stupebant omnes turbae et dicebant: «Numquid hic est filius David?». [24]Pharisaei autem audientes dixerunt: «Hic non eicit daemones nisi in Beelzebul, principe daemonum». [25]Sciens autem cogitationes eorum dixit eis: «Omne regnum divisum contra se desolatur, et omnis civitas vel domus divisa contra se non stabit. [26]Et si Satanas Satanam eicit, adversus se divisus est; quomodo ergo stabit regnum eius? [27]Et si ego in Beelzebul eicio daemones, filii vestri in quo eiciunt? Ideo ipsi iudices erunt vestri. [28]Si autem in Spiritu Dei ego eicio daemones, igitur pervenit in vos regnum Dei. [29]Aut quomodo potest quisquam intrare in domum fortis et vasa eius diripere, nisi prius alligaverit fortem? Et tunc domum illius diripiet. [30]Qui non est mecum, contra me est; et, qui non congregat mecum, spargit. [31]Ideo dico vobis: Omne peccatum et blasphemia remittetur hominibus, Spiritus autem blasphemia non remittetur. [32]Et quicumque dixerit verbum contra Filium hominis, remittetur ei; qui autem dixerit contra Spiritum Sanctum, non remittetur ei neque in hoc saeculo neque in futuro. [33]Aut facite arborem bonam et fructum eius bonum, aut facite arborem malam et fructum eius malum: siquidem ex fructu arbor agnoscitur. [34]Progenies viperarum, quomodo potestis bona loqui, cum sitis mali? Ex abundantia enim cordis os loquitur. [35]Bonus homo de

bono thesauro profert bona, et malus homo de malo thesauro profert mala. [36]Dico autem vobis: Omne verbum otiosum, quod locuti fuerint homines, reddent rationem de eo in die iudicii: [37]ex verbis enim tuis iustificaberis, et ex verbis tuis condemnaberis». [38]Tunc responderunt ei quidam de scribis et pharisaeis dicentes: «Magister, volumus a te signum videre». [39]Qui respondens ait illis: «Generatio mala et adultera signum requirit, et signum non dabitur ei nisi signum Ionae prophetae. [40]Sicut enim *fuit Ionas in ventre ceti tribus diebus et tribus noctibus*, sic erit Filius hominis in corde terrae tribus diebus et tribus noctibus. [41]Viri Ninevitae surgent in iudicio cum generatione ista et condemnabunt eam, quia paenitentiam egerunt in praedicatione Ionae; et ecce plus quam Iona hic! [42]Regina austri surget in iudicio cum generatione ista et condemnabit eam, quia venit a finibus terrae audire sapientiam Salomonis; et ecce plus quam Salomon hic! [43]Cum autem immundus spiritus exierit ab homine, ambulat per loca arida quaerens requiem et non invenit. [44]Tunc dicit: 'Revertar in domum meam unde exivi'; et veniens invenit vacantem, scopis mundatam et ornatam. [45]Tunc vadit et assumit secum septem alios spiritus nequiores se, et intrantes habitant ibi; et fiunt novissima hominis illius peiora prioribus. Sic erit et generationi huic pessimae». [46]Adhuc eo loquente ad turbas, ecce mater et fratres eius stabant foris quaerentes loqui ei. [47]Dixit autem ei quidam: «Ecce mater tua et fratres tui foris stant quaerentes loqui tecum». [48]At ille respondens dicenti sibi ait: «Quae est mater mea, et qui sunt fratres mei?». [49]Et extendens manum suam in discipulos suos dixit: «Ecce mater mea et fratres mei. [50]Quicumque enim fecerit voluntatem Patris mei, qui in caelis est, ipse meus frater et soror et mater est». **[13]** [1]In illo die exiens Iesus de domo sedebat secus mare; [2]et congregatae sunt ad eum turbae multae, ita ut in naviculam ascendens sederet, et omnis turba stabat in litore. [3]Et locutus est eis multa in parabolis dicens: «Ecce exiit, qui seminat, seminare. [4]Et dum seminat, quaedam ceciderunt secus viam, et venerunt volucres et comederunt ea. [5]Alia autem ceciderunt in petrosa, ubi non habebant terram multam, et continuo exorta sunt, quia non habebant altitudinem terrae; [6]sole autem orto, aestuaverunt et, quia non habebant radicem, aruerunt. [7]Alia autem ceciderunt in spinas, et creverunt spinae et suffocaverunt ea. [8]Alia vero ceciderunt in terram bonam et dabant fructum: aliud centesimum, aliud sexagesimum, aliud tricesimum. [9]Qui habet aures, audiat». [10]Et accedentes discipuli dixerunt ei: «Quare in parabolis loqueris eis?». [11]Qui respondens ait illis: «Quia vobis datum est nosse mysteria regni caelorum, illis autem non est datum. [12]Qui enim habet, dabitur ei, et abundabit; qui autem non habet, et quod habet, auferetur ab eo. [13]Ideo in parabolis loquor eis, quia videntes non vident et audientes non audiunt neque intellegunt; [14]et adimpletur eis prophetia Isaiae dicens: *"Auditu audietis et non intellegetis / et videntes videbitis et non videbitis. /* [15] *Incrassatum est enim cor populi huius, / et auribus graviter audierunt / et oculos suos clauserunt, / ne quando oculis videant / et auribus audiant / et corde intellegant et convertantur, / et sanem eos"*. [16]Vestri autem beati oculi, quia vident, et aures vestrae, quia audiunt. [17]Amen quippe dico vobis: Multi prophetae et iusti cupierunt videre, quae videtis, et non viderunt, et audire, quae auditis, et non audierunt! [18]Vos ergo audite parabolam seminantis. [19]Omnis, qui audit verbum regni et non intellegit, venit Malus et rapit, quod seminatum est in corde eius; hic est, qui secus viam seminatus est. [20]Qui autem supra petrosa seminatus est, hic est, qui verbum audit et continuo cum gaudio accipit illud, [21]non habet autem in se radicem, sed est temporalis; facta autem tribulatione vel persecutione propter verbum, continuo scandalizatur. [22]Qui autem est seminatus in spinis, hic est, qui verbum audit, et sollicitudo saeculi et fallacia divitiarum suffocat verbum, et sine fructu efficitur. [23]Qui vero in terra bona seminatus est, hic est, qui audit verbum et intellegit et fructum affert et facit aliud quidem centum, aliud autem sexaginta, porro aliud triginta». [24]Aliam parabolam proposuit illis dicens: «Simile factum est regnum caelorum homini, qui seminavit bonum semen in agro suo. [25]Cum autem dormirent homines, venit inimicus eius et superseminavit zizania in medio tritici et abiit. [26]Cum autem crevisset herba et fructum fecisset, tunc apparuerunt et zizania. [27]Accedentes autem servi patris familias dixerunt ei: "Domine, nonne bonum semen seminasti in agro tuo? Unde ergo habet zizania?". [28]Et ait illis: "Inimicus homo hoc fecit". Servi autem dicunt ei: "Vis, imus et colligimus ea?". [29]Et ait: "Non; ne forte colligentes zizania eradicetis simul cum eis triticum, [30]sinite utraque crescere usque ad messem. Et in tempore messis dicam messoribus: Colligite primum zizania et alligate ea in fasciculos ad comburendum ea, triticum autem congregate in horreum meum"». [31]Aliam parabolam proposuit eis dicens: «Simile est regnum caelorum grano sinapis, quod accipiens homo seminavit in agro suo. [32]Quod minimum quidem est omnibus seminibus; cum autem creverit, maius est holeribus et fit arbor, ita ut volucres caeli veniant et habitent in ramis eius». [33]Aliam parabolam locutus est eis: «Simile est regnum caelorum fermento, quod acceptum mulier abscondit in farinae satis tribus, donec fermentatum est totum». [34]Haec omnia locutus est Iesus in parabolis ad turbas et sine parabola nihil loquebatur eis, [35]ut adimpleretur, quod dictum erat per prophetam dicentem: *«Aperiam in parabolis os meum, / eructabo abscondita* a constitutione mundi». [36]Tunc dimissis turbis venit in domum, et accesserunt ad eum discipuli eius dicentes: «Dissere nobis parabolam zizaniorum agri». [37]Qui respondens ait: «Qui seminat bonum semen, est Filius hominis; [38]ager autem est mundus; bonum vero semen, hi sunt filii regni; zizania autem filii sunt Mali; [39]inimicus autem, qui seminavit ea, est Diabolus; messis vero consummatio saeculi est, messores autem angeli sunt. [40]Sicut ergo colliguntur zizania et igni comburuntur, sic erit in consummatione saeculi: [41]mittet Filius hominis angelos suos, et colligent de regno eius omnia scandala et eos, qui faciunt iniquitatem, [42]et mittent eos in caminum ignis; ibi erit fletus et stridor dentium. [43]Tunc iusti fulgebunt sicut sol in regno Patris eorum. Qui habet aures, audiat. [44]Simile est regnum caelorum thesauro abscondito in agro, quem qui invenit homo abscondit et prae gaudio illius vadit et vendit universa, quae habet, et emit agrum illum. [45]Iterum simile est regnum caelorum homini negotiatori quaerenti bonas margaritas. [46]Inventa autem una pretiosa margarita, abiit et vendidit omnia, quae habuit, et emit eam. [47]Iterum simile est regnum caelorum sagenae missae in mare et ex omni genere congreganti; [48]quam, cum impleta esset, educentes secus litus et sedentes collegerunt bonos in vasa, malos autem foras miserunt. [49]Sic erit in consummatione saeculi: exibunt angeli et separabunt malos de medio iustorum [50]et mittent eos in caminum ignis; ibi erit fletus et stridor dentium. [51]Intellexistis haec omnia?». Dicunt ei: «Etiam». [52]Ait autem illis: «Ideo omnis scriba doctus in regno caelorum similis est homini patri familias, qui profert de thesauro suo nova et vetera». [53]Et factum est cum consummasset Iesus parabolas istas, transiit inde. [54]Et veniens in patriam suam, docebat eos in synagoga eorum, ita ut mirarentur et dicerent: «Unde huic sapientia haec et virtutes? [55]Nonne hic est fabri filius? Nonne mater eius dicitur Maria, et fratres eius Iacobus et Ioseph et Simon et Iudas? [56]Et sorores eius nonne omnes apud nos sunt? Unde ergo huic omnia ista?». [57]Et scandalizabantur in eo. Iesus autem dixit eis: «Non est propheta sine honore nisi in patria et in domo sua». [58]Et non fecit ibi virtutes multas propter incredulitatem illorum.   [14] [1]In illo tempore audivit Herodes tetrarcha famam Iesu [2]et ait pueris suis: «Hic est Ioannes Baptista; ipse surrexit a mortuis, et ideo virtutes operantur in eo». [3]Herodes enim tenuit Ioannem et alligavit eum et posuit in carcere propter Herodiadem uxorem Philippi fratris sui. [4]Dicebat enim illi Ioannes: «Non licet tibi habere eam». [5]Et volens illum occidere, timuit populum, quia sicut prophetam eum habebant. [6]Die autem natalis Herodis saltavit filia Herodiadis in medio et placuit Herodi, [7]unde cum iuramento pollicitus est ei dare, quodcumque postulasset. [8]At illa, praemonita a matre sua: «Da mihi, inquit, hic in disco caput Ioannis Baptistae». [9]Et contristatus rex propter iuramentum et eos, qui pariter recumbebant, iussit dari [10]misitque et decollavit Ioannem in carcere; [11]et allatum est caput eius in disco et datum est puellae, et tulit matri suae. [12]Et accedentes discipuli eius tulerunt corpus et sepelierunt illud et venientes nuntiaverunt Iesu. [13]Quod cum audisset Iesus, secessit inde in navicula in locum desertum seorsum; et cum audissent, turbae secutae sunt eum pedestres de civitatibus. [14]Et exiens vidit turbam multam et misertus est eorum et curavit languidos eorum. [15]Vespere autem facto, accesserunt ad eum discipuli dicentes: «Desertus est locus, et hora iam praeteriit; dimitte turbas, ut euntes in castella emant sibi escas». [16]Iesus autem dixit eis: «Non habent necesse ire; date illis vos manducare». [17]Illi autem dicunt ei: «Non habemus hic nisi quinque panes et duos pisces». [18]Qui ait: «Afferte illos mihi huc». [19]Et cum iussisset turbas discumbere supra fenum, acceptis quinque panibus et duobus piscibus, aspiciens in caelum benedixit et fregit et dedit discipulis panes, discipuli autem turbis. [20]Et manducaverunt omnes et saturati sunt; et tulerunt reliquias fragmentorum duodecim cophinos plenos. [21]Manducantium autem fuit numerus fere quinque milia virorum, exceptis mulieribus et parvulis. [22]Et statim iussit discipulos ascendere in naviculam et praecedere eum trans fretum, donec dimitteret turbas. [23]Et dimissis turbis, ascendit in montem solus orare. Vespere autem facto, solus erat ibi. [24]Navicula autem iam multis stadiis a terra distabat, fluctibus iactata; erat enim contrarius ventus. [25]Quarta autem vigilia noctis venit ad eos ambulans supra mare. [26]Discipuli autem, videntes eum supra mare ambulantem, turbati sunt dicentes: «Phantasma est», et prae timore clamaverunt. [27]Statimque Iesus locutus est eis dicens: «Habete fiduciam, ego sum; nolite timere!». [28]Respondens autem ei Petrus dixit: «Domine, si tu es, iube me venire ad te super aquas». [29]At ipse ait: «Veni!». Et descendens Petrus de navicula ambulavit super aquas et venit ad Iesum. [30]Videns vero ventum validum timuit et, cum coepisset mergi, clamavit dicens: «Domine, salvum me fac!». [31]Continuo autem Iesus extendens manum apprehendit eum et ait illi: «Modicae fidei, quare dubitasti?». [32]Et cum ascendissent in naviculam, cessavit ventus. [33]Qui autem in navicula erant, adoraverunt eum dicentes: «Vere Filius Dei es!». [34]Et cum transfretassent, venerunt in terram Gennesaret. [35]Et cum cognovissent eum viri loci illius, miserunt in universam regionem illam et obtulerunt ei omnes male habentes, [36]et rogabant eum, ut vel fimbriam vestimenti eius tangerent; et, quicumque tetigerunt, salvi facti sunt. [15] [1]Tunc accedunt ad Iesum ab Hierosolymis pharisaei et scribae dicentes: [2]«Quare discipuli tui transgrediuntur traditionem seniorum? Non enim lavant manus suas, cum panem manducant». [3]Ipse autem respondens ait illis: «Quare et vos transgredimini mandatum Dei propter traditionem vestram?

[4]Nam Deus dixit: "*Honora patrem tuum et matrem*" et: "*Qui maladixerit patri vel matri, morte moriatur*". [5]Vos autem dicitis: "Quicumque dixerit patri vel matri: Munus est, quodcumque ex me profuerit, [6]non honorificabit patrem suum"; et irritum fecistis verbum Dei propter traditionem vestram. [7]Hypocritae! Bene prophetavit de vobis Isaias dicens: [8] "*Populus hic labiis me honorat, / cor autem eorum longe est a me; / [9] sine causa autem colunt me, / docentes doctrinas mandata hominum*"». [10]Et convocata ad se turba, dixit eis: «Audite et intellegite: [11]Non quod intrat in os, coinquinat hominem; sed quod procedit ex ore, hoc coinquinat hominem!». [12]Tunc accedentes discipuli dicunt ei: «Scis quia pharisaei, audito verbo, scandalizati sunt?». [13]At ille respondens ait: «Omnis plantatio, quam non plantavit Pater meus caelestis, eradicabitur. [14]Sinite illos: caeci sunt duces caecorum. Caecus autem si caeco ducatum praestet, ambo in foveam cadent». [15]Respondens autem Petrus dixit ei: «Edissere nobis parabolam istam». [16]At ille dixit: «Adhuc et vos sine intellectu estis? [17]Non intellegitis quia omne quod in os intrat, in ventrem vadit et in secessum emittitur? [18]Quae autem procedunt de ore, de corde exeunt, et ea coinquinant hominem. [19]De corde enim exeunt cogitationes malae, homicidia, adulteria, fornicationes, furta, falsa testimonia, blasphemiae. [20]Haec sunt, quae coinquinant hominem; non lotis autem manibus manducare non coinquinat hominem». [21]Et egressus inde Iesus, secessit in partes Tyri et Sidonis. [22]Et ecce mulier Chananaea a finibus illis egressa clamavit dicens: «Miserere mei, Domine, fili David! Filia mea male a daemonio vexatur». [23]Qui non respondit ei verbum. Et accedentes discipuli eius rogabant eum dicentes: «Dimitte eam, quia clamat post nos». [24]Ipse autem respondens ait: «Non sum missus nisi ad oves, quae perierunt domus Israel». [25]At illa venit et adoravit eum dicens: «Domine, adiuva me!». [26]Qui respondens ait: «Non est bonum sumere panem filiorum et mittere catellis». [27]At illa dixit: «Etiam, Domine, nam et catelli edunt de micis, quae cadunt de mensa dominorum suorum». [28]Tunc respondens Iesus ait illi: «O mulier, magna est fides tua! Fiat tibi, sicut vis». Et sanata est filia illius ex illa hora. [29]Et cum transisset inde, Iesus venit secus mare Galilaeae et ascendens in montem sedebat ibi. [30]Et accesserunt ad eum turbae multae habentes secum claudos, caecos, debiles, mutos et alios multos et proiecerunt eos ad pedes eius, et curavit eos, [31]ita ut turba miraretur videntes mutos loquentes, debiles sanos, et claudos ambulantes, et caecos videntes. Et magnificabant Deum Israel. [32]Iesus autem convocatis discipulis suis dixit: «Misereor turbae, quia triduo iam perseverant mecum et non habent, quod manducent; et dimittere eos ieiunos nolo, ne forte deficiant in via». [33]Et dicunt ei discipuli: «Unde nobis in deserto panes tantos, ut saturemus turbam tantam?». [34]Et ait illis Iesus: «Quot panes habetis?». At illi dixerunt: «Septem et paucos pisciculos». [35]Et praecepit turbae, ut discumberet super terram; [36]et accipiens septem panes et pisces et gratias agens fregit et dedit discipulis, discipuli autem turbis. [37]Et comederunt omnes et saturati sunt; et, quod superfuit de fragmentis, tulerunt septem sportas plenas. [38]Erant autem, qui manducaverant, quattuor milia hominum extra mulieres et parvulos. [39]Et dimissis turbis, ascendit in naviculam et venit in fines Magadan. **[16]** [1]Et accesserunt ad eum pharisaei et sadducaei tentantes et rogaverunt eum, ut signum de caelo ostenderet eis. [2]At ille respondens ait eis: «Facto vespere dicitis: 'Serenum erit, rubicundum est enim caelum'; [3]et mane: 'Hodie tempestas, rutilat enim triste caelum'. Faciem quidem caeli diiudicare nostis, signa autem temporum non potestis. [4]Generatio mala et adultera signum quaerit, et signum non dabitur ei nisi signum Ionae». Et, relictis illis, abiit. [5]Et cum venissent discipuli trans fretum, obliti sunt panes accipere. [6]Iesus autem dixit illis: «Intuemini et cavete a fermento pharisaeorum et sadducaeorum». [7]At illi cogitabant inter se dicentes: «Panes non accepimus!». [8]Sciens autem Iesus dixit: «Quid cogitatis inter vos, modicae fidei, quia panes non habetis? [9]Nondum intellegitis neque recordamini quinque panum quinque milium hominum, et quot cophinos sumpsistis? [10]Neque septem panum quattuor milium hominum, et quot sportas sumpsistis? [11]Quomodo non intellegitis quia non de panibus dixi vobis? Sed cavete a fermento pharisaeorum et sadducaeorum». [12]Tunc intellexerunt quia non dixerit cavendum a fermento panum, sed a doctrina pharisaeorum et sadducaeorum. [13]Venit autem Iesus in partes Caesareae Philippi et interrogabat discipulos suos dicens: «Quem dicunt homines esse Filium hominis?». [14]At illi dixerunt: «Alii Ioannem Baptistam, alii autem Eliam, alii vero Ieremiam, aut unum ex prophetis». [15]Dicit illis: «Vos autem quem me esse dicitis?». [16]Respondens Simon Petrus dixit: «Tu es Christus, Filius Dei vivi». [17]Respondens autem Iesus dixit ei: «Beatus es, Simon Bariona, quia caro et sanguis non revelavit tibi, sed Pater meus, qui in caelis est. [18]Et ego dico tibi: Tu es Petrus, et super hanc petram aedificabo Ecclesiam meam; et portae inferi non praevalebunt adversus eam. [19]Tibi dabo claves regni caelorum; et quodcumque ligaveris super terram, erit ligatum in caelis, et quodcumque solveris super terram, erit solutum in caelis». [20]Tunc praecepit discipulis, ut nemini dicerent quia ipse esset Christus. [21]Exinde coepit Iesus ostendere discipulis suis quia oporteret eum ire Hierosolymam et multa pati a senioribus et principibus sacerdotum et scribis et occidi et tertia die resurgere. [22]Et assumens eum Petrus coepit increpare illum dicens: «Absit a te, Domine, non erit tibi hoc». [23]Qui

conversus dixit Petro: «Vade post me, Satana! Scandalum es mihi, quia non sapis ea, quae Dei sunt, sed ea quae hominum!». [24]Tunc Iesus dixit discipulis suis: «Si quis vult post me venire, abneget semetipsum et tollat crucem suam et sequatur me. [25]Qui enim voluerit animam suam salvam facere, perdet eam; qui autem perdiderit animam suam propter me, inveniet eam. [26]Quid enim prodest homini, si mundum universum lucretur, animae vero suae detrimentum patiatur? Aut quam dabit homo commutationem pro anima sua? [27]Filius enim hominis venturus est in gloria Patris sui cum angelis suis, et tunc reddet unicuique secundum opus eius. [28]Amen dico vobis: Sunt quidam de hic stantibus, qui non gustabunt mortem, donec videant Filium hominis venientem in regno suo».   [17] [1]Et post dies sex assumit Iesus Petrum et Iacobum et Ioannem fratrem eius et ducit illos in montem excelsum seorsum. [2]Et transfiguratus est ante eos; et resplenduit facies eius sicut sol, vestimenta autem eius facta sunt alba sicut lux. [3]Et ecce apparuit illis Moyses et Elias cum eo loquentes. [4]Respondens autem Petrus dixit ad Iesum: «Domine, bonum est nos hic esse. Si vis, faciam hic tria tabernacula: tibi unum et Moysi unum et Eliae unum». [5]Adhuc eo loquente, ecce nubes lucida obumbravit eos; et ecce vox de nube dicens: «Hic est Filius meus dilectus, in quo mihi bene complacui; ipsum audite». [6]Et audientes discipuli ceciderunt in faciem suam et timuerunt valde. [7]Et accessit Iesus et tetigit eos dixitque eis: «Surgite et nolite timere». [8]Levantes autem oculos suos, neminem viderunt nisi solum Iesum. [9]Et descendentibus illis de monte, praecepit eis Iesus dicens: «Nemini dixeritis visionem, donec Filius hominis a mortuis resurgat». [10]Et interrogaverunt eum discipuli dicentes: «Quid ergo scribae dicunt quod Eliam oporteat primum venire?». [11]At ille respondens ait: «Elias quidem venturus est et restituet omnia. [12]Dico autem vobis quia Elias iam venit, et non cognoverunt eum, sed fecerunt in eo, quaecumque voluerunt; sic et Filius hominis passurus est ab eis». [13]Tunc intellexerunt discipuli quia de Ioanne Baptista dixisset eis. [14]Et cum venissent ad turbam, accessit ad eum homo genibus provolutus ante eum [15]et dicens: «Domine, miserere filii mei, quia lunaticus est et male patitur; nam saepe cadit in ignem et crebro in aquam. [16]Et obtuli eum discipulis tuis, et non potuerunt curare eum». [17]Respondens autem Iesus ait: «O generatio incredula et perversa, quousque ero vobiscum? Usquequo patiar vos? Afferte huc illum ad me». [18]Et increpavit eum Iesus, et exiit ab eo daemonium, et curatus est puer ex illa hora. [19]Tunc accesserunt discipuli ad Iesum secreto et dixerunt: «Quare nos non potuimus eicere illum?». [20]Ille autem dicit illis: «Propter modicam fidem vestram. Amen quippe dico vobis: Si habueritis fidem sicut granum sinapis, dicetis monti huic: "Transi hinc illuc!", et transibit, et nihil impossibile erit vobis». (21) [22]Conversantibus autem eis in Galilaea, dixit illis Iesus: «Filius hominis tradendus est in manus hominum, [23]et occident eum, et tertio die resurget». Et contristati sunt vehementer. [24]Et cum venissent Capharnaum, accesserunt, qui didrachma accipiebant, ad Petrum et dixerunt: «Magister vester non solvit didrachma?». [25]Ait: «Etiam». Et cum intrasset domum, praevenit eum Iesus dicens: «Quid tibi videtur, Simon? Reges terrae a quibus accipiunt tributum vel censum? A filiis suis an ab alienis?». [26]Cum autem ille dixisset: «Ab alienis», dixit illi Iesus: «Ergo liberi sunt filii. [27]Ut autem non scandalizemus eos, vade ad mare et mitte hamum; et eum piscem, qui primus ascenderit, tolle, et aperto ore eius invenies staterem. Illum sumens, da eis pro me et te».   [18] [1]In illa hora accesserunt discipuli ad Iesum dicentes: «Quis putas maior est in regno caelorum?». [2]Et advocans parvulum, statuit eum in medio eorum [3]et dixit: «Amen dico vobis: Nisi conversi fueritis et efficiamini sicut parvuli, non intrabitis in regnum caelorum. [4]Quicumque ergo humiliaverit se sicut parvulus iste, hic est maior in regno caelorum. [5]Et qui susceperit unum parvulum talem in nomine meo, me suscipit. [6]Qui autem scandalizaverit unum de pusillis istis, qui in me credunt, expedit ei, ut suspendatur mola asinaria in collo eius et demergatur in profundum maris. [7]Vae mundo ab scandalis! Necesse est enim ut veniant scandala; verumtamen vae homini, per quem scandalum venit! [8]Si autem manus tua vel pes tuus scandalizat te, abscide eum et proice abs te: bonum tibi est ad vitam ingredi debilem vel claudum, quam duas manus vel duos pedes habentem mitti in ignem aeternum. [9]Et si oculus tuus scandalizat te, erue eum et proice abs te: bonum tibi est unoculum in vitam intrare, quam duos oculos habentem mitti in gehennam ignis. [10]Videte, ne contemnatis unum ex his pusillis; dico enim vobis quia angeli eorum in caelis semper vident faciem Patris mei, qui in caelis est. (11) [12]Quid vobis videtur? Si fuerint alicui centum oves, et erraverit una ex eis, nonne relinquet nonaginta novem in montibus et vadit quaerere eam, quae erravit? [13]Et si contigerit ut inveniat eam, amen dico vobis quia gaudebit super eam magis quam super nonaginta novem, quae non erraverunt. [14]Sic non est voluntas ante Patrem vestrum, qui in caelis est, ut pereat unus de pusillis istis. [15]Si autem peccaverit in te frater tuus, vade, corripe eum inter te et ipsum solum. Si te audierit, lucratus es fratrem tuum; [16]si autem non audierit, adhibe tecum adhuc unum vel duos, *ut in ore duorum testium vel trium stet omne verbum*; [17]quod si noluerit audire eos, dic ecclesiae; si autem et ecclesiam noluerit audire, sit tibi sicut ethnicus et publicanus. [18]Amen dico vobis: Quaecumque alligaveritis super terram, erunt ligata in caelo, et quaecumque solveritis super terram, erunt soluta in caelo. [19]Iterum dico vobis: Si duo ex vobis consenserint super terram de omni re, quamcumque petierint, fiet illis a Patre meo, qui in caelis est. [20]Ubi enim sunt duo vel tres congregati in nomine meo, ibi sum in medio eorum». [21]Tunc accedens Petrus dixit ei: «Domine, quotiens peccabit in me frater meus, et dimittam ei? Usque septies?». [22]Dicit illi Iesus: «Non dico tibi usque septies sed usque septuagies septies. [23]Ideo assimilatum est regnum caelorum homini regi, qui voluit rationem ponere cum servis suis. [24]Et cum coepisset rationem ponere, oblatus est ei unus, qui debebat decem milia talenta. [25]Cum autem non haberet, unde redderet, iussit eum dominus venumdari et uxorem et filios et omnia, quae habebat, et reddi. [26]Procidens igitur servus ille adorabat eum dicens: "Patientiam habe in me, et omnia reddam tibi". [27]Misertus autem dominus servi illius dimisit eum et debitum dimisit ei. [28]Egressus autem servus ille invenit unum de conservis suis, qui debebat ei centum denarios, et tenens suffocabat eum dicens: "Redde, quod debes!". [29]Procidens igitur conservus eius rogabat eum dicens: "Patientiam habe in me, et reddam tibi". [30]Ille autem noluit, sed abiit et misit eum in carcerem, donec redderet debitum. [31]Videntes autem conservi eius, quae fiebant, contristati sunt valde et venerunt et narraverunt domino suo omnia, quae facta erant. [32]Tunc vocavit illum dominus suus et ait illi: "Serve nequam, omne debitum illud dimisi tibi, quoniam rogasti me; [33]non oportuit et te misereri conservi tui, sicut et ego tui misertus sum?". [34]Et iratus dominus eius tradidit eum tortoribus, quoadusque redderet universum debitum. [35]Sic et Pater meus caelestis faciet vobis, si non remiseritis unusquisque fratri suo de cordibus vestris».   [19] [1]Et factum est cum consummasset Iesus sermones istos, migravit a Galilaea et venit in fines Iudaeae trans Iordanem. [2]Et secutae sunt eum turbae multae, et curavit eos ibi. [3]Et accesserunt ad eum pharisaei tentantes eum et dicentes: «Licet homini dimittere uxorem suam quacumque ex causa?». [4]Qui respondens ait: «Non legistis quia, qui creavit ab initio, *masculum et feminam fecit eos* [5]et dixit: *"Propter hoc dimittet homo patrem et matrem et adhaerebit uxori suae, et erunt duo in carne una?"*. [6]Itaque iam non sunt duo sed una caro. Quod ergo Deus coniunxit, homo non separet». [7]Dicunt illi: «Quid ergo Moyses mandavit *dari libellum repudii et dimittere*?». [8]Ait illis: «Moyses ad duritiam cordis vestri permisit vobis dimittere uxores vestras; ab initio autem non sic fuit. [9]Dico autem vobis quia quicumque dimiserit uxorem suam, nisi ob fornicationem, et aliam duxerit, moechatur». [10]Dicunt ei discipuli eius: «Si ita est causa hominis cum uxore, non expedit nubere». [11]Qui dixit eis: «Non omnes capiunt verbum istud, sed quibus datum est. [12]Sunt enim eunuchi, qui de matris utero sic nati sunt; et sunt eunuchi, qui facti sunt ab hominibus; et sunt eunuchi, qui seipsos castraverunt propter regnum caelorum. Qui potest capere, capiat». [13]Tunc oblati sunt ei parvuli, ut manus eis imponeret et oraret; discipuli autem increpabant eis. [14]Iesus vero ait: «Sinite parvulos et nolite eos prohibere ad me venire; talium est enim regnum caelorum». [15]Et cum imposuisset eis manus, abiit inde. [16]Et ecce unus accedens ait illi: «Magister, quid boni faciam, ut habeam vitam aeternam?». Qui dixit ei: [17]«Quid me interrogas de bono? Unus est bonus. Si autem vis ad vitam ingredi, serva mandata». [18]Dicit illi: «Quae?». Iesus autem dixit: «*Non homicidium facies, non adulterabis, non facies furtum, non falsum testimonium dices,* [19] *honora patrem et matrem et diliges proximum tuum sicut teipsum*». [20]Dicit illi adulescens: «Omnia haec custodivi. Quid adhuc mihi deest?». [21]Ait illi Iesus: «Si vis perfectus esse, vade, vende, quae habes, et da pauperibus, et habebis thesaurum in caelo; et veni, sequere me». [22]Cum audisset autem adulescens verbum, abiit tristis; erat enim habens multas possessiones. [23]Iesus autem dixit discipulis suis: «Amen dico vobis: Dives difficile intrabit in regnum caelorum. [24]Et iterum dico vobis: Facilius est camelum per foramen acus transire, quam divitem intrare in regnum Dei». [25]Auditis autem his, discipuli mirabantur valde dicentes: «Quis ergo poterit salvus esse?». [26]Aspiciens autem Iesus dixit illis: «Apud homines hoc impossibile est, apud Deum autem omnia possibilia sunt». [27]Tunc respondens Petrus dixit ei: «Ecce nos reliquimus omnia et secuti sumus te. Quid ergo erit nobis?». [28]Iesus autem dixit illis: «Amen dico vobis quod vos, qui secuti estis me, in regeneratione, cum sederit Filius hominis in throno gloriae suae, sedebitis et vos super thronos duodecim, iudicantes duodecim tribus Israel. [29]Et omnis, qui reliquit domos vel fratres aut sorores aut patrem aut matrem aut filios aut agros propter nomen meum, centuplum accipiet et vitam aeternam possidebit. [30]Multi autem erunt primi novissimi et novissimi primi.   [20] [1]Simile est enim regnum caelorum homini patri familias, qui exiit primo mane conducere operarios in vineam suam; [2]conventione autem facta cum operariis ex denario diurno, misit eos in vineam suam. [3]Et egressus circa horam tertiam vidit alios stantes in foro otiosos [4]et illis dixit: "Ite et vos in vineam; et, quod iustum fuerit, dabo vobis". [5]Illi autem abierunt. Iterum autem exiit circa sextam et nonam horam et fecit similiter. [6]Circa undecimam vero exiit et invenit alios stantes et dicit illis: "Quid hic statis tota die otiosi?". [7]Dicunt ei: "Quia nemo nos conduxit". Dicit illis: "Ite et vos in vineam". [8]Cum sero autem factum esset, dicit dominus vineae procuratori suo: "Voca operarios et redde illis mercedem incipiens a novissimis usque ad primos". [9]Et cum venissent, qui circa undecimam horam venerant, acceperunt singuli denarium. [10]Venientes autem primi arbitrati sunt quod plus essent accepturi; acceperunt autem et ipsi singuli denarium. [11]Accipientes autem murmurabant adversus patrem familias [12]dicentes: "Hi novissimi una hora fecerunt, et pares illos nobis fecisti, qui portavimus pondus diei et aestum!". [13]At ille respondens uni eorum dixit: "Amice, non facio tibi iniuriam; nonne ex denario convenisti mecum? [14]Tolle, quod tuum est, et vade; volo autem et huic novissimo dare sicut et tibi. [15]Aut non licet mihi, quod volo, facere de meis? An oculus tuus nequam est, quia ego bonus sum?". [16]Sic erunt novissimi primi, et primi novissimi». [17]Et ascendens Iesus Hierosolymam assumpsit Duodecim discipulos secreto et ait illis in via: [18]«Ecce ascendimus Hierosolymam, et Filius hominis tradetur principibus sacerdotum et scribis, et condemnabunt eum morte [19]et tradent eum gentibus ad illudendum et flagellandum et crucifigendum, et tertia die resurget». [20]Tunc accessit ad eum mater filiorum Zebedaei cum filiis suis, adorans et petens aliquid ab eo. [21]Qui dixit ei: «Quid vis?». Ait illi: «Dic ut sedeant hi duo filii mei unus ad dexteram tuam et unus ad sinistram in regno tuo». [22]Respondens autem Iesus dixit: «Nescitis quid petatis. Potestis bibere calicem, quem ego bibiturus sum?». Dicunt ei: «Possumus». [23]Ait illis: «Calicem quidem meum bibetis, sedere autem ad dexteram meam et sinistram non est meum dare illud, sed quibus paratum est a Patre meo». [24]Et audientes decem indignati sunt de duobus fratribus. [25]Iesus autem vocavit eos ad se et ait: «Scitis quia principes gentium dominantur eorum et, qui magni sunt, potestatem exercent in eos. [26]Non ita erit inter vos, sed quicumque voluerit inter vos magnus fieri, erit vester minister; [27]et, quicumque voluerit inter vos primus esse, erit vester servus; [28]sicut Filius hominis non venit ministrari sed ministrare et dare animam suam redemptionem pro multis». [29]Et egredientibus illis ab Iericho, secuta est eum turba multa. [30]Et ecce duo caeci sedentes secus viam audierunt quia Iesus transiret et clamaverunt dicentes: «Domine, miserere nostri, fili David!». [31]Turba autem increpabat eos, ut tacerent; at illi magis clamabant dicentes: «Domine, miserere nostri, fili David!». [32]Et stetit Iesus et vocavit eos et ait: «Quid vultis, ut faciam vobis?». [33]Dicunt illi: «Domine, ut aperiantur oculi nostri». [34]Misertus autem Iesus, tetigit oculos eorum; et confestim viderunt et secuti sunt eum.   [21] [1]Et cum appropinquassent Hierosolymis et venissent Bethfage, ad montem Oliveti, tunc Iesus misit duos discipulos [2]dicens ei: «Ite in castellum, quod contra vos est, et statim invenietis asinam alligatam et pullum cum ea; solvite et adducite mihi. [3]Et si quis vobis aliquid dixerit, dicite: "Dominus eos necessarios habet", et confestim dimittet eos». [4]Hoc autem factum est, ut impleretur, quod dictum est per prophetam dicentem: [5]«Dicite filiae Sion: / Ecce Rex tuus venit tibi, / mansuetus et sedens super asinam / et super pullum filium subiugalis». [6]Euntes autem discipuli fecerunt, sicut praecepit illis Iesus, [7]et adduxerunt asinam et pullum, et imposuerunt super eis vestimenta sua, et sedit super ea. [8]Plurima autem turba straverunt vestimenta sua in via; alii autem caedebant ramos de arboribus et sternebant in via. [9]Turbae autem, quae praecedebant eum et quae sequebantur, clamabant dicentes: «Hosanna filio David! Benedictus, qui venit in nomine Domini! Hosanna in altissimis!». [10]Et cum intrasset Hierosolymam, commota est universa civitas dicens: «Quis est hic?». [11]Turbae autem dicebant: «Hic est Iesus propheta a Nazareth Galilaeae». [12]Et intravit Iesus in templum et eiciebat omnes vendentes et ementes in templo, et mensas nummulariorum evertit et cathedras vendentium columbas, [13]et dicit eis: «Scriptum est: "Domus mea domus orationis vocabitur". Vos autem facitis eam speluncam latronum». [14]Et accesserunt ad eum caeci et claudi in templo, et sanavit eos. [15]Videntes autem principes sacerdotum et scribae mirabilia, quae fecit, et pueros clamantes in templo et dicentes: «Hosanna filio David», indignati sunt [16]et dixerunt ei: «Audis quid isti dicant?». Iesus autem dicit eis: «Utique; numquam legistis: "Ex ore infantium et lactantium perfecisti laudem"?». [17]Et relictis illis, abiit foras extra civitatem in Bethaniam ibique mansit. [18]Mane autem revertens in civitatem, esuriit. [19]Et videns fici arborem unam secus viam, venit ad eam; et nihil invenit in ea nisi folia tantum et ait illi: «Numquam ex te fructus nascatur in sempiternum». Et arefacta est continuo ficulnea. [20]Et videntes discipuli mirati sunt dicentes: «Quomodo continuo aruit ficulnea?». [21]Respondens autem Iesus ait eis: «Amen dico vobis: Si habueritis fidem et non haesitaveritis, non solum de ficulnea facietis, sed et si monti huic dixeritis: "Tolle et iacta te in mare", fiet. [22]Et omnia, quaecumque petieritis in oratione credentes, accipietis». [23]Et cum venisset in templum, accesserunt ad eum docentem principes sacerdotum et seniores populi dicentes: «In qua potestate haec facis? Et quis tibi dedit hanc potestatem?». [24]Respondens autem Iesus dixit illis: «Interrogabo vos et ego unum sermonem, quem si dixeritis mihi, et ego vobis dicam, in qua potestate haec facio: [25]Baptismum Ioannis unde erat? A caelo an ex hominibus?». At illi cogitabant inter se dicentes: «Si dixerimus: "E caelo", dicet nobis: "Quare ergo non credidistis illi?"; [26]si autem dixerimus: "Ex hominibus", timemus turbam; omnes enim habent Ioannem sicut prophetam». [27]Et respondentes Iesu dixerunt: «Nescimus». Ait illis et ipse: «Nec ego dico vobis in qua potestate haec facio». [28]«Quid autem vobis videtur? Homo quidam habebat duos filios. Et accedens ad primum dixit: "Fili, vade hodie, operare in vinea". [29]Ille autem respondens ait: "Nolo"; postea autem paenitentia motus abiit. [30]Accedens autem ad alterum dixit similiter. At ille respondens ait: "Eo, domine"; et non ivit. [31]Quis ex duobus fecit voluntatem patris?». Dicunt: «Primus». Dicit illis Iesus: «Amen dico vobis: Publicani et meretrices praecedunt vos in regnum Dei. [32]Venit enim ad vos Ioannes in via iustitiae, et non credidistis ei; publicani autem et meretrices crediderunt ei. Vos autem videntes nec paenitentiam habuistis postea, ut crederetis ei. [33]Aliam parabolam audite. Homo erat pater familias, qui *plantavit vineam et saepem circumdedit ei et fodit in ea torcular et aedificavit turrim* et locavit eam agricolis et peregre profectus est. [34]Cum autem tempus fructuum appropinquasset, misit servos suos ad agricolas, ut acciperent fructus eius. [35]Et agricolae, apprehensis servis eius, alium ceciderunt, alium occiderunt, alium vero lapidaverunt. [36]Iterum misit alios servos plures prioribus, et fecerunt illis similiter. [37]Novissime autem misit ad eos filium suum dicens: "Verebuntur filium meum". [38]Agricolae autem videntes filium dixerunt intra se: "Hic est heres. Venite, occidamus eum et habebimus hereditatem eius". [39]Et apprehensum eum eiecerunt extra vineam et occiderunt. [40]Cum ergo venerit dominus vineae, quid faciet agricolis illis?». [41]Aiunt illi: «Malos male perdet et vineam locabit aliis agricolis, qui reddant ei fructum temporibus suis». [42]Dicit illis Iesus: «Numquam legistis in Scripturis: / *"Lapidem, quem reprobaverunt aedificantes, / hic factus est in caput anguli; / a Domino factum est istud / et est mirabile in oculis nostris"*? [43]Ideo dico vobis quia auferetur a vobis regnum Dei et dabitur genti facienti fructus eius. [44]Et, qui ceciderit super lapidem istum confringetur; super quem vero ceciderit, conteret eum». [45]Et cum audissent principes sacerdotum et pharisaei parabolas eius, cognoverunt quod de ipsis diceret; [46]et quaerentes eum tenere, timuerunt turbas, quoniam sicut prophetam eum habebant. **[22]** [1]Et respondens Iesus dixit iterum in parabolis eis dicens: [2]«Simile factum est regnum caelorum homini regi, qui fecit nuptias filio suo. [3]Et misit servos suos vocare invitatos ad nuptias, et nolebant venire. [4]Iterum misit alios servos dicens: "Dicite invitatis: Ecce prandium meum paravi, tauri mei et altilia occisa, et omnia parata; venite ad nuptias". [5]Illi autem neglexerunt et abierunt, alius in villam suam, alius vero ad negotiationem suam; [6]reliqui vero tenuerunt servos eius et contumelia affectos occiderunt. [7]Rex autem iratus est et, missis exercitibus suis, perdidit homicidas illos et civitatem illorum succendit. [8]Tunc ait servis suis: "Nuptiae quidem paratae sunt, sed qui invitati erant, non fuerunt digni; [9]ite ergo ad exitus viarum et quoscumque inveneritis, vocate ad nuptias". [10]Et egressi servi illi in vias, congregaverunt omnes, quos invenerunt, malos et bonos; et impletae sunt nuptiae discumbentium. [11]Intravit autem rex, ut videret discumbentes, et vidit ibi hominem non vestitum veste nuptiali [12]et ait illi: "Amice, quomodo huc intrasti, non habens vestem nuptialem?". At ille obmutuit. [13]Tunc dixit rex ministris: "Ligate pedes eius et manus et mittite eum in tenebras exteriores: ibi erit fletus et stridor dentium". [14]Multi enim sunt vocati, pauci vero electi». [15]Tunc abeuntes pharisaei consilium inierunt, ut caperent eum in sermone. [16]Et mittunt ei discipulos suos cum herodianis dicentes: «Magister, scimus quia verax es et viam Dei in veritate doces et non est tibi cura de aliquo; non enim respicis personam hominum. [17]Dic ergo nobis quid tibi videatur: Licet censum dare Caesari an non?». [18]Cognita autem Iesus nequitia eorum, ait: «Quid me tentatis, hypocritae? [19]Ostendite mihi nomisma census». At illi obtulerunt ei denarium. [20]Et ait illis: «Cuius est imago haec et suprascriptio?». [21]Dicunt ei: «Caesaris». Tunc ait illis: «Reddite ergo, quae sunt Caesaris, Caesari et, quae sunt Dei, Deo». [22]Et audientes mirati sunt et relicto eo abierunt. [23]In illo die accesserunt ad eum sadducaei, qui dicunt non esse resurrectionem, et interrogaverunt eum [24]dicentes: «Magister, Moyses dixit, *si quis mortuus fuerit non habens filios, ut ducat frater eius uxorem illius et suscitet semen fratri suo.* [25]Erant autem apud nos septem fratres: et primus, uxore ducta, defunctus est et non habens semen reliquit uxorem suam fratri suo; [26]similiter secundus et tertius usque ad septimum. [27]Novissime autem omnium mulier defuncta est. [28]In resurrectione ergo cuius erit de septem uxor? Omnes enim habuerunt eam». [29]Respondens autem Iesus ait illis: «Erratis nescientes Scripturas neque virtutem Dei; [30]in resurrectione enim neque nubent neque nubentur, sed sunt sicut angeli in caelo. [31]De resurrectione autem mortuorum non legistis, quod dictum est vobis a Deo dicente: [32]*"Ego sum Deus Abraham et Deus Isaac et Deus Iacob"*? Non est Deus mortuorum sed viventium». [33]Et audientes turbae mirabantur in doctrina eius. [34]Pharisaei autem audientes quod silentium imposuisset sadducaeis, convenerunt in unum. [35]Et interrogavit unus ex eis legis doctor tentans eum: [36]«Magister, quod est mandatum magnum in Lege?». [37]Ait autem illi: «*Diliges Dominum Deum tuum in toto corde tuo et in tota anima tua* et in tota mente tua: [38]hoc est magnum et primum mandatum. [39]Secundum autem simile est huic: *Diliges proximum tuum sicut teipsum.* [40]In his duobus mandatis universa Lex pendet et Prophetae». [41]Congregatis autem pharisaeis, interrogavit eos Iesus [42]dicens: «Quid vobis videtur de Christo? Cuius filius est?». Dicunt ei: «David». [43]Ait illis: «Quomodo ergo David in Spiritu vocat eum Dominum dicens: [44]*"Dixit Dominus Domino meo: Sede a dextris meis, / donec ponam inimicos tuos sub pedibus tuis"*? [45]Si ergo David vocat eum Dominum, quomodo filius eius est?». [46]Et nemo poterat respondere ei verbum, neque ausus fuit quisquam ex illa die eum amplius interrogare. **[23]** [1]Tunc Iesus locutus est ad turbas et ad discipulos suos ²dicens: «Super cathedram Moysis sederunt scribae et pharisaei. ³Omnia ergo, quaecumque dixerint vobis, facite et servate; secundum opera vero eorum nolite facere: dicunt enim et non faciunt. ⁴Alligant autem onera gravia et importabilia et imponunt in umeros hominum, ipsi autem digito suo nolunt ea movere. ⁵Omnia vero opera sua faciunt, ut videantur ab hominibus: dilatant enim phylacteria sua et magnificant fimbrias, ⁶amant autem primum recubitum in cenis et primas cathedras in synagogis ⁷et salutationes in foro et vocari ab hominibus Rabbi. ⁸Vos autem nolite vocari Rabbi; unus enim est Magister vester, omnes autem vos fratres estis. ⁹Et Patrem nolite vocare vobis super terram, unus enim est Pater vester, caelestis. ¹⁰Nec vocemini Magistri, quia Magister vester unus est, Christus. ¹¹Qui maior est vestrum, erit minister vester. ¹²Qui autem se exaltaverit, humiliabitur; et, qui se humiliaverit, exaltabitur. ¹³Vae autem vobis, scribae et pharisaei hypocritae, quia clauditis regnum caelorum ante homines! Vos enim non intratis nec introeuntes sinitis intrare. ⁽¹⁴⁾ ¹⁵Vae vobis, scribae et pharisaei hypocritae, quia circuitis mare et aridam, ut faciatis unum proselytum, et cum fuerit factus, facitis eum filium gehennae duplo quam vos! ¹⁶Vae vobis, duces caeci, qui dicitis: "Quicumque iuraverit per templum, nihil est; quicumque autem iuraverit in auro templi, debet". ¹⁷Stulti et caeci! Quid enim maius est: aurum an templum, quod sanctificat aurum? ¹⁸Et: "Quicumque iuraverit in altari, nihil est; quicumque autem iuraverit in dono, quod est super illud, debet". ¹⁹Caeci! Quid enim maius est: donum an altare, quod sanctificat donum? ²⁰Qui ergo iuraverit in altari, iurat in eo et in omnibus, quae super illud sunt; ²¹et, qui iuraverit in templo, iurat in illo et in eo, qui inhabitat in ipso; ²²et, qui iuraverit in caelo, iurat in throno Dei et in eo, qui sedet super eum. ²³Vae vobis, scribae et pharisaei hypocritae, quia decimatis mentam et anethum et cyminum et reliquistis, quae graviora sunt legis: iudicium et misericordiam et fidem! Haec oportuit facere et illa non omittere. ²⁴Duces caeci, excolantes culicem, camelum autem glutientes. ²⁵Vae vobis, scribae et pharisaei hypocritae, quia mundatis, quod de foris est calicis et paropsidis, intus autem pleni sunt rapina et immunditia! ²⁶Pharisaee caece, munda prius, quod intus est calicis, ut fiat et id, quod de foris eius est, mundum. ²⁷Vae vobis, scribae et pharisaei hypocritae, quia similes estis sepulcris dealbatis, quae a foris quidem parent speciosa, intus vero sunt ossibus mortuorum et omni spurcitia! ²⁸Sic et vos a foris quidem paretis hominibus iusti, intus autem pleni estis hypocrisi et iniquitate. ²⁹Vae vobis, scribae et pharisaei hypocritae, qui aedificatis sepulcra prophetarum et ornatis monumenta iustorum ³⁰et dicitis: "Si fuissemus in diebus patrum nostrorum, non essemus socii eorum in sanguine prophetarum"! ³¹Itaque testimonio estis vobismetipsis quia filii estis eorum, qui prophetas occiderunt. ³²Et vos implete mensuram patrum vestrorum. ³³Serpentes, genimina viperarum, quomodo fugietis a iudicio gehennae? ³⁴Ideo ecce ego mitto ad vos prophetas et sapientes et scribas; ex illis occidetis et crucifigetis et ex eis flagellabitis in synagogis vestris et persequemini de civitate in civitatem, ³⁵ut veniat super vos omnis sanguis iustus, qui effusus est super terram a sanguine Abel iusti usque ad sanguinem Zachariae filii Barachiae, quem occidistis inter templum et altare. ³⁶Amen dico vobis: Venient haec omnia super generationem istam. ³⁷Ierusalem, Ierusalem, quae occidis prophetas et lapidas eos, qui ad te missi sunt, quotiens volui congregare filios tuos, quemadmodum gallina congregat pullos suos sub alas, et noluistis! *³⁸Ecce relinquitur vobis domus vestra deserta!* ³⁹Dico enim vobis: Non me videbitis amodo, donec dicatis: "*Benedictus, qui venit in nomine Domini!*"». **[24]** ¹Et egressus Iesus de templo ibat, et accesserunt discipuli eius, ut ostenderent ei aedificationes templi; ²ipse autem respondens dixit eis: «Non videtis haec omnia? Amen dico vobis: Non relinquetur hic lapis super lapidem, qui non destruetur». ³Sedente autem eo super montem Oliveti, accesserunt ad eum discipuli secreto dicentes: «Dic nobis: Quando haec erunt, et quod signum adventus tui et consummationis saeculi?». ⁴Et respondens Iesus dixit eis: «Videte, ne quis vos seducat. ⁵Multi enim venient in nomine meo dicentes: "Ego sum Christus", et multos seducent. ⁶Audituri enim estis proelia et opiniones proeliorum. Videte, ne turbemini; oportet enim fieri, sed nondum est finis. ⁷Consurget enim gens in gentem, et regnum in regnum, et erunt fames et terrae motus per loca; ⁸haec autem omnia initia sunt dolorum. ⁹Tunc tradent vos in tribulationem et occident vos, et eritis odio omnibus gentibus propter nomen meum. ¹⁰Et tunc scandalizabuntur multi et invicem tradent et odio habebunt invicem; ¹¹et multi pseudoprophetae surgent et seducent multos. ¹²Et, quoniam abundavit iniquitas, refrigescet caritas multorum; ¹³qui autem permanserit usque in finem, hic salvus erit. ¹⁴Et praedicabitur hoc evangelium regni in universo orbe in testimonium omnibus gentibus; et tunc veniet consummatio. ¹⁵Cum ergo videritis *abominationem desolationis*, quae dicta est a Daniele propheta, stantem *in loco sancto*, qui legit, intellegat: ¹⁶tunc qui in Iudaea sunt, fugiant ad montes; ¹⁷qui in tecto, non descendat tollere aliquid de domo sua; ¹⁸et, qui in agro, non revertatur tollere pallium suum. ¹⁹Vae autem praegnantibus et nutrientibus in illis diebus! ²⁰Orate autem, ut non fiat fuga vestra hieme vel sabbato: ²¹erit enim tunc *tribulatio magna, qualis non fuit ab initio mundi usque modo* neque fiet. ²²Et nisi breviati fuissent dies illi, non fieret salva omnis caro; sed propter electos breviabuntur dies illi. [23]Tunc si quis vobis dixerit: "Ecce hic Christus" aut: "Hic", nolite credere. [24]Surgent enim pseudochristi et pseudoprophetae et dabunt signa magna et prodigia, ita ut in errorem inducantur, si fieri potest, etiam electi. [25]Ecce praedixi vobis. [26]Si ergo dixerint vobis: "Ecce in deserto est", nolite exire; "Ecce in penetralibus", nolite credere: [27]sicut enim fulgur exit ab oriente et paret usque in occidentem, ita erit adventus Filii hominis. [28]Ubicumque fuerit corpus, illuc congregabuntur aquilae. [29]Statim autem post tribulationem dierum illorum, *sol obscurabitur, et luna non dabit lumen suum, et stellae cadent* de caelo, *et virtutes caelorum* commovebuntur. [30]Et tunc parebit signum Filii hominis in caelo, et tunc *plangent omnes tribus terrae* et videbunt *Filium hominis venientem in nubibus caeli* cum virtute et gloria multa; [31]et mittet angelos suos cum tuba magna, et congregabunt electos eius a quattuor ventis, a summis caelorum usque ad terminos eorum. [32]Ab arbore autem fici discite parabolam: cum iam ramus eius tener fuerit, et folia nata, scitis quia prope est aestas. [33]Ita et vos, cum videritis haec omnia, scitote quia prope est in ianuis. [34]Amen dico vobis: Non praeteribit haec generatio, donec omnia haec fiant. [35]Caelum et terra transibunt, verba vero mea non praeteribunt. [36]De die autem illa et hora nemo scit, neque angeli caelorum neque Filius, nisi Pater solus. [37]Sicut enim dies Noe, ita erit adventus Filii hominis. [38]Sicut enim erant in diebus ante diluvium comedentes et bibentes, nubentes et nuptum tradentes, usque ad eum diem, quo introivit in arcam Noe, [39]et non cognoverunt, donec venit diluvium et tulit omnes, ita erit et adventus Filii hominis. [40]Tunc duo erunt in agro: unus assumitur, et unus relinquitur; [41]duae molentes in mola: una assumitur, et una relinquitur. [42]Vigilate ergo, quia nescitis qua die Dominus vester venturus sit. [43]Illud autem scitote quoniam si sciret pater familias qua hora fur venturus esset, vigilaret utique et non sineret perfodi domum suam. [44]Ideo et vos estote parati, quia, qua nescitis hora, Filius hominis venturus est. [45]Quis putas est fidelis servus et prudens, quem constituit dominus supra familiam suam, ut det illis cibum in tempore? [46]Beatus ille servus, quem cum venerit dominus eius invenerit sic facientem. [47]Amen dico vobis quoniam super omnia bona sua constituet eum. [48]Si autem dixerit malus servus ille in corde suo: "Moram facit dominus meus venire", [49]et coeperit percutere conservos suos, manducet autem et bibat cum ebriis, [50]veniet dominus servi illius in die, qua non sperat, et in hora, qua ignorat, [51]et dividet eum partemque eius ponet cum hypocritis; illic erit fletus et stridor dentium.   [25] [1]Tunc simile erit regnum caelorum decem virginibus, quae accipientes lampades suas exierunt obviam sponso. [2]Quinque autem ex eis erant fatuae et quinque prudentes. [3]Fatuae enim, acceptis lampadibus suis, non sumpserunt oleum secum; [4]prudentes vero acceperunt oleum in vasis cum lampadibus suis. [5]Moram autem faciente sponso, dormitaverunt omnes et dormierunt. [6]Media autem nocte clamor factus est: "Ecce sponsus! Exite obviam ei". [7]Tunc surrexerunt omnes virgines illae et ornaverunt lampades suas. [8]Fatuae autem sapientibus dixerunt: "Date nobis de oleo vestro, quia lampades nostrae exstinguuntur". [9]Responderunt prudentes dicentes: "Ne forte non sufficiat nobis et vobis, ite potius ad vendentes et emite vobis". [10]Dum autem irent emere, venit sponsus, et quae paratae erant, intraverunt cum eo ad nuptias; et clausa est ianua. [11]Novissime autem veniunt et reliquae virgines dicentes: "Domine, Domine, aperi nobis". [12]At ille respondens ait: "Amen dico vobis: Nescio vos". [13]Vigilate itaque, quia nescitis diem neque horam. [14]Sicut enim homo peregre proficiscens vocavit servos suos et tradidit illis bona sua. [15]Et uni dedit quinque talenta, alii autem duo, alii vero unum, unicuique secundum propriam virtutem, et profectus est. Statim [16]abiit, qui quinque talenta acceperat, et operatus est in eis et lucratus est alia quinque; [17]similiter qui duo acceperat, lucratus est alia duo. [18]Qui autem unum acceperat, abiens fodit in terra et abscondit pecuniam domini sui. [19]Post multum vero temporis venit dominus servorum illorum et ponit rationem cum eis. [20]Et accedens, qui quinque talenta acceperat, obtulit alia quinque talenta dicens: "Domine, quinque talenta tradidisti mihi; ecce alia quinque superlucratus sum". [21]Ait illi dominus eius: "Euge, serve bone et fidelis. Super pauca fuisti fidelis; supra multa te constituam: intra in gaudium domini tui". [22]Accessit autem et qui duo talenta acceperat, et ait: "Domine, duo talenta tradidisti mihi; ecce alia duo lucratus sum". [23]Ait illi dominus eius: "Euge, serve bone et fidelis. Super pauca fuisti fidelis; supra multa te constituam: intra in gaudium domini tui". [24]Accedens autem et qui unum talentum acceperat, ait: "Domine, novi te quia homo durus es: metis, ubi non seminasti, et congregas, ubi non sparsisti; [25]et timens abii et abscondi talentum tuum in terra. Ecce habes, quod tuum est". [26]Respondens autem dominus eius dixit ei: "Serve male et piger! Sciebas quia meto, ubi non seminavi, et congrego, ubi non sparsi? [27]Oportuit ergo te mittere pecuniam meam nummulariis, et veniens ego recepissem, quod meum est cum usura. [28]Tollite itaque ab eo talentum et date ei, qui habet decem talenta: [29]omni enim habenti dabitur, et abundabit; ei autem, qui non habet, et quod habet, auferetur ab eo. [30]Et inutilem servum eicite in tenebras exteriores: illic erit fletus et stridor dentium". [31]Cum autem venerit Filius hominis in gloria sua, et omnes angeli cum eo, tunc sedebit super thronum gloriae suae. [32]Et congregabuntur ante eum omnes gentes; et separabit eos ab invicem, sicut pastor segregat oves ab haedis, [33]et statuet oves quidem a dextris suis, haedos autem a sinistris. [34]Tunc dicet Rex his, qui a dextris eius erunt: "Venite, benedicti Patris mei; possidete paratum vobis regnum a constitutione mundi. [35]Esurivi enim, et dedistis mihi manducare; sitivi, et dedistis mihi bibere; hospes eram, et collegistis me; [36]nudus, et operuistis me; infirmus, et visitastis me; in carcere eram, et venistis ad me". [37]Tunc respondebunt ei iusti dicentes: "Domine, quando te vidimus esurientem et pavimus, aut sitientem et dedimus tibi potum? [38]Quando autem te vidimus hospitem et collegimus, aut nudum et cooperuimus? [39]Quando autem te vidimus infirmum aut in carcere et venimus ad te?". [40]Et respondens Rex dicet illis: "Amen dico vobis: Quamdiu fecistis uni de his fratribus meis minimis, mihi fecistis". [41]Tunc dicet et his, qui a sinistris erunt: "Discedite a me, maledicti, in ignem aeternum, qui praeparatus est Diabolo et angelis eius. [42]Esurivi enim, et non dedistis mihi manducare; sitivi, et non dedistis mihi potum; [43]hospes eram, et non collegistis me; nudus, et non operuistis me; infirmus et in carcere, et non visitastis me". [44]Tunc respondebunt et ipsi dicentes: "Domine, quando te vidimus esurientem aut sitientem aut hospitem aut nudum aut infirmum vel in carcere et non ministravimus tibi?". [45]Tunc respondebit illis dicens: "Amen dico vobis: Quamdiu non fecistis uni de minimis his, nec mihi fecistis". [46]Et ibunt hi in supplicium aeternum, iusti autem in vitam aeternam». **[26]** [1]Et factum est cum consummasset Iesus sermones hos omnes, dixit discipulis suis: [2]«Scitis quia post biduum Pascha fiet, et Filius hominis traditur, ut crucifigatur». [3]Tunc congregati sunt principes sacerdotum et seniores populi in aulam principis sacerdotum, qui dicebatur Caiphas, [4]et consilium fecerunt, ut Iesum dolo tenerent et occiderent; [5]dicebant autem: «Non in die festo, ne tumultus fiat in populo». [6]Cum autem esset Iesus in Bethania, in domo Simonis leprosi, [7]accessit ad eum mulier habens alabastrum unguenti pretiosi et effudit super caput ipsius recumbentis. [8]Videntes autem discipuli, indignati sunt dicentes: «Ut quid perditio haec? [9]Potuit enim istud venumdari multo et dari pauperibus». [10]Sciens autem Iesus ait illis: «Quid molesti estis mulieri? Opus enim bonum operata est in me; [11]nam semper pauperes habetis vobiscum, me autem non semper habetis. [12]Mittens enim haec unguentum hoc supra corpus meum, ad sepeliendum me fecit. [13]Amen dico vobis: Ubicumque praedicatum fuerit hoc evangelium in toto mundo, dicetur et quod haec fecit in memoriam eius». [14]Tunc abiit unus de Duodecim, qui dicebatur Iudas Iscariotes, ad principes sacerdotum [15]et ait: «Quid vultis mihi dare, et ego vobis eum tradam?». *At illi constituerunt ei triginta argenteos.* [16]Et exinde quaerebat opportunitatem, ut eum traderet. [17]Prima autem Azymorum accesserunt discipuli ad Iesum dicentes: «Ubi vis paremus tibi comedere Pascha?». [18]Ille autem dixit: «Ite in civitatem ad quendam et dicite ei: "Magister dicit: Tempus meum prope est; apud te facio Pascha cum discipulis meis"». [19]Et fecerunt discipuli, sicut constituit illis Iesus, et paraverunt Pascha. [20]Vespere autem facto, discumbebat cum Duodecim. [21]Et edentibus illis, dixit: «Amen dico vobis: Unus vestrum me traditurus est». [22]Et contristati valde, coeperunt singuli dicere ei: «Numquid ego sum, Domine?». [23]At ipse respondens ait: «Qui intingit mecum manum in paropside, hic me tradet. [24]Filius quidem hominis vadit, sicut scriptum est de illo; vae autem homini illi, per quem Filius hominis traditur! Bonum erat ei, si natus non fuisset homo ille». [25]Respondens autem Iudas, qui tradidit eum, dixit: «Numquid ego sum, Rabbi?». Ait illi: «Tu dixisti». [26]Cenantibus autem eis, accepit Iesus panem et benedixit ac fregit deditque discipulis et ait: «Accipite, comedite: hoc est corpus meum». [27]Et accipiens calicem, gratias egit et dedit illis dicens: «Bibite ex hoc omnes: [28]hic est enim sanguis meus novi testamenti, qui pro multis effunditur in remissionem peccatorum. [29]Dico autem vobis: Non bibam amodo de hoc genimine vitis usque in diem illum, cum illud bibam vobiscum novum in regno Patris mei». [30]Et hymno dicto, exierunt in montem Oliveti. [31]Tunc dicit illis Iesus: «Omnes vos scandalum patiemini in me in ista nocte. Scriptum est enim: *"Percutiam pastorem, et dispergentur oves gregis".* [32]Postquam autem resurrexero, praecedam vos in Galilaeam». [33]Respondens autem Petrus ait illi: «Et si omnes scandalizati fuerint in te, ego numquam scandalizabor». [34]Ait illi Iesus: «Amen dico tibi: In hac nocte, antequam gallus cantet, ter me negabis». [35]Ait illi Petrus: «Etiam si oportuerit me mori tecum, non te negabo». Similiter et omnes discipuli dixerunt. [36]Tunc venit Iesus cum illis in praedium, quod dicitur Gethsemani. Et dicit discipulis: «Sedete hic, donec vadam illuc et orem». [37]Et assumpto Petro et duobus filiis Zebedaei, coepit contristari et maestus esse. [38]Tunc ait illis: «Tristis est anima mea usque ad mortem; sustinete hic et vigilate mecum». [39]Et progressus pusillum, procidit in faciem suam orans et dicens: «Pater mi, si possibile est, transeat a me calix iste; verumtamen non sicut ego volo, sed sicut tu». [40]Et venit ad discipulos et invenit eos dormientes; et dicit Petro: «Sic non potuistis una hora vigilare mecum? [41]Vigilate et orate, ut non intretis in tentationem; spiritus quidem promptus est, caro autem infirma». [42]Iterum secundo abiit et oravit dicens: «Pater mi, si non potest hoc transire, nisi bibam illud, fiat voluntas tua». [43]Et venit iterum et invenit eos dormientes: erant enim oculi eorum gravati. [44]Et relictis illis, iterum abiit et oravit tertio, eundem sermonem iterum dicens. [45]Tunc venit ad discipulos et dicit illis: «Dormite iam et requiescite; ecce appropinquavit hora, et Filius hominis traditur in manus peccatorum. [46]Surgite, eamus; ecce appropinquavit, qui me tradit». [47]Et adhuc ipso loquente, ecce Iudas, unus de Duodecim, venit et cum eo turba multa cum gladiis et fustibus, missi a principibus sacerdotum et senioribus populi. [48]Qui autem tradidit eum, dedit illis signum dicens: «Quemcumque osculatus fuero, ipse est; tenete eum!». [49]Et confestim accedens ad Iesum dixit: «Ave, Rabbi!» et osculatus est eum. [50]Iesus autem dixit illi: «Amice, ad quod venisti!». Tunc accesserunt et manus iniecerunt in Iesum et tenuerunt eum. [51]Et ecce unus ex his, qui erant cum Iesu, extendens manum exemit gladium suum et percutiens servum principis sacerdotum amputavit auriculam eius. [52]Tunc ait illi Iesus: «Converte gladium tuum in locum suum. Omnes enim, qui acceperint gladium, gladio peribunt. [53]An putas quia non possum rogare Patrem meum, et exhibebit mihi modo plus quam duodecim legiones angelorum? [54]Quomodo ergo implebuntur Scripturae quia sic oportet fieri?». [55]In illa hora dixit Iesus turbis: «Tamquam ad latronem existis cum gladiis et fustibus comprehendere me? Cotidie sedebam docens in templo, et non me tenuistis». [56]Hoc autem totum factum est, ut implerentur scripturae Prophetarum. Tunc discipuli omnes, relicto eo, fugerunt. [57]Illi autem tenentes Iesum duxerunt ad Caipham principem sacerdotum, ubi scribae et seniores convenerant. [58]Petrus autem sequebatur eum a longe usque in aulam principis sacerdotum; et ingressus intro sedebat cum ministris, ut videret finem. [59]Principes autem sacerdotum et omne concilium quaerebant falsum testimonium contra Iesum, ut eum morti traderent, [60]et non invenerunt, cum multi falsi testes accessissent. Novissime autem venientes duo [61]dixerunt: «Hic dixit: "Possum destruere templum Dei et post triduum aedificare illud"». [62]Et surgens princeps sacerdotum ait illi: «Nihil respondes? Quid isti adversum te testificantur?». [63]Iesus autem tacebat. Et princeps sacerdotum ait illi: «Adiuro te per Deum vivum, ut dicas nobis, si tu es Christus Filius Dei». [64]Dicit illi Iesus: «Tu dixisti. Verumtamen dico vobis: Amodo videbitis *Filium hominis sedentem a dextris Virtutis et venientem in nubibus caeli*». [65]Tunc princeps sacerdotum scidit vestimenta sua dicens: «Blasphemavit! Quid adhuc egemus testibus? Ecce nunc audistis blasphemiam. [66]Quid vobis videtur?». Illi autem respondentes dixerunt: «Reus est mortis!». [67]Tunc exspuerunt in faciem eius et colaphis eum ceciderunt; alii autem palmas in faciem ei dederunt [68]dicentes: «Prophetiza nobis, Christe: Quis est, qui te percussit?». [69]Petrus vero sedebat foris in atrio; et accessit ad eum una ancilla dicens: «Et tu cum Iesu Galilaeo eras!». [70]At ille negavit coram omnibus dicens: «Nescio quid dicis!». [71]Exeunte autem illo ad ianuam, vidit eum alia et ait his, qui erant ibi: «Hic erat cum Iesu Nazareno!». [72]Et iterum negavit cum iuramento: «Non novi hominem!». [73]Post pusillum autem accesserunt, qui stabant et dixerunt Petro: «Vere et tu ex illis es, nam et loquela tua manifestum te facit». [74]Tunc coepit detestari et iurare: «Non novi hominem!». Et continuo gallus cantavit; [75]et recordatus est Petrus verbi Iesu, quod dixerat: «Priusquam gallus cantet, ter me negabis». Et egressus foras ploravit amare.

[27] [1]Mane autem facto, consilium inierunt omnes principes sacerdotum et seniores populi adversus Iesum, ut eum morti traderent. [2]Et vinctum adduxerunt eum et tradiderunt Pilato praesidi. [3]Tunc videns Iudas, qui eum tradidit, quod damnatus esset, paenitentia ductus, rettulit triginta argenteos principibus sacerdotum et senioribus [4]dicens: «Peccavi tradens sanguinem innocentem». At illi dixerunt: «Quid ad nos? Tu videris!». [5]Et proiectis argenteis in templo, recessit et abiens laqueo se suspendit. [6]Principes autem sacerdotum, acceptis argenteis, dixerunt: «Non licet mittere eos in corbanam, quia pretium sanguinis est». [7]Consilio autem inito, emerunt ex illis agrum Figuli in sepulturam peregrinorum. [8]Propter hoc vocatus est ager ille ager Sanguinis usque in hodiernum diem. [9]Tunc impletum est quod dictum est per Ieremiam prophetam dicentem: «*Et acceperunt triginta argenteos, pretium appretiati quem appretiaverunt a filiis Israel,* [10]*et dederunt eos in agrum Figuli, sicut constituit mihi Dominus*». [11]Iesus autem stetit ante praesidem; et interrogavit eum praeses dicens: «Tu es Rex Iudaeorum?». Dixit autem Iesus: «Tu dicis». [12]Et cum accusaretur a principibus sacerdotum et senioribus, nihil respondit. [13]Tunc dicit illi Pilatus: «Non audis quanta adversum te dicant testimonia?». [14]Et non respondit ei ad ullum verbum, ita ut miraretur praeses vehementer. [15]Per diem autem sollemnem consueverat praeses dimittere turbae unum vinctum, quem voluissent. [16]Habebant autem tunc vinctum insignem, qui dicebatur Barabbas. [17]Congregatis ergo illis dixit Pilatus: «Quem vultis dimittam vobis: Barabbam an Iesum, qui dicitur Christus?». [18]Sciebat enim quod per invidiam tradidissent eum. [19]Sedente autem illo pro tribunali, misit ad illum uxor eius dicens: «Nihil tibi et iusto illi. Multa enim passa sum hodie per visum propter eum». [20]Principes autem sacerdotum et seniores persuaserunt turbis, ut peterent Barabbam, Iesum vero perderent. [21]Respondens autem praeses ait illis: «Quem vultis vobis de duobus dimittam?». At illi dixerunt: «Barabbam!». [22]Dicit illis Pilatus: «Quid igitur faciam de Iesu, qui dicitur Christus?». Dicunt omnes: «Crucifigatur!». [23]Ait autem: «Quid enim mali fecit?». At illi magis clamabant dicentes: «Crucifigatur!». [24]Videns autem Pilatus quia nihil proficeret, sed magis tumultus fieret, accepta aqua, lavit manus coram turba dicens: «Innocens ego sum a sanguine hoc; vos videritis!». [25]Et respondens universus populus dixit: «Sanguis eius super nos et super filios nostros». [26]Tunc dimisit illis Barabbam; Iesum autem flagellatum tradidit, ut crucifigeretur. [27]Tunc milites praesidis suscipientes

Iesum in praetorio congregaverunt ad eum universam cohortem. [28]Et exuentes eum, clamydem coccineam circumdederunt ei [29]et plectentes coronam de spinis posuerunt super caput eius et arundinem in dextera eius et, genu flexo ante eum, illudebant ei dicentes: «Ave, rex Iudaeorum!». [30]Et exspuentes in eum acceperunt arundinem et percutiebant caput eius. [31]Et postquam illuserunt ei, exuerunt eum clamyde et induerunt eum vestimentis eius et duxerunt eum, ut crucifigerent. [32]Exeuntes autem invenerunt hominem Cyrenaeum nomine Simonem; hunc angariaverunt, ut tolleret crucem eius. [33]Et venerunt in locum, qui dicitur Golgotha, quod est Calvariae locus, [34]et *dederunt* ei vinum *bibere* cum *felle* mixtum; et cum gustasset, noluit bibere. [35]Postquam autem crucifixerunt eum, *diviserunt vestimenta* eius *sortem mittentes* [36]et sedentes servabant eum ibi. [37]Et imposuerunt super caput eius causam ipsius scriptam: «Hic est Iesus Rex Iudaeorum». [38]Tunc crucifiguntur cum eo duo latrones: unus a dextris et unus a sinistris. [39]Praetereuntes autem blasphemabant eum *moventes capita sua* [40]et dicentes: «Qui destruis templum et in triduo illud reaedificas, salva temetipsum; si Filius Dei es, descende de cruce!». [41]Similiter et principes sacerdotum illudentes cum scribis et senioribus dicebant: [42]«Alios salvos fecit, seipsum non potest salvum facere. Rex Israel est; descendat nunc de cruce, et credemus in eum. [43]*Confidit in Deo*; *liberet* nunc, *si vult eum*. Dixit enim: "Dei Filius sum"». [44]Idipsum autem et latrones, qui crucifixi erant cum eo, improperabant ei. [45]A sexta autem hora tenebrae factae sunt super universam terram usque ad horam nonam. [46]Et circa horam nonam clamavit Iesus voce magna dicens: «*Eli, Eli, lema sabacthani*?», hoc est: «*Deus meus, Deus meus, ut quid dereliquisti me*?». [47]Quidam autem ex illic stantibus audientes dicebant: «Eliam vocat iste». [48]Et continuo currens unus ex eis acceptam spongiam implevit aceto et imposuit arundini et *dabat* ei *bibere*. [49]Ceteri vero dicebant: «Sine, videamus an veniat Elias liberans eum». [50]Iesus autem iterum clamans voce magna emisit spiritum. [51]Et ecce velum templi scissum est a summo usque deorsum in duas partes, et terra mota est, et petrae scissae sunt, [52]et monumenta aperta sunt et multa corpora sanctorum, qui dormierant, surrexerunt [53]et exeuntes de monumentis post resurrectionem eius venerunt in sanctam civitatem et apparuerunt multis. [54]Centurio autem et, qui cum eo erant custodientes Iesum, viso terrae motu et his, quae fiebant, timuerunt valde dicentes: «Vere Dei Filius erat iste!». [55]Erant autem ibi mulieres multae a longe aspicientes, quae secutae erant Iesum a Galilaea ministrantes ei; [56]inter quas erat Maria Magdalene et Maria Iacobi et Ioseph mater et mater filiorum Zebedaei. [57]Cum sero autem factum esset, venit homo dives ab Arimathaea nomine Ioseph, qui et ipse discipulus erat Iesu. [58]Hic accessit ad Pilatum et petiit corpus Iesu. Tunc Pilatus iussit reddi. [59]Et accepto corpore, Ioseph involvit illud in sindone munda [60]et posuit illud in monumento suo novo, quod exciderat in petra, et advolvit saxum magnum ad ostium monumenti et abiit. [61]Erat autem ibi Maria Magdalene et altera Maria sedentes contra sepulcrum. [62]Altera autem die, quae est post Parascevem, convenerunt principes sacerdotum et pharisaei ad Pilatum [63]dicentes: «Domine, recordati sumus quia seductor ille dixit adhuc vivens: 'Post tres dies resurgam'. [64]Iube ergo custodiri sepulcrum usque in diem tertium, ne forte veniant discipuli eius et furentur eum et dicant plebi: 'Surrexit a mortuis', et erit novissimus error peior priore». [65]Ait illis Pilatus: «Habetis custodiam; ite, custodite, sicut scitis». [66]Illi autem abeuntes munierunt sepulcrum, signantes lapidem, cum custodia.   **[28]** [1]Sero autem post sabbatum, cum illucesceret in primam sabbati, venit Maria Magdalene et altera Maria videre sepulcrum. [2]Et ecce terrae motus factus est magnus: angelus enim Domini descendit de caelo et accedens revolvit lapidem et sedebat super eum. [3]Erat autem aspectus eius sicut fulgur, et vestimentum eius candidum sicut nix. [4]Prae timore autem eius exterriti sunt custodes et facti sunt velut mortui. [5]Respondens autem angelus dixit mulieribus: «Nolite timere vos! Scio enim quod Iesum, qui crucifixus est, quaeritis. [6]Non est hic: surrexit enim, sicut dixit. Venite, videte locum, ubi positus erat. [7]Et cito euntes dicite discipulis eius: "Surrexit a mortuis et ecce praecedit vos in Galilaeam; ibi eum videbitis". Ecce dixi vobis». [8]Et exeuntes cito de monumento cum timore et magno gaudio cucurrerunt nuntiare discipulis eius. [9]Et ecce Iesus occurrit illis dicens: «Avete». Illae autem accesserunt et tenuerunt pedes eius et adoraverunt eum. [10]Tunc ait illis Iesus: «Nolite timere; ite, nuntiate fratribus meis, ut eant in Galilaeam et ibi me videbunt». [11]Quae cum abiissent, ecce quidam de custodia venerunt in civitatem et nuntiaverunt principibus sacerdotum omnia, quae facta fuerant. [12]Et congregati cum senioribus, consilio accepto, pecuniam copiosam dederunt militibus [13]dicentes: «Dicite: "Discipuli eius nocte venerunt et furati sunt eum, nobis dormientibus". [14]Et si hoc auditum fuerit a praeside, nos suadebimus ei et securos vos faciemus». [15]At illi, accepta pecunia, fecerunt, sicut erant docti. Et divulgatum est verbum istud apud Iudaeos usque in hodiernum diem. [16]Undecim autem discipuli abierunt in Galilaeam, in montem ubi constituerat illis Iesus, [17]et videntes eum adoraverunt; quidam autem dubitaverunt. [18]Et accedens Iesus locutus est eis dicens: «Data est mihi omnis potestas in caelo et in terra. [19]Euntes ergo docete omnes gentes, baptizantes eos in nomine Patris et Filii et Spiritus Sancti, [20]docentes eos servare omnia, quaecumque mandavi vobis. Et ecce ego vobiscum sum omnibus diebus usque ad consummationem saeculi».

Explanatory Notes

Asterisks in the text of the New Testament refer to these "Explanatory Notes" in the RSVCE.

THE GOSPEL ACCORDING TO MATTHEW

1:1: The genealogy is given to show that Jesus had the descent required for Messiahship, i.e. from Abraham and, in particular, from David the king.

1:16: Joseph's, not Mary's, descent is given here, as the Jews did not usually reckon descent through the mother. Joseph was the legal and presumed father, and it was this fact that conferred rights of inheritance, in this case, the fulfilment of the Messianic promises.

1:25: This means only that Joseph had nothing to do with the conception of Jesus. It implies nothing as to what happened afterwards.

3:2, *Repent* implies an internal change of heart.

3:6: Not a Christian baptism but a preparation for it.

3:15: Though without sin, Jesus wished to be baptized by John, as this was the final preparation for his Messianic mission.

5:17: Jesus came to bring the old law to its natural fulfilment in the new while discarding what had become obsolete; cf. Jn 4:21.

5:29: An exaggeration to emphasize the need to avoid occasions of sin.

5:32, *unchastity*: The Greek word used here appears to refer to marriages which were not legally marriages, because they were either within the forbidden degrees of consanguinity (Lev 18:6–16) or contracted with a Gentile. The phrase *except on the ground of unchastity* does not occur in the parallel passage in Lk 16:18. See also Mt 19:9 (Mk 10:11–12), and especially 1 Cor 7:10–11, which shows that the prohibition is unconditional.

6:6: This does not, of course, exclude public worship but ostentatious prayer.

6:24, *mammon*: i.e., riches.

8:3: The miracles of Jesus were never performed to amaze people and shock them into belief. They were worked with a view to a real strengthening of faith in the recipient or beholder, from whom the proper dispositions were required.

8:29, *before the time:* Before the day of judgment the demons are permitted by God to tempt men and even to possess them.

10:5: The gospel, the Messianic salvation, had first to be preached and offered to the chosen people, Israel. Later it would be offered to the Gentiles.

11:3: The Baptist expected more obvious signs of the Messiah. By quoting the prophet Isaiah, Jesus showed that he was indeed inaugurating the Messianic kingdom—but by doing good rather than by glorious manifestations or sudden punishments.

11:27: This shows a profound relationship between the Son and the Father, far superior to adoptive sonship.

12:14: The Pharisees regarded healing as work and so forbade it on the sabbath.

12:24, *Beel-zebul:* Name of a Canaanite god meaning "the Prince-god". The Jews interpreted this name as "Prince of demons", because for them all false gods were demons.

12:31: To attribute to the devil the works of the Holy Spirit seems to imply a hardness of heart which precludes repentance.

12:46, *brethren*: The Greek word or its Semitic equivalent was used for varying degrees of blood relationship; cf. Gen 14:14; 29:12; Lev 10:4.

12:48: Jesus puts the work of salvation before family relationships. It is not said, however, that he refused to see them.

13:12: To those well-disposed Jews who have made good use of the old covenant will now be given the perfection of the new. On the other hand, from those who have rejected God's advances will now be taken away even that which they have, because the old covenant is passing away.

13:52: This is Matthew's ideal: that the learned Jew should become the disciple of Jesus and so add the riches of the new covenant to those of the old, which he already possesses; cf. verse 12.

13:55: See note on Mt 12:46.

14:33: Their realization of his Godhead was the prelude to Peter's confession of faith at Caesarea Philippi (Mt 16:16).

15:5: By dedicating his property to God, i.e. to the temple, a man could avoid having to help his parents, without actually giving up what he had. The scribes held such a vow to be valid without necessarily approving it.

15:24: See note on 10:5.

16:14: The title of prophet had a Messianic significance because the gift of prophecy, which had been extinct since Malachi, was expected to return at the beginning of the Messianic era, especially by an outpouring of the Spirit as foretold by the prophet Joel and as realized in Acts 2:16.

16:16: The context shows that Peter recognizes the sonship of Jesus as divine and not adoptive like ours. Mark and Luke in the parallel passages mention only the confession of the Messiahship.

16:18: The name "Peter" comes from the Greek word for "rock". Jesus makes him the foundation on which the Church is to be built. The word "church" means "assembly" or "society" of believers. The Hebrew equivalent is used in the Old Testament to indicate the chosen people. In applying it to the church Jesus shows it to be the Messianic community foretold by the prophets. See note on Mt 18:18.

16:19: *the kingdom of heaven*: Peter has the key to the gates of the city of God. This power is exercised through the church. "Binding" and "loosing" are rabbinic terms referring to excommunication, then later to forbidding or allowing something. Not only can Peter admit to the kingdom; he also has power to make authoritative decisions in matters of faith or morals.

16:25, *life* (both times): A play on the word "life"—natural and supernatural; cf. Mk 8:35–36.

17:4: Peter thought the glorious Messianic kingdom had come. In fact, Jesus allowed this glimpse of his glory to strengthen them for the coming passion.

18:9, *Gehenna* (see footnote **b**) was the name of a valley south of Jerusalem where human sacrifice had once been practised; cf. 2 Chron 33:6. Later it became a cursed place and refuse dump, and the name came to symbolize the Christian place of punishment.

18:18: To the other apostles is given a share in the authority given to Peter.

19:9: This appears to refer to the case in Mt 5:32, though the Greek word for "except" is different.

19:11–12: Jesus means that a life of continence is to be chosen only by those who are called to it for the sake of the kingdom of God.

21:9: The crowd openly recognize Jesus as the Messiah and he allows it for the first time.

21:23: They object to the assumption of authority implicit in the manner of his entry into the city and in his expulsion of the sellers from the temple.

21:33–44: This parable is really an allegory in which almost every detail represents something in God's dealings with Israel.

22:11: The wedding garment represents the dispositions necessary for admission to the kingdom.

23:5, *phylacteries*: Little leather boxes containing, on a very small scroll, the principal words of the law; cf. Deut 6:4–9. Taking the command literally, they fastened these to their arms and their foreheads.

23:9: i.e., "Do not use the title without reference to God's universal fatherhood." He cannot mean that the title is never to be used by a son to his father.

24:1—25:46: The "eschatological discourse," as it is called, deals with the fall of Jerusalem and the end of the world. The two themes seem to be inextricably intermingled in the Gospels as we now have it, but it is possible that originally they were in separate discourses. However, the fusion of the two does bring out their connection. The one prefigures the other. Moreover, in the reverse direction, so to speak, the language used to describe the day of the Lord in Joel and elsewhere is here applied to the fall of Jerusalem, the details of which must therefore not be taken too literally (24:29).

25:29: See note on 13:12.

26:17: The passover was celebrated this year on the Friday evening (Jn 18:28). Jesus must have anticipated the passover meal because he would be dead the following day and because the meal prefigured his death.

26:26: The details of the Eucharist are superimposed on the ritual of the passover.

26:51: It was Peter, as John in his later Gospel tells us (Jn 18:10), though Matthew is reluctant to say so.

26:59: They sought evidence against him and this was necessarily false.

26:64–65: For the first time Jesus speaks clearly of his own identity. Caiaphas evidently understands him to claim divinity.

27:46: Jesus applies Psalm 22 (Vulgate 21) to himself.

Explanatory Notes

27:66: The sealing and guarding only helped to make the subsequent resurrection more obvious.

28:1–20: The resurrection appearances. There are divergent traditions in the Gospels, Galilean and Judean. Paul adds his own record (1 Cor 15). The accounts do not easily fit together, but this is surely evidence of their genuineness. There is no attempt to produce an artificial conformity.

Changes in the RSV for the Catholic Edition

| | TEXT | | FOOTNOTES | |
	RSV	RSVCE	RSV	RSVCE
Mt 1:19	divorce her	send her away		
Mt 12:46,47 (note), 48, 49	brothers	brethren		
Mt 13:55	brothers	brethren		
Mt 18:24			fDelete existing note and substitute:	fA talent was more than fifteen years' wages of a labourer
Mt 18:28			gDelete existing note and substitute:	gThe denarius was a day's wage for a labourer
Mt 19:9		. . . commits adultery; and he who marries a divorced woman commits adultery."k		kOther ancient authorities omit *and he . . . adultery*
Mt 20:2			mDelete existing note and substitute:	mThe denarius was a day's wage for a labourer
Mt 21:44		q+44 And he who falls on this stone will be broken to pieces; but when it falls on any one, it will crush him		qOther ancient authorities omit verse 44
Mt 25:15			dDelete existing note and substitute:	dA talent was more than fifteen years' wages of a labourer
Mt 27:24		lthis righteous man's blood		lOther ancient authorities omit *righteous* or *man's*

Headings added to the Biblical Text

1. BIRTH AND INFANCY OF JESUS
The ancestry of Jesus Christ 1:1
The virginal conception of Jesus, and his birth 1:18
The adoration of the Magi 2:1
The flight into Egypt. The massacre of the Innocents 2:13
Return to Nazareth 2:19

2. PRELUDE TO THE PUBLIC MINISTRY OF JESUS
John the Baptist preaching in the wilderness 3:1
Jesus is baptized 3:13
Jesus fasts and is tempted 4:1

Part One: Jesus' ministry in Galilee

Jesus begins to preach 4:12
The first disciples are called 4:18

3. THE SERMON ON THE MOUNT
The Beatitudes 5:1
Salt of the earth and light of the world 5:13
Jesus and his teaching, the fullness of the Law 5:17
An upright intention in almsgiving, prayer and fasting 6:1
Trust in God's fatherly providence 6:19
Various precepts. Do not judge 7:1
Respect for holy things 7:6
Effectiveness of prayer 7:7
The golden rule 7:12
The narrow gate 7:13
False prophets 7:15
Doing the will of God 7:21
Building on rock 7:24
Jesus teaches with authority 7:28

4. MIRACLES OF THE MESSIAH
Curing of a leper 8:1
The centurion's faith 8:5
Curing of Peter's mother-in-law 8:14
Other cures 8:16
Following Christ is not easy 8:18
The calming of the storm 8:23
The demoniacs of Gadara 8:28
Curing of a paralyzed man 9:1
The call of Matthew 9:9
A discussion on fasting 9:14
The raising of Jairus' daughter and the curing of the woman with a haemorrhage 9:18
Curing of two blind men. The dumb devil 9:27
The need for good pastors 9:35

5. FROM THE OLD TO THE NEW PEOPLE OF GOD
The calling of the twelve apostles 10:1
The apostles' first mission 10:5
Jesus' instructions to the apostles 10:16
Messengers from John the Baptist 11:1
Jesus reproaches his contemporaries 11:16
Jesus reproaches cities for their unbelief 11:20
Jesus thanks his Father 11:25
The law of the sabbath 12:1
Curing of the man with a withered hand 12:9
Jesus, the servant of God 12:15
Allegations by the Pharisees. The sin against the Holy Spirit 12:22
The sign of Jonah 12:38
The true kinsmen of Jesus 12:46

6. THE PARABLES OF THE KINGDOM
Parable of the sower. The meaning of parables 13:1
The parable of the weeds 13:24
The mustard seed; the leaven 13:31
The parable of the weeds explained 13:36
The hidden treasure; the pearl; the net 13:44

7. JESUS WITHDRAWS TO THE BORDER COUNTRY
No one is a prophet in his own country 13:53
The martyrdom of John the Baptist 14:1
First miracle of the loaves and fish 14:13
Jesus walks on the water 14:22
Cures in Gennesaret 14:34
The tradition of the elders. True cleanness 15:1
The Canaanite woman 15:21
Curing of many sick people 15:29
Second miracle of the loaves and fish 15:32
The Pharisees and Sadducees try to test Jesus 16:1
Peter's profession of faith and his primacy 16:13

Headings added to the Biblical Text

Part Two: Jesus' ministry on the way to Jerusalem

8. TOWARDS JUDEA AND JERUSALEM
Jesus foretells his passion and resurrection. The law of Christian renunciation 16:21
The Transfiguration 17:1
Curing of an epileptic boy 17:14
Second announcement of the Passion. The temple tax 17:22

9. THE DISCOURSE ON THE CHURCH
The "little ones" and the Kingdom. On leading others astray. The lost sheep 18:1

Fraternal correction. The apostles' authority 18:15
Forgiveness of injuries. Parable of the unforgiving servant 18:21
Marriage and virginity 19:1
Jesus blesses the children 19:13
The rich young man. Christian poverty and renunciation 19:16
Parable of the labourers in the vineyard 20:1
Third announcement of the Passion 20:17
The mother of the sons of Zebedee makes her request 20:20
Curing of the blind men of Jericho 20:29

Part Three: Jesus' ministry in Jerusalem

10. CLEANSING OF THE TEMPLE. CONTROVERSIES
The Messiah enters the Holy City 21:1
Jesus in the temple 21:12
The cursing of the fig tree 21:18
The authority of Jesus is questioned 21:23
Parable of the two sons 21:28
Parable of the wicked tenants 21:33
Parable of the marriage feast 22:1
Paying tax to Caesar 22:15
The resurrection of the dead 22:23
The greatest commandment of all 22:34
The divinity of the Messiah 22:41
Jesus berates the scribes and Pharisees 23:1
Jerusalem admonished 23:37

11. THE ESCHATOLOGICAL DISCOURSE
Announcement of the destruction of the temple 24:1
The beginning of tribulations. Persecution on account of the Gospel 24:3
The great tribulation 24:15
The coming of the Son of man 24:29
The end will surely come. The lesson of the fig tree 24:32
The time of the second coming of Christ 24:36
Parable of the faithful servant 24:45

Parable of the wise and foolish maidens 25:1
Parable of the talents 25:14
The Last Judgment 25:31

12. THE PASSION, DEATH AND RESURRECTION OF JESUS
Last announcement of the Passion. The conspiracy against Jesus 26:1
The anointing at Bethany. Judas betrays Jesus 26:6
Preparations for the Last Supper and announcement of Judas' treachery 26:17
The institution of the Eucharist 26:26
The disciples' desertion foretold 26:30
Gethsemane—the agony in the garden 26:36
Arrest of Jesus 26:47
Jesus before the chief priests 26:57
Peter's denials 26:69
Jesus is brought before Pilate 27:1
Judas' despair and death 27:3
Jesus' trial before Pilate 27:11
The crowning with thorns 27:27
The crucifixion and death of Jesus 27:32
The burial of Jesus 27:57
Jesus rises from the dead and appears to the women 28:1
The soldiers are bribed 28:11
Appearance in Galilee. The mission to the world 28:16

Sources quoted in the Navarre Bible New Testament Commentary

1. DOCUMENTS OF THE CHURCH AND OF POPES

Benedict XII
Const. *Benedictus Deus*, 29 January 1336
Benedict XV
Enc. *Humani generis redemptionem*, 15 June 1917
Enc. *Spiritus Paraclitus*, 1 September 1920
Clement of Rome, St
Letter to the Corinthians
Constantinople, First Council of
Nicene-Constantinopolitan Creed
Constantinople, Third Council of
Definitio de duabus
    in Christo voluntatibus et operationibus
Florence, Council of
Decree *Pro Jacobitis*
Laetentur coeli
Decree *Pro Armeniis*
John Paul II
Addresses and homilies
Apos. Exhort. *Catechesi tradendae*, 16 October 1979
Apos. Exhort. *Familiaris consortio*, 22 November 1981
Apos. Exhort. *Reconciliatio et paenitentia*, 2 December 1984
Apos. Letter. *Salvifici doloris*, 11 February 1984
Bull, *Aperite portas*, 6 January 1983
Enc. *Redemptor hominis*, 4 March 1979
Enc. *Dives in misericordia*, 30 November 1980
Enc. *Dominum et Vivificantem*, 30 May 1986
Enc. *Laborem exercens*, 14 September 1981
Letter to all priests, 8 April 1979
Letter to all bishops, 24 February 1980
Gelasius I
Ne forte
Gregory the Great, St
Epistula ad Theodorum medicum contra Fabianum
Exposition on the Seven Penitential
Ne forte
In Evangelia homiliae
In Ezechielem homiliae
Moralia in Job

Regulae pastoralis liber
Innocent III
Letter *Eius exemplo*, 18 December 1208
John XXIII
Pacem in terris, 11 April 1963
Enc. *Ad Petri cathedram*, 29 June 1959
Lateran Council (649)
Canons
Leo the Great, St
Homilies and sermons
Licet per nostros
Promisisse memememi
Leo IX
Creed
Leo XIII
Enc. *Aeterni Patris*, 4 August 1879
Enc. *Immortale Dei*, 1 November 1885
Enc. *Libertas praestantissimum*, 20 June 1888
Enc. *Sapientiae christianae*, 18 January 1890
Enc. *Rerum novarum*, 15 May 1891
Enc. *Providentissimus Deus*, 18 November 1893
Enc. *Divinum illud munus*, 9 May 1897
Lateran, Fourth Council of (1215)
De fide catholica
Lyons, Second Council of (1274)
Doctrina de gratia
Profession of faith of Michael Palaeologue
Orange, Second Council of (529)
De gratia
Paul IV
Const. *Cum quorumdam*, 7 August 1555
Paul VI
Enc. *Ecclesiam suam*, 6 August 1964
Enc. *Mysterium fidei*, 9 September 1965
Apos. Exhort. *Marialis cultus*, 2 February 1967
Apos. Letter *Petrum et Paulum*, 27 February 1967
Enc. *Populorum progressio*, 26 March 1967
Enc. *Sacerdotalis coelibatus*, 24 June 1967
Creed of the People of God: Solemn Profession of Faith, 30 June 1968
Apos. Letter *Octagesima adveniens*, 14 June 1971

Sources quoted in the Commentary

Apos. Exhort. *Gaudete in Domino*, 9 May 1975
Apos. Exhort. *Evangelii nuntiandi*, 8 Dec. 1975
Homilies and addresses
Pius V, St
Catechism of the Council of Trent for Parish Priests or *Pius V Catechism*
Pius IX, Bl.
Bull *Ineffabilis Deus*, 8 December 1854
Syllabus of Errors
Pius X, St
Enc. *E supreme apostolatus*, 4 October 1903
Enc. *Ad Diem illum*, 2 February 1904
Enc. *Acerbo nimis*, 15 April 1905
Catechism of Christian Doctrine, 15 July 1905
Decree *Lamentabili*, 3 July 1907
Enc. *Haerent animo*, 4 August 1908
Pius XI
Enc. *Quas primas*, 11 December 1925
Enc. *Divini illius magistri*, 31 December 1929
Enc. *Mens nostra*, 20 December 1929
Enc. *Casti connubii*, 31 December 1930
Enc. *Quadragesimo anno*, 15 May 1931
Enc. *Ad catholici sacerdotii*, 20 December 1935
Pius XII
Enc. *Mystici Corporis*, 29 June 1943
Enc. *Mediator Dei*, 20 November 1947
Enc. *Divino afflante Spiritu*, 30 September 1943
Enc. *Humani generis*, 12 August 1950
Apost. Const. *Menti nostrae*, 23 September 1950
Enc. *Sacra virginitas*, 25 March 1954
Enc. *Ad caeli Reginam*, 11 October 1954
Homilies and addresses
Quierzy, Council of (833)
Doctrina de libero arbitrio hominis et de praedestinatione
Trent, Council of (1545–1563)
De sacris imaginibus

De Purgatorio
De reformatione
De sacramento ordinis
De libris sacris
De peccato originale
De SS. Eucharistia
De iustificatione
De SS. Missae sacrificio
De sacramento matrimonio
Doctrina de peccato originali
Doctrina de sacramento extremae unctionis
Doctrina de sacramento paenitentiae
Toledo, Ninth Council of (655)
De Redemptione
Toledo, Eleventh Council of (675)
De Trinitate Creed
Valence, Third Council of (855)
De praedestinatione
Vatican, First Council of the (1869–1870)
Dogm. Const. *Dei Filius*
Dogm. Const. *Pastor aeternus*
Vatican, Second Council of the (1963–1965)
Const. *Sacrosanctum Concilium*
Decree *Christus Dominus*
Decl. *Dignitatis humanae*
Decl. *Gravissimum educationis*
Decl. *Nostrae aetate*
Decree *Optatam totius*
Decree *Ad gentes*
Decree *Apostolicam actuositatem*
Decree *Perfectae caritatis*
Decree *Presbyterorum ordinis*
Decree *Unitatis redintegratio*
Dogm. Const. *Dei Verbum*
Dogm. Const. *Lumen gentium*
Past. Const. *Gaudium et spes*

Liturgical Texts

Roman Missal: Missale Romanum, editio typica altera (Vatican City, 1975)
The Divine Office (London, Sydney, Dublin, 1974)

Other Church Documents

Code of Canon Law
Codex Iuris Canonici (Vatican City, 1983)
Congregation for the Doctrine of the Faith
Declaration concerning Sexual Ethics, December 1975
Instruction on Infant Baptism, 20 October 1980
Inter insigniores, 15 October 1976
Letter on certain questions concerning Eschatology, 17 May 1979

Libertatis conscientia, 22 March 1986
Sacerdotium ministeriale, 6 August 1983
Libertatis nuntius, 6 August 1984
Mysterium Filii Dei, 21 February 1972
Pontifical Biblical Commission
Replies
New Vulgate
Nova Vulgata Bibliorum Sacrorum editio typica altera (Vatican City, 1986)

214

Sources quoted in the Commentary

2. THE FATHERS, ECCLESIASTICAL WRITERS AND OTHER AUTHORS

Alphonsus Mary Liguori, St
Christmas Novena
The Love of Our Lord Jesus Christ reduced to practice
Meditations for Advent
Thoughts on the Passion
Shorter Sermons
Sunday Sermons
Treasury of Teaching Material
Ambrose, St
De sacramentis
De mysteriis
De officiis ministrorum
Exameron
Expositio Evangelii secundum Lucam
Expositio in Ps 118
Treatise on the Mysteries
Anastasius of Sinai, St
Sermon on the Holy Synaxis
Anon.
Apostolic Constitutions
Didache, or *Teaching of the Twelve Apostles*
Letter to Diognetus
Shepherd of Hermas
Anselm, St
Prayers and Meditations
Aphraates
Demonstratio
Athanasius, St
Adversus Antigonum
De decretis nicaenae synodi
De Incarnatio contra arianos
Historia arianorum
Oratio I contra arianos
Oratio II contra arianos
Oratio contra gentes
Augustine, St
The City of God
Confessions
Contra Adimantum Manichaei discipulum
De Actis cum Felice Manicheo
De agone christiano
De bono matrimonii
De bono viduitatis
De catechizandis rudibus
De civitate Dei
De coniugiis adulterinis
De consensu Evangelistarum
De correptione et gratia
De doctrina christiana
De dono perseverantiae
De fide et operibus

De fide et symbolo
De Genesi ad litteram
De gratia et libero arbitrio
De natura et gratia
De praedestinatione sanctorum
De sermo Domini in monte
De spiritu et littera
De Trinitate
De verbis Domini sermones
Enarrationes in Psalmos
Enchiridion
Expositio epistulae ad Galatas
In I Epist. Ioann. ad Parthos
In Ioannis Evangelium tractatus
Letters
Quaestiones in Heptateuchum
Sermo ad Cassariensis Ecclesiae plebem
Sermo de Nativitate Domini
Sermons
Basil, St
De Spiritu Sancto
Homilia in Julittam martyrem
In Psalmos homiliae
Bede, St
Explanatio Apocalypsis
In Ioannis Evangelium expositio
In Lucae Evangelium expositio
In Marci Evangelium expositio
In primam Epistolam Petri
In primam Epistolam S. Ioanis
Sermo super Qui audientes gavisi sunt
Super Acta Apostolorum expositio
Super divi Iacobi Epistolam
Bernal, Salvador
Monsignor Josemaría Escrivá de Balaguer, Dublin, 1977
Bernard, St
Book of Consideration
De Beata Virgine
De fallacia et brevitate vitae
De laudibus novae militiae
Divine amoris
Meditationes piissimae de cognitionis humanae conditionis
Sermons on Psalm 90
Sermon on Song of Songs
Sermons
Bonaventure, St
In IV Libri sententiarum
Speculum Beatae Virgine
Borromeo, St Charles
Homilies

Sources quoted in the Commentary

Catherine of Siena, St
Dialogue
Cano, Melchor
De locis
Cassian, John
Collationes
De institutis coenobiorum
Clement of Alexandria
Catechesis III, De Baptismo
Commentary on Luke
Quis dives salvetur?
Stromata
Cyprian, St
De bono patientiae
De dominica oratione
De mortalitate
De opere et eleemosynis
De unitate Ecclesiae
De zelo et livore
Epist. ad Fortunatum
Quod idola dii non sint
Cyril of Alexandria, St
Commentarium in Lucam
Explanation of Hebrews
Homilia XXVIII in Mattheum
Cyril of Jerusalem, St
Catecheses
Mystagogical Catechesis
Diadochus of Photike
Chapters on Spiritual Perfection
Ephrem, St
Armenian Commentary on Acts
Commentarium in Epistolam ad Haebreos
Eusebius of Caesarea
Ecclesiastical History
Francis de Sales, St
Introduction to the Devout Life
Treatise on the Love of God
Francis of Assisi, St
Little Flowers
Reflections on Christ's Wounds
Fulgentius of Ruspe
Contra Fabianum libri decem
De fide ad Petrum
Gregory Nazianzen, St
Orationes theologicae
Sermons
Gregory of Nyssa, St
De instituto christiano
De perfecta christiana forma
On the Life of Moses
Oratio catechetica magna
Oratio I in beatitudinibus
Oratio I in Christi resurrectionem

Hippolytus, St
De consummatione saeculi
Ignatius of Antioch, St
Letter to Polycarp
Letters to various churches
Ignatius, Loyola, St
Spiritual Exercises
Irenaeus, St
Against Heresies
Proof of Apostolic Preaching
Jerome, St
Ad Nepotianum
Adversus Helvidium
Comm. in Ionam
Commentary on Galatians
Commentary on St Mark's Gospel
Contra Luciferianos
Dialogus contra pelagianos
Expositio in Evangelium secundum Lucam
Homilies to neophytes on Psalm 41
Letters
On Famous Men
John of Avila, St
Audi, filia
Lecciones sobre Gálatas
Sermons
John Chrysostom, St
Ante exilium homilia
Adversus Iudaeos
Baptismal Catechesis
De coemeterio et de cruce
De incomprehensibile Dei natura
De sacerdotio
De virginitate
Fifth homily on Anna
Hom. De Cruce et latrone
Homilies on St Matthew's Gospel, St John's
*   Gospel, Acts of the Apostles, Romans,*
*   Ephesians, 1 and 2 Corinthians, Colossians,*
*   1 and 2 Timothy, 1 and 2 Thessalonians,*
*   Philippians, Philemon, Hebrews*
II Hom. De proditione Iudae
Paraeneses ad Theodorum lapsum
Second homily in praise of St Paul
Sermon recorded by Metaphrastus
John of the Cross, St
A Prayer of the Soul enkindled by Love
Ascent of Mount Carmel
Dark Night of the Soul
Spiritual Canticle
John Damascene, St
De fide orthodoxa
John Mary Vianney, St
Sermons

Sources quoted in the Commentary

Josemaría Escrivá, St
Christ Is Passing By
Conversations
The Forge
Friends of God
Furrow
Holy Rosary
In Love with the Church
The Way
The Way of the Cross
Josephus, Flavius
Against Apion
Jewish Antiquities
The Jewish War
Justin Martyr, St
Dialogue with Tryphon
First and Second Apologies
à Kempis, Thomas
The Imitation of Christ
Luis de Granada, Fray
Book of Prayer and Meditation
Guide for Sinners
Introduccíon al símbolo de la fe
Life of Jesus Christ
Sermon on Public Sins
Suma de la vida cristiana
Luis de Léon, Fray
Exposición del Libro de Job
Minucius Felix
Octavius
Newman, J.H.
Biglietto Speech
Discourses to Mixed Congregations
Historical Sketches
Origen
Contra Celsum
Homilies on Genesis
Homilies on St John
In Exodum homiliae
Homiliae in Iesu nave
In Leviticum homiliae
In Matth. comm.
In Rom. comm.
Philo of Alexandria
De sacrificio Abel
Photius
Ad Amphilochium
Polycarp, St
Letter to the Philippians
del Portillo, A.
On Priesthood, Chicago, 1974
Primasius
Commentariorum super Apocalypsim B. Ioannis libri quinque
Prosper of Aquitaine, St
De vita contemplativa

Pseudo-Dionysius
De divinis nominibus
Pseudo-Macarius
Homilies
Severian of Gabala
Commentary on 1 Thessalonians
Teresa of Avila, St
Book of Foundations
Exclamations of the Soul to God
Interior Castle
Life
Poems
Way of Perfection
Tertullian
Against Marcion
Apologeticum
De baptismo
De oratione
Theodore the Studite, St
Oratio in adorationis crucis
Theodoret of Cyrrhus
Interpretatio Ep. ad Haebreos
Theophylact
Enarratio in Evangelium Marci
Thérèse de Lisieux, St
The Autobiography of a Saint
Thomas Aquinas, St
Adoro te devote
Commentary on St John = Super Evangelium S. Ioannis lectura
Commentaries on St Matthew's Gospel, Romans, 1 and 2 Corinthians, Galatians, Ephesians, Colossians, Philippians, 1 and 2 Timothy, 1 and 2 Thessalonians, Titus, Hebrews
De veritate
Expositio quorumdam propositionum ex Epistola ad Romanos
On the Lord's Prayer
On the two commandments of Love and the ten commandments of the Law
Summa contra gentiles
Summa theologiae
Super Symbolum Apostolorum
Thomas More, St
De tristitia Christi
Victorinus of Pettau
Commentary on the Apocalypse
Vincent Ferrer, St
Treatise on the Spiritual Life
Vincent of Lerins, St
Commonitorium
Zosimus, St
Epist. Enc. "Tractoria" ad Ecclesias Orientales